WOODTURNING TECHNIQUES

MIKE
DARLOW

STOBART DAVIES
HERTFORD

First published 2001

Woodturning Techniques is the third book in Mike Darlow's woodturning series. The first two books in the series are *The Fundamentals of Woodturning* and *Woodturning Methods*.

Published in 2001 by Stobart Davies Ltd., Priory House, 2 Priory Street, Hertford SG14 1RN.

Printed by H & Y Printing Limited, Hong Kong.

British Library Cataloguing-in-Publication Data

A catalogue record for this book is available from the British Library

ISBN 0-85442-092-4

CONTENTS

ACKNOWLEDGEMENTS

I thank the people, companies, and organizations listed below for their advice and information; the supply of transparencies, photographs and scans; and for allowing me to photograph and trial equipment. Their contributions have been essential to the success of this book.

Antonia Fraser in the author's note to her biography of Oliver Cromwell suggests that there should be a campaign medal bestowed to the families of authors. I am sure my wife, Aliki, and sons, Joshua and Samuel, agree. I also thank Aliki for her proofreading.

Australia
Narendra Aniy, State Forests of New South Wales; Chemco Adhesives; Gorgi Armen, Uni-Jig; Neil Ellis, U-Beaut Polishes; John Ewart, The Woodturning Centre; Jo Foley, Ballarat Fine Art Gallery; John Hawkins, John Hawkins Antiques; Chris Thompson, Selleys Chemical Company; Mike Jeffreys, The Wood Works Book & Tool; Jennifer Nursey, Fewings Joinery; Michael Richter, MIK International; Vic Verrecchio, Vicmark Machinery.

Jack Crawford, Peter Herbert, Alf Jordan, Bruce Leadbeatter, Michelle Kane, John Morgan, Dennis Moulang, Ernie Newman, Keith Torey, Vic Wood.

Canada
Debbie Shay and Leonard Lee, Lee Valley Tools; Paul Ross, Chalet Woodcraft; Kevin and Cathy Clay, Oneway Manufacturing.

Stephen Hogbin, Andre Martel.

Germany
Carl Heidtmann GmbH.

Gottfried Bockelmann, Gerhard Christmann, Johannes Volmer.

New Zealand
Kel McNaughton, Kelton Industries; Ken Port, Woodcut Tools International.

Scotland
Michael O'Donnell.

United Kingdom
Victoria Emmanuel and Iain Harrison, Birmingham Museums and Art Gallery; Chris Child, Peter Child; David Levi, David Levi Antiques; Jim Bright, The Leeds Museum Resource Center, and James Lomax, a curator at Temple Newsam House, Leeds; Rev. Michael Knight, vicar of St Mary and All Saints Anglican Church, Chesterfield; Angela Murphy, Science Museum; Mark Baker, then at Robert Sorby; Dennis Abdy, Henry Taylor Tools.

John Ambrose, E.W. (Bill) Newton, A.L. Robinson.

United States
Judith Beall, The Beall Tool Company; Alan Giagnocavo and Ayleen Stellhorn, Fox Chapel Publishing; Bruce Bradley, Linda Hall Library; Darrel Nish, Craft Supplies USA; Dean S. Levy, Bernard & S. Dean Levy; IBM, New York.

The late Ray Allen, Philip Bowman, Jerry Glaser, Gary Johnson, Bonnie Klein, Jane Newport, Michael Shuler.

INTRODUCTION

I started to write a book on woodturning methods in early 1998. A year later it had become clear that 200 pages would not suffice. I selected about half the methods, and detailed them in *Woodturning Methods* published in November 1999. Almost all of the remaining methods are described in this book. As the two books are closely related, most of the introduction to *Woodturning Methods* applies here and I shall not therefore repeat its content.

The layout format introduced in *The Fundamentals of Woodturning* is continued here. The two-column format restricts the layout and sizing of illustrations, but the three- and more-column formats result in lines of text which are too short to be read comfortably. As the text here is important, and because readers gain because the positioning of the illustrations is predictable, I have stuck with two columns. Due to a shortage of space, I have however had to make the size of the type in the index smaller than elsewhere, and reduce the number of entries.

I again include historical background, a feature of *Woodturning Methods* which pleased many readers because it was both interesting in itself and a source of ideas. I also again include references and endnotes, both to aid those readers who wish to investigate more deeply and to acknowledge the prior input of others. I therefore disagree with Anatole France (1844-1924) who said (tongue-in-cheek?), "When a thing has been said and well said, have no scruple: take it and copy it. Give references? Why should you? Either your readers know where you have taken the passage and the precaution is needless, or they do not know and you humiliate them." Should I have mentioned that Anatole France was the author of this quotation?

One advantage of an integrated series of books is that the author can return to topics. I have thus revisited tool grinding in chapter 2, and chucking in chapter 4. As in earlier books, I use the italicized *cut* to refer to a true cut made at a large rake angle to distinguish it from an undefined type of cut which could even be a scraping cut. Also, I often refer to *The Fundamentals of Woodturning*, and usually do so using the contraction FOW.

A few readers have found the thoroughness of the descriptions and explanations in my series of woodturning books difficult to cope with; most have welcomed it. While an author cannot please everyone, I have tried to make the detail accessible. I have also again included some maths, but it is, as before, at the level school students learn in their mid-teens. If you are prepared to follow it, it will aid your understanding; if you are not, you can still gain from using the results. For example, when making boxes with threaded lids, it is quicker and more certain to calculate the diameters of the lid socket and base spigot than to use trial and error.

Woodturning seems to bring out the inventor in its practitioners. The products of their inspiration and perspiration are important content in this and in my other books. I have learnt about some of the inventions through personal contacts. To learn about others I have followed Alexander Pope (1688-1744) who acknowledged "I freely confess that I have served myself all I could by reading." But I hope that the addition of my in-lathe research and thinking and this book's presentation will assist readers to a greater knowledge and understanding than would otherwise be possible.

The importance of knowledge and understanding was highlighted recently in a radio talk by an Indian musician. He discussing the importance of what he termed "technical freedom". He stated that because of his technical mastery he was able to impart to his playing the nuances and feelings that he desired. He knew that knowledge and expertise which were both wide and deep, and the efficiency which flowed from them, were not a straightjacket which repressed his expression, but the opposite, the most direct route to artistic freedom.

If this is the first book of my woodturning series that you have read, I hope that you will be encouraged to read the two earlier books in the series. And there are more books to come.

Mike Darlow, March, 2001.

KEY

Saw cuts and future cut surfaces

Center lines and axes

Hidden detail

Pointing and dimensioning

Diameter

Force

Movement

Cuts

Vertical distance from bottom of object

Make pencil mark on revolving wood surface

Wood in elevation

Wood in section

Cast iron, mild steel, in elevation

Cast iron, mild steel, in section

Tool and special steels

Tool cuts

Grinding wheels, in elevation

Ditto, in section

Note, there may some departures from the colors specified.

Chapter One

GLUING

Gluing wood together is often termed laminating, a word properly reserved for gluing *sheets* of wood together. Thus plywood is laminated. Pieces of wood not in sheet form are glued together, or conglutinated. And I prefer conglutinated to agglutinated because the former has a greater sense that the separate pieces become rigidly bonded together.

The nouns glue and adhesive are synonymous. Adhesive is thought by some to be more dignified; some use it to denote a synthetic origin and reserve glue for glues derived from animal or vegetable matter. I shall use glue for both.

You glue pieces of wood together to:

1. Produce a bigger and/or stronger workpiece. A simple example of the former is the technique of split rings described on page 55 of *Woodturning Methods*.
2. Conglutinate a hollow workpiece. This reduces weight, the quantity of wood used, and the likelihood of cracking.
3. Produce a container which needs little hollowing.
4. Reduce weight and/or cost by forming a core in a wood of lower density or cost than the exposed external wood.
5. Save wood by conglutinating a shape which would otherwise have to be turned or carved out of a larger volume.
6. Eliminate zones where the grain is not suitably aligned for appearance or strength.
7. Improve dimensional stability by using small component pieces which are fully seasoned and/or by arranging the pieces' grain directions more compatibly.
8. Use up small pieces of wood which would otherwise be scrapped.
9. Create decorative effects.

This chapter starts by looking at glues and the problems of wood as a subject for gluing, before describing some of the applications for gluing in woodturning.

1.1 GLUES

Hide (often called Scotch) glue, made by boiling animal skins, and casein glue, made from milk curds, were the only wood glues of importance until the development of synthetic-resin glues started in the 1930s. (A resin is a liquid which hardens when exposed to air. Tree sap is a resin. The term has unfortunately now been widened to include compounds which need to be mixed with a hardener to set within a reasonable time).

The first synthetic glue was phenol-formaldehyde resin. It was used extensively for gluing wood and in plywood manufacture. Synthetic-resin glues are unaffected by molds and can be formulated to suit particular applications to a much greater extent than the animal-based glues. Thus you can now buy glues which:

1. Glue both porous and nonporous materials.
2. Create a strong joint even when there are gaps between the two surfaces to be glued together.
3. Make joints which are highly resistant to water and other solvents, and are little affected by high or low temperatures.
4. Make joints which are rigid, have some flexibility, or can creep under stress.
5. Have short, long, or variable grabbing and setting times.
6. Do not require the pieces of wood to be clamped together.
7. Can be softened by heat or dissolved with a solvent.
8. Can be clear or colored.

These options partially explain the bewildering ranks of bottles, cans, and packets at glue suppliers. However there are only about a dozen main glue types, and they are described in table 1.1. If you have a special application, consult a specialist supplier. Glue manufacturers also offer extensive technical literature and advice.

Figure 1.1 A pot conglutinated in a variety of woods by the late Ray Allen of Yuma, Arizona. Its design echoes American Indian motifs, and it is 7 in. (180 mm) high and 9 in. (230 mm) in diameter.

Table 1.1 Glue details.[1]

Glue type	*Description and use*	*Materials bonded*	*Bond*	*Gap filling*
Aliphatic resin (yellow glue)	Dyed pale yellow, creamy consistency, use direct from bottle	Porous: wood, paper, cloth	Dries clear. Harder and creeps less than PVA	Slightly
Casein	Cream-colored powder. Mix into about $1^1/_4$ x volume of stirred water. Allow to stand for 15 minutes before use	Porous	Stains tannin-rich woods yellow	Good
Contact	Natural yellow or dyed other colors. Brushable and sprayable forms,	Porous and nonporous	Weak, heat resistant	Poor
Cross-linking PVA	Dyed yellow, creamy consistency, use direct from bottle	Porous	Harder and creeps less than aliphatic resin	Up to 0.5 mm
Cyanoacrylate (CA or Super)	Available in a range of viscosities	Metal, rubber, wood, some plastics	Brittle	Poor
Epoxy	Resin milky or pale yellow. Hardener yellower or amber. Avaible in various viscosities from liquid to thick pastes	Most except thermoplastics such as polyethylene and polypropylene	Dries clear or cloudy. Hard.	Excellent, often bulked with cotton microfibres to save cost
Hide (Scotch)	Joints can be disassembled with hot water or steam. Takes stains	Porous	Strong and hard. Flexible with <10% glycerine	Poor
Hot-melt	In pale sticks. Dispensed as a tacky viscous liquid at about 350° F from electrically-heated guns. Also in sheets. Used for quick temporary gluing	Porous	Glue penetrates poorly, is flexible, and has low strength	Good, but strength less with bigger gap
Polyurethane	Amber colored, available in a range of viscosiities. Use direct from container	One or both substrates must be porous. Does not bond thermoplastics	High strength, even with woods of high moisture content	Foams in open joints to leave a weakened layer
PVA (white glue, polyvinyl acetate)	White creamy liquid. Use direct from bottle	Porous	Clear glue line. Creeps under sustained load.	Poor
Resorcinol	Red/brown liquid resin and fawn powder hardener	Porous	Red, hard, and solvent resistant	Good, to 1.3 mm
Urea-formaldehyde	Resin can be a pale creamy liquid with brown powder or liquid hardeners. Resin can also be a powder with a water or liquid hardener	Porous	Hard, clear or tan colored glue line	Good with gap-filling hardeners

Table 1.1 Glue details continued.

Glue type	*Water-proof*	*Hazards*	*Open assembly time*	*Hardening*	*Cleanup solvent*	*Storage life*	*Cost*
Aliphatic resin	Fair	None	5 minutes	Clamp until squeeze-out has dried clear	Water	6 months	Low
Casein	Fair	None	10 to 15 minutes	12 hours	Water	12 months	Very low
Contact	Good	Difficult to remove, wear gloves, unpleasant vapor from solvent types	When touch dry (maximum 40 minutes) immediate set on contact	Maximum strength 24 hours	Toluol, lacquer thinners*	12 months, longer if evaporation prevented	Medium
Cross-linking PVA	Fair	None	5 minutes	1 hour, full strength 24 hours	Up to 0.5 mm	12 months	Medium
Cyano-acrylate	Excellent	Sticks fingers together, wear gloves	10 to 30 seconds depending on type	Good strength after several minutes, maximum 12 hours	Acetone	12 months	Very high
Epoxy	Excellent	Avoid contact with skin and eyes, and beathing vapor.	Variable according to formulation	Setting time 5 mins to 8 hours, full strength after 16 hrs to 3 days depending on tyrpe	Acetone	Long, scrap if solutions start to go granular	High
Hide	Poor	None	2 to 3 minutes	3 hours, full strength after 24 hours	Hot water	Several years	Low
Hot-melt	High	None	Sets in 15–20 seconds	Doesn't harden, retains some flexibility	Min'l spirit, lacquer thinners.* Often peels off	Long	Medium
Polyurethane	Excellent	Bonds skin if left to cure	20–45 minutes	6 hours, maximum strength 24 to 48 hours	Alcohol, mineral spirit*	Skins if air or moisture in container	Medium
PVA	Poor	None	5 minutes	30 mins, maximum after 12 hours	Water	12 months	Low
Resorcinol	Excellent	Avoid contact and breathing vapor	15 minutes	Clamp for several hours	Water	12 months	High
Urea-formaldehyde	Good	Avoid contact and breathing vapor	15 minutes	Clamp for several hours	Water	3 m'ths for liquid resin, 24 for resin powder	Medium

* Mineral spirit, white spirit, and turpentine substitute are the same; as are lacquer thinners and cellulose thinners.

GLUING NOTES

1. The data in table 1.1 is approximate. The formulation of each brand of glue is unique, and for accurate data contact its stockist or manufacturer. Setting times are often greatly affected by temperature, and to a lesser extent by humidity.
2. Clamping pressure should not be so high that the joint is squeezed dry. Clamping pressures of 50 to 100 psi (350 to 700 kPa) are recommeneded.
3. Blunt rotating cutters or those set without clearance can compress and glaze the wood's surface and limit glue penetration. Coarsely sand such surfaces before gluing.
4. The glues which set hard will rapidly blunt and can chip tool cutting edges.
5. Some woods contain extractives which impede bonding or have surfaces which have been contaminated. Wipe such surfaces with acetone shortly before gluing.
6. PVA glue softens during sanding and pulls out of the joint leaving a groove which is highlighted when the piece is polished.
7. Adding 10% of PVA to urea-formaldehyde resin improves the penetration, and reduces the brittleness of the joint.
8. Do not laminate substantial numbers of thin layers of wood such as veneers with glues which set by evaporation such as PVA or casein. If you do, setting can take many hours.
9. Glue storage life is affected by temperature. Water-based liquid glues deteriorate with every freeze-thaw cycle. Some other glues last better if stored at low temperature or below freezing. As you use glue, more air and moisture can occupy the container and speed deterioration unless you reduce the container's volume or use an inert filler.
10. Liquid glues and resins deteriorate and produce weaker joints over time. For example, urea-formaldehyde resin in liquid form deteriorates within three months even under good storage conditions.
11. Always do a trial assembly first. You may wish to test the glue's open assembly time in the then current conditions if time is critical. Have clamps adjusted to their optimum lengths and everything arranged and ready before you start gluing.
12. End-grain absorbs glue, leading to a starved and therefore weak joint. Size the end-grain with glue (if aqueous, dilute it a little), and allow the glue to set before applying the second and final coat.
13. Changes in the wetnesses (moisture contents) of conglutinations subjects the glue joints to stress, and are a common cause of joint failure. The next section therefore discusses moisture in wood.

SUMMARY

All the glues in table 1.1 have applications in woodturning. However:

1. For most gluing use a cross-linking PVA or aliphatic resin. Both these PVA glues are usually dyed yellow to distinguish them from white glue. The cross-linking form sets harder and is more water resistant because the long chain molecules link to one another as the glue sets.
2. When the joint must not show through the finish or allow movement, use a glue which sets hard. Urea-formaldehyde, hide, polyurethane, or epoxy are preferred. If the urea resin is in liquid form, it must be fresh or the hardened glue with be very brittle and the joint will fail. Therefore for occasional use, buy the resin in powder form as it keeps for much longer.
3. Where a strong, rigid joint and gap filling is needed and cost is not a major consideration, use epoxy resin.
4. For quick gluing use a five-minute epoxy. Where faster setting is needed, use cyanoacrylate for a rigid permanent joint, or hot-melt, particularly for a temporary joint. Both glues are used by woodturners for chucking. Cyanoacrylate is often used for running repairs on workpieces.

1.2 THE EFFECTS OF MOISTURE ON WOOD AND ON GLUE JOINTS

Anyone who has worked with wood knows it doesn't keep still; it warps, expands, and contracts. There are two causes:

1. The relaxation of internal stresses which was discussed on pages 70 to 72 of *Woodturning Methods*. When you conglutinate a workpiece from internally stressed components, the relaxation of the component pieces of wood is usually complete before you start gluing. Only later when you cut wood away from the workpiece do the highly stressed pieces of wood want to relax again into a new equilibrium and stress the glue joints.
2. A change in the wetness of the wood. This is the most common cause of wood movement and attendant joint failure.

A living tree is saturated with water; the proportion being between 30% and 200% of the dry weight of the wood. Dense hardwood trees contain far less water than fast growing softwoods; sapwood contains more water than heartwood. This water is held within the cells (bound water), and between them (free water). As wood dries the free water evaporates first—during this stage there is no change in the wood's volume. But as the bound water held within the cells evaporates, the wood shrinks. Unfortunately for wood users shrinkage is not equal in all directions (figure 1.2),

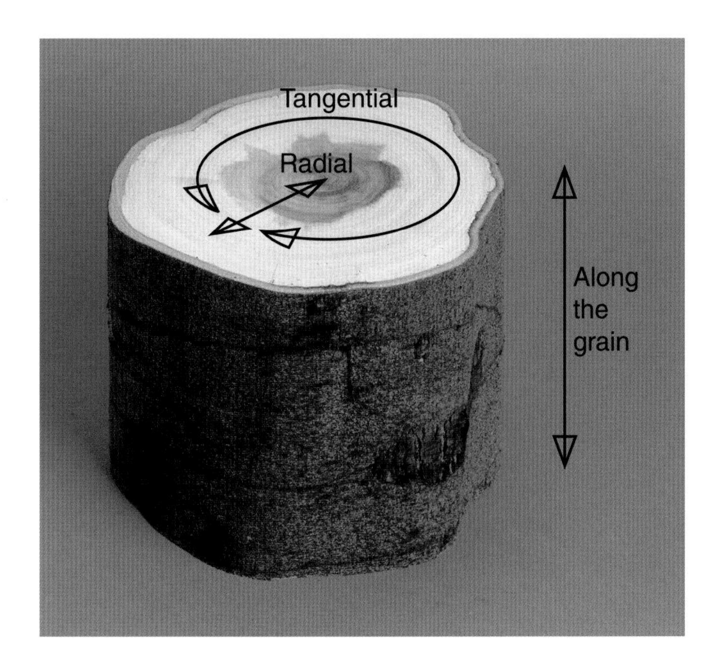

Figure 1.2 **A log showing the three directions in which shrinkage is measured.** It is now usual to quote a shrinkage as the average percentage reduction in dimension as the species seasons from green to 12% moisture content.

The circumstances of a tree's growth will affect its wood's shrinkage values.

Typically the shrinkage along the grain is negligible, and the tangential is between $1^1/_2$ and 2 times the radial. Dry wood will also absorb water, and will then expand. Typical shrinkage values vary from species to species, and some are given in Table 1.2.

Table 1.2 Percent shrinkages from green to 12% moisture content for various woods.[2]

Species	*Radial*	*Tangent-ial*
Indonesian kauri, *Agathis alba*	1.1	1.7
Redwood, *Sequoia sempervirens*	1.5	2.5
Honduras mahogany, *Swietenia macrophylla*	1.5	3.0
Western red cedar, *Thuja plicata*	1.5	3.0
Baltic pine, *Picea abies*	1.5	4.0
European walnut, *Juglans regia*	2.0	4.0
New Zealand kauri, *A. australis*	2.5	4.0
Black walnut, *Juglans nigra*	3.0	4.5
Radiata pine, *Pinus radiata*	3.0	4.5
European oak, *Quercus robur*	3.0	6.0
Europ'n beech, *Fagus sylvatica*	4.0	6.0
Turpentine, *Syncarpia glomulifera*	7.0	14.5
Peppermint, *Eucalyptus piperita*	9.5	20.5

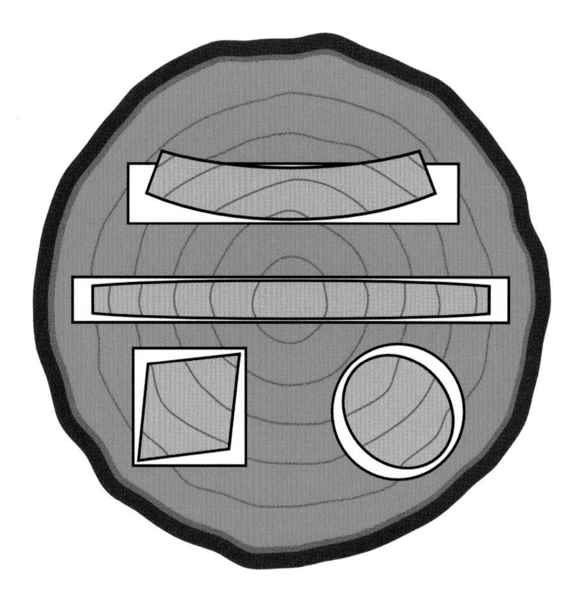

Figure 1.3 **How cross sections cut from a freshly felled trunk distort during seasoning.** The distortions happen because the tangential shrinkage is much larger than the radial. *Top*: the most common cross sections, backsawn planks, cup away from the heart as they season. *Center*: quartersawn planks are the most stable, and are preferred where wide planks need to be used in situations where cupping would be undesirable. Another solution is to glue narrow boards edge-to-edge (figure 1.9).

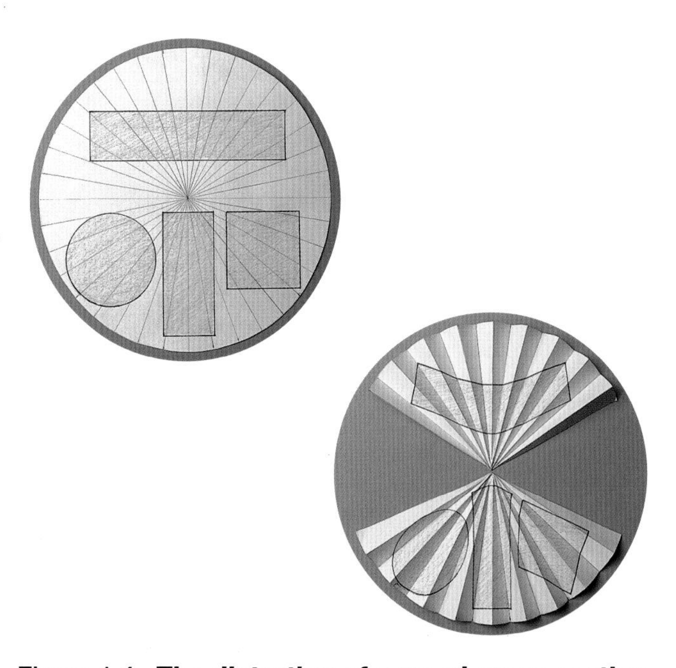

Figure 1.4 **The distortion of a wood cross section during seasoning can be demonstrated by drawing it on a fan.** This idea was previously shown in John A. Walton, *Woodwork in Theory and Practice* (Sydney: Random Century Australia, 1990), p. 217.

and it varies with the species (table 1.2). Figures 1.3, 1.4, 1.8, and 1.9 illustrate the distortions which differential shrinkages cause; figure 1.7 doesn't.

Wood should be seasoned for most of its applications. Seasoning is a drying process in which the bulk of the moisture which was present in the living wood is removed. Relatively great shrinkage occurs during seasoning. But once wood is seasoned and if it is kept out of the weather, changes in the wetness of the surrounding (ambient) air will cause only minor fluctuations in the wood's dimensions. Seasoned wood is also:

1. Stronger and harder.
2. Lighter in weight.
3. Less liable to decay, bacterial staining, and insect attack.
4. Better able to be finished and glued.

Seasoned wood still contains some water, the amount being best defined by the term moisture content, the total weight of water present expressed as a percentage of the dry weight of the wood:

$$\text{Moisture content} = \frac{\text{Weight of moisture}}{\text{Dry weight of wood}} \times 100\%$$

$$= \frac{\text{Wet weight of wood} - \text{Dry weight of wood}}{\text{Dry weight of wood}} \times 100\%$$

The moisture content of a piece of wood is most accurately determined by taking a wood sample back from the ends which you weigh, oven dry, and then weigh again. This is destructive and time-consuming. You can store the wood indoors, weigh it regularly, and assume that once it has ceased to lose weight it is seasoned. But the most convenient way to measure moisture content is with a battery-operated meter (figure 1.5).

Air contains moisture. There is a maximum amount of water vapor which air can hold at a given temperature. If air at that same temperature contains less than that maximum, the lesser amount expressed as a percentage of the maximum is the relative humidity. For example air at 85°F (29°C) can hold a maximum of 1.7 grams of water per kilogram of dry air. If air at the same temperature is holding only 0.85 grams per kilogram, its relative humidity is 50%.

Although the outside air's relative humidity is continuously changing, there will be an average value for any locality. The average relative humidity in a heated or air-conditioned building is likely to differ from that outdoors in the locality.

Wood is hygroscopic; its moisture content and dimensions are affected by changes in the ambient air's relative humidity. Therefore for wood to be fairly stable, its moisture content needs to be brought to the value that corresponds to the average relative humidity of the ambient air. Figure 1.6 provides the ideal wood moisture contents

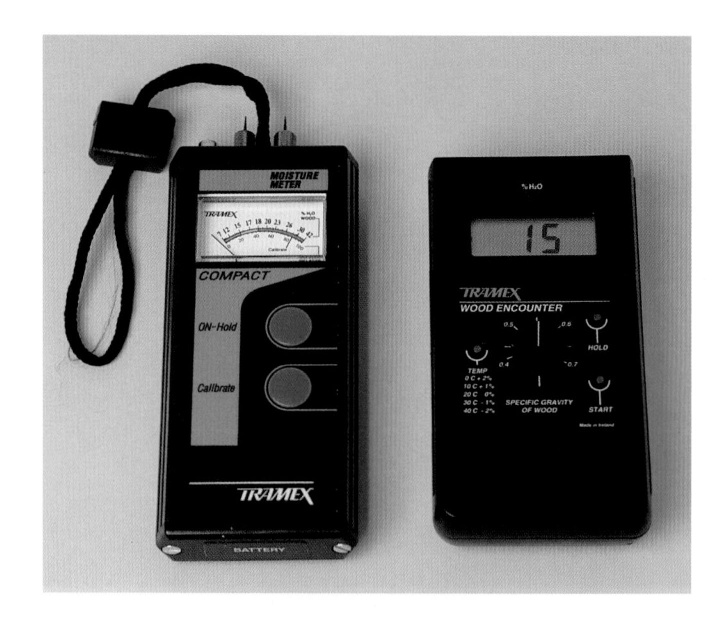

Figure 1.5 Probed and probeless moisture content meters, here by Tramex Ltd of Shankhill, Ireland.

Top left: the probed meter has pointed steel electrodes which are driven into the wood along the line of the grain. The electrical impedance between them is then measured—the higher the moisture content, the lower the impedance. Wood's impedance is also affected by the wood's specific gravity and by temperature, and these are input by the user. From the three pieces of information the moisture content is calculated within the meter and then displayed.

Top right and bottom: the probeless meter sends a low frequency signal to a depth of about 1 in. (25 mm) into the wood between the two rubber electrodes on its back. The electrical impedance is measured, and the moisture content calculated and displayed, again using the wood's specific gravity and the ambient temperature.

for different ambient air average relative humidities.

When a conglutinated workpiece is in contact with air which is not at the corresponding relative humidity, the wood's moisture content will gradually change. As the moisture content of each wooden component changes, the shape of each will try to change. This exerts forces which may cause cracking within the component pieces of wood and failure of the glue joints between them. The joints can also fail if the glue absorbs water and softens. Figures 1.8 and 1.9 show how to lessen the effects of moisture content changes in conglutinations. Other steps you can take are:

1. Use the same species or species with similar shrinkages to eliminate stresses caused by the different shrinkages of different species.
2. Use species with low shrinkages and thus lessen the size of the dimensional changes which the components will try to make.
3. Conglutinate so that the grain directions of the component pieces are sympathetically arranged,
4. Finish all exposed surfaces, including those hidden, so that changes in moisture content are slower, decreased, and smoother.

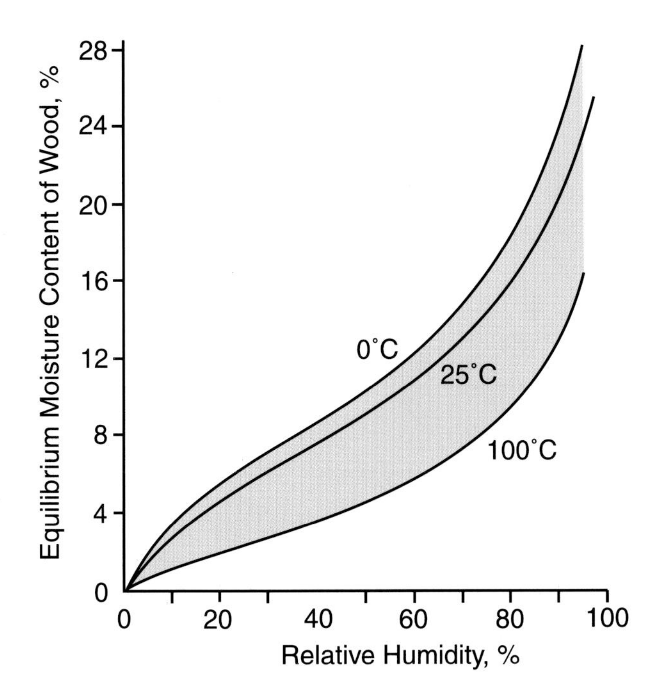

Figure 1.6 The relationship between the relative humidity of the ambient air, the equilibrium moisture content of wood, and the temperature.[3] Wood at its equilibrium moisture content will neither lose nor gain moisture unless the ambient conditions change.

The average equilibrium moisture content differs from region to region: for example, it is 12% for Sydney, Australia, a temperate coastal region.

Figure 1.7 **The twisted spire of St Mary and All Saints** at Chesterfield, Yorkshire. Although sometimes cited as an extreme example of the problems which can result from constructing with unseasoned wood which then seasons, the spire was built with the twist.

Spires originated in the twelfth century.[4] Perhaps the designer of this fourteenth-century spire was among the first to realise that rifling would help propel parishioners' prayers and aspirations to heaven more accurately.

The Reverend Michael Knight, vicar of St Mary and All Saints, informed me that the spire leaned 104.63 in. (2.657 m) to the south and 45.17 in. (1.147 m) to the west due to failures in stays at the base—obviously the lean of this spire is monitored as closely as that of a teetering tower in Pisa.

1.3 STRUCTURAL CONGLUTINATION

In figures 1.8 to 1.13 this section discusses structural conglutinations using wood in the form of boards .

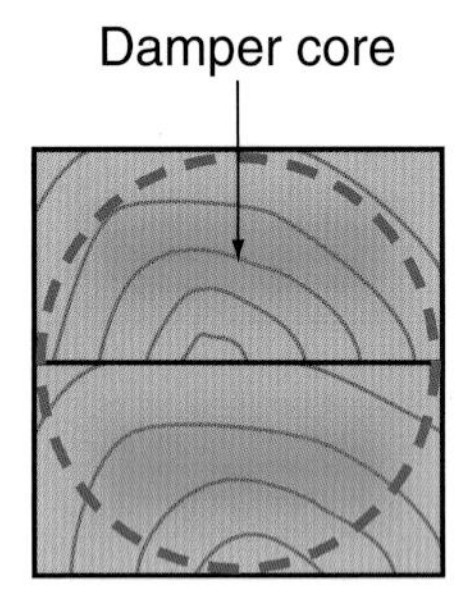

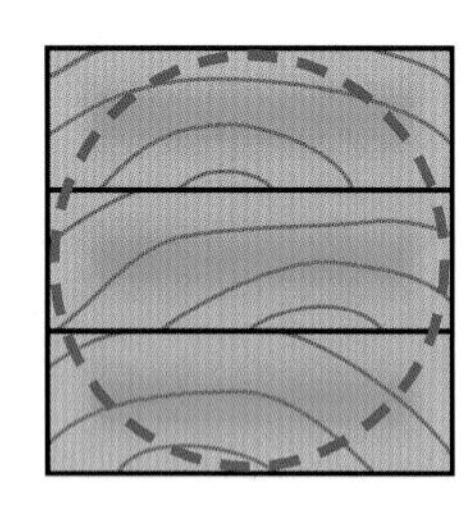

Figure 1.8 Stack conglutination of spindle blanks. The core of a seasoned wood section usually has a higher moisture content than the wood at and near its surfaces. Turning a conglutination of seasoned boards exposes the damper cores which will then each season, and attempt to cup. By arranging the component boards with their hearts to the same sides as shown, the boards are more likely to cup in sympathy and so stress the glue joints less. Also the joints will be less visible because the grain patterns along the edges will be more alike.

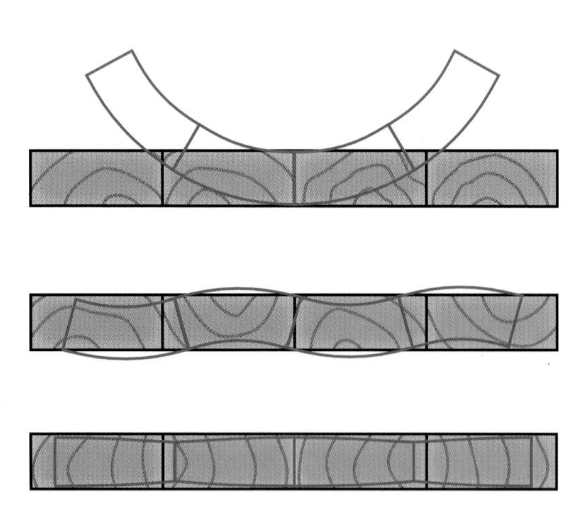

Figure 1.9 The warping of edge-to-edge glued workpieces. Seasoned sawn boards will probably season further after dressing, especially if the conglutination is moved into a heated atmosphere. *Top and middle*: if you use backsawn boards, you can minimize the effects by alternating their heart sides. *Bottom*: the ideal is to use quartersawn boards arranged as shown.

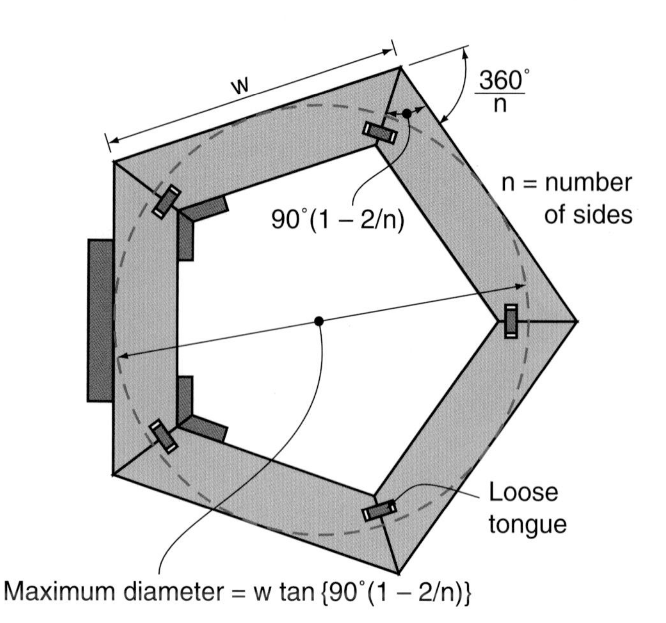

Figure 1.10 Coopering is often used for large-diameter cylindrical turnings. *Left, colored darker*: where the finished thickness at the joints will be too small, strips of wood can be added locally at the inside edges of the boards before the edges are cut. Adding a narrow strip of wood to the center of the outside of staves is undesirable—the strips' leading edges will often break out during turning, and subsequent seasoning is likely to cause the glue joints holding the strips to fail.

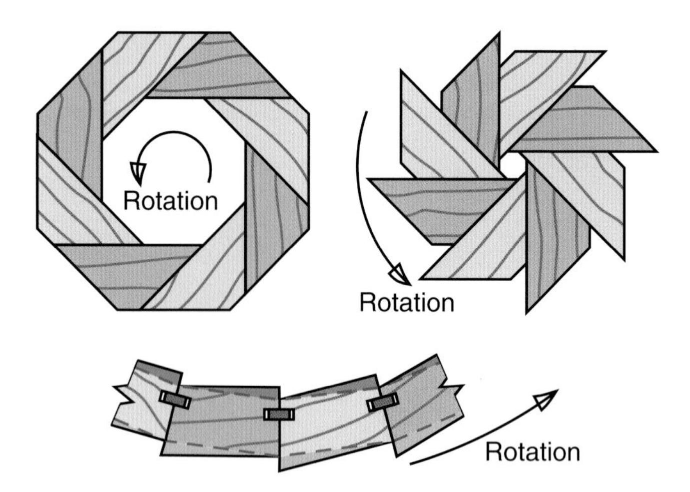

Figure 1.11 Coopering and framing to avoid turning against the grain can be desirable, and is essential if staves are of laminated board such as MDF (medium-density fibreboard). When the joints are other than radial the assembly is unstable as the two top drawings show. Such assemblies cannot be cramped in one operation just with band cramps. *Bottom*: the other solution is to use more staves or segments, here 24, and/or to orientate the grain or laminations so that turning against the grain is avoided. You do not have to trim off the inner waste, colored dark green, before gluing.

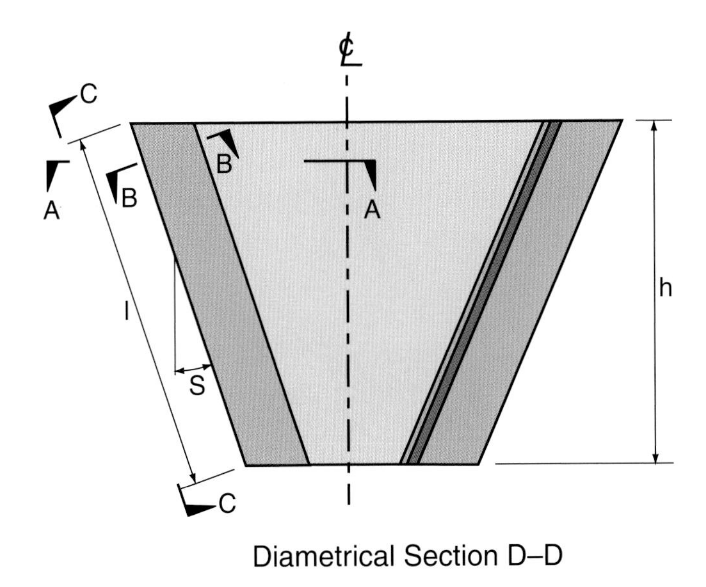

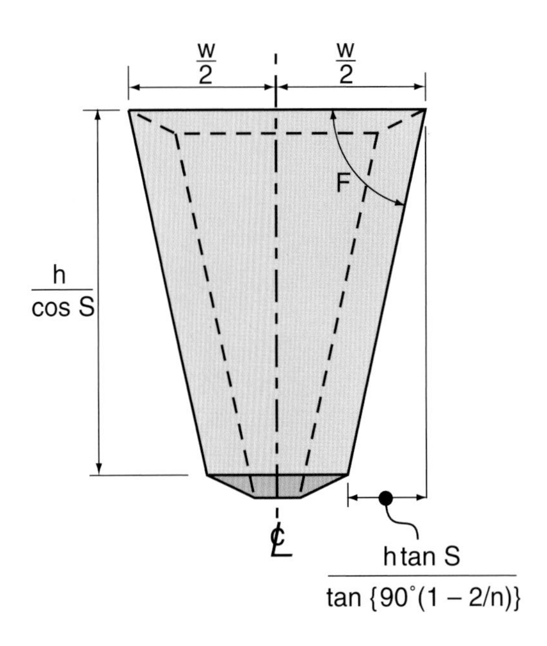

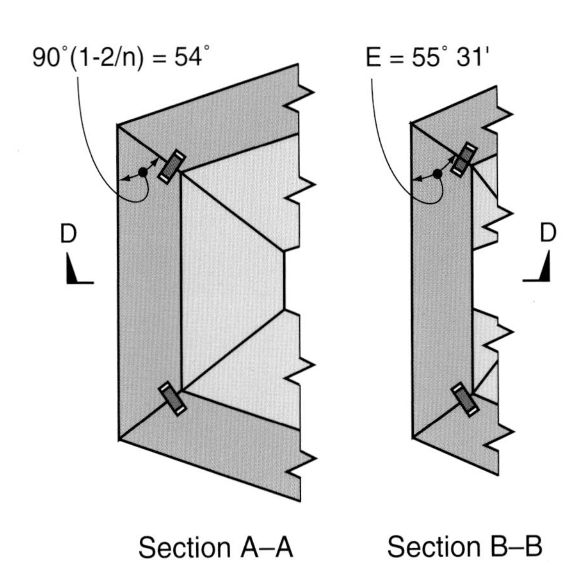

Figure 1.12 Tapered coopering, here with five staves.

When the coopered workpiece is not tapered, $S = 0°$, and the board edges are cut to the angle $90°(1 - 2/n)$. As the taper of the coopering (angle S measured at the center of a stave) increases, the angle of the board edges must increase, and can be calculated by the formula

$$\tan E = \frac{\tan\{90°(1 - 2/n)\}}{\cos S}$$

Here for $S = 19°$

$$\tan E = \frac{\tan\{90°(1 - 2/5)\}}{\cos 19°} = \frac{\tan 54°}{\cos 19°} = \frac{1.376}{0.9455} = 1.456$$

$E = 55° 31'$

Figure 1.13 The geometry of staves, here those in the preceding figure. Angle F can be found using

$$\tan F = \frac{\tan\{90°(1–2/n)\}}{\sin S}$$

1.4 LOCATING AND CLAMPING JOINTS

During assembly and clamping, glue is at its most lubricious. It is usually wise, and sometimes essential, to restrict or prevent sliding during gluing, especially when the components are long (figure 1.14) or many, by:

1. Machining locating features: sockets and spigots; and profiled edges such as tongue-and-groove, finger, reverse, and lock miter. Note that these profiled edges are visually far more obtrusive than square butt joints if later turned through obliquely.
2. Adding locators such as biscuits, dowels, and loose tongues. The loose tongues can be of plywood, or of solid wood with its grain at 90° to the plane of the joint.
3. Hammering small brads partially into areas which are to be coated with glue, then pinching off the brads' tops leaving short protruding chisel points.
4. Providing checkouts, glue blocks, or similar to enable temporary clamping (figure 1.15).

Take care when deciding where to locate such features if you do not want them to be exposed during later turning.

There are also two methods of combined clamping and location: slot screwing (figures 1.16 and 1.17), and feather jointing which is described in the next section.

Figure 1.14 **A pattern for precast concrete columns,** the shaft coopered from radiata pine planks.[5]

Figure 1.15 **Clamping stave ends.** When conglutinating long staves such as those in the preceding figure, you may need to supplement the usual locating features such as loose tongues. End clamping with nuts and bolts, C clamps, or similar stabilizes the assemblage while you place and tighten the band cramps at intervals along its length.

Figure 1.16 **The end of a slot-screwed joint.**[6] Screws, holes and slots are regularly spaced along the two boards. The screw heads project about $^3/_8$ in. (10 mm), and the screws lean here a little to the left to help pull the joint tighter. Notice that the screw hole is a little further from the end of its board than the screw.

Figure 1.17 **Hammering a slot-screwed joint.** One or two crisp taps will tighten the joint as the tilted screw heads are forced along and deeper into the slots.

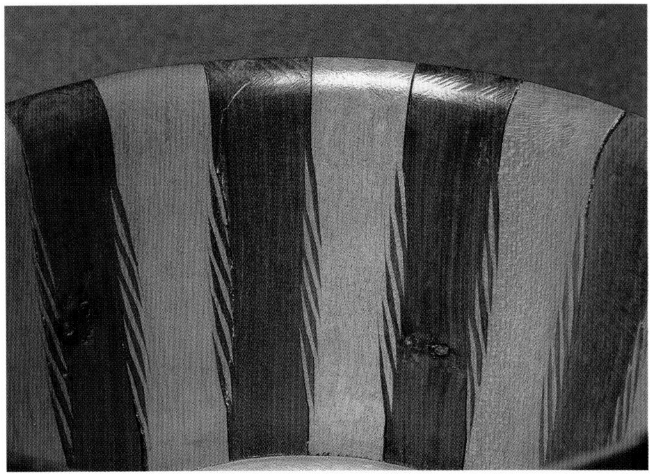

Figure 1.18 **A bicker in the Pinto Collection.** The length of these barbs is about 6 to 8 times their thickness, and they start 3 to 4 barb thicknesses apart.

The barbs are not cut symmetrically into a stave. The reason is explained in the next figure. *Photographs courtesy of Birmingham Museums & Art Gallery, England.*

1.5 BICKERS AND FEATHER JOINTS

Bickers, the name is derived from the same root word as the English beaker, were made in Scotland during the eighteenth and nineteenth centuries.[7] Small bickers were used for whisky, larger sizes for ale. Very large bickers were called cogs or coggies; small, shallow bickers were called quaiches.

Bickers have alternating dark and light staves and feather joints (figure 1.18). The pale wood was usually sycamore; the dark wood was often Scotch mahogany, alder which had been steeped in peat bogs. The joints between the staves are called feather joints. When cut accurately the fingerlike barbs interlock like the barbs of a bird's feather or zip-fastener to produce decorative joints which are watertight and largely self-clamping (figures 1.19 to 1.22). Thus the staves were not glued together, but bound with willow; so, like Chesterfield's spire, feather joints have no business in this chapter.

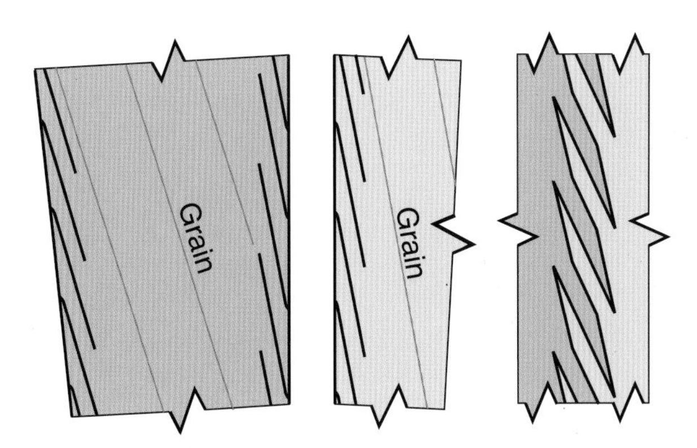

Figure 1.19 **The relative directions of the grain in the staves and the cutting of the barbs.** *Left and center*: these elevations show that the grain is angled so that the barbs do not rive across between the bottoms of the cuts and become detached. *Right*: showing how the barbs deform when the staves are pushed together.

Figure 1.20 Starting to cut a barb. Here the cuts start $^3/_8$ in. (10 mm) apart. The knife bade must be sharp and thin to avoid bending the barbs too much and breaking them. Each cut has two parts:

1. A very shallow vertical cut to define the free end of the barb and start the cut.
2. A long straight cut angled down at about 10°, and described in the next figure.

Figure 1.21 "Sawing" a barb. Once you have started a cut as in the preceding figure, tilt the blade back to 10° to the stave edge. Use a sawing action for this second part of a cut as it gives more control. Don't change the angle of descent—lessening it would effectively thicken the free ends of the barbs which could not then pass each other and interlock.

Figure 1.22 The completed feather joint shown almost twice life-size.

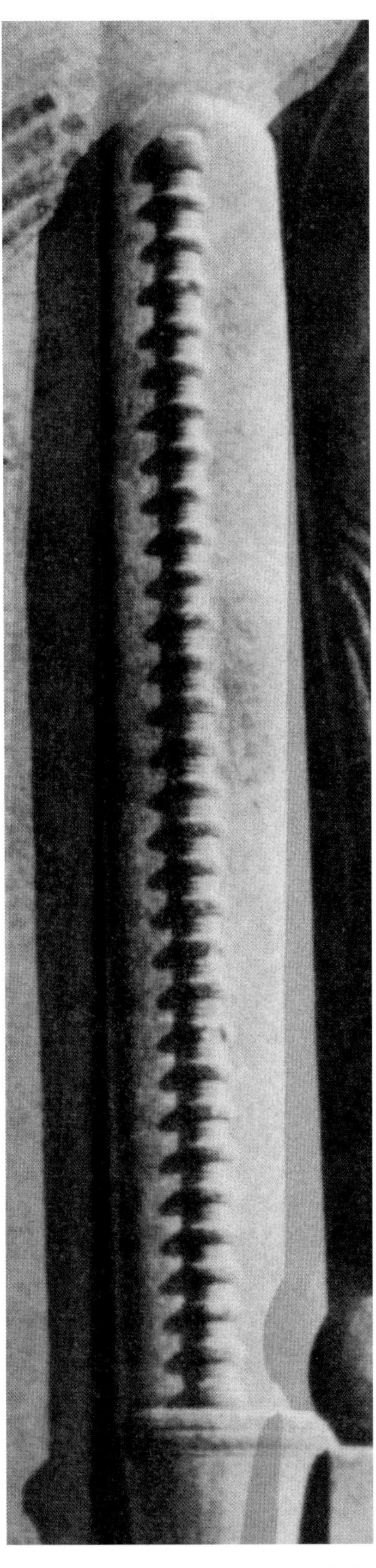

1.6 SPLIT TURNINGS AND PAPER JOINTS

Sawing or riving turnings into two or more parts known as split turnings dates from before Christ (figure 1.23). Split turnings are usually produced by splitting spindles axially, but the technique can be applied to any type of turning (figure 1.54).

Split turnings are applied as decoration (figures 1.23, 1.24 and 1.27), can be butted end to end to form long moldings (figures 1.25 and 1.26), or can be arranged in other ways, for example as a frame. Split turnings are used structually, for example as engaged columns or balusters at the ends of colonnades or balustrades (figure 1.29), and as vertical spindles or *sticks* in chair backs. Another major use is in patterns for casting (figure 1.28).

You can saw a turning into halves or into other proportions, but:

1. Significant thickness is lost in the kerf. The two halves of a spindle sawn longitudinally would have segment-shaped cross sections less than semicircular.
2. You may not be able to saw accurately because the shape of the turning may not fit nicely against a fence, properly support the turning during bandsawing, or lend itself to accurate hand sawing.
3. The faces left after sawing may need planing and/or sanding flat and smooth—processes which can be difficult, inexact, and which destroy more thickness.

There is a faster alternative which has none of the above drawbacks (figures 1.30 to 1.34). You prepare a blank for each split turning, weakly glue the blanks together, turn the conglutination, and rive the conglutination apart along the weak glue joints to separate the split turnings. To make the glue joints weak you interlay paper rather than dilute the glue.

Figure 1.23 A limestone relief at Persepolis, Iran, of Xerxes on his turned throne, circa 600 BC. Observant readers will have already spotted the split turning on the throne's back upright in figure 1.1 of *FOW*. Whether the spindle was halved by riving down a papyrus joint or by some other means is unknown.

Figure 1.24 **A panelled lift top chest with split turnings.** Probably made in Boston, Massachusetts, circa 1680. The woods are red oak and white pine, with the split turnings in maple. Height 29 in., width 46 in., depth 20 in. *Photograph courtesy of Bernard & S. Dean Levy, Inc., New York.*

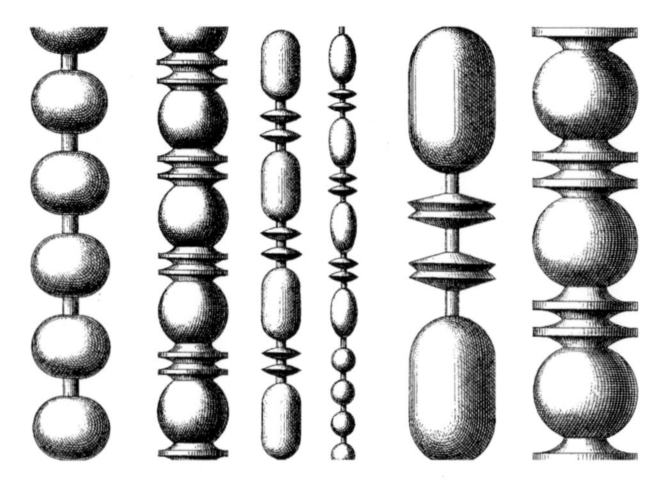

Figure 1.25 **Six late nineteenth-century split-turned moldings.**[8]

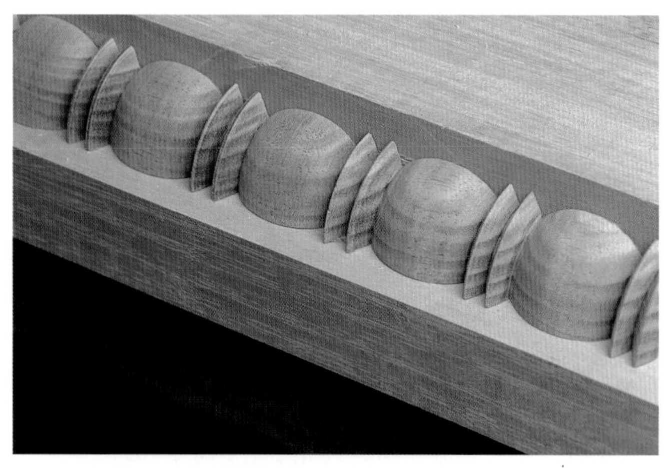

Figure 1.26 **A bead-and-reel molding** used to decorate the edge of a table top.

Figure 1.27 Split turnings and paterae on a Tasmanian red cedar sideboard, circa 1830. *Photograph courtesy of Ballarat Fine Art Gallery, Victoria, Australia.*

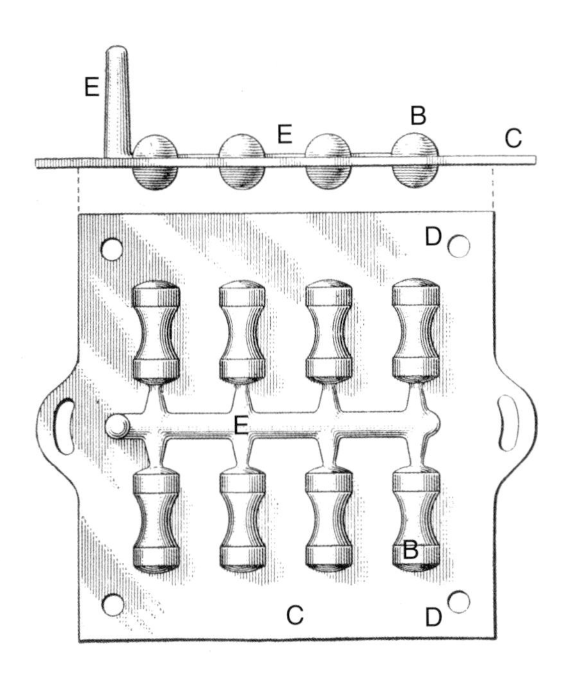

Figure 1.28 A pattern for a plate molding of eight rollers.[9]

The roller patterns are made by gluing spindle workpieces together with paper joints as shown in figure 1.30. Each workpiece is then turned to the same shape as a finished roller, but to a slightly larger size to allow for the shrinkage of the casting metal as it solidifies and cools. After the workpieces are split into two along their paper joints, each half *B* is fixed exactly opposite its mate (registered) on a plate *C*. Pieces of wood *E* are then fixed to the top of plate *C* to act as runners to allow the molten metal to enter and flow through the mold.

The plate *C* has holes *D* near its corners which locate on the pins of a molding box which is in two parts. With the plate between, sand is rammed into both parts of the box. The top part is removed, the pattern is removed, the top part of the box is located on the bottom part, and the metal is poured in. Once the metal has cooled, the two halves of the molding box are separated, and the casting removed. The runners are broken off the rollers and will be remelted and used in a future casting operation. Finally, each roller casting is cleaned and machined.

Figure 1.29 **A comparison of engaged columns.** *Left*: splitting at 60% to 7.0% produces a far more substantial look, but is an inefficient use of wood and time. *Right*: splitting down a diameter produces a weak looking form.

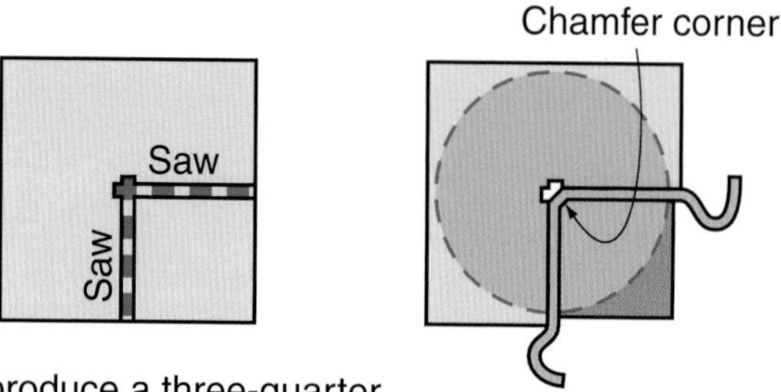

To produce a three-quarter molding: saw out a quarter, ideally on a table saw, glue the quarter back in with a paper joint, turn, then rive away the waste quarter.

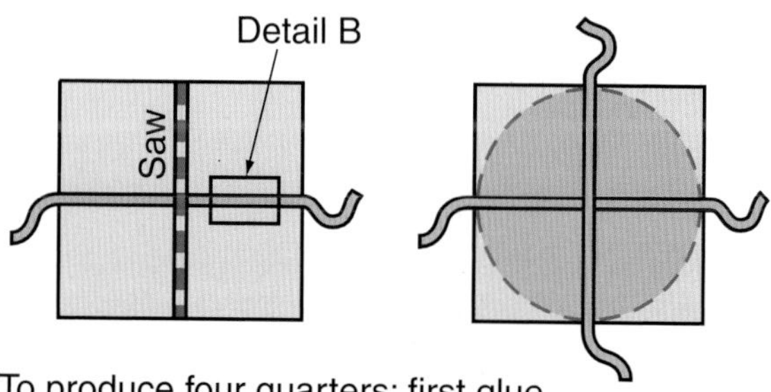

To produce four quarters: first glue two halves together with a paper joint, allow the glue to set, rip the conglutination in half at right angles, glue the two new halves together with a second paper joint, turn, and rive.

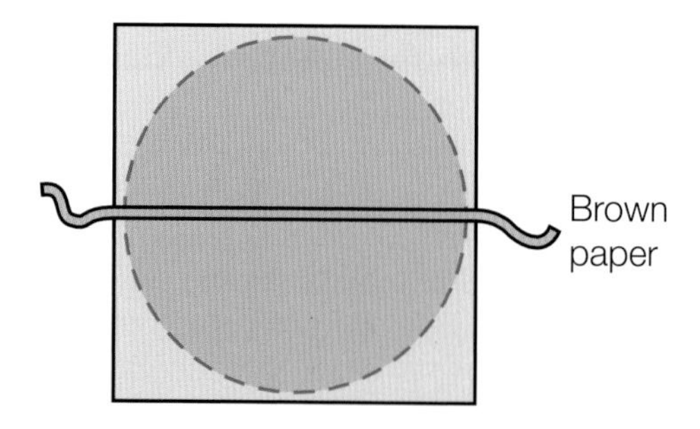

Figure 1.30 **Producing two perfect semicircular split turnings.** Two rectangular cross sections, or one squarish cross section ripped into halves, are glued together with a paper joint, turned, and then rived along the joint.

When column or baluster split turnings are to be planted against a wall, the paper joint is often put off-center, and only the larger of the split turnings is used.

Sectors which are quarters and three-quarters of a circle are also produced using paper joints.

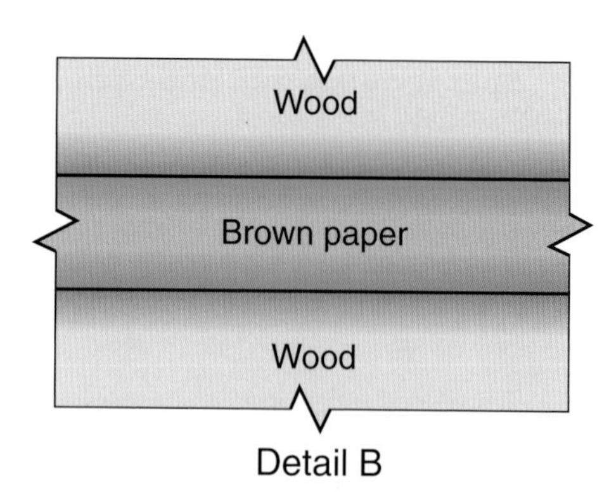

Detail B

Figure 1.31 **How to produce cross sections which are sectors of a quarter and three-quarters of a circle.**

Detail B shows a magnified section through a paper joint. By limiting the amount of glue applied to the two wood surfaces to a generous, even smear, the glue, shown green, will penetrate into but not through heavy, good quality brown paper. This leaves the central band of unimpregnated paper as a plane of weakness which will fail easily when the conglutinated and turned workpiece is rived apart. The use of paper joints in the production of the bead-and-reel molding pictured in figure 1.26 is described in the next three figures.

Figure 1.32 The second gluing operation to produce four quarter split turnings. Two rectangular pieces of wood were earlier glued together face-to-face with paper between (preceding figure). When dry that conglutination was sawn in half at 90° to the first paper joint. The two revealed faces have just been generously smeared with PVA glue—too little glue and the joint will fail during turning, too much and the joint will not rive nicely. The joint will then be clamped together with the brown paper between.

PVA and hide are the preferred glues. PVA is more convenient, but both are soluble in hot water—this helps you to remove the brown paper from the wood joint faces after riving.

The ideal paper is thick, good quality brown paper. It is strong and is therefore unlikely to split through its thickness during the turning. It also has the desirable limited absorbency, and is slow to, or does not, blister and wrinkle as it absorbs the glue.

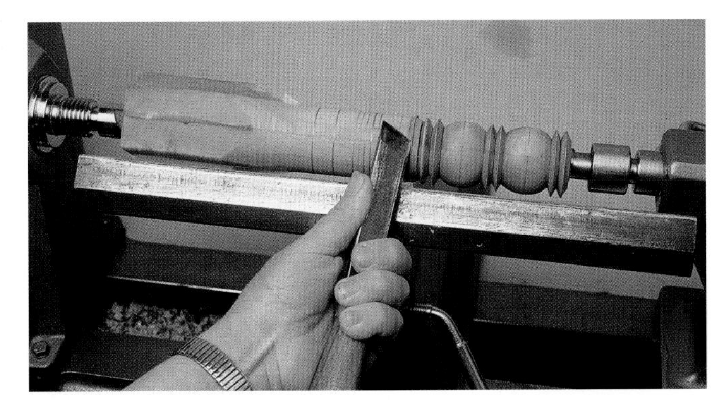

Figure 1.33 Turning the four-piece conglutination from the preceding figure to the bead-and-reel profile shown in figure 1.26.

To prevent the workpiece splitting in the lathe, use a cup rather than a cone live tail center, and ensure that your drive center's prongs bite into wood not into the joint. You might also fasten the ends of the workpiece together mechanically, and this is wise if the workpiece is coopered. You should also lower your lathe's speed.

Figure 1.34 Riving split turnings apart along the paper joints. To the left are split turnings similar to those planted onto some seventeenth-century chests. On the right beneath the bead-and-reel moldings are split turnings similar to those used in seventeenth-century chair backs.

You can sand the remnants of the brown paper away; or if the glue is water soluble, rub the paper and glue away with a rag dampened with boiling water, or steam and scrape the softened paper and glue away.

1.7 COMBINED TURNINGS

Turnings can be combined together after being trimmed as necessary (figures 1.35 and 1.36). The trimming can be done using paper joints as shown in the preceding section, or by sawing and/or planing. Conglutinations of turnings such as those in this section are sometimes called cluster turnings.[10] However there is nothing in the term cluster which suggests that the components are combined into a whole and so lose their individuality. I have therefore discussed the clustering of separate turnings in section 3.2.

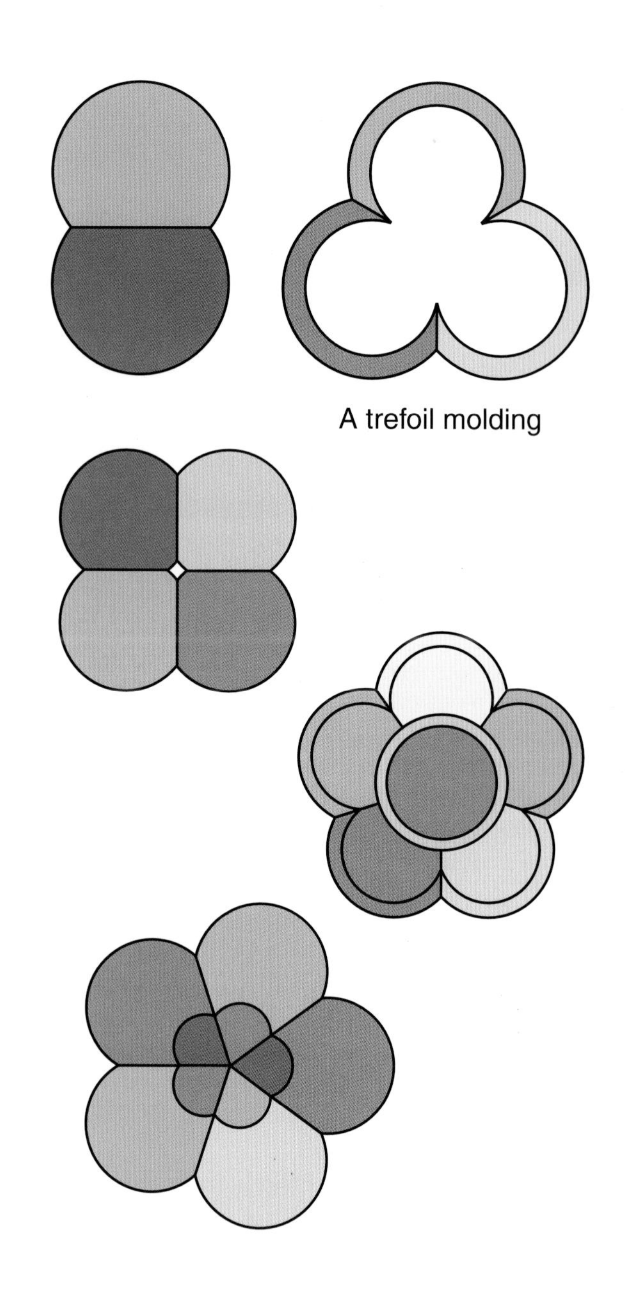

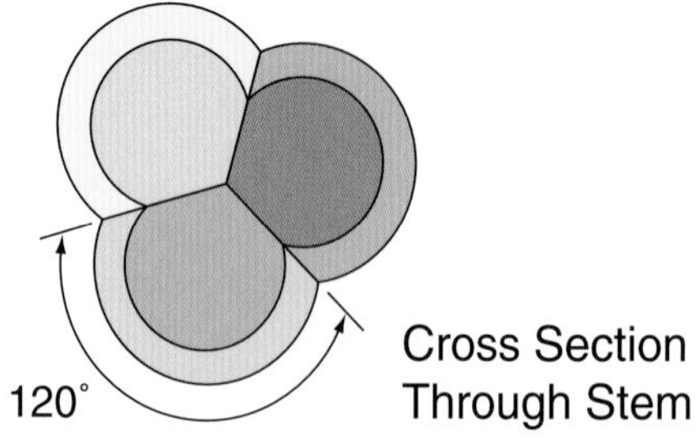

Figure 1.35 **A stem made by combining three spindles.** The cross section shows where flat faces were planed on the three spindles. To plane its faces I held each spindle between the jaws of a clamp, the body of the clamp being held in a vise.

Figure 1.36 **Symmetrically combined turnings.** (Turnings can of course be combined asymmetrically, but there are restrictions if the joints are to be neat). The technique need not be confined to the combining of spindle turnings; cupchuck, faceplate, and bowl turnings can also be combined as the trefoil molding above illustrates. The bottom combination is of turnings similar to club feet (*Woodturning Methods*, pages 130 to 132) turned on two parallel turning-axes.

Figure 1.37 **Candlesticks, combined turnings by Stephen Hogbin** of Ontario. Each was made by turning one face of a square plate, sawing the plate into four squares, and gluing the squares together in a different configuration.

Stephen Hogbin has lead exploration into cutting through turnings to reveal new and unexpected faces and forms, and into the recombination of cut-through turnings. Although out of print, Stephen's first book *Wood Turning: The Purpose of the Object* (Sydney: John Ferguson, 1980) is worth searching out.

Figure 1.38 **Vases by Bruce Leadbeatter** of Sydney, conglutinated from rings turned from offcuts from a coffin manufacturer.[11]

1.8 STACKED RINGS

You can conglutinate a workpiece from radially-grained rings. Dramatic effects can be achieved just by orientating the grain differently in adjacent rings even when the rings are of the same species (figure 1.38). The technique can be used to make a bowl from a single disk of wood (figures 1.39 to 1.41). A turning can be conglutinated from stacked rings of different thicknesses and of different woods, or the rings can conglutinated from several or many pieces of wood in a host of ways as is illustrated in section 1.11.

The first essential is a full-size drawing (figure 1.42). The rings can all be parted through at the same angle, or at whatever angles and to whatever internal and external diameters are most efficient.

To minimize waste, the parting cuts should be as narrow as possible, and angled accurately. Figures 1.43 to 1.47 describe parting rings free in the lathe, but rings can be cut out using a jigsaw or bandsaw.

For bandsawing, the starting disk is prepared as two semicircles. After bandsawing each semicircle into half rings, each corresponding pair is glued end-to-end to produce a full ring. The full rings are then conglutinated into a stack. This technique is used to produce some of the bowls and vessels shown in section 1.11.

Figure 1.39 **A bowl made by Bruce Leadbeatter** from a single disk of wood which was parted into one base and four rings. The rings are separated by light-colored veneer. The theory is described in the next two figures.

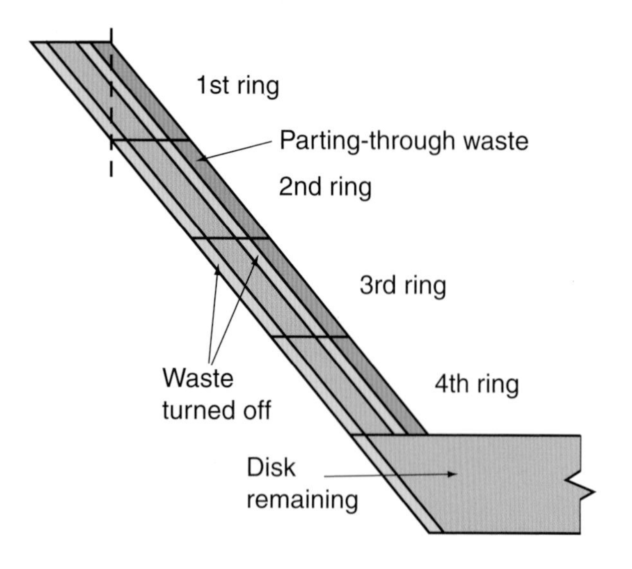

Figure 1.40 **A diagonal section through a bowl made from a single disk,** such as that in the preceding figure.

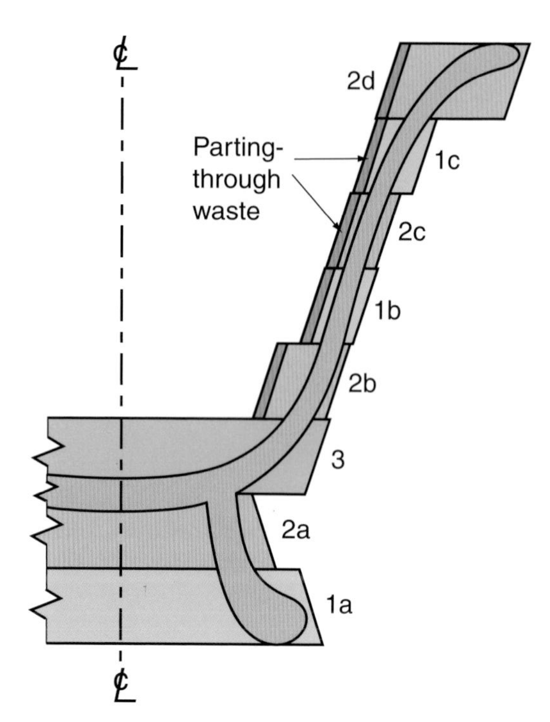

Figure 1.42 **A drawing showing how a bowl with a footrim can be conglutinated** from three disks and five rings, all cut from three disks. When the number of rings is large, it is easier to glue them together into several stacks which are later and after any internal turning glued together to produce the whole workpiece.

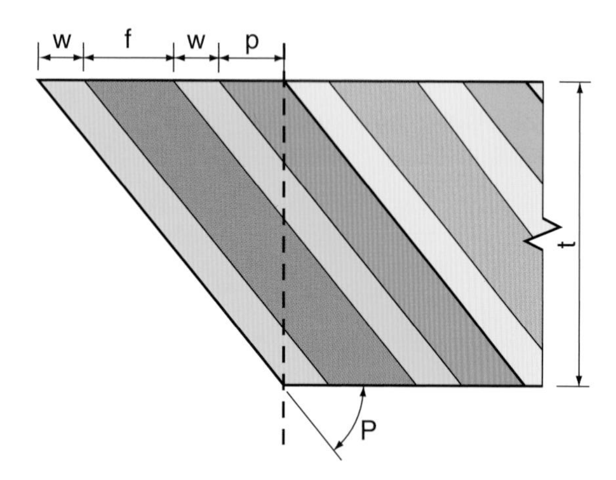

Figure 1.41 **A diagonal section through the edge of the disk which will be parted into rings to make the bowl in the preceding figure.** Angle P, the angle at which to make the parting cut, can be obtained by drawing or calculated from:

$$\tan P = \frac{t}{(2w + f) + p}$$

where: w is the waste which will be turned off the walls
f is the finished wall thickness of the bowl, and
p is the width of the parting cut used to separate the rings

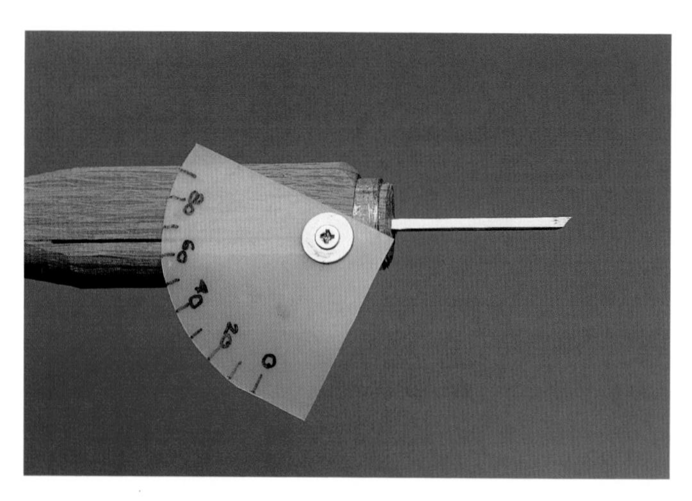

Figure 1.43 **A ring-parting tool.** The blade is a 4 mm x 4 mm HSS toolbit. Setting the angle P (figure 1.41) on the plastic sector enables the tool to be accurately angled in plan when presented to the disk.

Another device which sets the angle P is the Marrison System, sold by Craft Supplies of Derbyshire, England. It includes a horizontal bar of rectangular cross section mounted on a stem which fits in the lathe banjo. In the top of the bar are regularly spaced grooves which guide a $3/16$ in. parting tool. Two bars are available, with angles P at 62.5° and 50°.

Figure 1.44 Parting through a ring.

It is desirable that as a ring is parted through it falls forwards towards the tailstock—the rings spins around the faceplate boss or chuck if pushed backwards. A short toolrest allows the ring to fall forwards freely. The other essential is that the parting tool's cutting edge be sufficiently angled, and this is explained in the next figure.

Figure 1.46 The Leady Ringcutter by Bruce Leadbeatter. The distance between the cutter-holding arms is adjustable. Turning the handle clockwise and counterclockwise moves the pair of cutters to-and-fro as a unit, it does not change the clear distance between the cutter tips.

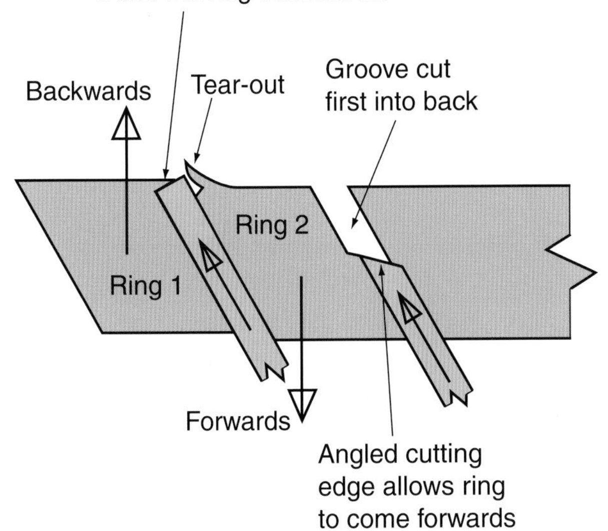

Figure 1.45 Parting rings. *Left*: parting from the front with a cutting edge square in plan pushes the freed ring 1 backwards and causes tear-out around the back of the disk left on the chuck or faceplate. *Right*: both problems are avoided by parting halfway first from the back with an angled cutting edge, and then from the front.

Figure 1.47 The Leady Ringcutter in use. The lathe speed should be low. After setting the Ringcutter to cut at the parting angle P, you first cut halfway through from the front (*right*), then turn the handle in the reverse direction to part through from the back (*left*) and push the ring forwards.

Figure 1.48 **Gluing rings together with a simple yoke cramp.** You can also cramp rings between your lathe's centers, or with G cramps—preferable to the quick-release types which exert a sideways force making it more difficult to keep the rings aligned.

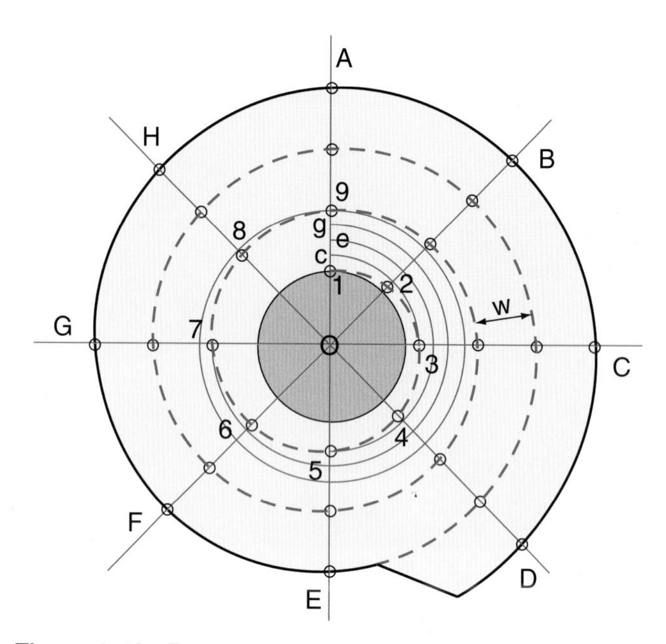

Figure 1.49 **Drawing an Archimedian spiral,** a spiral formed by a band of constant width.[12] Draw the base with a compass, and through its center *0* draw several diameters, here four, spaced at equal vectorial angles. On radius *A* draw the spiral band's width (*1–9*), and divide it into equal lengths, the number of lengths being twice the number of diameters. Draw an arc about *O* from each point *b*, *c*, *d*, etc., from radius *A* until it intersects the corresponding radius *B*, *C*, *D*, etc. (Only alternate arcs are shown). You thus obtain points *1*, *2*, *3*, etc.—you can also obtain them by measurement. Then with dividers set to the band width *w*, scribe the rest of the points on the spiral along the radiuses. The best device to join the points with is a flexible curve which is obtainable from drafting suppliers and resembles a plastic snake. You could also generate the spiral in a computer, and transfer the lines to the wood with carbon paper.

1.9 SPIRAL BOWLS

There are four stages in making a spiral bowl from plywood or wood:

1. Draw an Archimedian spiral on the top face of the wood or plywood (figure 1.49).
2. Saw along the spiral. To achieve tight glue joints the sawcut should not be perpendicular to the workpiece's faces (figure 1.50) and the kerf should be thin.
3. Spring the spiral into a bowl shape (if using solid wood take care not to snap it), and glue it to hold that shape. You cannot properly clamp the spiral, but the self-clamping geometry in figure 1.50 and the gap-filling properties of yellow glue are adequate.
4. The workpiece walls are not concentric about the axis through O in figure 1.49. Therefore take care to mount the workpiece for turning in the position relative to the lathe axis which will give the greatest even wall thickness over the whole wall area.

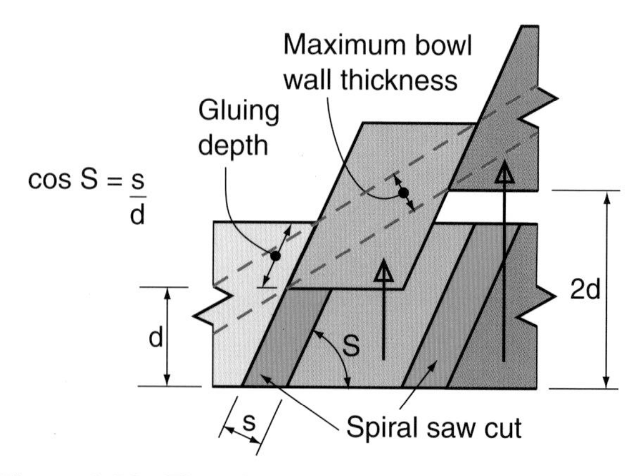

Figure 1.50 **The theory of the spiral bowl** shown in radial section. You can calculate the angle *S*, and if you cut the spiral at an angle slightly less than *S*, most of the spiral will be self-clamping.

Figure 1.51 Gluing a spiral bowl. The width *w* of the spiral was 3/8 in. (10 mm) and the plywood 1/2 in. (13 mm) thick.

Figure 1.52 The completed spiral bowl.

1.10 DECORATIVE CONGLUTINATION

By conglutinating pieces of wood of different colors and grain patterns you can achieve geometric, figurative, and communicative effects. Spectacular decorative effects can even be achieved by conglutinating small pieces cut from the same large piece of wood, especially if the wood has chatoyance (a greater ability to reflect light). Additional effects can be achieved by using colored epoxies, pewter, and other materials as inlay, as a filling, or as a matrix .

In decorative conglutinations there are three adverse factors in addition to any resulting from differences and changes in the moisture contents of the component pieces:

1. End-grain absorbs finishes to a greater extent than side-grain, and therefore tends to be darkened more by tinted finishes (figure 1.39).
2. When you sand a conglutination of woods of different hardnesses, the softer wood will be abraded faster and the smooth circularity of the surface will be marred.
3. Ultraviolet light and oxidation changes the colors of woods over time.
4. Polishes yellow, turn brown, fade, or whiten over time. Therefore the brilliance of a freshly exposed wood surface will fade over time, and the colors can change and dull (or mellow) significantly. There is a positive; lanolin from hands, and waxing and rubbing, can build a glowing patina.

The endnotes list some of the books and articles which detail decorative conglutination.[13] I shall not attempt to replicate their content in this and the next section for it would need a large book. But to summarize, there are nine main methods of decorative conglutination which can be used alone or in a variety of combinations:

1. Edge-to-edge, and face-to-face conglutination.
2. Repeated conglutinations with resawing between.
3. Simple rings glued together face-to-face.
4. Rings conglutinated from sectors or cut from edge-to-edge and face-to-face conglutinations.
5. Layers not of equal thickness, nor of constant thickness.
6. Drilling holes and gluing in turned plugs.
7. Inlaying disks and rings.
8. Building a Platonic solid not from layers, but from identical component pieces with their edges not at right angles to their faces which glue together to form the basic shape directly. For example, Jack Cox on pages 204 to 216 of *Beyond Basic Turning* shows how to conglutinate hollow spheres from four, six, eight, twelve, or twenty component pieces.
9. Conglutinations in which the glue joints are curved not flat.

Figure 1.53 A Tunbridge ware box lid. Woodware with polychrome wood mosaic patterns and pictures was made in Tunbridge Wells, Kent, England, from about 1830. Production declined from 1880, and ceased at the outbreak of WWII.[14] The mosaic retains excellent definition because the tiny pieces of wood are all seen side-grain. It would have been far easier to show end-grain, but the picture would have been darker, with less color differentiation between the species.

Figure 1.54 Bookends, a souvenir in New Zealand native woods. Planks of different woods were conglutinated face-to-face to produce a composite plank which was then planed, and bandsawn into disks. After turning, each disk was split along a diameter.

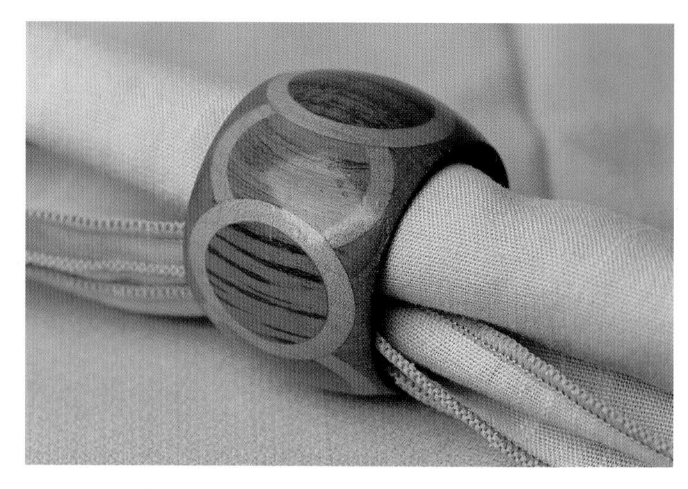

Figure 1.56 A napkin ring. It holds a napkin—only "non-U" types use the genteelism serviette, perhaps to avoid any association with nappy (diaper to North American readers).[15] Napkin is derived from napery (table linen), and does not have any etymological connection with nape, the back of the neck, although the practice of tucking the edge of the tablecloth or a large napkin into one's collar has much to recommend it. The procedure for making this napkin ring is shown in the next figure.

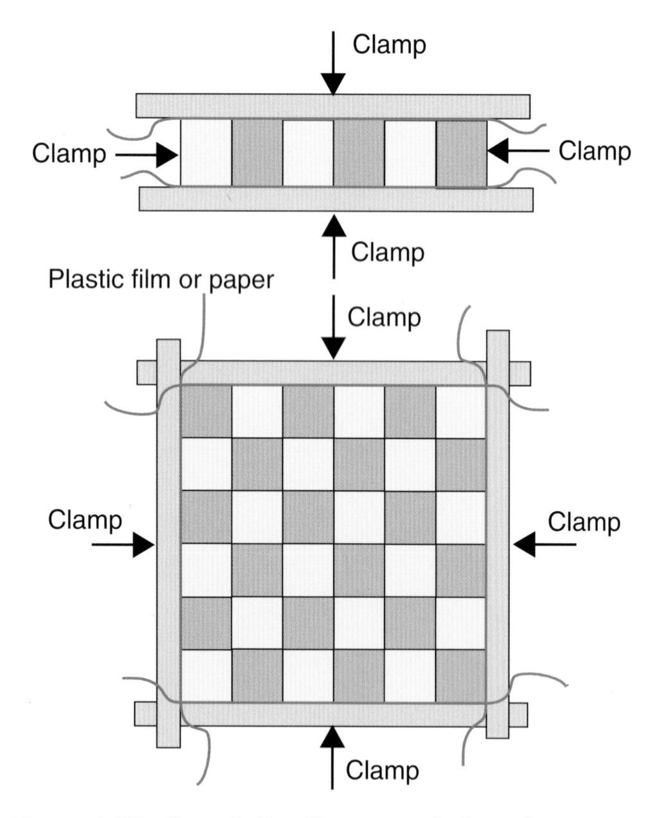

Figure 1.55 Conglutinating a workpiece in a checkerboard pattern. (In both drawings the strips of wood are shown end-grain). *Top*: first conglutinate a row of long strips face-to-face. Use an even number of strips which are slightly rectangular in cross section. When the glue is set, plane one face and thickness the conglutination. Then crosscut it, here to produce six lengths. *Bottom*: The six lengths are glued together.

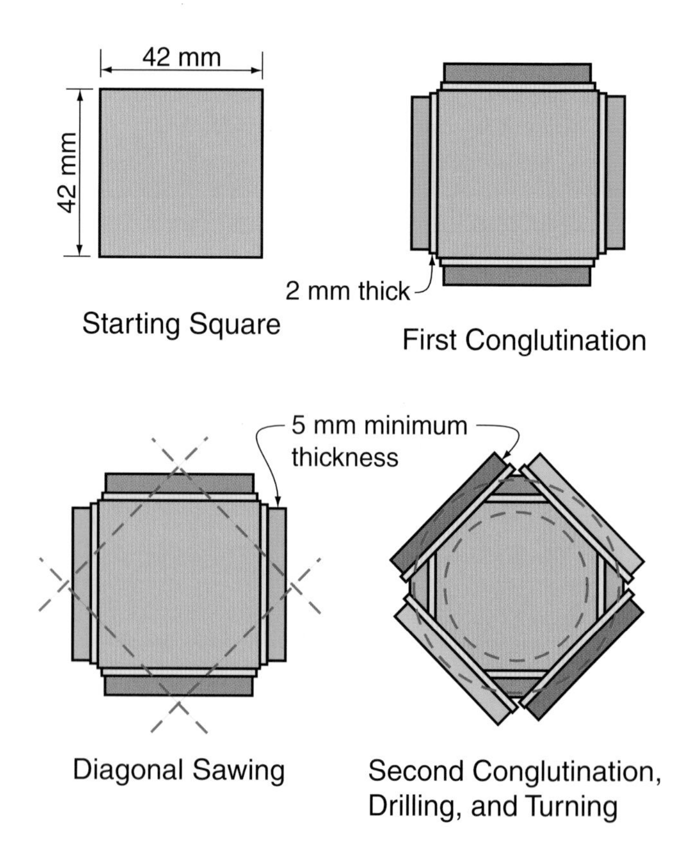

Figure 1.57 The procedure for making the napkin ring in the preceding figure. All wood is viewed in cross section and end grain.

1.11 MORE-COMPLEX DECORATIVE EFFECTS

The preceding sections described relatively simple conglutinations. You can build a workpiece from rings or layers which are themselves conglutinated from pieces of one, several, or many species. These pieces are commonly sectors, but they can be shaped and assembled in an infinite number of ways. Nor need the rings or layers be perpendicular to a piece's axis of symmetry. And the patterns formed can be seemingly random, geometric, figurative, or communicative. Figures 1.58 to 1.68 show just a few of the possibilities.

Figure 1.58 Chok-te-kok bowl by Michael Shuler of Santa Cruz, California; diameter 12 in. (300 mm), height 5 in (125 mm). The woods are satinwood, Gabon ebony, and chok-te-viga.

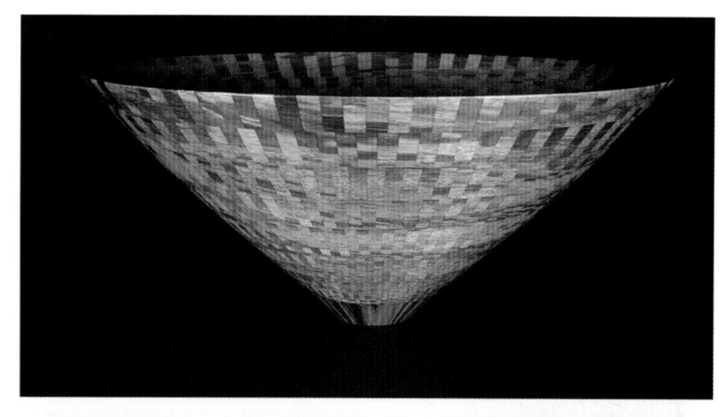

Figure 1.59 A Brazilian tulipwood bowl by Michael Shuler, 12 in. (300 mm) diameter, 5 in. (125 mm) high. Michael started making similar bowls in 1985.[16]

Michael builds his bowls from two disks of sectors or wedges, all cut from the same plank in the above bowl.[15] The smaller disk is used for the bowl base, and consists of 20 wedges. These wedges are ripcut because they must end at sharp points at the center of the disk.

The larger disk is used for the walls of the bowl, and consists of 104 (an unusually large number) of crosscut wedges glued together. This larger disk is first conglutinated as two semicircles, which are then bandsawn with the table tilted according to the geometry described in figures 1.40 and 1.41. The resulting, corresponding half rings are joined, and these full rings and the base disk are glued together and clamped in a yoke similar to that in figure 1.48. The conglutination is then turned.

Figure 1.60 A pair of pots by Ray Allen which recall a veneering technique.[17] In veneering the "waste" veneer left after cutting the primary pattern can be assembled to produce the reverse pattern. For example after cutting an ebony circle to go within a maple square, the premiere partie, the waste pieces of veneer can be assembled to create a maple circle within an ebony background, the contre-partie or deuxieme partie.[18] Premiere- and contre-partie are also called Boulle and counter Boulle after Andre-Charles Boulle (1642–1732), the celebrated French marquetry cutter.[19]

Figure 1.61 Vases with their maker Keith Tory of Queensland. Conglutination enables you to produce big items without the problems of seasoning thick sections, turning heavy lumps of wood, or large-scale hollow turning.

Keith, a retired builder, self-published *A Step by Step Guide to Polychromatic Woodturning* in 2000.[20]

Figure 1.62 **A hollow turning by Keith Tory featuring Australian fauna.**

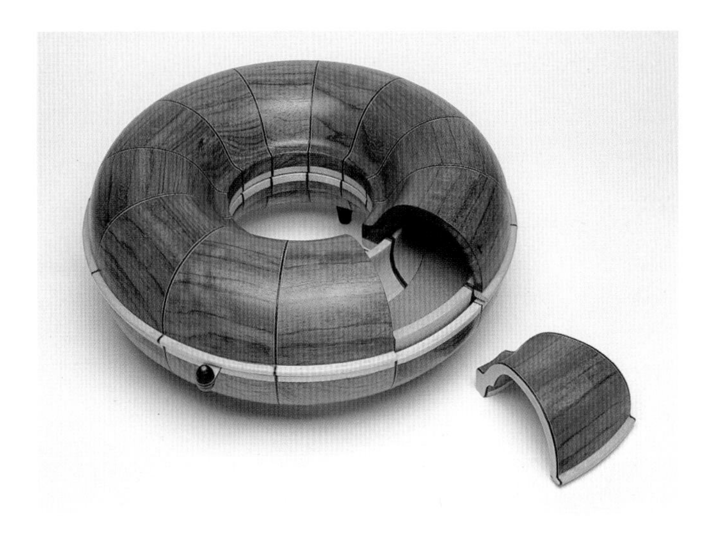

Figure 1.64 **"Toroid", a jewellery box by Philip Bowman** of Newton Highlands, Massachusetts. The top revolves, and the single removable sector lifts off to gain access. The diameter is 12 in. (300 mm), and the woods are bubinga, maple, ebony, and dyed veneer.

Figure 1.63 **A pot by Ray Allen,** 7 in. (180 mm) high. The layers were tapered in thickness before being glued together. *Photograph by Gary Zeff.*

Figure 1.65 **A vase by Philip Bowman,** 10 in. (250 mm) high, 5 in. (125 mm) in diameter, in bloodwood, bird's-eye maple, ebony, maple, and dyed veneer.

Figure 1.66 A "basket" bowl by Gary Johnson of Bridgeton, Missouri. His technique is similar to Michael Shuler's, is detailed in two articles,[21] and is in brief:

1. Design and draw a diametrical section through the bowl similar to that in figure 1.40, and design the mosaic pattern of the wall.
2. Glue together several thin planks (four in figure 1.68) face-to-face to produce sandwiches. The planks are sandwiched in the designed order which may not be the same for all sandwiches. Each plank has the same thickness and is of a species of the desired color.
3. Crosscut each sandwich into 48 sectors with an included angle of 7.5°.
4. Arrange the 48 sectors into a disk. Depending on the complexity of the mosaic pattern, the sectors in a disk may come from some or all of the sandwiches, and some sectors may be reversed top to bottom. Glue all joints except for two opposite joints, so that the resulting disk will be in the form of two semicircles. Gary recommends a band clamp and a slow-setting epoxy for this gluing as the assembly time can be as long as an hour.
5. Using hot-melt glue, fix each pair of semicircles to a backing plate, and skim both faces flat (figure 1.67).
6. Mark out and bandsaw each semicircle into several half rings. For each the bandsaw table is tilted according to the design. This process is akin to the parting off of rings in figures 1.44 and 1.47.
7. Glue the corresponding pairs of half rings into rings.
8. Lightly disk sand the rings' faces flat if required. Clamp and glue together the stack of rings (four in figure 1.68) with each ring correctly orientated, the base disk, and any rim ring.
9. Chuck the bowl blank by its rim, and turn a chucking spigot on the base disk (figure 1.68).
10. Finish-turn the bowl.

Figure 1.67 A disk of two semicircles, each of 24 sectors, being skimmed flat.

Figure 1.68 About to turn a spigot on the base disk to enable accurate bowl alignment for the finish-turning. The mosaic body is conglutinated from four rings.

1.12 ENDNOTES

1 References for table 1.1 and section 1.1 include:

Niall Barrett, "Polyurethane Glue," *Fine Woodworking* 113 (July/Aug 1995): pp. 46–47.

Chris Minick, "Adhesives for Woodworking," *Fine Woodworking* (Sept/Oct 1992): pp. 44–50.

William Tandy Young, *The Glue Book* (Newtown, CT: The Taunton Press, 1998).

Product information from Chemco Adhesives P/L, Marrickville, NSW, Australia.

Product information from Selleys Chemical Company P/L, Moorebank, NSW, Australia.

2. Most of the data and information in table 1.2 and section 1.2 was sourced from Keith Bootle, *Wood in Australia* (Sydney: McGraw Hill, 1983).

3. Graph based on David Johnston, *The Wood Handbook for Craftsmen* (London: B.T. Batsford, 1983), p. 17, fig. 8.
4. *Encyclopaedia Britannica.*
5. Not much has been published on coopering columns. Of interest is John Leeke, "Coopered Columns," *Fine Woodworking* 28 (May/June 1981): pp. 78–83. However I advocate gluing in one or at most two operations, and turning with cutting tools, either hand-held or carriage-mounted, is both quieter and faster than using a router.
6. Charles H. Hayward, *Woodwork Joints* (London: Evans Brothers, 1960), pp. 13–15.
7. Edward H. Pinto, *Treen and Other Wooden Bygones* (London: G. Bell & Sons, 1969), pp. 53–54, pl. 46.
8. A. Graef and M. Graef, *Moderner Drechslerarbeiten* (1889; reprint, Hannover: Verlag Th. Schafer, 1982), pl. XXIII.
9. I. C. S. Reference Library, *Wood Working, etc.* (London: International Correspondence Schools Ltd, 1914), pp. 14–15 of Patternmaking.
10. Judith Miller, *A Closer Look at Antiques* (Noble Park, Australia: The Five Mile Press, 2000), p. 155.
11. Bruce Leadbeatter described his techniques in "Turning Boards into Bowls," *Australian Woodworker* (Sept/Oct 1997): pp. 82–82.
12 .W. Abbott, *Practical Geometry and Engineering Graphics* (London: Blackie & Son, 1962), pp. 54–55.
13. Books which concentrate on decorative conglutination for woodturners include:

    Emmett E. Brown and Cyril Brown, *Polychromatic Assembly for Woodturning* (Fresno, CA: Linden Publishing, 1982).

    Jack Cox, *Beyond Basic Turning* (Hertford, UK: Stobart Davies, 1993).

    Clarence Rannefeld, *Laminated Designs in Wood* (Asheville, NC: Lark Books, 1998).

    Articles on decorative conglutination for woodturners include:

    Gianfranco Angeling, "Composite Bowls," *American Woodturner* (September 1994): pp. 30–33.

    Bob Armstrong, "Turning Laminated Bowls and Vases," *American Woodturner* (December 1988): pp. 4–7.

    Jim Armstrong, "Segmented Turnings," *American Woodturner* (December 1989): pp. 3–5.

    Dick Bew, "Stickwork for Use in Woodturning," *Woodturning* 6 (January/February 1992): pp. 48–51.

    Virginia Dotson, "Laminated Turnings," *American Woodturner* (June 1995): pp. 8–11.

    Addie Draper and Bud Latven, "Segmented Turning," *Fine Woodworking* 54 (September/October 1985): pp. 64–67.

    Ron Hampton, "A Touch of Class," *Woodturning* 64 (June 1998): pp. 36–39.

    Gordon Harrison, "Curve-Segmented Plates," *American Woodturner* (September 1996): pp. 24–26.

    Jim Hume, "Segmented Urns," *American Woodturner* (December 1994): pp. 32–35.

    John Hunnex, "Stripping Down," *Woodturning* 77 (July 1999): pp. 13–16.

    Willis M. Hunt, "Eight-Piece Ring Turnings," *American Woodturner* (March 1996): pp. 18–23.

    Dale Larson, "Stacked-Ring Bowls," *American Woodturner* (September 1992): pp. 10–13.

    Terry Lawrence "Blockwork," a series of eight articles running in *Woodturning* between issues 56 and 65 (October 1997–July 1998).

    Jenelle Lenser, "Multiple-Segment Turnings," *Fine Woodworking* 83 (Aug 1990): pp. 46–47.

    David May, "Part and Parcel," *Woodturning* 80 (October 1999): pp.13–16.

    Dave Ramsey, "Tall Segmented Vessels," *American Woodturner* (Winter 1998): pp. 13–15.

    Lincoln Seitzman, "Polychromatic Assembly," *American Woodturner* (December 1989): pp. 8–9.

    Robert Sterba, "Bricklaid Bowls," *Fine Woodworking* 64 (May/June 1987): pp. 48–53.

    Vic Wood, "The Ring Master," *Woodturning* 27 (November 1994): pp. 42–47.
14. Margaret A.V. Gill, *Tunbridge Ware* (Aylesbury, Buckinghamshire: Shire Publications), 1985.
15. Nancy Mitford, *Nobless Oblige* (London: Hamish Hamilton, 1956), p.42; and R.W. Burchfield, *The New Fowler's Modern English Usage* (Oxford: Clarendon Press, 1996).
16. Michael detailed his basic method for making a bowl in "Segmented Turning," *Fine Woodworking* 76 (May/June 1989): pp. 72–75. He detailed further thoughts and progress in "Monochrome Assembly," *American Woodturner* (December 1989): pp. 14–15; and "Rediscovering Polychrome," *American Woodturner* (June 1995): pp. 12–13.
17. Ray Allen, "Ray Allen's Segmented Turnings," *American Woodturner* (March 1993): pp. 2–8.
18. George Savage, *French Decorative Art* 1638–1793 (London: Allen Lane The Penguin Press, 1969), p. 61.
19. Ernest Joyce, *The Technique of Furniture Making* (London: B.T. Batsford, 1970), p. 240.
20. Keith Tory, *Step by Step Guide to Polychromatic Woodturning*. Self-published in 2000, and available direct from Keith at P.O. Box 785, Maryborough, Queensland, Australia 4650.
21. Gary Johnson, "Basket Bowls," *American Woodturner* (Summer 1998): pp. 22–25; and Albert LeCoff, "Double Vision," *Woodturning* 35 (September 1995): pp. 20–21.

Chapter Two

TOOL GRINDING

Chapter 4 of FOW gave an overview of turning-tool sharpening. This chapter focusses on how you can best grind turning tools on grinding wheels, but ends with an alternative to grinding for sharpening scrapers.

Cutting tools must be honed to achieve a sharp, long-lasting edge. After a grinding followed by about three honings, you need to regrind. Regrinding the bevel(s) on a convex abrasive surface to produce the same sharpening angle each time has five advantages (figure 2.1). But you cannot regrind to this accuracy without a jig. Even then grinding, truing and dressing continually reduce the diameter of your grinding wheel. You may therefore have to continually alter your grinding jig settings; and this chapter shows how.

Improved grinding methods and technology have little value if you grind your tool tips to inferior shapes. Pages 53 to 65 of FOW show the preferred tool tip shapes and sharpening angles. These recommendations may differ from tool manufacturers' grindings and from those specified in other texts, grinding-jig instruction booklets, and videos—for example, some recommend a 45° sharpening angle for roughing gouges rather than the 30° which I favor.

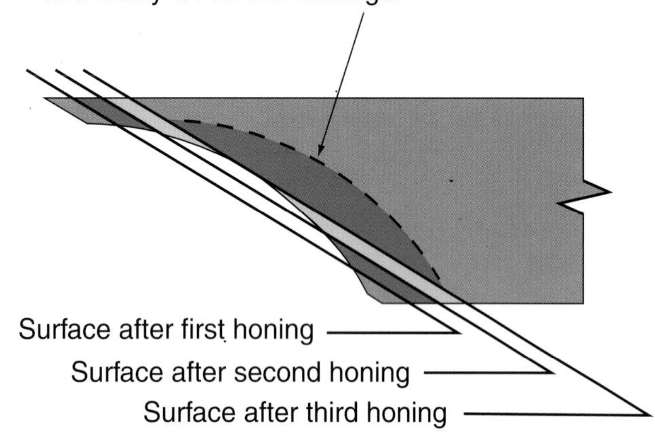

Figure 2.1 **The ideal regrinding and honing procedure for a bevel,** originally figure 4.27 of *FOW*. In this longitudinal section the amount of hollow grind is exaggerated, and the honing of the tool's top surface is omitted.

The procedure in the drawing maximizes:

1. Cutting edge durability because the steel remains cool during the brief regrindings.
2. Tool life because the blade is shortened only by honing.
3. The speed of resharpening. Honing is quicker than regrinding, and jigged regrinding is usually quicker than regrinding by hand.
4. Tool predictability. Because each tool's sharpening angle remains constant, you will automatically present each tool to the wood correctly.
5. The life of your abrasive belt, or grinding wheel and dresser.

But to maximize these gains you have to regrind the same sharpening angle each time, and ideally leave very narrow honed bands along the bevel heel and adjacent to the cutting edge. These narrow bands then support the tool at the correct angle for the subsequent honing.

2.1 THE PROBLEM OF GRINDING-WHEEL WEAR

Three types of abrasive surface are used to grind turning tools:

1. A flat surface such as over the flat platen of a belt sander, the side of a grinding wheel, or the top face of a grinding wheel which rotates about a vertical axis.
2. A cylindrical surface of fixed curvature and position such as that formed by a sanding belt passing over a driving or jockey wheel, or a curved platen.
3. The cylindrical periphery of a grinding wheel.

Flat grinding surfaces produce flat bevels which are slow to hone because you have to keep the whole bevel in contact with the hone if you want to preserve the ground sharpening angle. I do not therefore recommend flat grinding surfaces for turning tools. When grinding over the wheel of a belt sander or similar, accurate jigging is straightforward because the curvature and position of the grinding surface remain fixed. This means of grinding was detailed in figures 4.30 and 4.31 of FOW, but is usually too expensive for most turners. This chapter therefore concentrates on grinding on grinding wheels.

You will grind far more accurately on a grinding wheel if you use a jig. However, as figure 2.2 confirms, you need to continually adjust your jig's settings to compensate for wheel wear. Figure 2.3 clarifies the nomenclature of bevels.

The resetting of tilting-platform jigs is discussed in the next section 2.2. The O'Donnell Tool Sharpening System, the first commercial jig to incorporate a formal means for adjusting for wheel wear, is described in section 2.3.

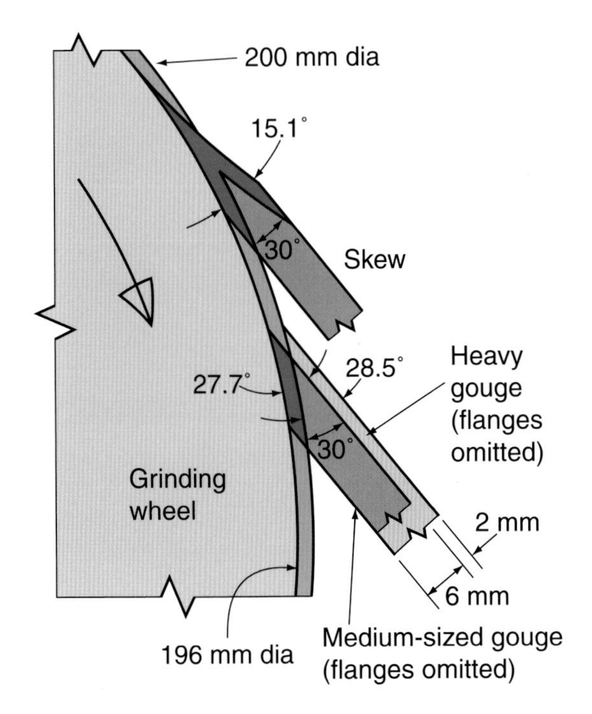

Figure 2.2 How grinding-wheel wear reduces tool sharpening angles. This vertical section shows a grinding wheel at 200 mm diameter, and after it has worn to 196 mm diameter.

The 30°, 30° and 28.5° sharpening angles were ground when the grinding wheel diameter was 200 mm. The same platform settings continued to be used as the wheel wore and was dressed to 196 mm diameter. The diagram confirms that sharpening angles:

1. Decrease at a greater rate for tools with smaller nominal sharpening angles. The decrease is therefore negligible for scrapers, and greatest for skews—here from 30° (2 x 15°) to 15.1° (2 x 7.55°).
2. Decrease at a greater rate for tools with bigger bevel thicknesses. (The term bevel thickness is defined in the next figure).
3. Vary with bevel thickness. The sharpening angles of 30° for the medium-sized gouge and the 28.5° for the heavy gouge show that the sharpening angle ground using a particular platform setting is smaller for thicker bevels.

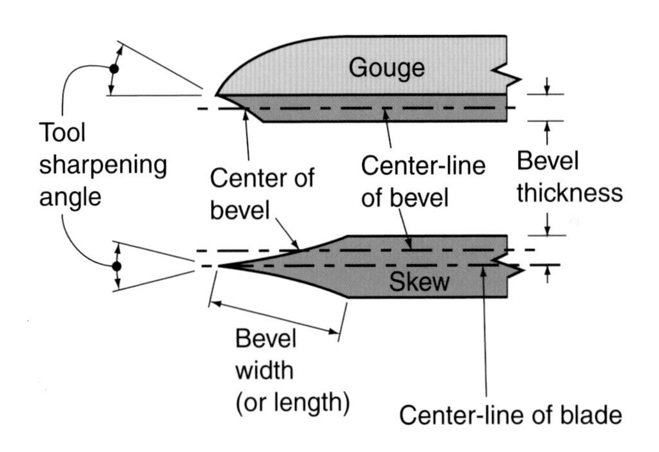

Figure 2.3 Bevel nomenclature illustrated in longitudinal sections.

2.2 TILTING-PLATFORM JIGS

Tilting-platform grinding jigs receive less attention than they deserve. Perhaps accurate grinding is mistakenly thought to be so difficult that only the more elaborate and expensive jigs can ensure success—I am not against such jigs and acknowledge that they have enabled many turners to greatly improve their tool grinding, but platform jigs can be both accurate and quick to adjust.

Figures 2.4 to 2.6 show the three types of commercially available tilting-platform jig. Homemade versions are common and some, for example that shown by Hugh O'Neill,[1] incorporate features for quickly adjusting the platform settings for different sharpening angles. Unfortunately there is rarely any attempt to compensate for wheel wear.

To regrind a tool with your preferred sharpening angle every time during the life of a wheel, you can reset the platform's tilt and occasionally its closeness to the wheel by using the tool itself as a template as shown in figures 2.4 and 2.5. This method is however not reliably accurate for tools with bevels which are narrow, much honed, or were last ground when the grinding wheel diameter was substantially greater. Also, as there will be some wheel wear during a single regrinding, the sharpening angle ground will be minutely less than that present before the regrinding. Over the life of a wheel this could cause a perceptible reduction in each tool's sharpening angle. The alternative is to use separate templates. Their geometry and use is detailed in figures 2.7 to 2.20: the compensating type in figures 2.15 to 2.20 is patented.

Figure 2.4 **Resetting the tilt of a single-pivot platform jig by using the bevel of the gouge about to be ground as a template.**

You first place the bevel heel on the wheel with the tool blade in light but full contact with the platform. To bring the bevel into full contact with the wheel, you pull the handle back and up. This causes the blade to slide down and across the platform, the platform to rotate counterclockwise, and the wheel to rotate forwards. With two-pivot jigs, such as that shown in the next figure, the tool blade does not have to slide across the platform.

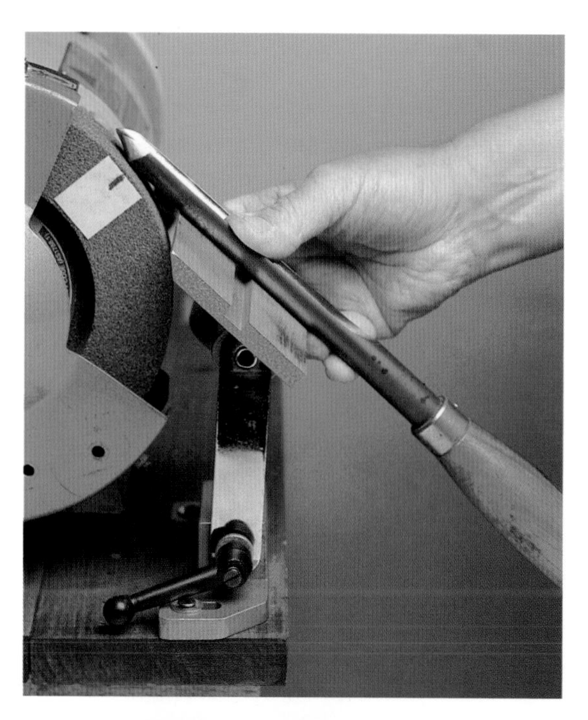

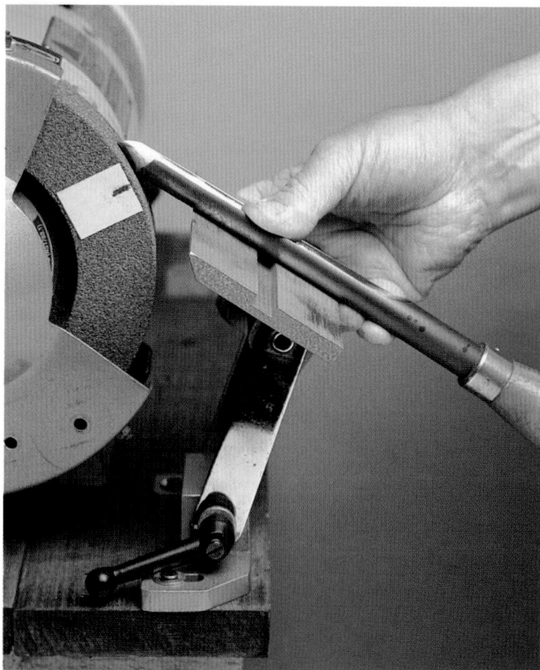

Figure 2.5 **Setting the platform of a two-pivot platform jig,** the CJ-04, made in Taiwan and widely available. The groove in the platform is to guide slides which jig wheel dressing and tool grinding (figure 2.23).

You hold the tool onto the platform with the tool tip projecting from the platform's front edge the distance that you desire for grinding. With both pivots free, place the bevel heel onto the wheel. Gently lift the tool handle until the tool bevel comes into full contact with the wheel periphery. Then lock the two pivots without moving the tool or the platform. (This method is also used to set the Heli-Grind jig which is described in section 2.9).

Figure 2.6 **A one-pivot platform jig,** the Platform Attachment of the Wolverine Grinding Jig. You can adjust this platform as though it were two-pivot by having the slide and the pivot free. If you lock the slide beforehand, you have adjust the platform's tilt as though the jig were of the single-pivot type shown in figure 2.4.

Under the right-hand wheel is the second housing supplied with the Wolverine system. It houses a handle-end jig, a jig type described in section 2.5. Either Wolverine jig type can be mounted in either housing. Oneway's Wolverine grinding system, first developed in Stratford, Ontario in 1993, has since been extended by the introduction of new attachments.

Tilting-platform jigs do not have to be set from your tools' bevels, they can also be set from templates.

Figure 2.7 **A simple template** designed to set the CJ-04 platform to produce a 30° sharpening angle. The screw head locates in the channel in the top face of the platform, and helps maintain the template in the desired position on the platform while setting the platform tilt (see next figure).

Figure 2.8 **Setting a platform jig with the simple template of the preceding figure.** This template is similar to that shown in figure 4.39 of *FOW*. Although recommended in the instructions for some commercial platform jigs, templates of this type are not accurate over a range of grinding wheel diameters as the next figure shows.

Inaccurate platform setting necessitates more grinding: a 1° error in resetting the platform for regrinding a 10 mm wide bevel, means that an extra $^1/_6$ mm thickness of steel will have to be ground off one end of the bevel.

Some platform jigs have defined settings for different sharpening angles. These settings may ignore the need to continually adjust the settings to compensate for grinding-wheel wear and differences in bevel thickness. The effects of both are illustrated in the next figure.

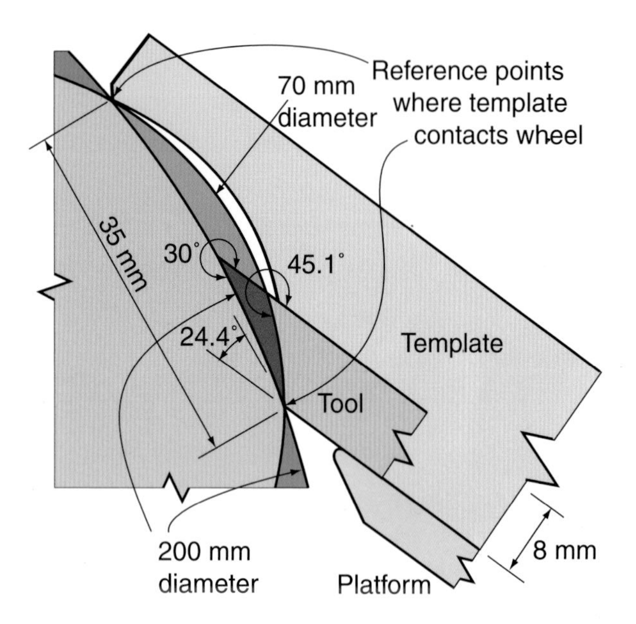

Figure 2.9 **The geometry of a simple template** similar to that shown in the preceding two figures. The grinding wheel is shown in side elevation at 200 mm diameter, and worn to 70 mm diameter.

If the template is designed to set the platform tilt to produce a sharpening angle of 30° with a 200 mm wheel on an 8 mm bevel thickness, the same template will lead to a 45.1° sharpening angle on the same bevel thickness when the wheel has worn to 70 mm. A realistic situation, that of grinding a 4 mm bevel thickness on a 200 mm diameter wheel wearing to 150 mm, would not show the effects clearly in a diagram, but is detailed in table 2.1. This table shows that for the same bevel thickness, the increase in sharpening angle in degrees as a wheel wears is largely independent of the magnitude of the sharpening angle. But if the increase is measured as a proportion of the nominal sharpening angle, the increase is greater for smaller sharpening angles.

The template in the diagram references to the grinding wheel at two points 35 mm apart measured along a chord. This chord does not lie at the nominal included angle of 30° to the template's bottom edge, but at 24.5°. This lesser angle is necessary to give the desired 30° sharpening angle on a bevel 8 mm thick ground on a 200 mm diameter wheel. Only when the bevel width equals the distance between the two reference points will the angle between the chord and the bottom straight edge of the template equal the nominal sharpening angle.

A major reason for the inaccuracy of simple templates is that their two reference points have to be held against the wheel on one side of the platform, here above. This shortcoming is not present in the templates shown in the next figure.

Table 2.1 Sharpening angles for 4 mm bevel thicknesses, the platform tilt set using the simple type of template.

Nominal sharpening angle	*Grinding-wheel diameter 200 mm*	*150 mm*
12.5°	12.5°	15.7°
30°	30.0°	32.9°
70°	70.0°	73.0°

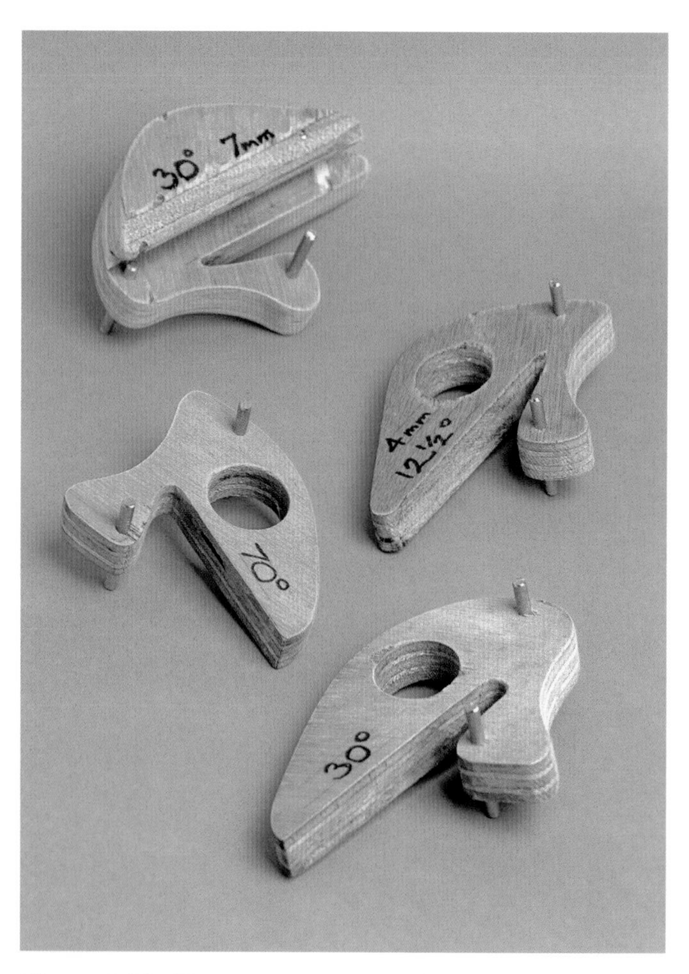

Figure 2.10 **Four two-pin templates.** The three front templates are used to set the tilts of platforms (next two figures). The rear template is used to position a tool directly on a grinding wheel (figure 2.32). Figures 2.13 to 2.20 show how the designs of these patented templates are derived.

Figure 2.11 **Setting the platform tilt to grind a 70° sharpening angle with a two-pin template.**

The 32 mm diameter thumb hole makes the template easier to hold in place. The two pins which are held against the periphery of the grinding wheel are 5 mm in diameter and 70 mm apart—this long separation increases the template's accuracy.

You may need to pack your grinder or your grinding jig up so that the platform is at the optimum level relative to the grinding wheel. If your jig is too high relative to your grinder:

1. When grinding a detail gouge, the tool tip may have to go under the guard when grinding near the tops of the flanges as figure 2.30 illustrates.
2. If you wanted to use a two-pin template to set the platform tilt, there might be insufficient clearance between the platform and the guard to fit the template.

Figure 2.12 **Setting the tilt of a Oneway Platform Attachment** for a grinding a skew chisel with a two-pin template.

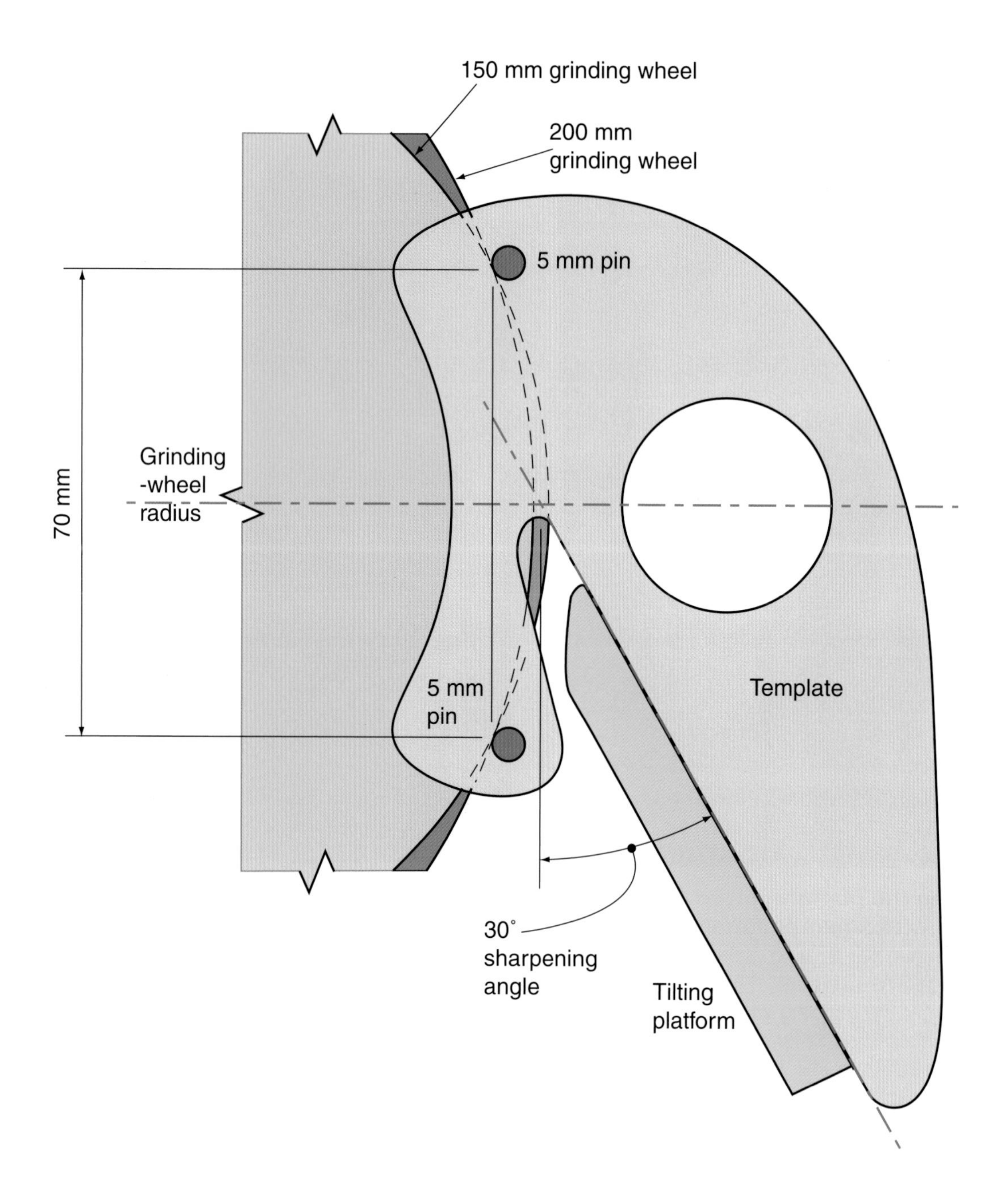

Figure 2.13 **An uncorrected two-pin template,** here for a nominal 30° sharpening angle. To improve its accuracy the template is designed to be used on a diameter halfway between the 200 mm diameter of a new wheel, and 150 mm, the diameter at which a 200 mm wheel would typically be replaced.

Unfortunately, this two-pin template design does not guarantee the desired sharpening angle as table 2.2 demonstrates. The attempt to minimize the effects of wheel wear by using the average wheel diameter is not totally successful. Also, the template ignores the effects that variations in bevel thickness have on the sharpening angle ground, a factor which the template design in the next figure largely corrects.

Table 2.2 The sharpening angles ground on different bevel thicknesses at different wheel diameters. The nominal sharpening angle is 30°.

Bevel thickness	*Grinding wheel-diameter*	
	200 mm	*150 mm*
3 mm	28.6°	26.9°
5 mm	27.2°	25.9°
7 mm	25.1°	23.9°

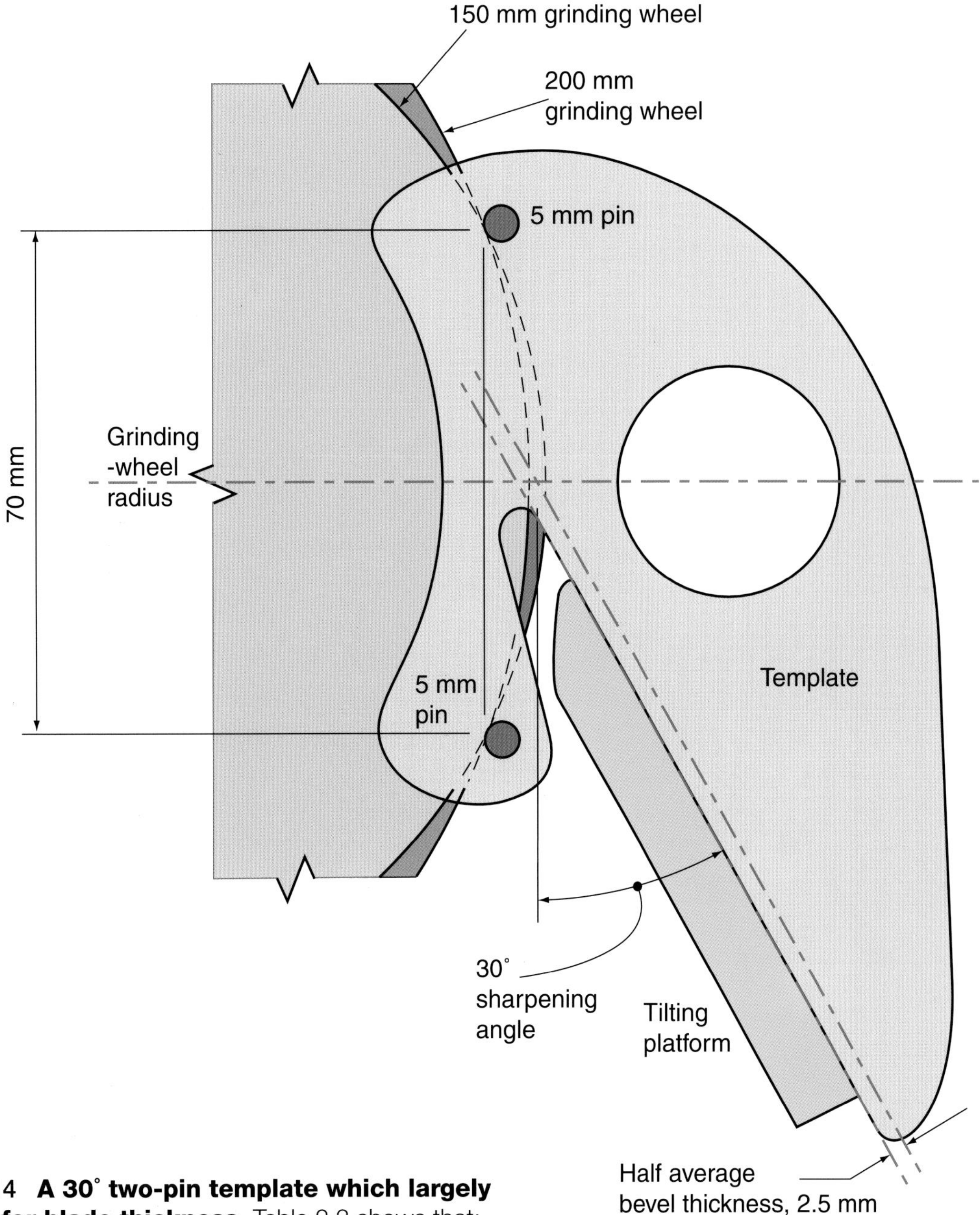

Figure 2.14 A 30° two-pin template which largely corrects for blade thickness. Table 2.3 shows that:

1. The increase in the sharpening angle ground as the wheel wears is acceptable.
2. The differences in sharpening angle between tools with different bevel thicknesses is less than 3° which is also acceptable.

With sharpening angles bigger than 30° this type of template is acceptably accurate. However for tools with sharpening angles below 30°, and especially skews, you want greater accuracy. The templates in figures 2.15 to 2.20 provide that greater accuracy over the full range of sharpening angles.

If your jig's platform is iron or steel, you could incorporate a pot magnet into the template body to hold the template to the platform.

Table 2.3 The sharpening angles ground on different bevel thicknesses at different grinding-wheel diameters. Nominal sharpening angle 30°.

Bevel thickness	*Grinding-wheel diameter*	
	200 mm	*150 mm*
3 mm	30.7°	31.8°
5 mm	29.0°	30.8°
7 mm	27.5°	29.3°

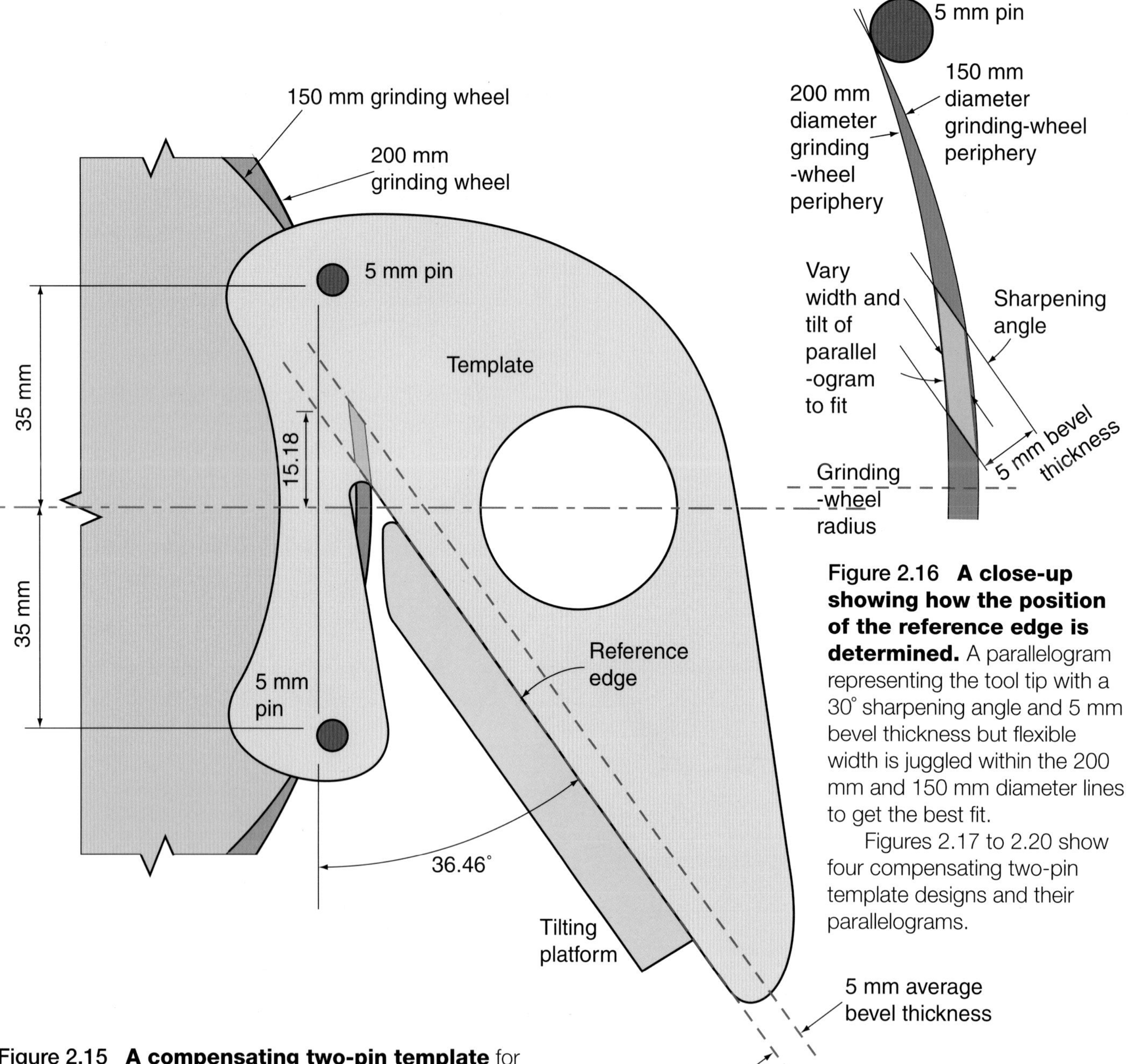

Figure 2.16 **A close-up showing how the position of the reference edge is determined.** A parallelogram representing the tool tip with a 30° sharpening angle and 5 mm bevel thickness but flexible width is juggled within the 200 mm and 150 mm diameter lines to get the best fit.

Figures 2.17 to 2.20 show four compensating two-pin template designs and their parallelograms.

Figure 2.15 **A compensating two-pin template** for a 30° sharpening angle and a 5 mm bevel thickness. This template retains the correction for bevel thickness of the preceding template. Table 2.4 shows that it also almost eliminates variations in the sharpening angles ground caused by wheel wear, but that the gain in accuracy over the preceding template is small for sharpening angles bigger than 30°.

The difference between this compensating template and that in the preceding figure is that the straight edge which references the platform is no longer at 30° to the line of the two reference pins, and is also higher relative to them. The exact position of this edge is determined by trial and error for each combination of sharpening angle, bevel thickness, and maximum and minimum grinding wheel diameters. The method is shown in the next figure.

Table 2.4 The sharpening angles resulting from different bevel thicknesses and wheel diameters. The nominal sharpening angle is 30° .

Bevel thickness	*Grinding-wheel diameter* 200 mm	150 mm
3 mm	30.8°	31.6°
5 mm	30.0°	30.1°
7 mm	28.1°	28.0°

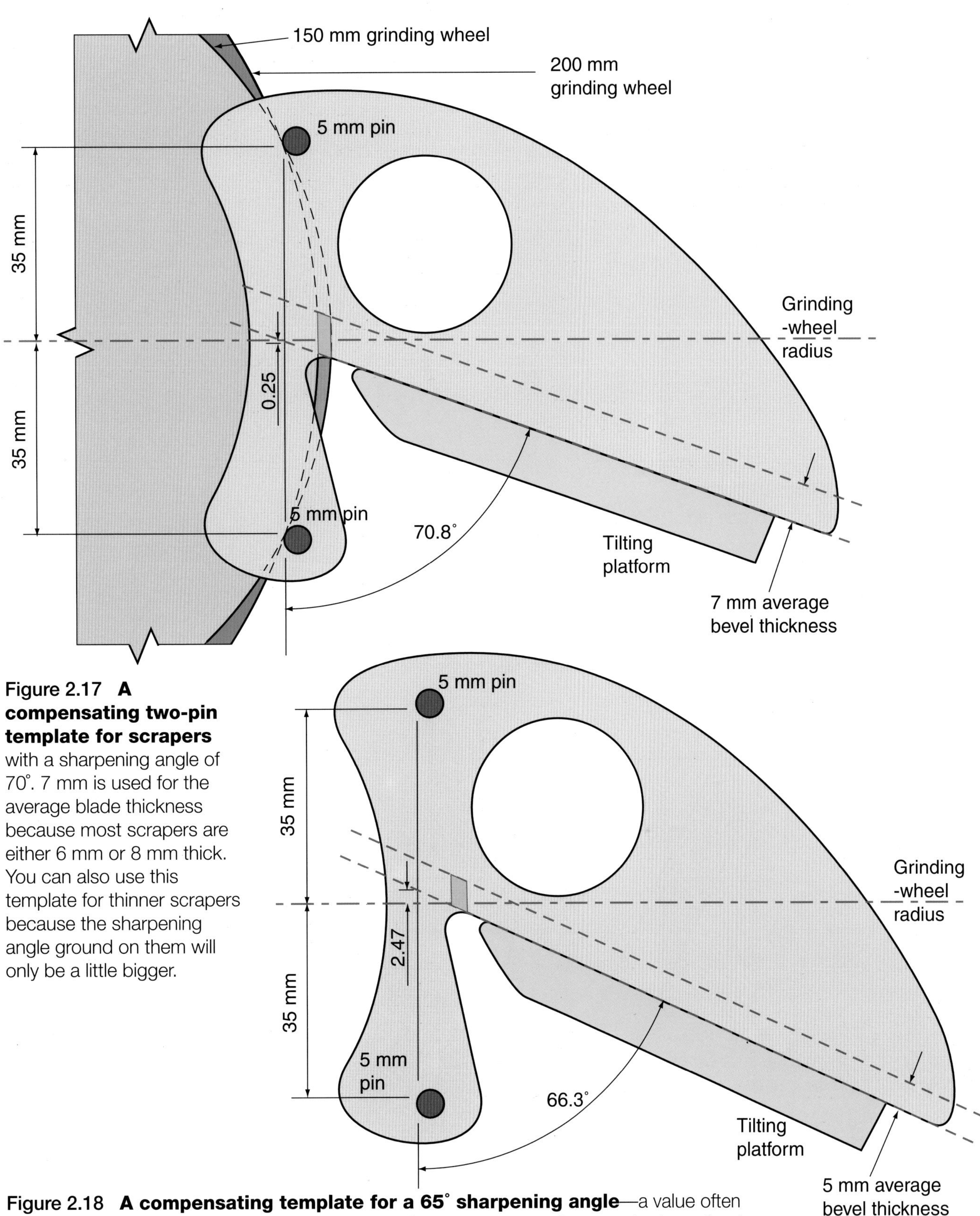

Figure 2.17 **A compensating two-pin template for scrapers** with a sharpening angle of 70°. 7 mm is used for the average blade thickness because most scrapers are either 6 mm or 8 mm thick. You can also use this template for thinner scrapers because the sharpening angle ground on them will only be a little bigger.

Figure 2.18 **A compensating template for a 65° sharpening angle**—a value often specified for the tip of swept-back bowl gouges. Such gouges are sharpened using a fanning action (figure 2.45). The average bevel thickness for swept-back bowl gouges is about 5 mm, but as the nominal sharpening angle at the tip is big, variations in bevel thickness will not significantly alter the sharpening angle ground.

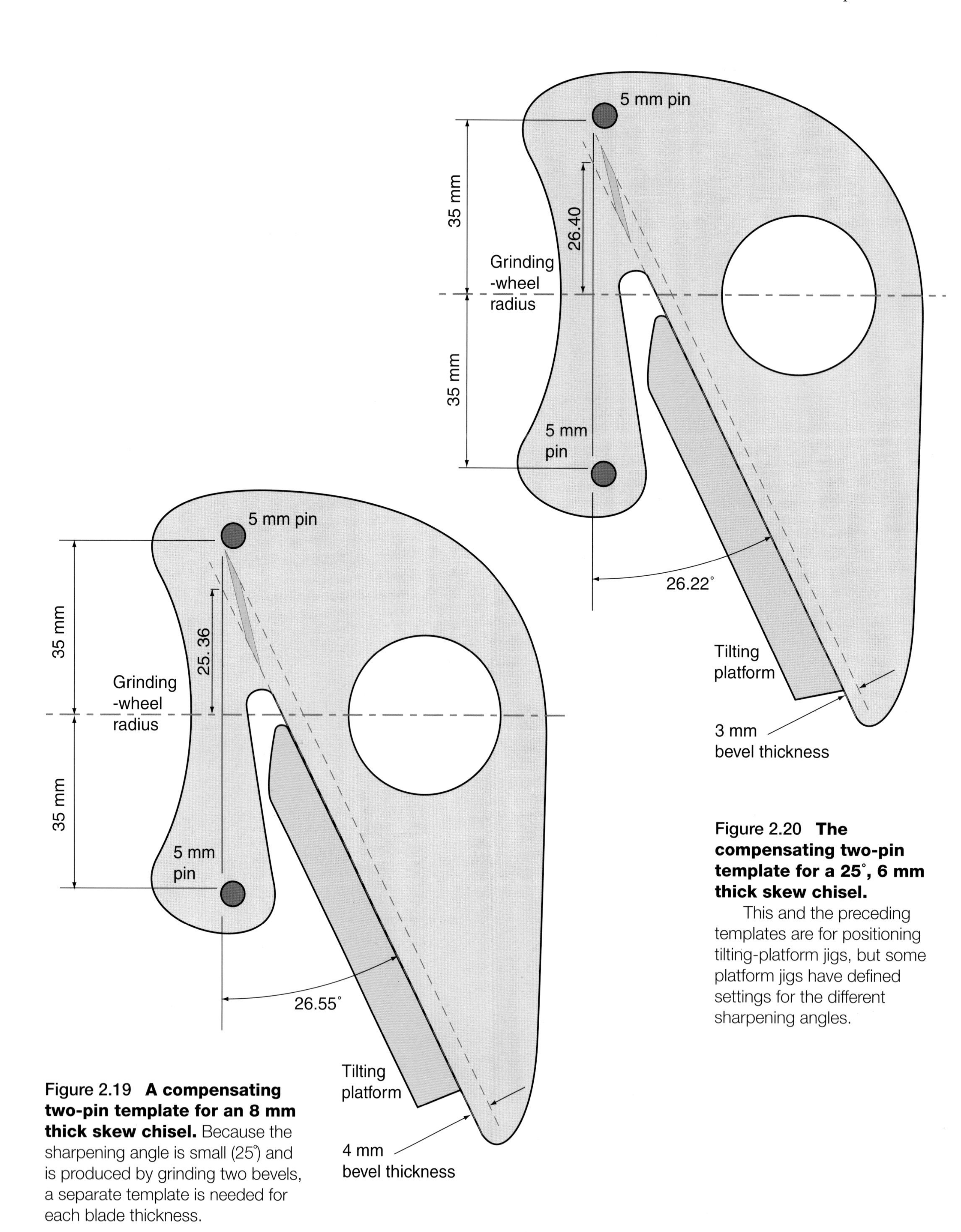

Figure 2.19 **A compensating two-pin template for an 8 mm thick skew chisel.** Because the sharpening angle is small (25°) and is produced by grinding two bevels, a separate template is needed for each blade thickness.

Figure 2.20 **The compensating two-pin template for a 25°, 6 mm thick skew chisel.**

This and the preceding templates are for positioning tilting-platform jigs, but some platform jigs have defined settings for the different sharpening angles.

2.3 THE O'DONNELL TOOL SHARPENING SYSTEM

This robust and nicely machined jig was introduced in 1993 by Cullen and Michael O'Donnell. They market the jig from their home in Scotland.[2] It was the first commercial jig to include a formal method of adjustment to compensate for wheel wear, and it has stops to set sharpening angles between 15° and 45° at 5° intervals. Figures 2.21 and 2.22 describe the jig. My test results are shown in table 2.5.

There are different variants of the jig for 200 mm, 175 mm, and 150 mm grinding-wheel grinders. The jig's instructions recommend that a grinding wheel should be replaced when its diameter has worn by 25 mm.

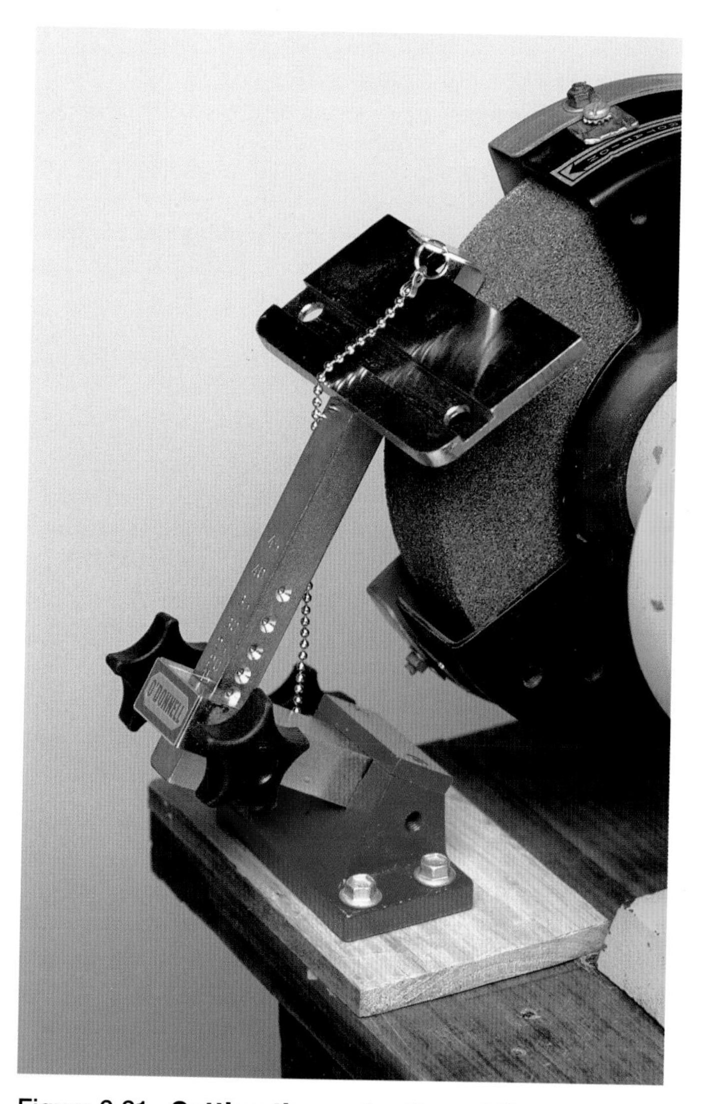

Figure 2.21 **Setting the projection of the wheel wear bar of the O'Donnell Tool Sharpening System** using the slip gauge provided. Like most jigs it has instructions which detail how to mount the jig, and how to set the jig to grind the common tool types.

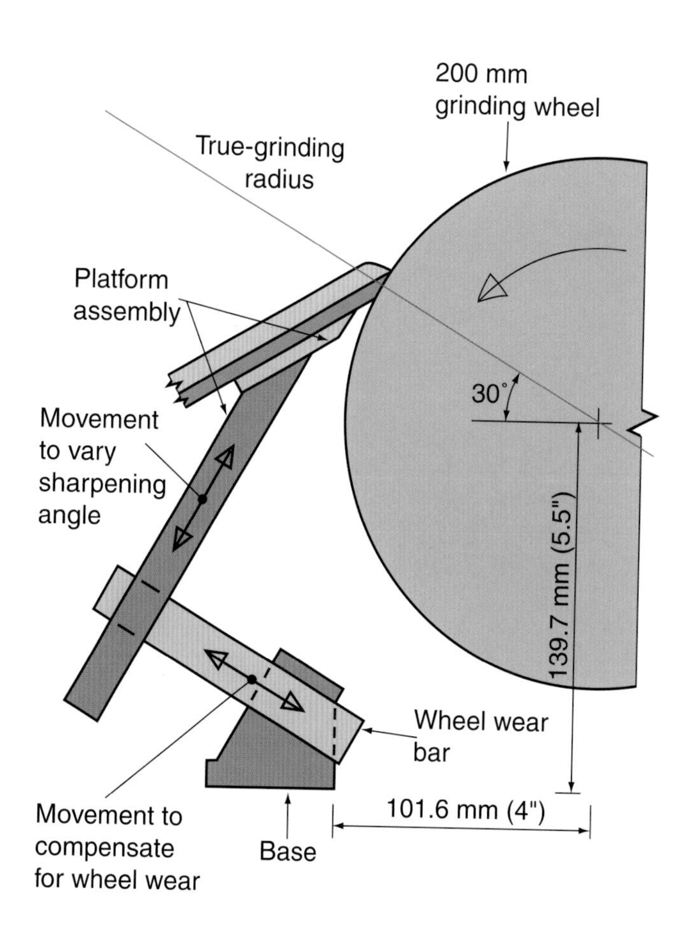

Figure 2.22 **The geometry of the O'Donnell jig** drawn in vertical section. As the grinding wheel wears the jig needs to be reset. To do this the platform assemby is raised to the 15° setting. The wheel wear bar is then adjusted until the clearance between the front of the platform checkout and the wheel periphery is the thickness of the slip gauge supplied. This wheel wear bar setting is then used for all tools whatever their sharpening angles until the wheel wears significantly and the wheel wear bar should be reset.

After adjusting for wheel wear, the bevels of tools with a 30° sharpening angle continue to be centered on and be aligned at 90° to a radius at 30° above the horizontal when in contact with the wheel periphery. This radius, although a straight line, I call a "true-grinding curve". Other examples will be discussed in section 2.8.

For sharpening angles other than 30° the platform is still moved to the right parallel to the true-grinding radius as the wheel wears. Therefore the sharpening angles ground vary with wheel diameter, but these variations are small within the specified range of grinding-wheel diameter as table 2.5 illustrates.

Table 2.5 Sharpening angles actually ground using O'Donnell jig.

Bevel thick-ness	Nominal bevel angle, set by stop	Bevel angle ground	
		200 mm grinding wheel	Wheel worn to 175 mm
3 mm	15° *	17.7° *	15.6° *
6 mm	30°	30.5°	30.4°
6 mm	45°	44.8°	46.7°

*Based on the angles being measured in a plane parallel to the long edge of a skew with a 60° included angle at its long point (see *FOW*, fig. 4.47, elev. A-A).

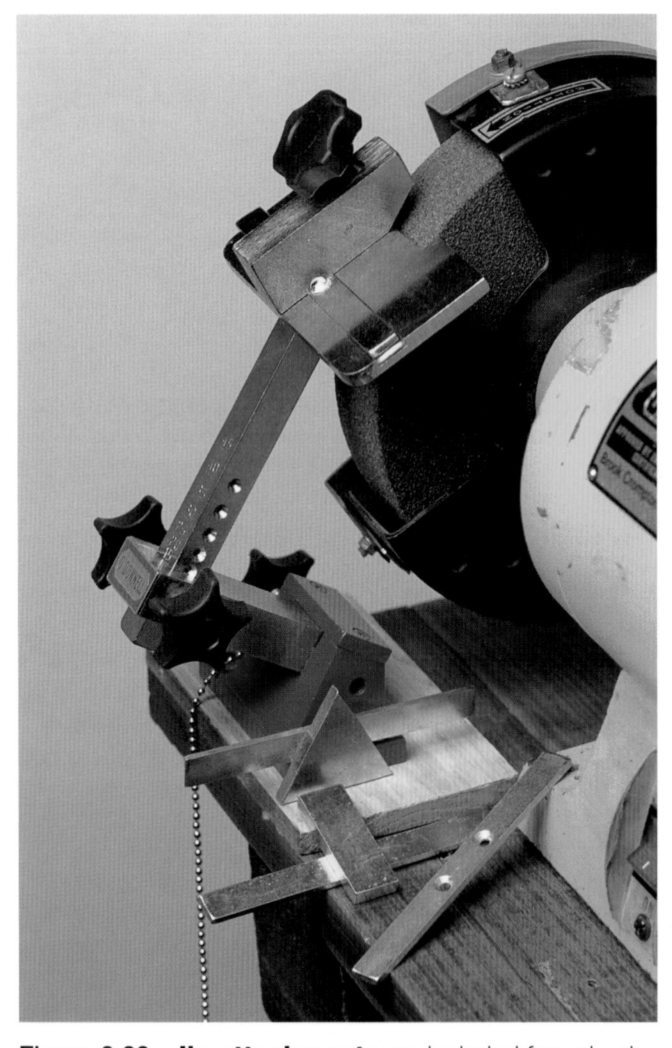

Figure 2.23 **Jig attachments** are included for: wheel dressing (*top*), grinding blades square across, and grinding skews with an angle of 60° at the long point. The attachments slide in the channel in the platform. Also provided is a slide which you can customize.

2.4 GRINDING PROBLEM TOOLS

If you use a platform jig, being able to set the tilt of its platform accurately may not solve all your grinding problems. Some tools have such long, heavy handles that maintaining their blades in flat contact with a platform during grinding is difficult. While long, heavy handles are desirable for tools such as those for deep hollowing, their popularity is largely due to the mistaken belief that massive force and inertia are a sensible alternative to proper tool presentation. If such handles are used when not needed, they make turning slower and more tiring.

To overcome the problems of grinding tools with heavy handles you can:

1. Use tools with separate, replaceable tool tips which fit into a steel shaft. However, some tips may be too short to hold alone for regrinding or to hone easily.
2. Use easily removable handles. These have merit, especially for those turners who travel. Some commercial removeable handles are too heavy for general use. A design for homemade handles is shown in figure 2.24.
3. Add a support. You can effectively widen the platform of a platform jig with a crossarm similar to that described in figure 2.57.
4. Use a pivoting jig. The simplest is the handle-end type shown in the next section. More complex pivoting jigs are discussed in section 2.6.

Another grinding problem is that some tools have blades which have worn too short to fit flat onto most platforms. (These blades are also usually too short to be held in pivoting jigs). To grind short blades you can add a narrower supplementary platform (figure 2.25).

Figure 2.24 **A removable handle** with a saw cut and hoseclip, based on handles made by Clay Foster of Texas.

Figure 2.25 **A supplementary narrow steel platform** for grinding short-bladed tools which fits onto the two-pivot jig's wide platform.

2.5 HANDLE-END JIGS

Handle-end jigs locate the ends of tool handles, making accurate manipulation of the tools during grinding easier.

The earliest commercial handle-end jig incorporated a platform jig with a fixed tilt (figure 2.26). Disappointingly the combination of platform jig and handle-end jig does not seem to be presently manufactured, but the concept is resurrected in section 2.7. Figure 2.27 shows the arrangement used for Oneway's Wolverine Vee-Arm (shown in use in figure 2.28), which was developed in 1993. It uses the sliding arm as the mounting for two other sharpening attachments, a skew grinding attachment pictured in figure 2.29, and a pivoting jig shown in figures 2.39 and 2.40.

Handle-end jigs are well suited for grinding tools with short blades or heavy handles, tools which can be a problem to grind on tilting-platform jigs. However handle-end jigs are only suitable for grinding detail gouges (figure 2.30) and *cutting* tools with a sharpening angle measured parallel to the tool's longitudinal axis which is constant along the cutting edge: these tools are skew chisels, parting tools, square-across and ground-back bowl gouges, and roughing gouges.

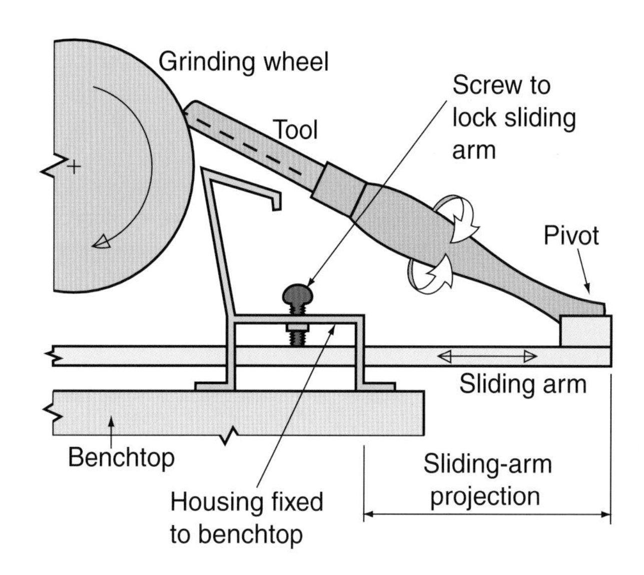

Figure 2.26 **The first commercial handle-end jig,** designed by Jeff Parsons of Ontario. (This elevation is not true to proportion). Chalet Woodcraft of Waterford, Ontario, marketed the jig throughout North America between 1980 and 1998. The sliding-arm housing incorporated a fixed platform.[3]

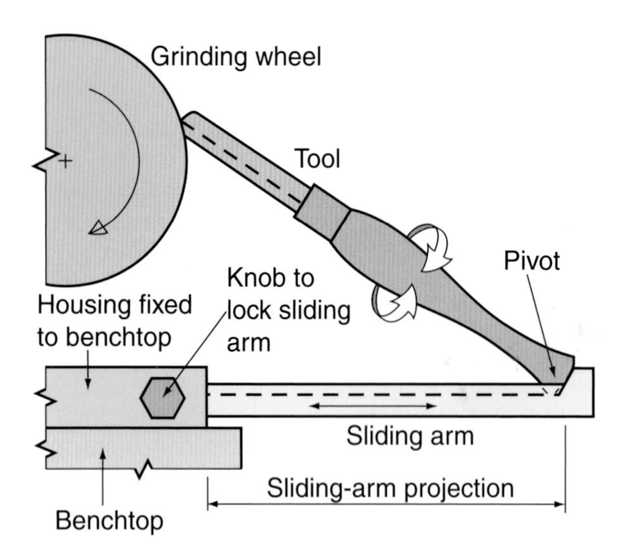

Figure 2.27 A handle-end jig. The right-hand end of the sliding arm has a pocket, V-shaped groove, or similar which locates the end of the tool handle while the tool is being rotated. You set the optimum sliding-arm projection by:

1. Using the tool's bevel as a template. You adjust the projection of the sliding arm until the tool's bevel lies flush on the grinding-wheel periphery.
2. Using a template to set the inclination of the tool while adjusting the sliding-arm projection (figures 2.31 and 2.32).
3. First setting the tilt of a tilting-platform jig mounted above the sliding-arm housing with a two-pin template. Then, while holding the tool onto the platform, set the sliding arm. The now redundant platform can then be dropped out of the way. Alternatively you can use the tilting platform to support the tool, and have a crossarm fixed to the sliding arm to provide supplementary support rather than positively locate the handle; this is shown in figure 2.57.

With handle-end jigs and all forms of pivoting jig, the sharpening angle ground on each tool increases during a grinding operation. And if you continually reset the jig by using the bevel as a template, the tool's sharpening angle will continue to increase during the life of the tool. Accasionally you will therefore need to grind back the sharpening angle to your preferred value.

For a smooth grinding action your handles' ends should be round and even.

If all your tools are longer than standard, you may need to pack your grinder up more than usually recommended, or use a longer sliding arm.

You should not use handle-end jigs to grind the large sharpening angles used with scrapers as the tool is likely to jam.

Figure 2.28 **Grinding a roughing gouge to a 30° sharpening angle using the Wolverine Vee-Arm** made by Oneway Manufacturing. Once the sliding arm is set, the gouge is rotated first in one direction, then the other.

Handle-end jigs require room in front of the grinder to slide the arm out for longer tools, and enough room behind the grinder to use the arm at short projections. (The Oneway arm is 28 in. [700 mm] long).

Square-across bowl gouges are ground in the same way as roughing gouges. For ground-back bowl gouges, you grind the flanges back merely by grinding for a shorter duration at the bottom of the flute than at the tops of the flanges.

The orientation of the vee in which the handle locates enables this jig to be used to grind detail gouges (next figure), an advantage over the vee of the Parsons jig shown in figure 2.26.

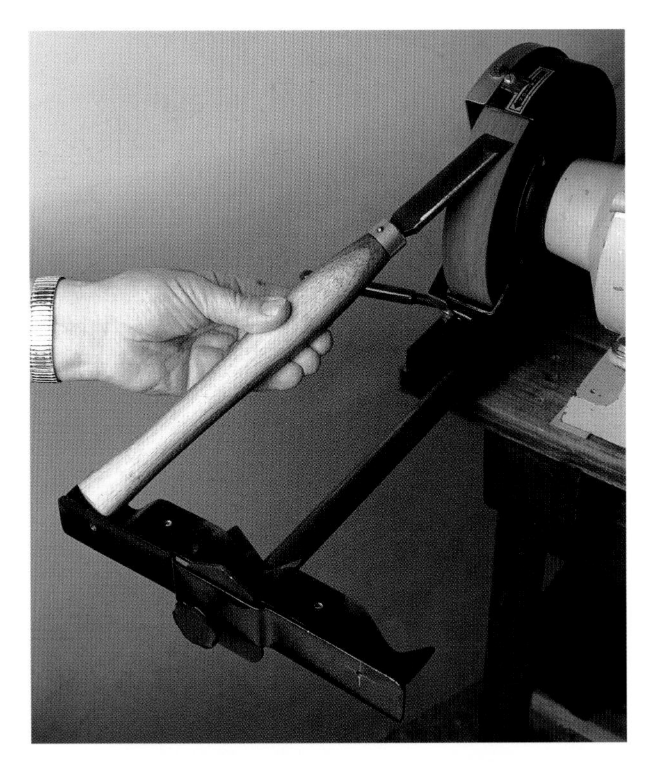

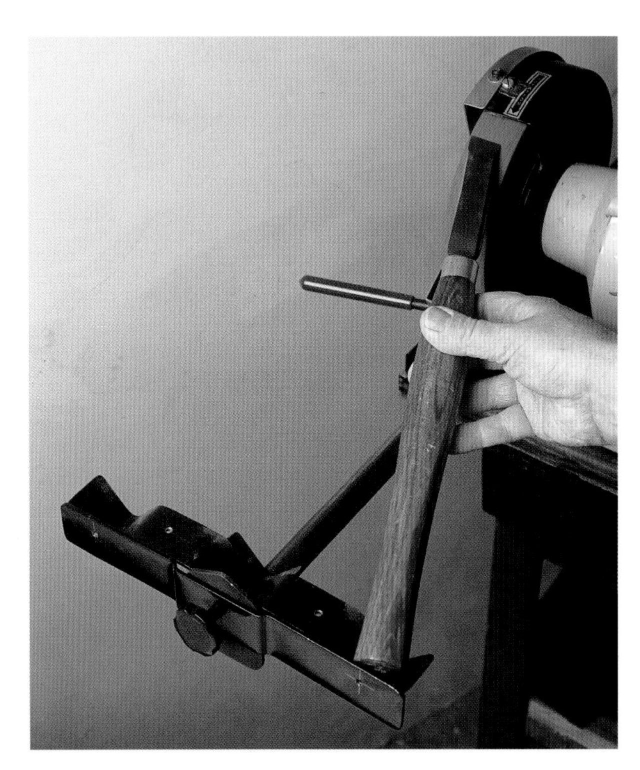

Figure 2.29 **Grinding a skew with the Oneway Skew Grinding Attachment** fixed to the Wolverine Vee-Arm. You locate the end of the skew's handle in each of the two pockets in turn. However:

1. There is no aligning support to the lower flat face of a skew's blade as there is from a platform jig. Therefore the bevels and cutting edge are less likely to be ground parallel to the blade's faces.
2. If you fan the tool across the width of the wheel periphery, you will tend to grind a larger sharpening angle at the long point than at the short point because when the long point is ground it is lower on the wheel. If you grind without fanning the chisel, the edge will have the same sharpening angle along its full length.
3. The shorter the skew the smaller the angle of skewness between the cutting edge and long edge.

Although the three drawbacks of this attachment are minor, there do not seem to be any compensating advantages apart from not having to swop the Vee-Arm for the platform. The skew attachment can however be used as the mounting for a crossarm (figure 2.57), a device which supports a tool handle but does not locate it.

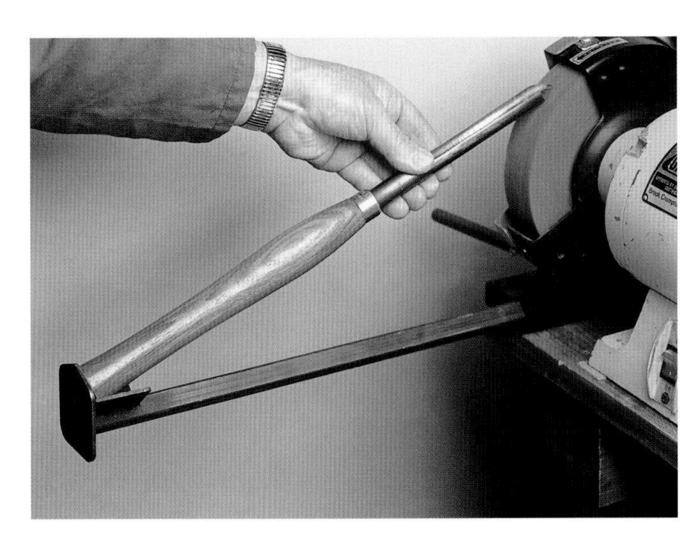

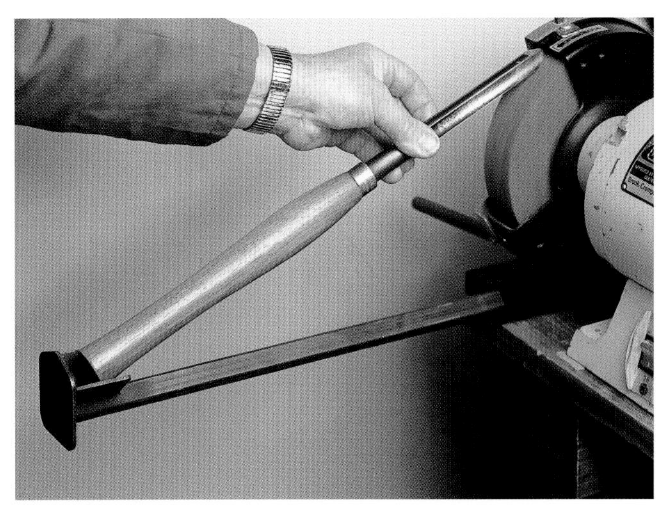

Figure 2.30 **Grinding a detail gouge with a handle-end jig.** (I have not used my right hand to avoid obscuring the end of the gouge handle). The long downward-pointing vee of the Oneway Vee-Arm allows you to keep the handle end located in the vee while you push the gouge nose up the wheel and rotate it onto its sides and vice-versa.

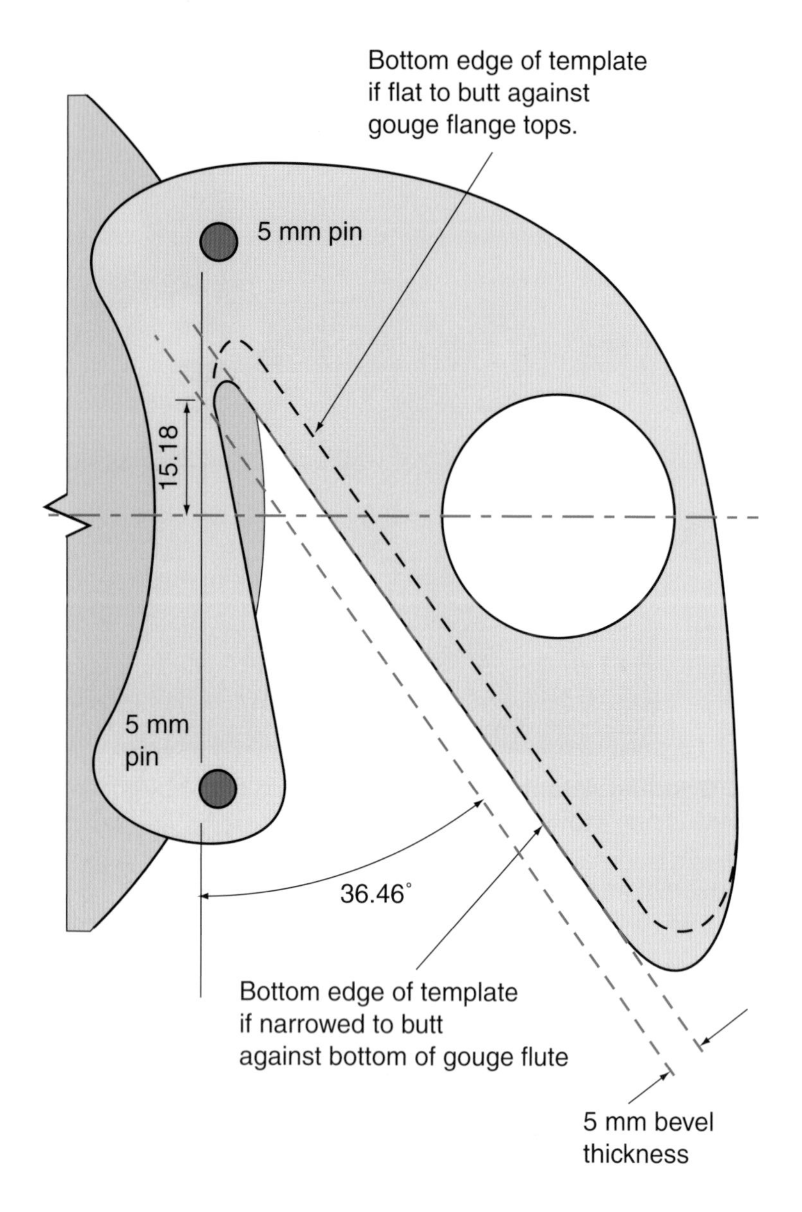

Figure 2.31 **A two-pin on-top template** for a 30° sharpening angle and a 5 mm bevel thickness. The edge which references and butts against the tool should lie centrally along the grinding wheel periphery, and therefore needs to be packed away from the face of the template which you hold against the circular face of the wheel. The next figure shows the the template in use.

Figure 2.32 **Using a two-pin on-top template** to set the sliding-arm projection of a handle-end jig.

You have to hold the tool blade in full contact with the template's reference edge while holding the tool bevel in full contact with the grinding wheel periphery. At the same time you have to adjust and lock the jig!

Two types of two-pin template have been described so far. A third, a supporting type is shown in the next figure, and two further types are described in section 2.6.1.

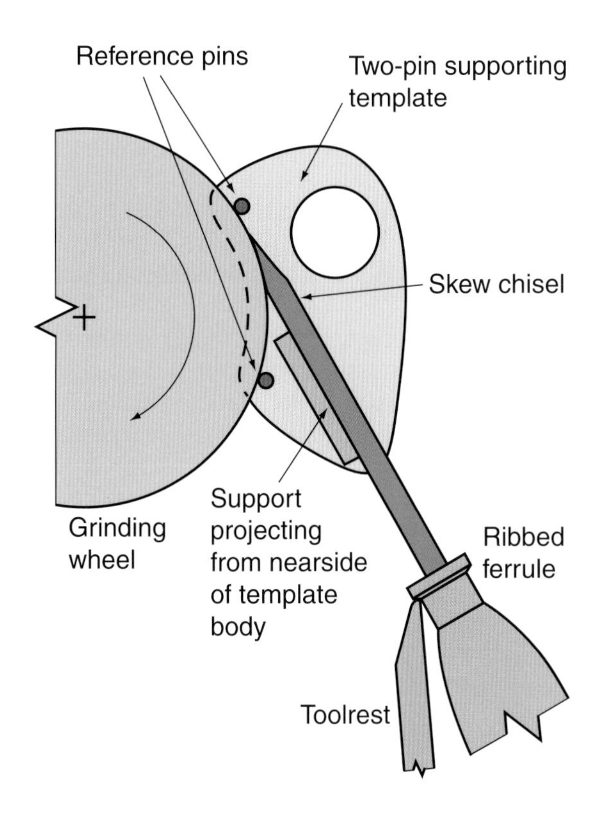

Figure 2.33 **The Craft Supplies ribbed ferrule,** a handle-front jig. To position the platform's front edge you would have to use:

1. An on-top two-pin template like that shown in the preceding figure.
2. A two-pin supporting template like that shown in the drawing. The support has its top surface level with the reference edge for a platform.
3. The tool's bevel as a template.

2.6 PIVOTING JIGS

Pivoting jigs are similar to pencil compasses, and are descended from the ball-ended goniostat (figure 2.34). The geometry and working of pivoting jigs is explained in figure 2.35.

The first commercial pivoting jig for grinding woodturning tools was introduced by Jerry Glaser of Los Angeles in 1993 (figures 2.36 to 2.38).

Later jigs include the Uni-Jig 5 which was developed in Australia by Gorgi Armen in 1998,[4] and the Wolverine Vari-Grind. The ends of their legs pivot in a recess at the end of a sliding arm. They are pictured in figures 2.39 to 2.41, and are fairly representative of the brands of short pivoting jigs introduced during the 1990s. The Robert Sorby Universal Sharpening System shown in figures 2.54 and 2.55 combines a pivoting jig with a two-pivot tilting platform jig.

Pivoting jigs are ideal for the grinding of swept-back bowl gouges, and are good for grinding detail gouges. Their suitability for grinding other tool types depends in part on the detailed design of the tool holder.

Some manufacturers recommend that you set their pivoting jigs by using the tool as a template. Other manufacturers recommended settings which if valid for a new grinding wheel become increasingly inaccurate as the wheel wears. This section therefore details three ways to set pivoting jigs accurately.

Figure 2.34 **A ball-ended goniostat,** figure 8 from J.H. Evans, *Ornamental Turning* (1886; reprint, Mendham, New Jersey: Astragal Press, 1993). This little known device is used to hone the bevels of round-ended ornamental-turning cutters on each of the three successively-finer abrasive plates on the left.

The projection of the cutter in the ball-ended goniostat can be varied, but the variation is limited because the cutters are usually short. The jig therefore has only one effective adjustment, the projection of the leg with the ball end. Varying this projection alters the sharpening angle honed at the tip of the cutter, but does not alter the sharpening angle honed along the sides of the cutter—this sharpening angle is about 90°, the exact value being dependant on the width of the cutter and the diameter of the ball.

Unlike this goniostat, pivoting jigs are used with a grinding wheel and usually have two adjustments. These enable the sharpening angles both at the point of the tool tip and along the sides to be varied.

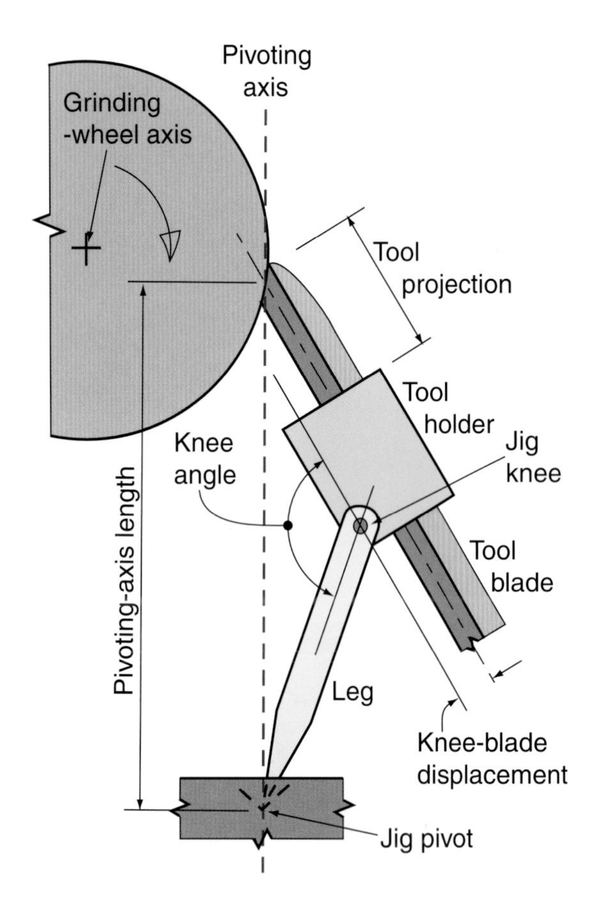

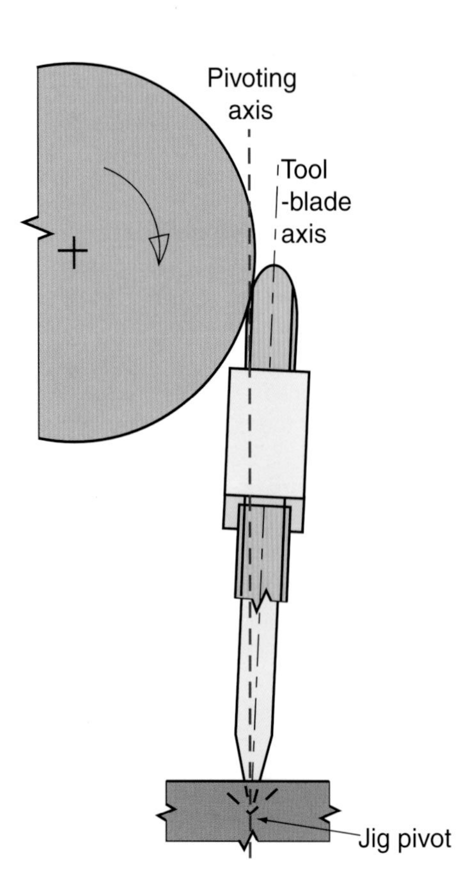

Figure 2.35 Side elevations showing the geometry of pivoting jigs.

Most pivoting jigs have leg lengths and knee angles which can be varied. The knee–blade displacement is usually not adjustable, but varies according to the blade's cross section. Minor adjustments to the tool projection are sometimes recommended, but are not significant. Some jigs include a packer to use with blades of smaller cross sections.

The essential property of a pivoting jig is that the pivoting axis always passes through both the jig pivot and the point where the bevel center contacts the grinding wheel periphery. In the top drawing the jig is in its upright position with the axis of the tool at a significant angle to the pivoting axis. But, as the bottom drawing shows, when a pivoting jig is rotated 90° onto its side, the pivoting axis and the tool's blade axis always lie almost in the same plane, a plane parallel to the grinder's axis. Therefore to set pivoting jigs for tools such as gouges which require the jig to be rotated during grinding the steps are:

1. Mount the tool in the tool holder with the recommended tool projection. Set the knee angle and sliding-arm length about midway through their ranges.
2. Rotate the jig onto its side so that the bevel at the top of the gouge flange lies on the grinding wheel periphery as in the lower drawing. Adjust the leg length until that bevel will be ground with the desired sharpening angle. With some jigs, for example the Glaser and Sorby, the leg length is adjusted directly; with jigs such as the Wolverine and Uni-Jig 5 the leg length is adjusted indirectly by changing the sliding-arm's projection and with it the location of the jig pivot.
3. Rotate the jig into the upright position and adjust the knee angle so that the correct sharpening angle will be ground at the bottom of the flute. This adjustment will usually alter the sharpening angle which will be ground at the tops of the flanges, and you therefore need to repeat steps 2 and 3—these repeats I call steps 4 and 5.
4. Rotate the jig back to 90°, and adjust the leg or sliding arm length to give the correct sharpening angle at the tops of the flanges.
5. Rotate the jig to upright and correct the knee angle to give the required sharpening angle at the bottom of the flute. Two cycles of adjustment should be sufficient.
6. Record the knee angle and leg or sliding-arm length. When you next regrind this same tool you can reuse these settings if there has been negligible wheel wear in the interim; or if there has been wheel wear, start from these recorded settings, and you will not need to use steps 4 and 5.

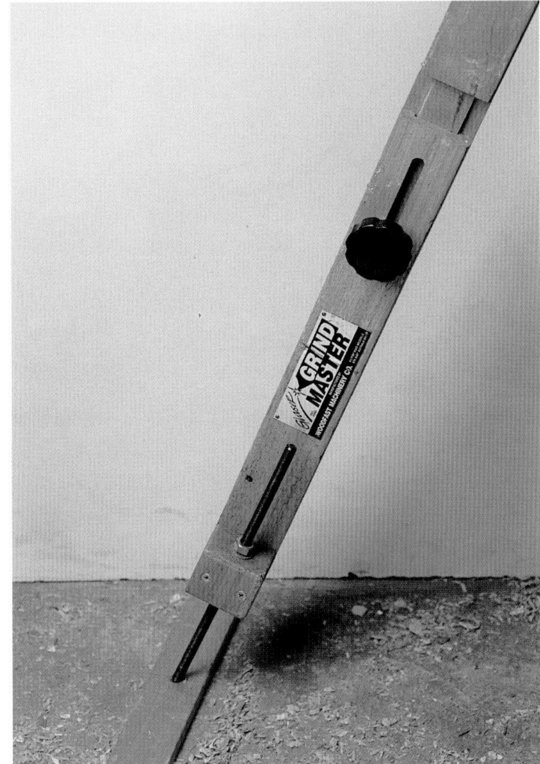

Figure 2.36 The Glaser Joystick or Grindmaster has a leg length which is far longer than those of pivoting jigs which have their jig pivots at about benchtop level. This long leg has the advantage over short legs that the sharpening angles ground if the jig is not adjusted vary less with wheel wear.

The lower photograph shows the two leg adjustments of the Glaser jig. The first adjustment, the projection of the screwed rod from the bottom of the wooden part, is adjusted only when you first set up the jig. The bottom end of this screwed rod is pointed and locates in a conical jig pivot hole, here in a piece of wood fixed to the floor. The length of the wooden part of the leg is also adjustable, and there are particular leg length and knee angle settings recommended for each tool type.

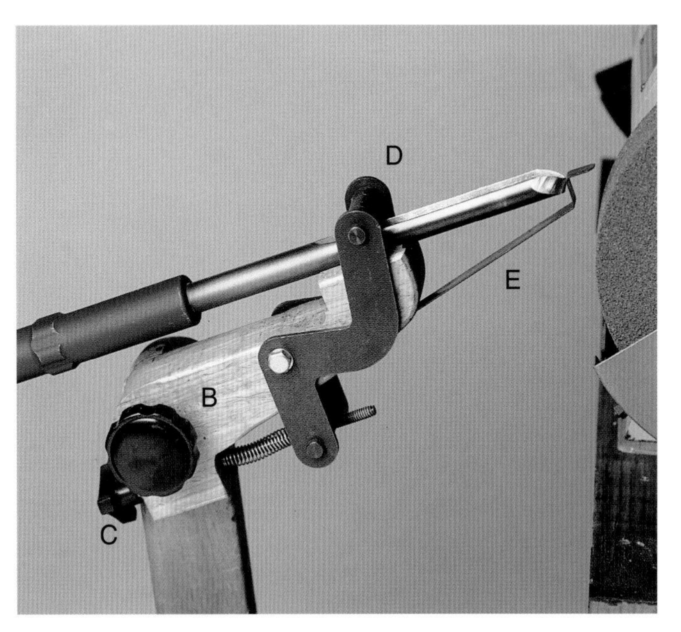

Figure 2.37 The knee and tool holder of the Glaser jig. The larger knob *B* locks the knee angle. Tightening the smaller knob *C* pulls down the top of the yoke *D* to clamp the tool. The cranked strip of spring steel *E* pulls out to ensure that the tool projection is correct.

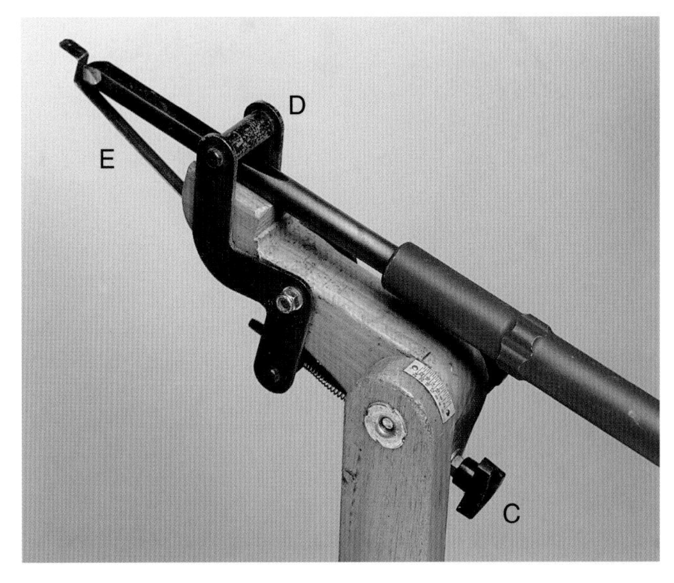

Figure 2.38 Another view of the Glaser jig's knee showing the knee-angle scale.

Figure 2.39 **The Oneway Vari-Grind Attachment** pivots in the vee at the end of the Wolverine Vee-Arm.

Figure 2.40 **The knee and tool holder of the Oneway Vari-Grind.** The largest diameter of tool which it can hold is 13/16 in. (21 mm).

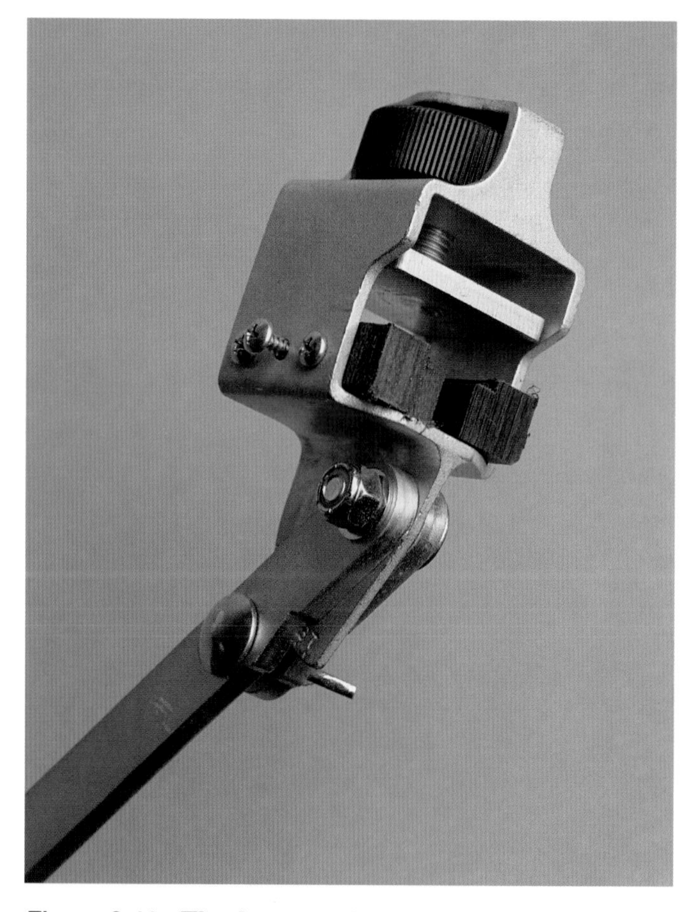

Figure 2.41 **The knee and tool holder of the Uni-Jig 5.** The knee angle is calibrated, and the tool holder is unusually capacious and can accomodate tools up to 44 mm wide and 40 mm deep. It can therefore be used to grind many brands of roughing gouge.

Figure 2.42 **About to regrind a roughing gouge with the Uni-Jig 5.** The knee angle is set to 180°, and the sliding-arm projection was set using the bevel under the bottom of the flute as a template. The error resulting from using this incorrect setting method is revealed in the next two figures.

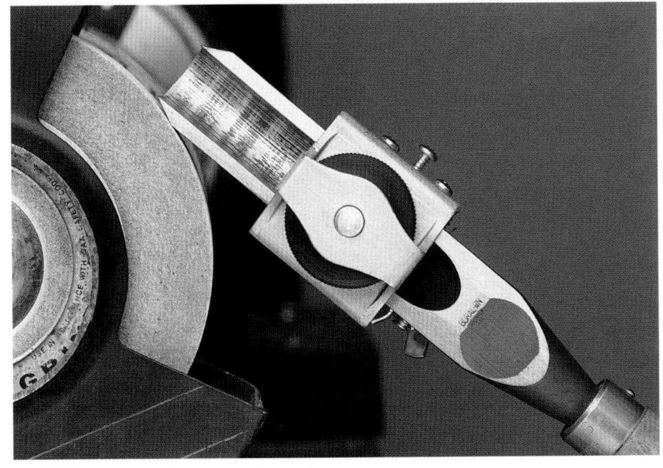

Figure 2.43 **Close-ups of the roughing gouge before regrinding was started.** The gouge was previously ground on a platform jig and therefore has the same sharpening angle along its whole cutting edge. In the upper photograph the bevel is in full contact with the grinding-wheel periphery. In the lower photograph there is clearance under the cutting edge. Therefore after regrinding, the sharpening angle will be coarser at the base of the flute than at the tops of the flanges. Had the Uni-Jig 5 settings been made using the correct method described in the legend of figure 2.35, the resulting knee angle setting would have been greater than 180°.

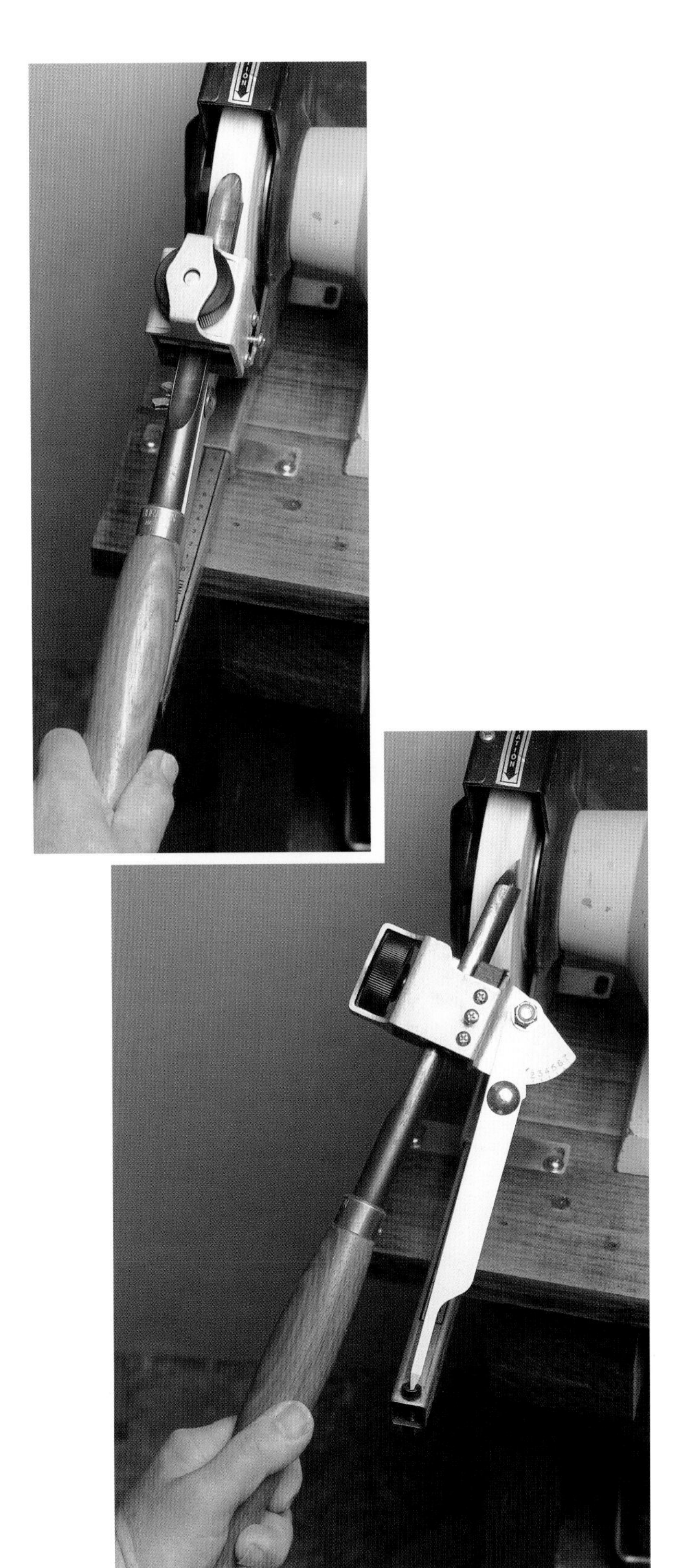

Figure 2.44 **Grinding a detail gouge with the Uni-Jig 5.**

The instruction booklet gives sound settings for a new grinding wheel, but as the wheel wears the sliding-arm projection should be shortened.

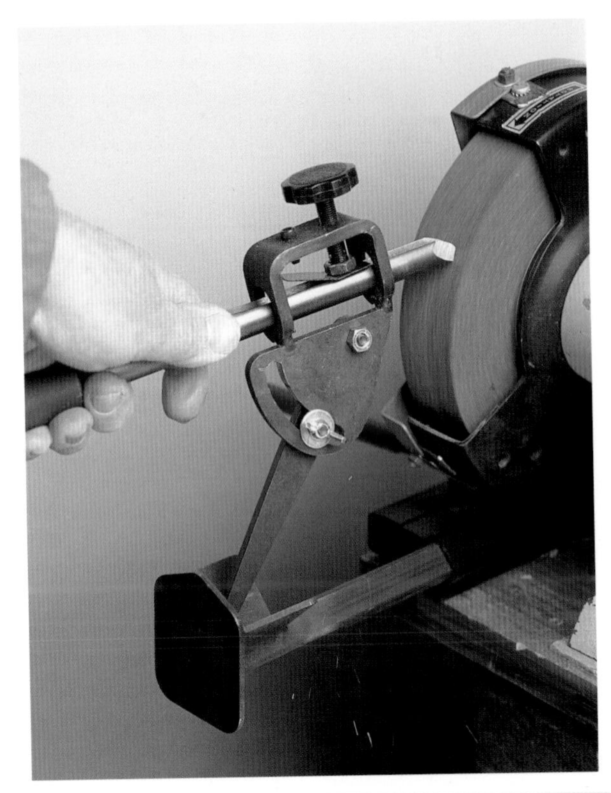

Figure 2.45 **Grinding a swept-back bowl gouge with the Oneway Vari-Grind.** The jig was set as described in the figure 2.35 legend.The sharpening angle at the tops of the flanges is 20°, and that at the base of the flute is 65°. The knee angle is substantially less than that set to sharpen the detail gouge in the preceding figure.

Figure 2.46 **Grinding a skew as recommended in the Uni-Jig 5's instructions.** Although the sharpening angle and angle of skewness are jigged, the skew's blade faces are not jigged parallel to the wheel periphery as they are with a tilting-platform jig. If you don't keep the blade faces parallel to the grinding wheel periphery:

1. The cutting edge may not be parallel to the two blade faces.
2. The bevels may not being of constant width.
3. The cutting edge may not be at the preferred 70° angle of skewness to the long edge.

The jig with the chisel still clamped in it is rotated 180° to grind the skew's second bevel.

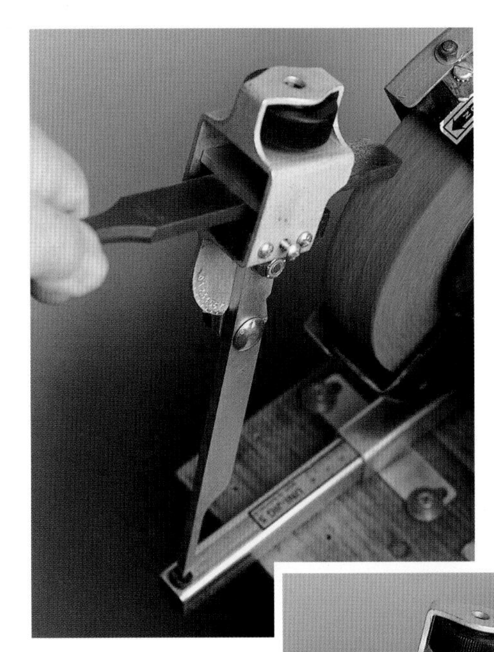

Figure 2.47 **Grinding a scraper to a sharpening angle of 70° using a Uni-Jig 5.** The jig was set using the tool as a template in the procedure described in the figure 2.35 legend. However with a pivoting jig the sharpening angle coarsens during a single grinding operation due to the shortening of the tool projection and any wheel wear. And if a tool is continually reground at the same jig settings or these later jig settings are determined by using the tool as the template, the sharpening angle(s) ground will continue to grow. To continually grind your preferred sharpening angle(s) you therefore need to:

1. Use the same recorded knee angle, but increase the leg length or shorten the sliding-arm projection by using the bevel with a touch of clearance at the cutting edge as a template .
2. Rather than use the tool as a template, use a pivoting jig two-pin template to establish the new leg length. Two types are described in figures 2.48 to 2.53.

2.6.1 SETTING PIVOTING JIGS WITH TEMPLATES

The two templates shown in figures 2.48 to 2.53 enable the correct leg length or sliding-arm projection to be set whatever the grinding wheel diameter. The knee angle and tool projection remain unchanged, and are first decided by using the tool as a template.

Figure 2.48 **A swept-back bowl gouge held in a correctly-set pivoting jig.** The sharpening angle at the base of the gouge flute is 65°. The grinding wheel is wedged and a piece of masking tape has been pressed onto its periphery. A red band has been drawn on the tape where the bevel contacts the wheel.

Figure 2.49 **Fixing the geometry of a two-pin template.** The geometry of the template's plywood body is identical to that of the 65° template shown in figure 2.18. The sliding arm's projection is unchanged from that shown in the preceding figure.

With both template reference pins in contact with the wheel, the red band drawn on the template body representing the bevel thickness was aligned with the red band drawn on the masking tape. The point of the steel leg was then held into the jig pivot at the right-hand end of the sliding arm, and the top of the steel leg was then screwed to the plywood. The template could then be used to accurately set the sliding-arm projection whatever the grinding-wheel diameter as shown in the next figure.

Figure 2.50 **Setting the sliding arm projection from the template** before regrinding the swept-back bowl gouge on the worn wheel. The swept-back bowl gouge will then be locked into the Uni-Jig 5 with the same knee angle and tool projection as in figure 2.48, and reground.

The next three figures show the use of a different but related two-pin template.

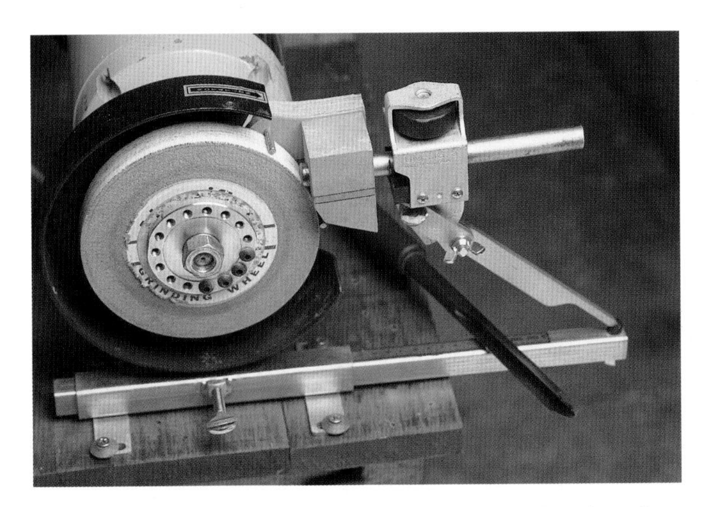

Figure 2.51 **Setting the sliding-arm projection for a swept-back bowl gouge with a two-pin template** which uses the Uni-Jig's leg to set the correct sliding-arm projection.

This template is based on that in figure 2.18. The red band drawn on the wood is at the same level and inclination as the bevel-thickness dashed lines in figure 2.18. The steel bar in the template slides within a hole, and the length from the left-hand tip of the rod to the red-filled saw cut is the 60 mm tool projection specified for the Uni-Jig.

To set the sliding-arm projection the Uni-Jig is first locked at the correct knee angle. The Uni-Jig is then locked onto the template rod with 60 mm of rod projecting. The left-hand end of the rod is then pressed against the wheel periphery as are the template's two reference pins. With the wheel free to rotate, the sliding-arm projection is adjusted until the pointed end of the Uni-Jig leg fits into the pivot point. The arm is then locked, the template is removed from the Uni-Jig, and the tool is locked into the Uni-Jig and reground.

Figure 2.53 **Close-ups of the template.** The red band is drawn to the thickness, level, and inclination of the bevel. The steel rod slides in the hole through the wooden block, and the length from the red line scribed on the rod to its end is the recommended tool projection for the Uni-Jig.

Figure 2.52 **A close-up of the preceding figure.**

2.7 COMBINING JIGS

The three jig types discussed so far are complementary, but have up to early 2001 been combined commercially only in twos. Jeff Parsons' jig shown in figure 2.26 is possibly the earliest example, with the Robert Sorby Universal Sharpening System shown in figures 2.54 and 2.55 being the most recent.

You can however combine the three main jig types relatively easily. This is a useful option if you want to reserve only one wheel for tool grinding, and is illustrated in figures 2.56 to 2.58.

Figure 2.54 **Grinding a swept-back bowl gouge with the pivoting-jig component of the Robert Sorby Universal Sharpening System.** The way the tilting platform and pivoting jig are combined is novel, but two different-sized Allen keys are needed to adjust the leg length and the knee angle.

Figure 2.55 **Setting the platform of the Robert Sorby Universal Sharpening System** for grinding a skew chisel with a two-pin template. The platform is just long enough parallel to the grinder's axis to grind skews and the sides of scrapers, but its top pivot mechanism impedes the setting of the platform tilt with a two-pin template. The lower photograph shows the platform reversed—simple to do and better for use with two-pin templates.

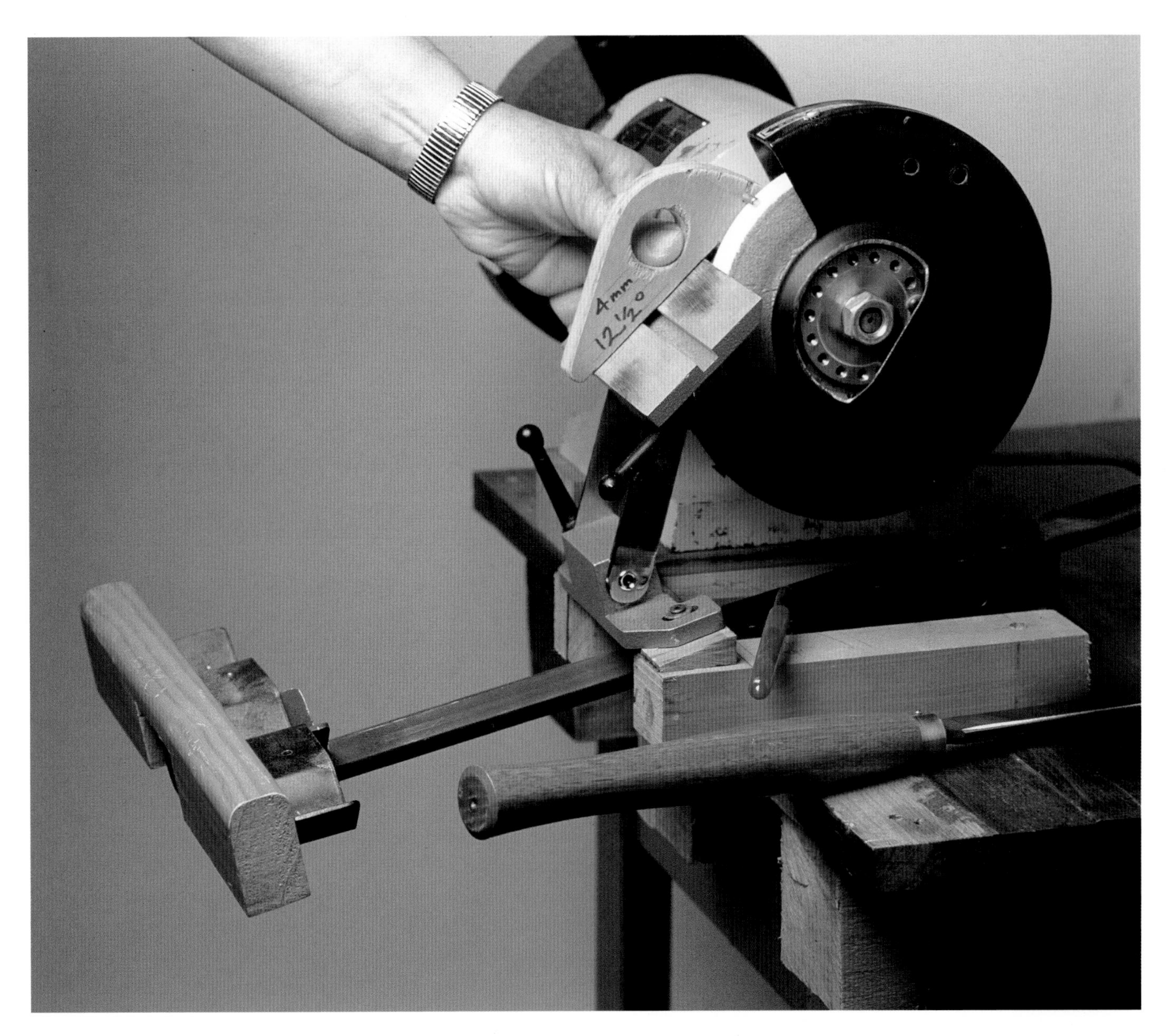

Figure 2.56 Setting a two-pivot platform jig for grinding a skew chisel. Also mounted beneath the wheel is a Oneway Vee-Arm. This handle-end jig provides the pivot point for a Vari-Grind pivoting jig, and can carry a crossarm. The crossarm is merely a piece of wood screwed to the Oneway Skew Grinding Attachment.

When we mount bench grinders and sliding-arm housings directly onto horizontal bench tops there is usually insufficient clearance to mount a tilting-platform jig. The solution is to raise the grinder substantially. Here I have also tilted the mountings of both the Vee-Arm housing and the two-pivot platform jig to allow the platform to be folded lower when not in use, and to bring grinding lower on the wheel periphery when either jig is in use.

Figure 2.57 **Grinding a skew using both a platform and a crossarm** to support the chisel and ensure its correct presentation. The crossarm acts as a support which effectively widens the platform, but does not prevent the tool moving backwards towards you. A crossarm is particularly useful for tools with short blades which are ground on a narrowed platform (figure 2.25), and for tools with heavy handles.

2.8 TRUE-GRINDING CURVES

You can set jigs and tools held in jigs with templates or by using the tool about to be ground as a template. You can also position a tool for grinding by centering the tool's bevel on what I call that tool's true-grinding curve. Figure 2.22 shows that the O'Donnell jig is based upon a true-grinding curve which is a radius rising at 30° to the horizontal. The jig shown in figure 4.38 of FOW also uses the same true-grinding radius, and has two additional mechanisms: the first adjusts the tilt of the platform to vary the sharpening angle ground, the second raises or lowers the platform to compensate for different bevel thicknesses.

Figures 2.59 and 2.60 show how to determine and use the true-grinding curve for a handle-end jig. True-grinding curves can also be used to set pivoting jigs (figures 2.61 to 2.63) and platform jigs. However because the articulating pivots for platform jigs are invariably below the top surface of the platform and therefore considerably displaced from the axis of a tool being ground, the true-grinding curves for platform jigs are complicated to derive, and so will not be pursued here.

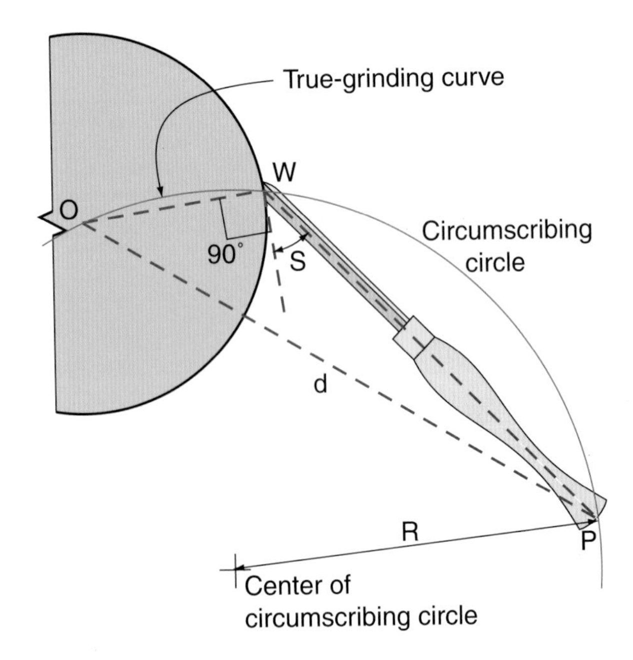

Figure 2.59 **The geometry of the true-grinding curve for a handle-end jig.** The true-grinding curve is part of the circumscribing circle which passes through the end of the gouge handle *P*, where the bevel center-line intersects with the grinding wheel periphery *W*, and the axis of the grinding wheel *O*.

As the wheel wears, if the end of the gouge's handle remains at *P*, and if the bevel is reground where the true-grinding curve crosses the grinding wheel periphery, the

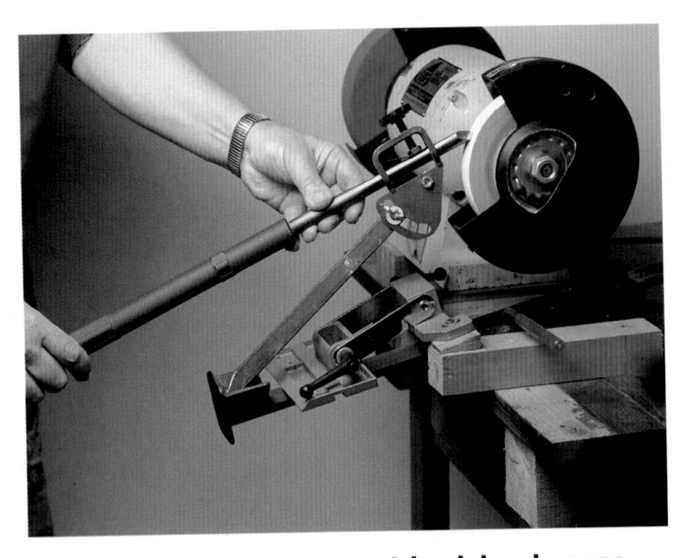

Figure 2.58 **Grinding a swept-back bowl gouge** which is held in a Vari-Grind pivoting jig with a homemade longer leg. The Vari-Grind's jig pivot is at the left-hand end of the Vee-Arm, and the CJ-04 two-pivot platform jig is pivoted down to lie flat on the sliding arm.

sharpening angle ground will always be *S*.

The radius of the true grinding curve *R* can be calculated using the sine formula:

$$R = \frac{d}{2 \times \sin(90^\circ + S)} = \frac{d}{2 \times \sin(90^\circ - S)}$$

Where:

S = the sharpening angle for that tool type.
d = the distance between the axis of the grinding wheel and the jig pivot.

The practical application for this type of true-grinding curve is however limited because the tool's length has to be increased as the grinding wheel wears to maintain the end of the tool's handle at *P*. Figure 2.60 shows how this can be done.

Figure 2.60 Setting up to grind a roughing gouge on the true-grinding curve. The 200 mm grinding wheel was wedged, the position of jig pivot P was decided, and the length of the pivoting axis d was measured, and was 437 mm. R was then calculated (R = 437/[2 x sin (90° – 30°)] = 252.3 mm). W is where the center of the bevel lies on the wheel periphery. The true grinding curve was then drawn on the card using compasses or dividers, and the bottom end of the guard marked so that the card can be replaced in the same orientation in future.

To regrind as wheel wears, wedge the wheel, replace the card in the same position, and using the two nuts, extend the projection of the screwed rod from the end of the handle. This extension is increased until the point of the rod locates in the jig pivot, and the bevel center lies on the intersection of the true-grinding curve and the wheel periphery. The wedge and card are then removed and the guard replaced, and regrinding can begin.

The next three figures show the use of true-grinding curves with pivoting jigs.

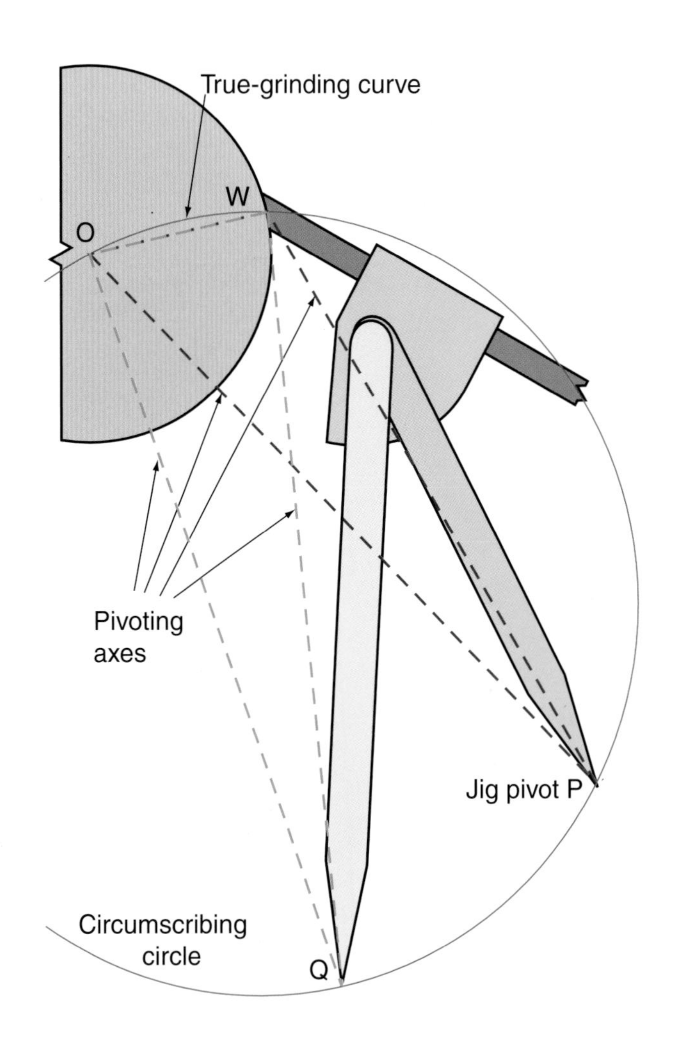

Figure 2.61 The geometry of true-grinding curves for pivoting jigs. The true-grinding curve is again part of the circumscribing circle which passes through the jig pivot P, where the bevel center-line intersects the wheel periphery W, and the grinding wheel axis O.

For jig pivot P, as the grinding wheel wears the distance of the tool bevel from the jig pivot has to increase, and that increase must effectively take place along the pivoting axis. This would require the leg to lengthen and the knee angle to increase. This need to make such complicated adjustments can be avoided by moving the pivot point from P to Q so that triangle OWQ becomes isosceles. Moving the jig pivot from P to Q would require the jig leg to be lengthened and the knee angle to be reduced. But once done, for all subsequent regrinding the same pivot point Q, leg length and knee angle can be retained.

There are obviously an infinite number of combinations of the variables—the next figure shows how the first pivot point P can be still be retained.

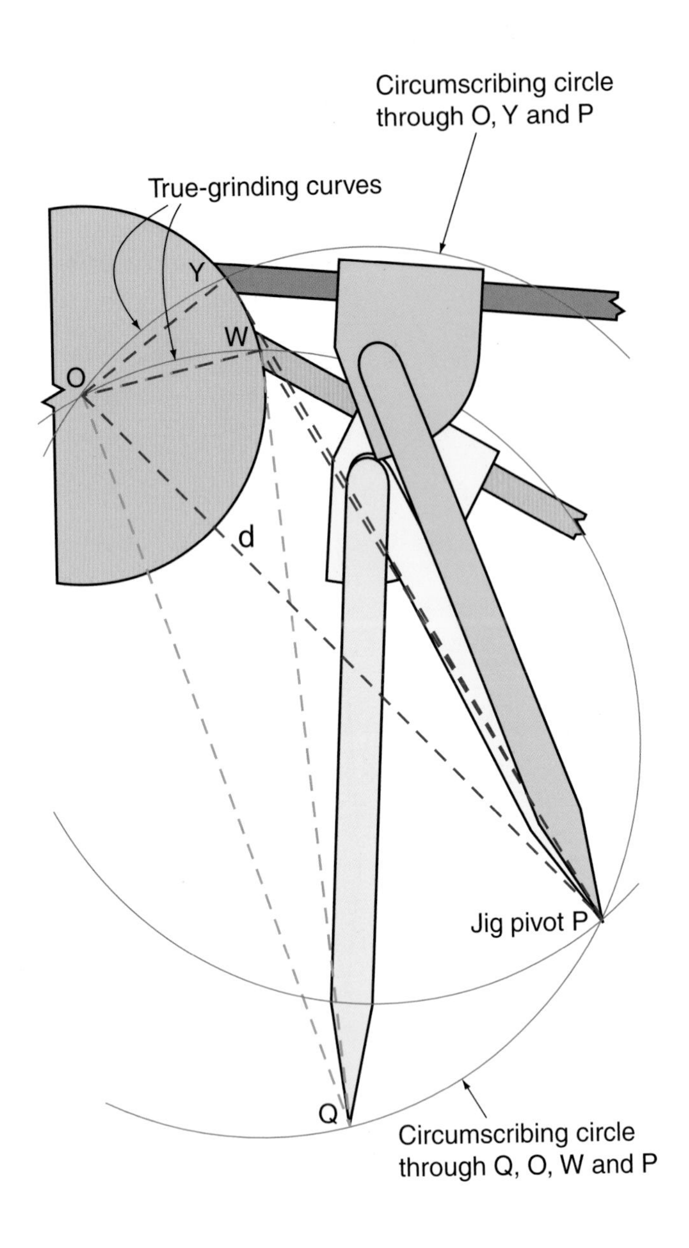

Figure 2.62 The true-grinding arc OY for jig pivot P.

The next figure shows how to grind a skew chisel on a true-grinding curve.

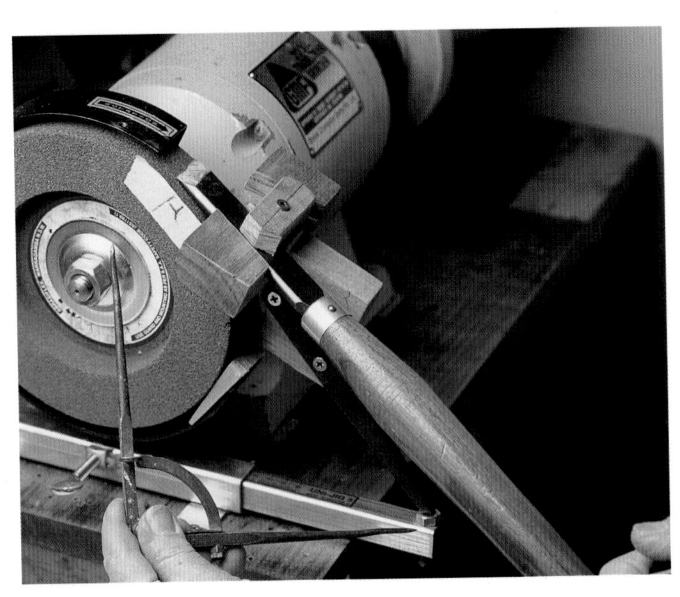

Figure 2.63 Grinding a skew on a true-grinding arc with a homemade jig.

To set the jig first you:

1. Decide upon a suitable position for the jig pivot P (see preceding diagram).
2. Measure the distance d from O to P—dividers or compasses are good for this. Do not alter the setting of the dividers or compasses because you will use it in step 4.
3. Wedge the grinding wheel stationary, and put masking tape on the side of the wheel on which to mark Y.
4. Mark Y by holding a point of your dividers or compasses in the jig pivot P, and swinging the free end from O to mark Y on the masking tape at the edge of the wheel.
5. Without changing the position of P, mount the tool into the pivoting jig and adjust the jig settings so that the correct sharpening angle will be ground with the tool bevel centered on Y.
6. Note the jig settings, tool projection, and how to reestablish P.
7. To regrind in the future, reestablish the same P, and set the tool in the pivoting jig with the same tool projection and jig settings, and regrind. There is no need to find the new Y, the bevel will automatically be centered on the true-grinding arc.

2.9 THE HELI-GRIND JIG

With the Heli-Grind you can easily and closely mimic the manipulations of hand grinding even with a detail gouge. And you use the tool you are about to regrind as a template which overcomes the problems associated with grinding-wheel wear except that of the gradual increase in sharpening angle characteristic of pivoting jigs. Invented in 1999 by Jack Crawford and Mike Irvine of Sydney, Australia, the Heli-Grind is a grinding system incorporating several accessories which all attach to a bench-mounted horizontal support.[5] The jig is described in figures 2.64 to 2.70.

Figure 2.64 The Heli-Grind horizontal support. All the accessories slide and/or pivot and/or fix onto the horizontal 12 mm diameter stainless-steel bar of the horizontal support. The stainless-steel bar can be swung nearer to or further from the periphery of a grinding wheel, and is freed and locked in the desired position by socket-head cap screw *B*. For this an Allen key is supplied.

The horizontal support has to be fixed to the benchtop to which the grinder is fixed, and accurately positioned relative to the grinding wheel. The Heli-Grind can be used with any nominal diameter of grinding wheel. With wheels smaller than 8 in. (200 mm) diameter the grinder will usually need to be packed up; with wheels greater than 8 in. the horizontal support usually needs to be packed up. The minimum grinding wheel thickness is 1 in. (25 mm), and this allows skew chisels up to 1 in. wide to be ground. A wheel thickness of 1$^5/_8$ in. (40 mm) allows wider skews to be ground, and a specially-formulated BLU-MAX wide wheel is available. Some grinders may not be able to accomodate this wider wheel unless the outer guard is shifted further out. The three homemade fishplates shown beneath the grinder switch allow this. The wooden jig just to the right of the the fishplates is to speed setting the correct tool projection—a similar device is useful for correctly mounting tools in all pivoting jigs.

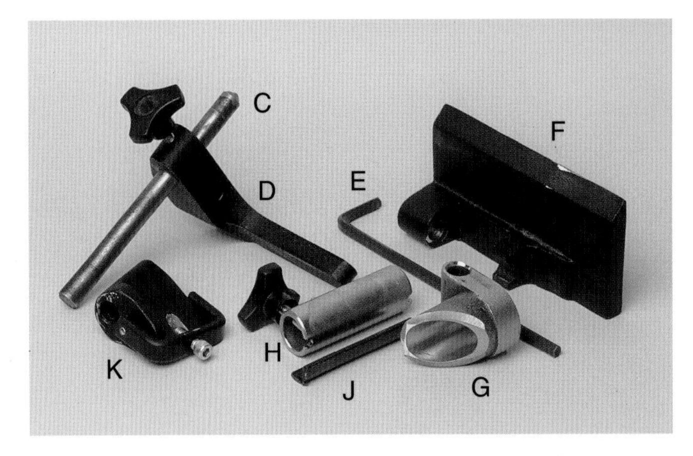

Figure 2.65 The Heli-Grind accessories: *C*, a single-point diamond dresser; *D*, the diamond dresser support; *E*, the Allen key to operate the horizontal support; *F*, the platform table for hand grinding; *G* and *H*, the helix head and guide tube for grinding detail and bowl gouges; *J*, the helix inner half spacer for use with small gouges; *K*, the skew guide. The slot cut in the top of the skew guide allows the yoke containing the fixing screw to be swung from one side of the guide to the other without having to fully unscrew the screw.

The platform *F* is used to grind tools which are not suitable to be ground using the helix or skew heads.

Figure 2.66 Wheel truing and dressing with a single-point diamond dresser. Lock the dresser into the support so that diamond tip projects about 1⁵/8 in. (40 mm) from the support. With the grinding wheel stationary, lock the horizontal support when the diamond is almost touching the wheel. Then switch the grinder on, and move the dresser fairly briskly across the wheel . The grip shown helps to move the dresser without jerking while pushing towards the wheel to control the depth of dressing.

To help the arm to slip smoothly across the horizontal support, rub the two contacting surfaces together to remove any roughness, and lubricate with graphite.

A single-point diamond dresser moved at a constant and relatively brisk speed across the rim leaves the abrasive grains sharper than does any other dressing method. It is therefore worth practicing a little to get the knack, and taking care to set a very small dressing "depth of cut".

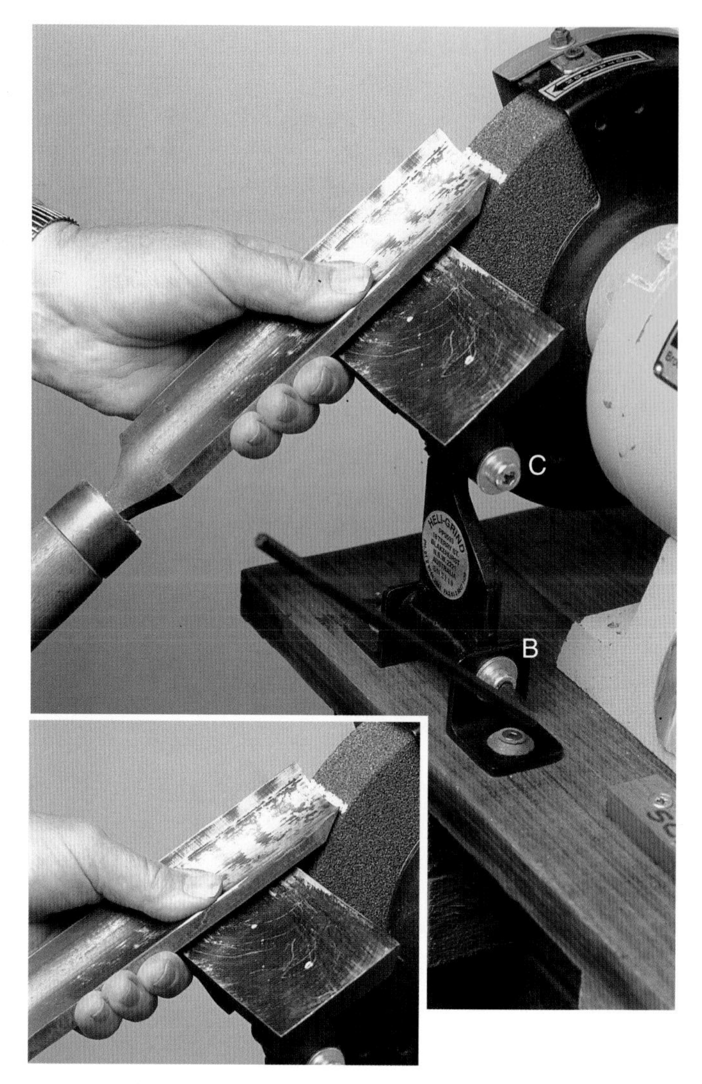

Figure 2.67 Setting the tilt of the platform table to grind a roughing gouge. This gouge is 2 in. (50 mm) wide, too wide to be held in the helix head.

Top: the grinder is off, the platform is loose on the stainless-steel bar, and the horizontal support is free to pivot. The gouge is held in full contact with the platform and projects forward from its edge a suitable amount. The gouge handle is then slowly swung up and forwards until the whole of the gouge bevel is felt to be in contact with the grinding wheel periphery as shown in the inset. You then tighten cap screws *B* and *C*, do a visual check from the side, and after any readjustments, are ready to regrind. The process is identical to that shown earlier with a two-pivot platform jig in figure 2.5. This same process is used to set the sharpening angle with the Heli-Grind for every tool, irrespective of the accessory you will use to support that tool. Your first task if you buy a Heli-Grind is therefore to check that your tools are sharpened correctly. If any are not, correct their tip grindings using the Heli-Grind with checking and adjusting. You will then be able to set the jig for subsequent regrindings directly from the correctly angled bevels.

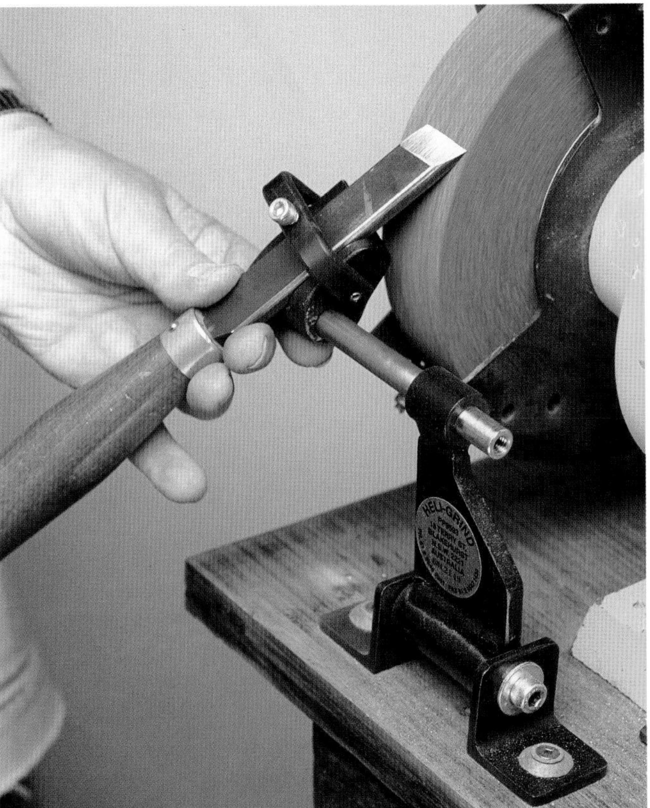

Figure 2.68 Regrinding a skew in the skew guide. After grinding the first bevel, the skew is remounted on the other side of the guide to regrind the other bevel.

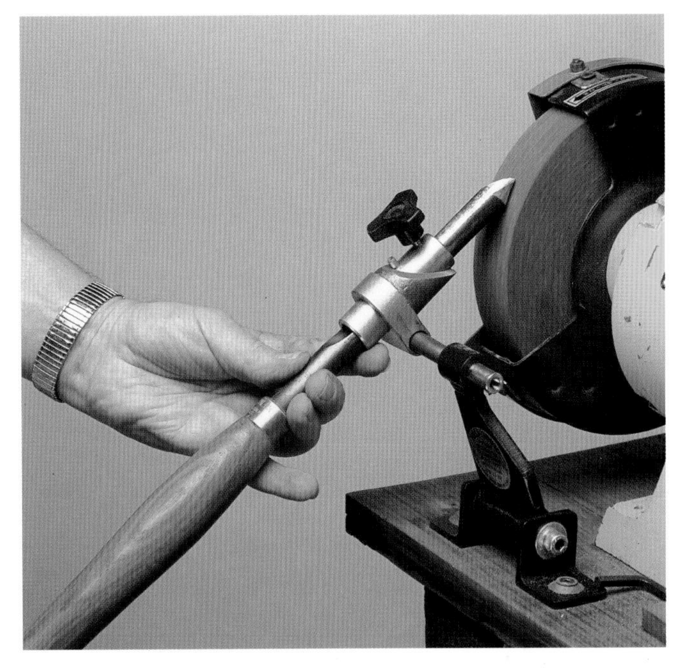

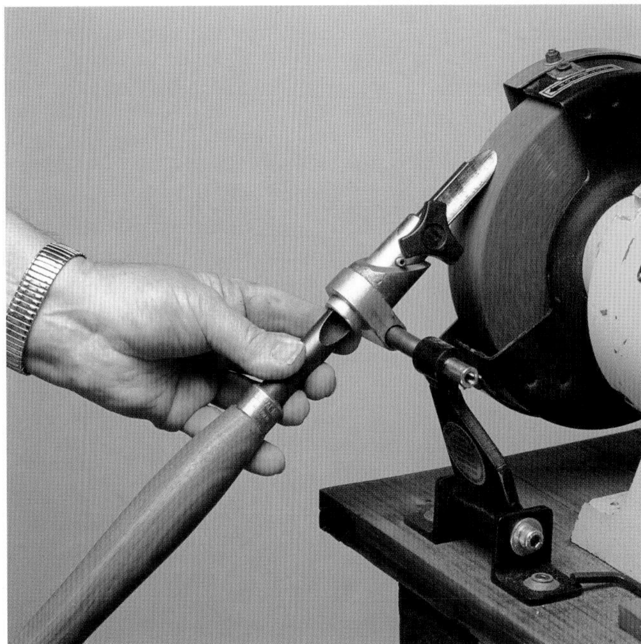

Figure 2.69 Regrinding a detail gouge. The helix guide tube is first inserted into the helix head. The gouge is then locked into the guide tube with about 50 mm projecting, using the half spacer if the gouge cross section is small. After sliding the helix head onto the stainless-steel bar, the gouge is held with its flute facing up and its bevel in full contact with the wheel, and the horizontal support is locked. To regrind, rotate the gouge clockwise and counterclockwise with its bevel in light contact with the wheel. As you grind further from the nose tip, the gouge is automatically pushed up the grinding wheel by the pin projecting from the helix guide tube bearing on the sloping end of the helix guide. The tool thus follows a helical path, hence system's name.

Figure 2.70 **Grinding a square-across or ground-back bowl gouge.** The helix head but not the guide tube are reversed on the pivot support bar.

There is a third, common bowl-gouge nose, the swept-back. This nose shape tends to be favored by those turners who have to turn bowls inboard on non-swivelling-headstock lathes. You can grind a swept-back bowl-gouge nose with the helix head providing that the cutting edges along the flanges are not too long. For this you first freehand grind the tops of the flanges with the gouge flute down so that the nose has the correct shape in profile. You then grind the bevel using the helix head and grind tube in the detail gouge presentation shown in the preceding figure. You continue to grind until the bevel just meets the edge of the flute, thereby producing a cutting edge. To produce a swept-back nose with very long cutting edges along the flanges, you would have to first to set the platform table to give a coarse sharpening angle (typically 65°) at the tip, and then fan the tool by hand.

2.10 SUMMARY

I continue to believe that a sanding belt running over a wheel or convex platen is the simplest apparatus for grinding turning tools. The simplicity stems from the absense of grinding-wheel wear, and the procedure is detailed in figures 4.30 and 4.31 of FOW. But for most turners a bench grinder is the sensible grinding apparatus because it is far cheaper.

Bench grinders can accomodate two wheels. Can you spare both for turning-tool grinding? If so, how will you split the sharpening tasks between them? If you are a keen bowl turner, you may opt for a flat-rimmed wheel at one end of your grinder and a concave-rimmed wheel (FOW figure 4.35) in preference to a second flat-rimmed wheel at the other. You may want to employ a felt wheel, honing wheel, or buff; if so you might need a second grinder.

If you already have a turning jig, I hope this chapter will help you to grind more accurately with it. If you intend to buy a sharpening jig, which one? There is no easy answer because the different jigs vary in their suitability for grinding the different tool types, and because jig design will continue to advance. Jig prices and values also cover a wide range. But the main shortcoming with grinding jigs in 2000 is not their constructions but their instructions which are usually scanty, and ignore the problems of wheel wear.

Platform jigs are usually the cheapest type, and can be used for every tool type and size, a quality rare in the more complicated jigs. Platform jigs can easily be set with two-pin templates, while the O'Donnell jig has inbuilt settings. My preference is for a steel platform. Diecast platforms tend to wear quickly, and have an intrinsic stickiness. Platform jigs do demand more skill to manipulate the tools, but isn't the desire to learn new skills one of the reasons why people turn? Adding a handle-end jig and crossarm is worthwhile if you have long, heavy tools. The sliding arm can also be used to provide the female part of a pivoting-jig pivot.

Pivoting jigs tend to require multiple adjustments, which makes them slower to use than platform jigs, but they are the only jigs which jig the grinding of very swept-back bowl gouges. Few pivoting jigs can cope with extremes of blade cross section, or with tools with short blades. Some pivoting jigs hinder wheel dressing. A dresser must be supported during use; hand-holding a dresser will lead to a non-circular grinding-wheel periphery.

Although they are similar, there are currently differences between the three pivoting jigs shown in this section. The Glaser Joystick and Uni-Jig 5 have their knee-angles and leg length or sliding-arm projection calibrated which aids their resetting: the Vari-Grind does not have these calibrations. On the plus side for the Vari-Grind, it has a wheel-dressing attachment, a platform which can be substituted for the Vee-Arm/Vari-Grind combination, and a crossarm.

The Heli-Grind is quick and easy to operate, enables you to dress your grinding wheel accurately, and it includes a platform jig which offers the flexibility to grind any tool. It does not however jig the grinding of very swept-back bowl gouges. And as with all pivoting-type jigs, when you use the bevel as a template you will have to correct for the gradual increase in sharpening angle.

Some woodturners are ever ready to copy commercially made equipment. Sharpening equipment is relatively simple in its construction and therefore easy to copy: sometimes how to construct homemade versions of commercial jigs appears in the woodturning media.[6] If the commercial equipment is patented, making even one copy for your private use is illegal. Whether copying something which is not protected by patent or design registration is morally wrong is a judgement you must make yourself, although your conscience may be lightened when a commercial product is clearly a rip-off or a reintroduction of a device invented long ago.

2.11 GRINDING WHEELS

Grinding wheels are available in an increasing range of colors, formulations, and structures; although in countries with small populations the choice may be restricted. If you have properly jigged your tool regrinding, your grinding and dressing will be minimized . And if you do dress your wheels as soon as required, your grinding should be both cool and quick. It can, however, be cooler and quicker if you take advantage of the progress in grinding-wheel technology.

Most double-ended bench grinders are equipped when new with grey-colored aluminum oxide wheels, one coarse and one fine. These wheels are composed of grains of impure aluminum oxide which are strongly bonded together. There are other forms of aluminum oxide and wheel compositions which are better suited to grind HSS turning tools:[7]

1. White aluminum oxide is more than 99% pure, and harder and more friable than the grey form. There is also a superior single-crystal white form.
2. The aluminum oxide in pink wheels is alloyed with a small percentage of chrome oxide.
3. High-chrome wheels contain about 3% of chrome oxide and are ruby colored.
4. Sol-gel, sometimes called seeded-gel, aluminum oxide is made by a multi-stage process which includes jelling, dehydration, crushing, and firing. One form is pale blue due to the presence of cobalt. Sol-gel abrasive has a fine-crystal microstructure.

To grind tool steel well the abrasive grains want to be very hard, and not too tough but friable so that they fracture leaving sharp edges. To take full advantage of friable grains, the ceramic bond holding the grains must be just soft enough to allow the worn grain particles to fracture and escape. The hardness of the bond is signified by a capital letter, the later the letter in the alphabet, the harder the bond. The usual grey wheels often have bonds of P or Q hardness, the ideal bond for our wheels is J.

An advance which is being adopted for turning-tool grinding wheels is a porous structure. The bonding compound is mixed with a combustible material. When the wheel is fired, the combustible material burns away leaving a porous structure which allows air to pass through it and therefore grinds cooler and cloggs less.

I have not done the necessary testing to determine the best wheel for turning-tool grinding. Factors which would influence the choice include: the purchase price, cost per grind, rate of wheel wear, and rate of steel removal. The grain size is significant, and although 56 or 60 grit are excellent for reshaping, the less aggresive 80 grit might be preferred for faster-grinding wheels.

2.12 WHEEL DRESSING AND BALANCING

Dressing with a single-point diamond wheel leaves the wheel's abrasive grains sharpest. The dresser needs to be moved across the periphery fairly briskly. If the movement is too fast, the diamond cuts a helical groove in the periphery leaving it serrated in cross section. If the movement is too slow, abrasive grains are dressed more than once, the second and any later contacts blunting the sharpness of the grain edges. Single-point dressers should be mechanically held or jigged in position, it being between difficult and impossible to achieve a flat rim with the dresser hand-held (figures 2.71 to 2.73).

Star-wheel dressers should be axially tilted about 15° and again moved across the wheel rim briskly; multipoint diamond dressers leave somewhat blunt grains, dressing sticks blunter grains. The dressing stick is the cheapest dresser, and the best for dressing concave rims (FOW figure 4.35).

The geometry of grinding wheels is rarely perfect, and their density is rarely uniform. You can make your grinder run more smoothly by using balancing hubs (figures 2.74 and 2.75).

Figure 2.71 **A single-point diamond dresser held in a homemade wood collar.** A screw runs through a clearance hole above the saw cut and in a pilot hole below. Tightening the screw clamps the collar around the dresser. The projection of the diamond from the face of the collar should be a little more than the width of the tilting platform. To increase the diamond's life, rotate it occasionally in the collar.

Figure 2.72 Using the dresser and homemade collar from the preceding figure on a tilting-platform jig.

With the grinder off, lock the tilting platform so that the diamond almost touches the wheel periphery. The dresser should point about 10° below the radius from the center of the wheel to the diamond. Dress by moving the dresser across the periphery, here from right to left. The gripping shown enables you to pull the dresser steadily without jerking while pressing the collar against the back of the platform—as most tilting platforms flex a little this force will press the diamond against the wheel. The cuts should be light, removing about 1/100 in. (0.25 mm) thickness of abrasive per pass.

Figure 2.73 **The Wolverine Dressing Attachment** has two large components: the diamond arm support *B* fits into a Oneway Wolverine housing; and the diamond arm *C* pivots about the adjusting screw *D*. The projection of the diamond *E* from the diamond arm is locked with a socket screw. To dress the wheel the diamond support is fanned, while being pressed against the horizontal bar welded to the top of the diamond arm support. The diamond should be advanced by quarter turns of the adjusting screw to equalize wear.

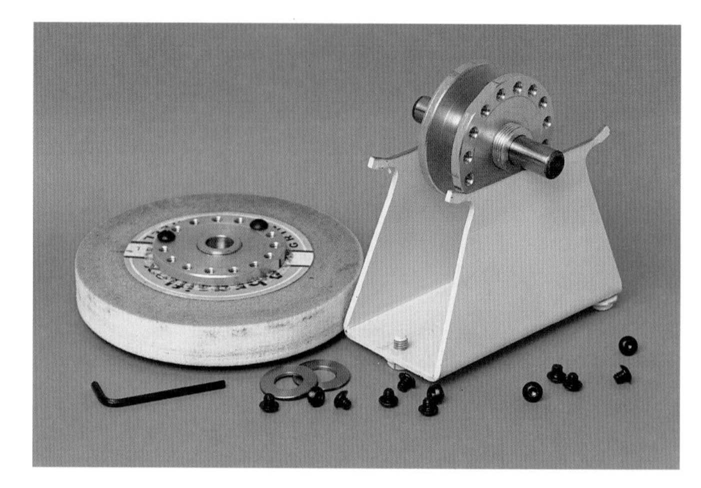

Figure 2.74 **The Oneway Balancing System** for grinding wheels with a 1 in. bore. The System consists of left- and right-hand flange assemblies, a cradle, a hardened and ground pin, and counterweights in the form of buttonhead socket screws.

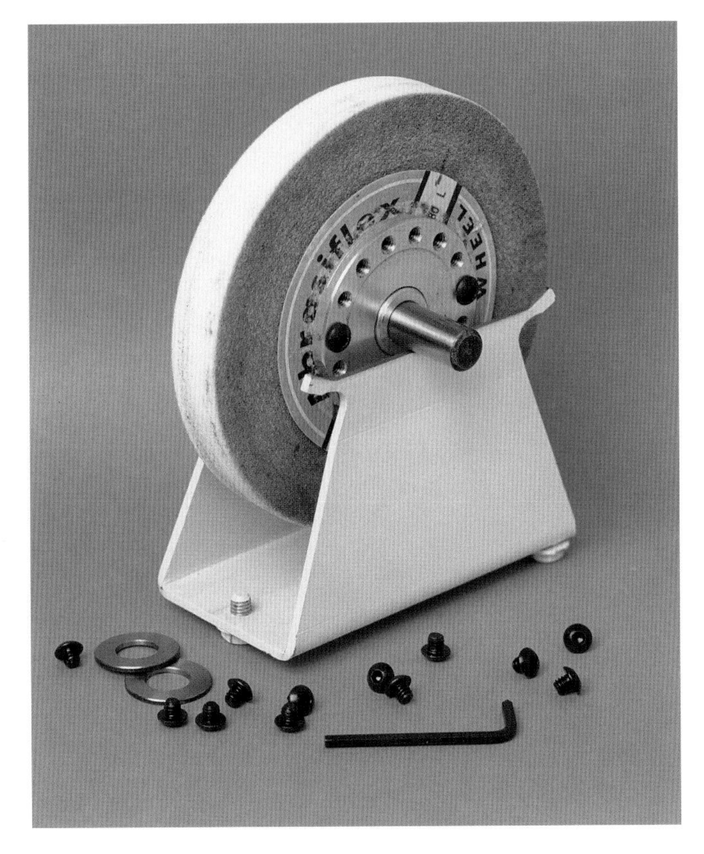

Figure 2.75 Balancing a grinding wheel. You first follow a simple procedure to level the balancing cradle. After mounting the grinding wheel on the appropriate flange assembly, you pass the pin through the assembly and place the ends of the pin on the machined edges of the cradle. You then screw buttonhead socket screws into the flange assembly using the described procedure until the wheel does not want to roll along the cradle and is balanced.

The two flange assemblies supplied are labelled left-hand and right-hand. If you mount a grinding wheel on a flange assembly on the wrong side of your grinder, the separate flange of the assembley will unscrew, and the grinding wheel will be free to spin on the flange assembly.

Before investing in a balancing system, run your grinder with bare spindles to check that it runs without vibration and is therefore balanced: if it does not, return it to the supplier.

2.13 SHARPENING FLAT SCRAPERS

Most turners resharpen scrapers by regrinding the bevel. This method is quick and effective when the scraper's end is simple in plan. But regrinding the bevel is too crude for ends which are intricate or precise in plan—it removes too much steel, and the risk of destroying the accuracy of the end's plan is high. There are three other techniques which can be used instead:

1. Hone the scraper's top face.
2. Ticket a burr.
3. Hone the bevel to produce a sharp edge without a burr.

Honing the top face can require a lot of steel to be removed, but is the ideal method for thread chasers where you don't want to affect the accuracy of the teeth. Ticketing is not a process which is easy to repeat consistently. Honing the bevel is quick and accurate with a coarse diamond hone, and the edge can be further refined with finer-grained hones. You can hone the bevel by hand, or make a simple jig (figures 2.76 and 2.77).

Figure 2.76 A scraper honer.
When required the bevel is reground to leave a sharpening angle of 70°. The diamond hone slopes at 10° to the vertical, and thus hones a microbevel at the top of the bevel. The coarseness of the hone is changed by loosening the wing nut and thus the steel arm.
For intricate scrapers a similar device could be made which used a rattail diamond hone instead of a flat one.

Figure 2.77 Close-ups of the scraper honer. The diamond hone is clamped at 10° to the vertical and supported at its bottom in the slot in the steel plate. By varying the projection of the hone above the steel plate you can spread the wear.

2.14 ENDNOTES

1. Hugh O'Neil, *Woodturning A Manual of Techniques* (Marlborough, Wiltshire: The Crowood Press, 1989), pp. 35–39.
2. C. & M. O'Donnell, Brough, Thurso, Caithness, Scotland KW14 8YE.
3. Combined handle-end and platform jigs are also shown in: Ron Roszkiewicz, *The Woodturner's Companion* (New York: Sterling Publishing 1984), p.65; and Ernie Conover, *The Lathe Book* (Newtown CT: The Taunton Press, 1993), p. 70. Leonard Lee, *The Complete Guide to Sharpening* (Newtown CT: The Taunton Press,1995), p. 124 shows a homemade handle-end jig without the platform jig.
4. Uni-Jig Products, 68 Oliver Street, Harbord, NSW 2096, Australia.
5. You can buy the Heli-Grind from some specialist woodturning suppliers and from John Crawford, 18 Terry Street, Blakehurst, NSW 2221, Australia.
6. King Heiple, "Shop-Built Sharpening System," *American Woodturner* (Winter 1999): pp. 28–31; and Tobias Kaye, "Grinding fingernail gouges," *Good Woodworking* (November 1996): pp. 46–51.
7. William Wellborn, "Modern Abrasive Recipes," *Cutting Tool Engineering* (April 1994): pp. 42–47.

Chapter Three

SPINDLE TURNING

This short chapter discusses wire burning, then cluster legs.

3.1 WIRE BURNING

You can easily produce black rings on spindles and on radially grained workpieces with wire burning. A similar effect can be created by holding any hard, high-melting-point material against a fast-revolving wood surface. As with decorative V-cutting, the technique can be overused.

Figure 3.1 **Burning black rings.** You first make fine V-cuts in which to locate the wire. Keeping both hands above the workpiece is safer than running the wire under the toolrest and having one hand low and one high. The handles ensure that if you lose control you will not cut though your fingers.

The length of wire between the handles is here $6^1/_2$ in. (165 mm). The wire can be single or multiple strand, but should be flexible enough to conform to the workpiece surface. The diameter of the wire will influence the width of the burning. Steel is the most durable metal for the wire, but non-ferrous metals can be used.

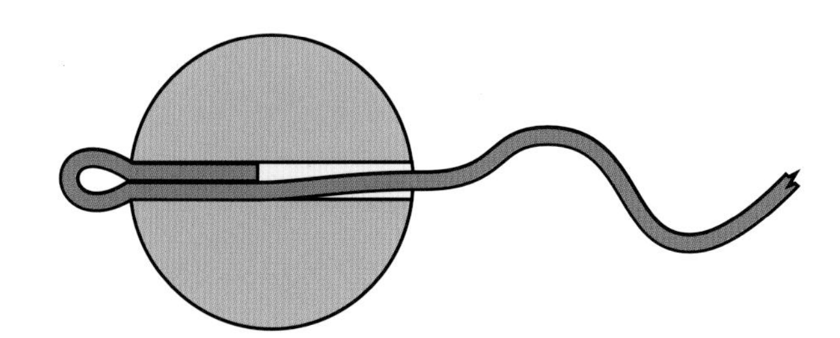

Figure 3.2 **A cross section through a handle showing how the wire is held.** Drill a hole through each handle about twice the diameter of the wire. Pass the ends of the wire through the holes, then push each end back into the hole leaving a loop of wire. Pull the handles apart hard, and the loops will contract and jam.

3.2 CLUSTER LEGS

Turned cluster legs (figure 3.3) were introduced at the middle of the eighteenth century, and were at their most fashionable around 1760. They enabled furniture designers to achieve visual bulk with delicacy. Cluster legs were most used on small rectangular tables, and clusters of spindles were occasionally incorporated into bed posts. The spindles were sometimes turned to simulate bamboo, reflecting the cluster leg's descent from the legs of imported Chinese furniture assembled from several stems of bamboo.

Cluster columns and legs usually have three or four spindles per tier, and can be constructed in two ways as figure 3.4 shows.

Figure 3.3 **An English chair in mahogany and beech with cluster legs, circa 1760.** Although there can be four spindles in the cluster, three without the inside spindle, as here, is more common. This chair is in the collection at Temple Newsam House, Leeds, England. The furniture collection at Temple Newsam is described in Christopher Gilbert, *Furniture at Temple Newsam House and Lotherton Hall*, 3 vols. (National Art-Collections Fund and the Leeds Art Collections Fund, 1978–98). *Photograph by James Lomax.*

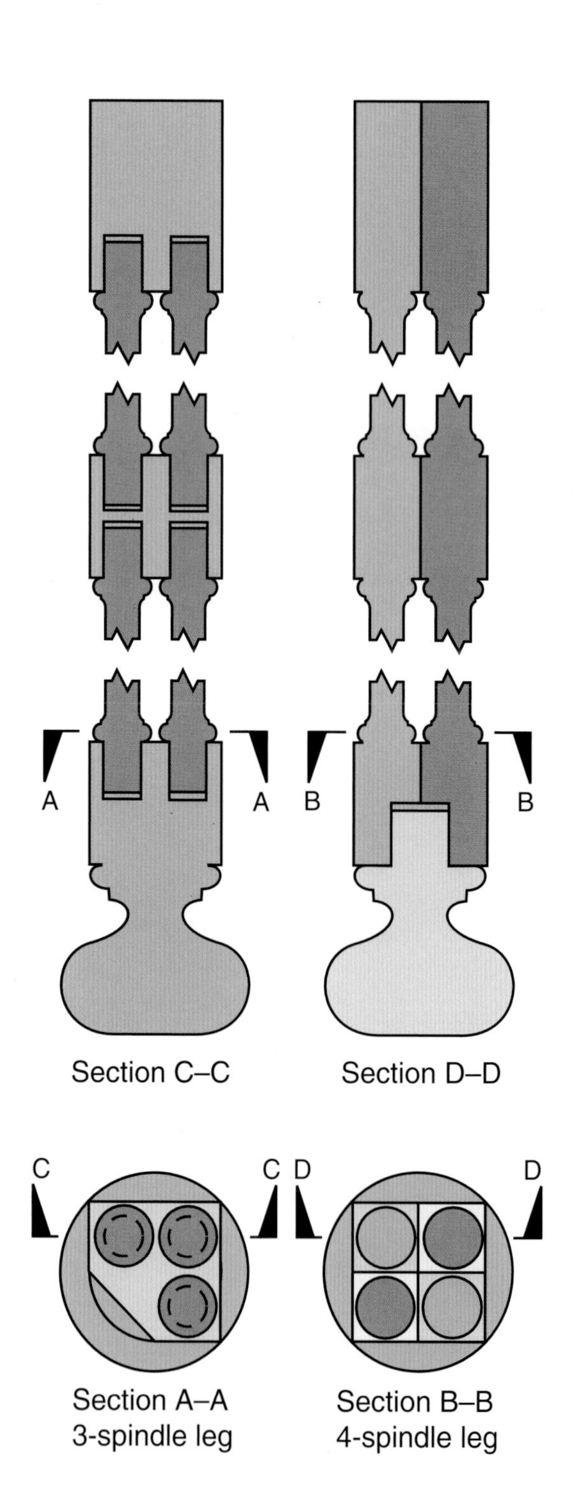

Figure 3.4 **The constructions of cluster legs.** Note, the bun feet at the bottoms of sections *C–C* and *D-D* are shown in diametrical section.

Left: the leg is conglutinated from drilled blocks joined by clusters of spindles with pins at each end.

Right: this leg is the stronger being conglutinated from full-length turnings. The vertical glue joints in the blocks will barely be visible if the medullary rays in each spindle are similarly orientated, but could be hidden by veneering around the outsides of the compound blocks.

Chapter Four

CUPCHUCK TURNING

This chapter details:

1. The flute-down hollowing method.
2. A new scraper for finish-turning hollows.
3. Hollowing with a hook or ring tool.
4. The Martel hook tool.
5. Turning nests of thin cups
6. Chatterwork.
7. Leonardo's true contribution to self-centering chucking, and three new chucks by Bruce Leadbeatter.

The basics of cupchuck turning are covered in chapter 7 of FOW.

4.1 THE FLUTE-DOWN METHOD OF CUPCHUCK HOLLOWING

Figures 722 to 7.25 of FOW show the most useful method for end-grain hollowing. There is an alternative method which I could label German on the slight grounds that most of the books which describe it are German.[1] But both methods are, I suspect, centuries old, and their origins unknown. In the method described in FOW you use the detail gouge with its flute facing up and to the left, whereas in the method described here you use the detail gouge with its flute facing down and to your right. Perhaps flute-up and flute-down would be more appropriate labels for the two methods.

Compared with the flute-up method, the flute-down method:

1. Is slightly more difficult to master.
2. Cannot be used for the later cuts for very deep or large-diameter hollows.
3. Uses the gouge in a *cutting* presentation and therefore enables you to remove waste more quickly. In the flute-up method the gouge is usually scraping or shear-scraping. You can however by withdrawing the detail gouge tip not at lathe axis height but lower along the surface of the hollow make the action nearer to a *cut*.
4. Always uses the bevel or the bevel heel to provide support. Additional support is often gained by bearing the detail-gouge blade against the rim of the hollow. The flute-down technique cannot therefore be used to finish-turn thin-walled and/or thin-rimmed hollows.

The flute-down method is described in figures 4.1 to 4.11.

Figure 4.1 **Starting a first flute-down hollowing cut.** You should position the toolrest at about 60° in plan to, and about half your gouge's diameter below, the lathe axis. The first cut is essentially a pointing cut. As you push the gouge nose, first the bevel and then the bevel heel bear against the rim of the hollow and provide a fulcrum.

The workpiece is here held firmly in a scroll chuck mounted inboard. Only if the chucking is secure can you cut forcefully and hollow quickly.

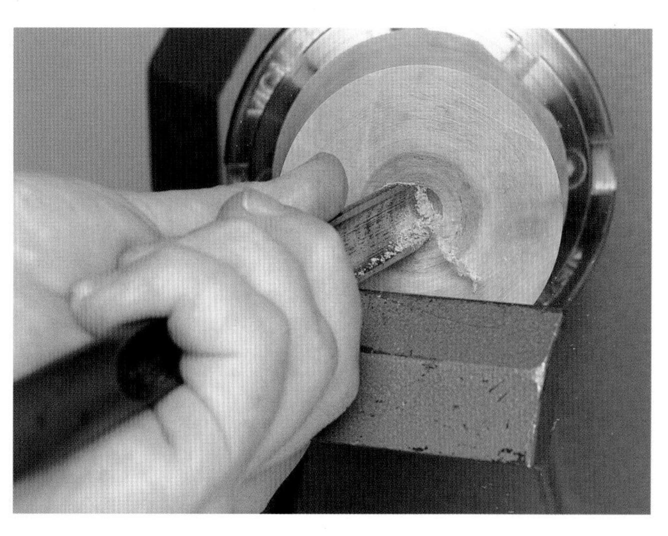

Figure 4.2 **Completing the first cut.** The tip of the detail gouge has reached the lathe axis.

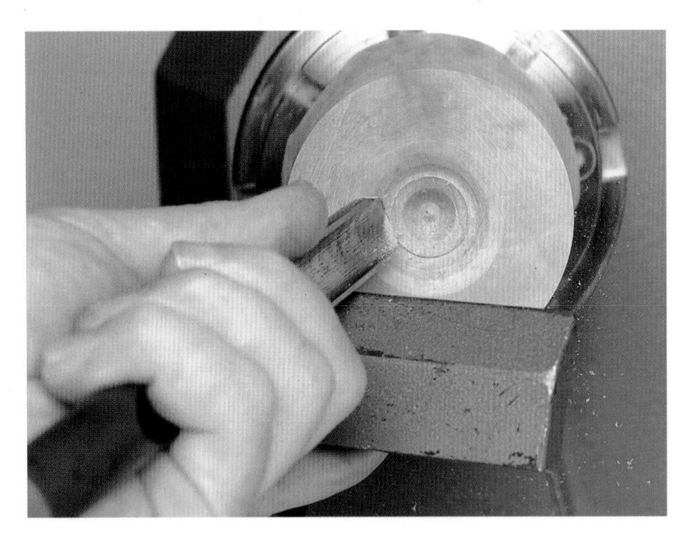

Figure 4.3 **Starting the second cut,** again a pointing cut.

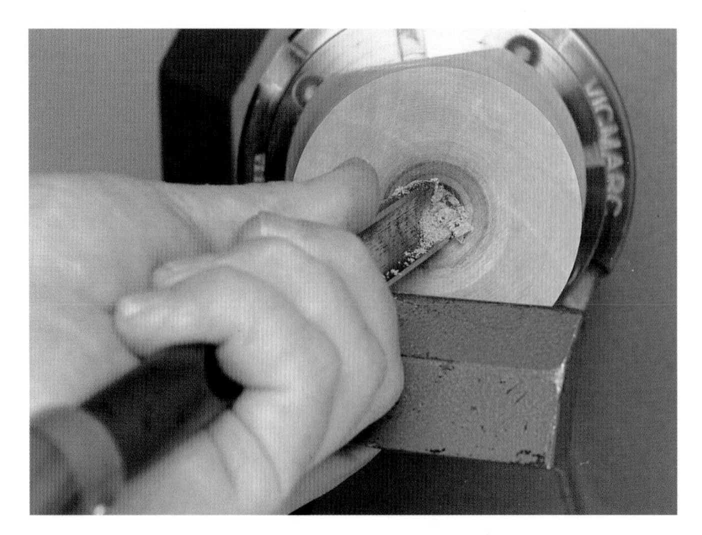

Figure 4.4 **The completion of the pointing part of the second cut.** The rest of the cut is made as the tool is withdrawn, and is described in figures 4.5 to 4.7.

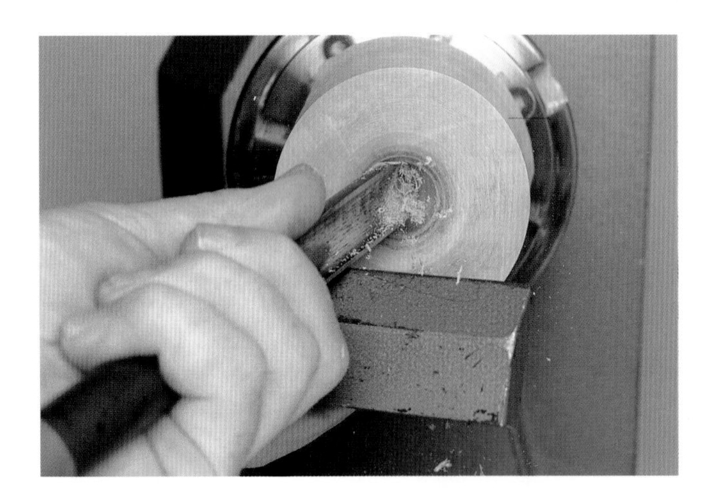

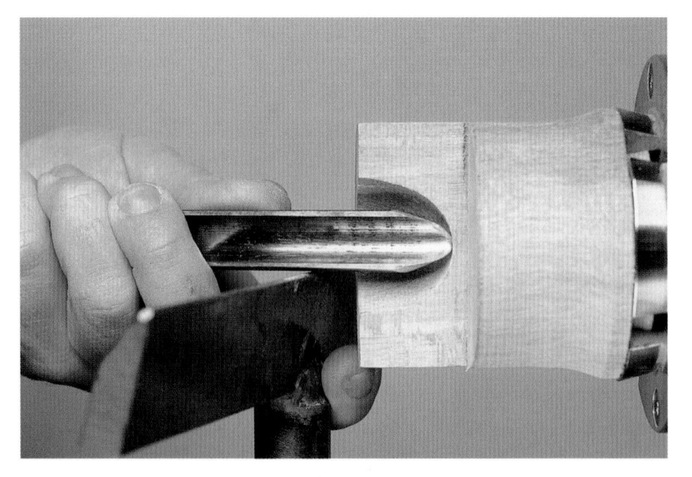

Figure 4.5 **Starting the flute-down part of the second cut.** While starting to axially rotate the gouge clockwise, the gouge nose is levered up. The back of the gouge blade is bearing against the rim of the hollow.

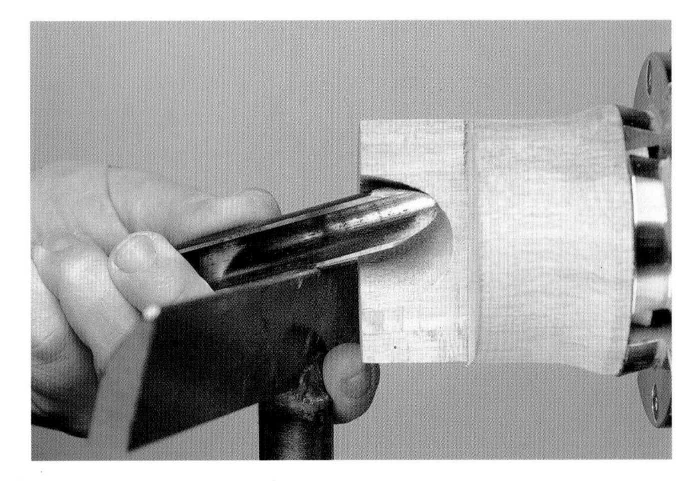

Figure 4.6 **Continuing to axially rotate the gouge clockwise** while levering the gouge tip up and out of the hollow.

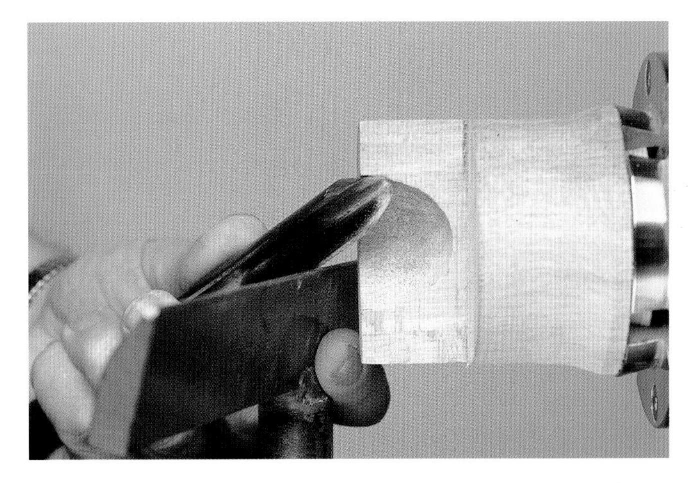

Figure 4.7 **Completing the second cut.** The back of the blade and the heel of the bevel are both supported by the rim of the hollow.

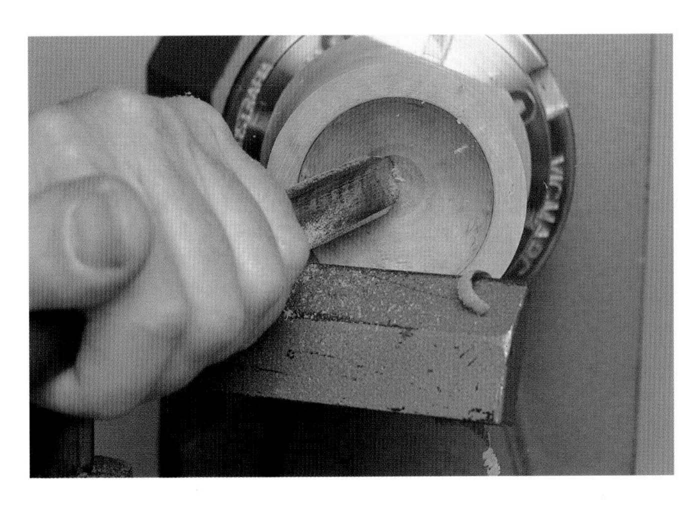

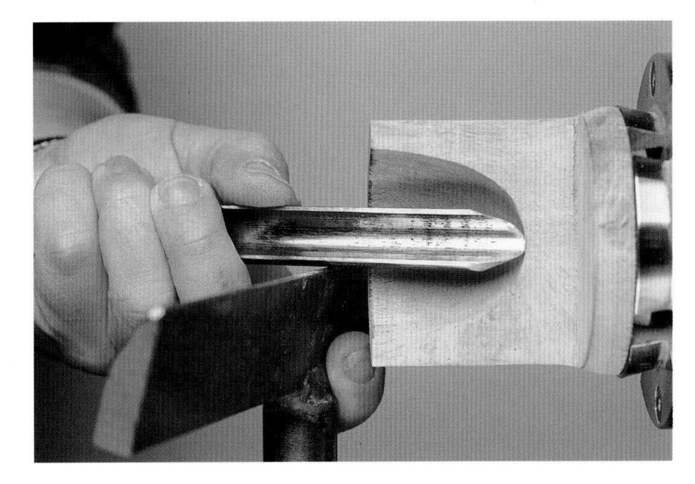

Figure 4.8 **Starting the third flute-down hollowing cut.** With the back of the blade bearing against the rim of the hollow, the gouge point penetrates the end of the hollow a little to the left of the lathe axis, and is pushed forwards until it reaches the lathe axis.

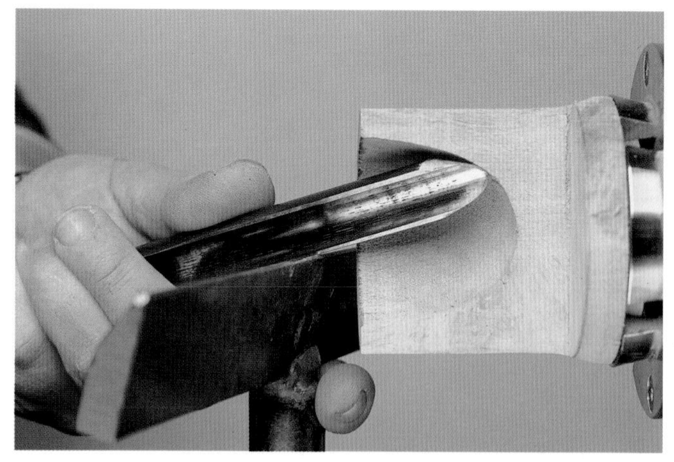

Figure 4.9 Starting to cut on the pull during the third cut. The back of the gouge blade is bearing on the rim of the hollow. The clockwise rotation of the gouge proceeds at the rate which gives minimal clearance and therefore the sweetest and most controlled *cut*.

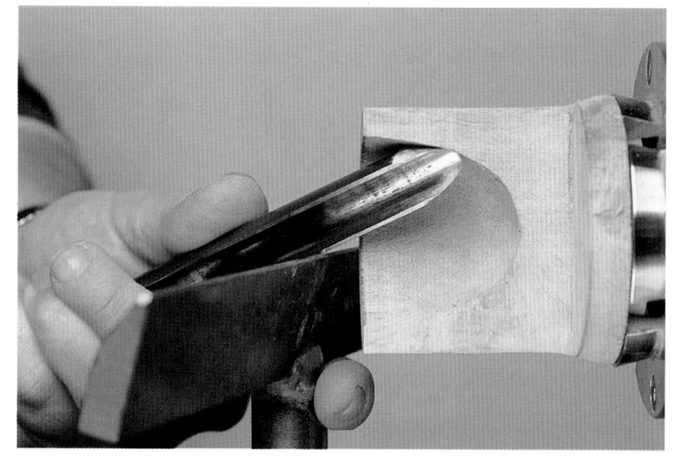

Figure 4.10 Nearing the end of the third cut. Although the back of the blade is supported by the hollow's rim, if the shape of the hollow makes it impossible to also retain bevel or bevel-heel support, control will be lost.

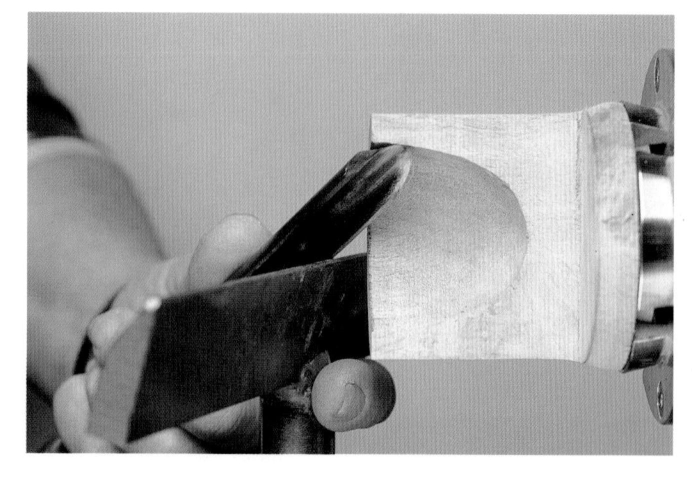

Figure 4.11 Completing the third, and here final, flute-down hollowing cut. The bevel heel and the back of the blade are supported by the rim. The inside of the hollow could then be finish-turned using a detail gouge, a flat scraper, a shear scraper, or any of the three tools described in the next section.

4.2 FINISH-TURNING HOLLOWS

Turners often use flat scrapers to refine the shapes and surfaces of hollows, but there are alternative tools. This section describes three.

4.2.1 A TOOTHED SHEAR SCRAPER

Figure 4.12 **A toothed shear scraper** with overlapping edges invented by your author. The tool is sharpened by honing the upper faces of the teeth with a diamond lap.

Figure 4.13 **Smoothing a hollow by pulling the toothed shear scraper out and to the left.**

4.2.2 THE RING OR HOOK TOOL

You should present ring and hook tools with minimum clearance and about 45° side rake to cut securely and leave an excellent finish. Figures 4.14 to 4.18 demonstrate the presentations.

Figure 4.14 **Cutting at the bottom of a hollow without side rake** will leave a poorer surface than that produced with the 45° side rake presentation shown in the next figure. Also, this stable presentation with the cutting edge facing vertically up becomes unstable as the tool is pulled out and left, towards the rim.

This hook tool manufactured by Robert Sorby has two circular cutting edges of diameters $^5/_8$ in. and $^1/_2$ in. (17 mm and 13 mm). The second cutting edge allows the tool to be used to cut nearer to the rim of shallow hollows.

When buying a hook or ring tool, test that the shaft is stiff enough not to flex at longer overhangs.

Figure 4.15 **The optimum presentation to cut safely at the bottom of a hollow.** The clearance angle is near zero and the side rake about 45°. As the cut continues, the handle must be swung to the right to prevent the clearance angle increasing.

Figure 4.16 **Continuing the cut started in the preceeding figure.** However even with a hollow this shallow, the tool will not be able to cut much further without the movement of the shaft being blocked by the rim of the hollow on the right.

Figure 4.17 **A catch is almost certain with conventional hook and ring tools in this presentation** because the downward force applied by the wood is applied at a lever arm equal in length to the radius of the cutting edge. Any imbalance in the vertical forces on the cutting edge will cause the hook or ring to catch and jerk counterclockwise.

Figure 4.18 **With the smaller-diameter cutting edge you can cut to the rim of shallow hollows,** but to *cut* along the wall of a deep hollow with side rake you will need the tool described in the next section.

4.2.3 THE MARTEL HOOK TOOL

You can safely use conventional hook and ring tools to cut finished surfaces at the bottom of hollows in cupchuck turnings as shown in figures 4.15, 4.16, and 4.18. But attempt to cut from the bottom and out along the wall of a deep hollow, and you will not be able you retain the safe cutting presentation because the rim of the hollow will prevent you swinging the handle far enough to the right (figure 4.16). Andre Martel has invented a new design of hook tool which is stable and safe when used in even deep hollows, and which cuts with side rake to leave an excellent off-the-tool surface even on softer woods (figures 4.19 to 4.22). Andre produces and markets the tool himself from 167 Rang des Ecossais, St-Cesaire, Quebec, Canada JOL 1TO.

Figure 4.20 **Cutting at the bottom of the hollow.** To achieve the safe cutting presentation with the minimum clearance and a high side rake, you have to angle the tool in from the right. If the hole is narrower than that shown, you would have to use a detail gouge, scraper, shear scraper, or conventional hook or ring tool in this area.

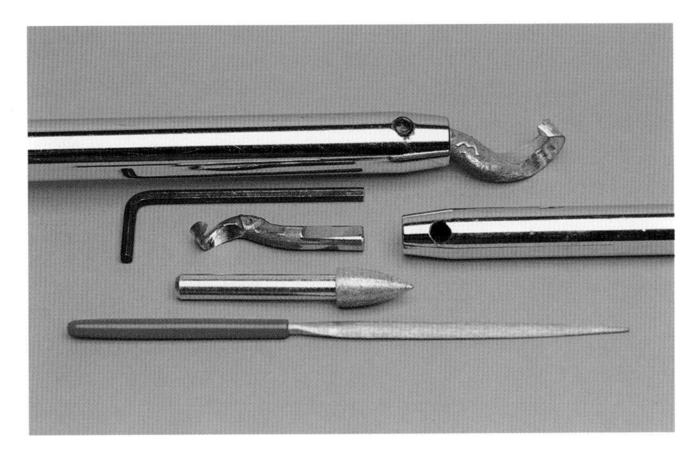

Figure 4.19 **Martel hook tools.** The 1/4 in. (6 mm) and 3/8 in. (10 mm) hooks (there is also a 1/2 in. (13 mm)) lock into stiff steel shanks which are available in a range of diameters and lengths. The shanks fit into most popular brands of metal handle, or you can fit wooden handles.

The fine-grit, diamond hone is used to refresh the cutting edges. The 150-grit diamond burr is used to grind the bevels after several honings. Because the number of resharpenings is limited, you should use a detail gouge in the flute-up or flute-down presentation to first rough the hollow to close to its final shape.

Figure 4.21 **Cutting round the bend** from the bottom into the side of the hollow. After cutting the bottom, the tool has to be represented as shown to achieve the desirable combination of rake and side rake.

Figure 4.22 Cutting almost parallel to the lathe axis. The MHT was slowly and continuously rotated clockwise from the presentation in the preceeding figure to maintain the same rake and side rake presentation. With care this tool will leave a superb surface.

4.3 NESTS OF CUPS

Among the many neglected gems in the Holtzapffel series *Turning and Mechanical Manipulation* is John Jacob Holtzapffel's description of the technique for turning nests of cups on pages 562 to 564 of volume IV, *Hand or Simple Turning*. Even Edward H. Pinto seems to have missed it, for in describing nests of cups on page 40 of *Treen and Other Wooden Bygones* (London: G. Bell & Sons, 1969) he makes no mention of the procedure. The challenge of turning nests has been answered only occasionally, mainly in the eighteenth and nineteenth centuries (figure 4.23)—perhaps the description which follows in figures 4.24 to 4.33 will attract a new generation who wish to demonstrate their skills and patience.

The technique is used for axially-grained workpieces. You must use a hard, near-white, fine-grained wood which turns well if you want to produce cups which are of paper thickness. You also need two chucks, one which you use to chuck each nest cup workpiece, the other which holds what John Jacob calls the chuck, and which I shall call the mandrel.

The stages in turning a nest of cups are:

1. Rough (including hollow) a workpiece for each cup and allow them to relax and season (figure 4.24). I advise you to rough a few extra, because you are likely to have some failures.
2. Chuck and turn a mandrel to the inside shape of the outer cup—in figure 4.23 the outer cup is the footed, lidded (also called covered) one.
3. Cupchuck the outer cup workpiece and hollow it to exactly conform to the shape of the mandrel using chalking to monitor progress. As the hollow approaches the correct shape, the inside area left chalked will increase, and the mandrel will jam in the hollow with little axial force.
4. The outer cup contains and protects the nest of thin cups, and will have thicker walls. Its outside and lid can therefore be turned in the usual way described in FOW pages 140 to 149.
5. Mount the mandrel back on the lathe and skim off it a thickness equal to the clearance you want between the inside of the outer cup and the outside of the first of the thin nest cups, plus the thickness of this cup.
6. Cupchuck the outer nest cup workpiece, hollow it to exactly conform to the shape of the mandrel using chalking to monitor progress (figures 4.25 and 4.26), then part it off (figure 4.27).
7. Stain the outside of the mandrel black except for its left-hand end. Glue the workpiece to the mandrel at their left hand ends (figure 4.28).
8. Turn the outside of the nest cup (figure 4.29). The finish-turning should work backwards from the right-hand end so that the very thin wood you are turning is supported by the thicker wood to its left. Holtzapffel maintains that as the wood gets very thin, the black of the mandrel becomes visible through the thin wood, and this allows you to turn a constant and very thin wall thickness.
9. Part off the nest bowl just to the right of the glued joint (figure 4.30).
10. Repeat steps 5 (figure 4.31) to 9 for the rest of the nest bowl blanks.

When I attempted to turn the outside of several nest boxes, the wood was not sufficiently translucent to enable me to see the stained mandrel before I turned through the cup bottoms. John Jacob's description may not be complete because he does not discuss whether any means was used to increase the translucency of the cups while turning their outsides. Perhaps the cups were glued to the mandrel with dilute Scotch glue and steamed off. Perhaps the final thickness was removed with abrasive paper or cloth rather than a *cutting* tool. Although an internally lit mandrel could not have been used, that shown in figures 4.32 and 4.33 may be a less risky alternative to the method used historically, whatever it was.

Figure 4.23 **A nest of cups** in the collection of A. L. Robinson. The height of the cup and cover is $10^1/_2$ in. (267 mm). This nest is also pictured in Jonathan Levi, *Treen for the Table* (Woodbridge, Suffolk: Antique Collector's Club, 1998), p. 49, pl. 3/13. A similar lidded cup with sixteen nest cups is pictured in Edward H. Pinto, *Treen and other Wooden Bygones,* pl. 27. I have seen an engine-turned lidded cup containing a nest of many more cups, each literally paper thin, but it was sold before I could photograph it. Perhaps it was the German specimen mentioned by Holtzapffel!

Figure 4.24 **The mandrel and roughed cup blanks.** The mandrel is here chucked in a screw cupcuck and turned to the shape of the inside of the outer cup. The circle towards the left-hand end of the mandrel is where each of the nest cups will be parted off, and is a known distance from the left-hand end of the mandrel.

Figure 4.25 **About push the mandrel into the cup** (the lathe is off). The mandrel has been coated with chalk, and when inside will be rotated by hand to leave chalk on the projecting bands on the inside of the cup.

Figure 4.26 **The inside of the cup amost wholly covered with chalk** and therefore almost ready for any light sanding. As the shape of the inside of the cup is turned to approach the shape of the mandrel, more chalk rubs off the mandrel onto the inside surface of the cup. When the two shapes are very close the mandrel will jam in the cup with a very light axial thrust.

Figure 4.27 **Parting off the cup.**

Figure 4.28 **About to glue the cup by its rim onto the mandrel.** Spread the glue only on the mandrel, just to the left of where you will part the cup off. You might also be able to hold the rim of the cup onto the mandrel with a hose clip.

I have brushed the black stain onto the mandrel in rings rather over the whole surface in a vain attempt to make the mandrel more visible through the nest cup.

Figure 4.29 **Turning off the outside of the cup.** Work from the bottom of the nest cup towards the left so that the band being turned is supported by the thicker wood to its left. The principle is that as the wood gets very thin (less than 1/32 in. (1 mm), the black of the mandrel becomes visible, thereby enabling you to monitor the thickness. It didn't work for me, and I turned through the cup each time. Wetting, oiling, waxing, or polishing the wood did not significantly increase its translucency.

Figure 4.30 **After Cutting off the cup at its correct height** with the long point of a skew. All the cups should be cut off at the same distance (here 30 mm) from the mandrel's left-hand end. There is no finished cup to photograph as I didn't succeed in completing one to my satisfaction.

Figure 4.31 **Turning an even thickness off the whole mandrel surface.** This thickness should equal the sum of the radial clearance between the inside of the cup just turned and the outside of the cup about to be turned, plus the wall thickness of the cup about to be turned. It would typically be about $^{1}/_{16}$ in. (1 to 2 mm). The process in figures 4.25 to 4.31 is then repeated as many times as required.

Figure 4.33 **Batteries mounted outboard to power the internally lit mandrel in the preceeding figure.** An alternative would be to mount a simple commutator outboard which was connected to an electicity source which was not mounted on the headstock spindle—if using this method ensure that the source is low voltage so that there will be no danger if the lathe accidentally becomes live.

Figure 4.32 **An internally lit mandrel** with batteries mounted outboard (see next figure).

4.4 CHATTERWORK

As Richard Raffan so appositely puts it on page 127 of *Turning Boxes* "My turning education instilled in me the belief that chatter marks are a sign of extreme ineptitude". However the production of rings of low-relief patterning by scraping with a flexing spring-steel blade is now a valid technique (figures 4.34 to 4.40). Although chatterwork could only be confused with low-relief ornamental-turning in a dim light from a long distance, it is far quicker to produce and needs minimal special equipment. The technique was popularized through Denis Stewart including chatter blades in his Stewart System, and by several magazine articles and at least one video.[2]

If a chatter blade can be held against a plain-turned workpiece and induced to flex away and back an integral number of times during each workpiece rotation, a clear chatter pattern should result. The technique is not precise, and to produce a clear strong pattern you may need to experiment to achieve an effective combination of variables. These variables include:

1. The exposed length of your chatter blade. As you shorten the blade it becomes stiffer, and the ridges of the chatter pattern grow closer together as it approaches the plain surface which would be left by a stiff scraper. The pattern loses definition as the blade is lengthened past the optimum.To achieve a strong pattern the blade should be held rigidly onto the shaft.

2. Your tool presentation. Have the toolrest close to the front end of the shaft which holds the blade. Figure 4.35 discusses the positioning of the toolrest.
3. The tilt of the blade relative to the wood's velocity has little effect compared with whether the tip is moved across the face radially inwards or outwards. However if the tip is rotated, say, a little clockwise, the tilt does encourage movement to the right. You can alter the angle of the ridges by varying the tilt of your blade relative to the velocity of the wood at the point of contact of the blade with the wood.
4. You can alter the pattern by altering the profile of the tip of the chatter blade.
5. The velocity of the wood relative to the blade affects the spacing of the pattern ridges. The optimum velocity range is 2000 to 3000 rpm for a workpiece about 75 mm diameter. The faster the lathe speed, the wider the spacing of the ribs of the pattern.
6. The hardness of the wood, and the grain direction. The harder the wood the shallower but crisper the patterning.

You could therefore increase the variety of patterning on the one surface by varying the lathe speeds, moving the tip radially inwards or outwards, and using different profiles of chatter tool tip

Chatter patterns are best produced on end-grain hard wood. You can also produce chatter-like patterns on cupchuck work by thinning the waste spigot which supports the workpiece adjacent to the chuck so that the spigot flexes rather than the blade. Related patterns occur when you turn slender spindles without steadying. After producing the pattern it can be highlighted with contrasting scumbles. You can produce a crisper effect by defining and retaining the chatter work in annular bands by say plain-turned V-cuts, grooves, ridges, or on annular planes at different levels.

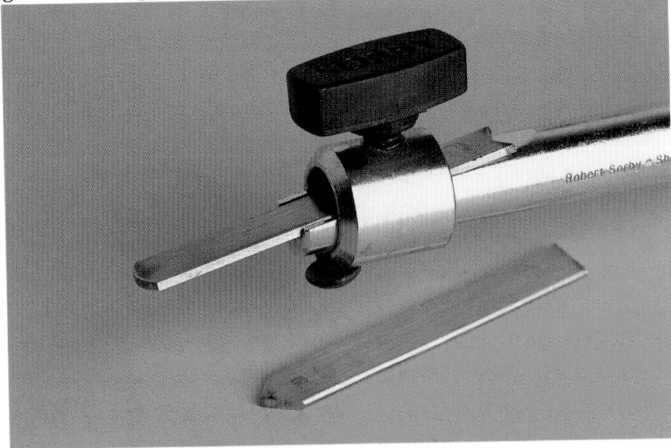

Figure 4.34 A chatter tool by Robert Sorby. The spring-steel chatter blades are 10 mm x 1.5 mm x 65 mm, and should project 30 to 35 mm. The two blades supplied are double-ended giving four different tip profiles.

A chatter tip should be ground and honed square to its top and bottom faces. These faces should also be honed to produce sharp, square edges without burrs.

Figure 4.35 Cutting end-grain hard wood with a chatter tool. The blade must trail, with the angle between the top face of the blade and the wood's surface upstream about 65°. You can achieve this by raising the toolrest a lot, and cutting at lathe axis height; or by raising the toolrest less, and cutting along a radius running to the left and at about 45° below horizontal. When the technique is working properly an unpleasant, piercing screeching sound is produced.

Figure 4.36 Chatter patterns made with a V-shaped chatter tip on end-grain hard wood of 2 1/2 in. (65 mm) diameter. The lathe speed was 3000 rpm. There are three bands of chatter patterning. When patterning the outside and inside bands the tip was being moved radially outwards; for the band between the two others the tip was being moved radially inwards.

Figure 4.37 **Chatter patterns made with a dome-ended chatter tool.** The tip was moved radially outwards while patterning the inside annular band. For the other bands the tip was moved radially inwards.

Figure 4.38 **The chatter pattern from the preceeding figure accentuated by scumbling with a black felt-tipped pen at a low lathe speed.**

Figure 4.39 **Patterns produced with a V-shaped tip with its end radiused at about 1/16 in. (1.5 mm).** This is perhaps the easiest tip shape to use.

Figure 4.40 **A lidded box showing side-grain chatter patterns.** The *center* and *right-hand* chatter patterns were made with the vee and domed chatter tool tips respectively before the waste spigot was thinned. For both bands of chatter pattern the tools worked from the outsides to the centers of the bands.

Left: with a small detail gouge, the waste spigot attaching the box the the chuck reduced to 1/4 in. (6 mm) diameter. The use of this chatter technique on both end and side grain is more fully described in articles by Remi Marchot and Stephen Paulsen.[3]

4.5 CHUCKS

Chapter 7 of FOW and chapter 1 of *Woodturning Methods* provide a comprehensive introduction to chucks. This section corrects information on Leonardo da Vinci's self-centering chuck, and shows three new chucks.

4.5.1 LEONARDO'S CIRCULAR RACK

Page 13 of *Woodturning Methods* includes the sentence: "The scroll principle had been foreseen by Leonardo da Vinci in a pipe-boring mill". I had not seen Leonardo's sketch of the mill when quoting that sentence, but now show it in figure 4.41.[4] Figure 4.42 shows a model of the mill. It is clear that the chuck mechanism which Leonardo had sketched was not the scroll but the circular rack and pinions later developed by A. F. Cushman (*Woodturning Methods*, figure 1.19). Whether Cushman knew of Leonardo's sketch is unknown, but Cushman's invention was the converse in that he rotated a pinion to rotate a circular rack. Cushman also introduced the concept of screwing the rack along the chuck body to engage or disengage with the pinions fixed to the jaw screws. This feature enabled a chuck to have self-centering or independent jaw movement.

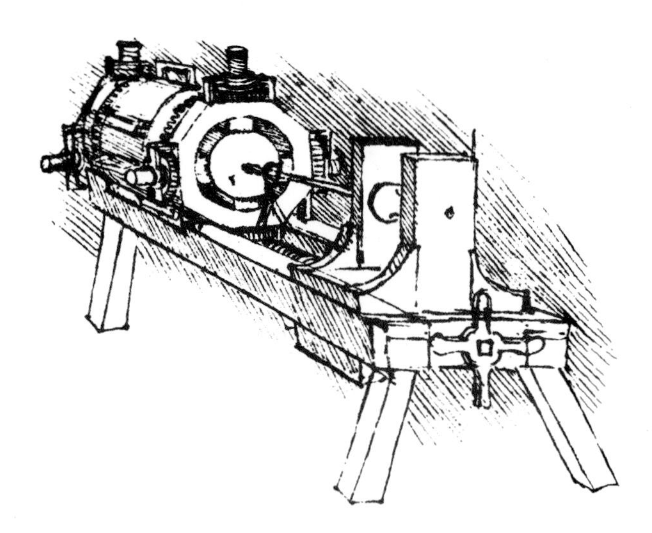

Figure 4.41 **Leonardo da Vinci's sketch of a horizontal boring machine with a self-centering chuck** (Codice Atlantico, folio 393, recto. Ambrosiana Library, Milan).

The chuck is fixed to the bed and does not rotate. The chuck's mechanism presages Cushman's, but is not fully resolved. Handles are fixed to a collar which has an integral circular rack at each end. Wrenching the handles around the chuck body causes the racks to rotate all eight pinions in unison. The jaw screws which pass through the pinions must be prevented from rotating if the jaws are to move axially and concentrically. No means are shown, although keys in the chuck body mating with keyways in the jaw screws would do.

Leonardo was born near Vinci, Italy, in 1452. He died in 1519 at Cloux in France, and is buried there.

Figure 4.42 **A model of Leonardo's boring machine.** This view clarifies the integral nature of the handles, collar and circular racks.

The drill projects from a simple headstock, and is rotated by a belt (not shown) acting on the pulley between the headstock bearings. To feed the drill, the headstock is pushed to the left. *Photograph courtesy IBM, New York.*

4.5.2 THREE CHUCKS BY BRUCE LEADBEATTER

Woodturning seems to bring out the inventor in its adherents. An outstanding example is Bruce Leadbeatter of Sydney. Three new chucks from him are shown in figures 4.43 to 4.47.

Figure 4.43 **The Leady Chuck,** an improved version of Bruce's Super Chuck which was manufactured by Woodfast Machinery of South Australia between 1985 and 2000.

Figure 4.44 **The Leady Chuck apart.** The improvement is that the outsides of the jaws are housed in a groove in the chuck body. This prevents the cone locking, and the jaws tilting as the chuck is tightened if the recess in the workpiece has been bored too large.

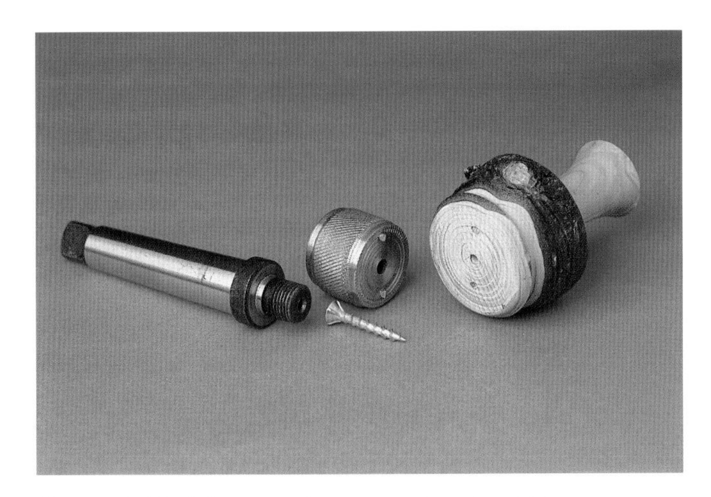

Figure 4.45 **The Leady screwchuck** which can accommodate a range of screw lengths and gauges. You screw through the small hole in the right-hand end of the collar into the workpiece, then screw the collar with the workpiece attached onto the threaded stub of the Morse taper arbor. Ideally the small-diameter end of the arbor would be tapped to take a drawbar.

Figure 4.47 **How the two halves of the Leady Eccentric Chuck locate.** The front half can be indexed relative to the back half in 30° steps.

Bottom right, the spigot of a workpiece after removal from the screw cupchuck.

Figure 4.46 **A Leady Eccentric Chuck** for multi-axis cupchuck turning. It holds the workpiece in a screw cupchuck (*FOW,* figure 7.5). To change the tilt you remove the chuck from the lathe, loosen an internal socket-head screw with an Allen key, rotate the two main parts of the chuck relative to one another, and then lock the two parts together again by tightening the screw.

Figure 6.8 of *Woodturning Methods* shows a similar chuck invented by Jean-Francois Escoulen. It holds the work in a plain cupchuck and the tilt is adjusted with external screws.

4.6 ENDNOTES

1. The earliest description of the flute-up technique that I have found is in Fritz Spannagel, *Das Drechslerwerk* (1940; reprint, Hannover: Verlag Th. Schafer, 1981), p. 76, fig. 319. Other descriptions of the technique are given in:

   Gottfried Bockelmann, *Handbuch Drechseln* (Ravensburg, Germany: Ravensburger Buchverlag, 1997), pp.73–76.

   Klaus Pracht, *Woodturning* (London: Dryad Press, 1988), pp. 60, 61, and 116.

   Richard Raffan, *Turning Wood* (Newtown, Connecticut: The Taunton Press, 1985), pp. 84-87.
2. Bonnie Klein, "Chatterwork," *American Woodturner* (March 1996): p. 30.

   Terry Lawrence, "Chatter Boxes," *Woodturning* 68 (October 1998): pp. 77–78.
3. Remi Verchot, "Large Chatterwork," *American Woodturner* (June 1997): p. 35.

   Stephen Paulsen, "Chatterwork," *Fine Woodworking* 49 (November/December 1984): pp. 81–85.
4. Figure 4.41 was sourced from Charles Gibbs-Smith and Gareth Rees, *The Inventions of Leonardo da Vinci* (Oxford: Phaidon Press, 1978), a book which provides an excellent introduction to the many devices and mechanisms which Leonardo foresaw and drew.

Chapter Five

FACEPLATE TURNING

Chapter 8 of *The Fundamentals of Woodturning* describes the three basic faceplate-turning cuts: rim-skimming, face-peeling, and face-scraping. This chapter shows how you can use these cuts to produce radially-grained rings, frames, moldings (figure 5.1), and paterae. The last section shows how to make platters and boxes with polygonal peripheries.

Figure 5.1 A circular architrave being turned in 1994 by Dale Hageman, foreman at Mike Darlow Woodturning. The workpiece was screwed onto a backing plate of $1^{1}/_{4}$ in. (32 mm) thick MDF which was in turn screwed to a steel faceplate of 24 in. (600 mm) diameter.

This architrave had to be turned outboard because of its diameter, but any rings with concave sections in their faces are also best turned outboard or on a swivelling headstock. This is because to *cut* (not scrape or shear scrape) concave details you need to present your detail gouge with its handle low as in figures 5.72 and 5.81.

5.1 RINGS WITH CIRCULAR CROSS SECTIONS

The turning of circular rings from and on spindles was described in pages 46 to 55 of *Woodturning Methods*. Such rings are generally small in overall diameter. Rings with larger overall diameters are usually turned from disks cut from planks, and are therefore stronger and show more attractive side-grain patterning.

If you have the necessary equipment you can save time and increase accuracy by jointing (planing flat) and thicknessing the plank(s) to the rings' finished thickness. If the rings are small in overall diameter, you may also be able to drill the rings' center holes to their finished diameter before bandsawing around the rings' peripheries. For those less-well equipped, the steps in figures 5.2 to 5.18 show how to turn a ring starting from a disk bandsawn from a sawn plank. You can modify these steps according to the state of your planks, and the machinery and equipment you decide to use. And because there are not any concave surfaces on circular rings, you can readily turn them inboard.

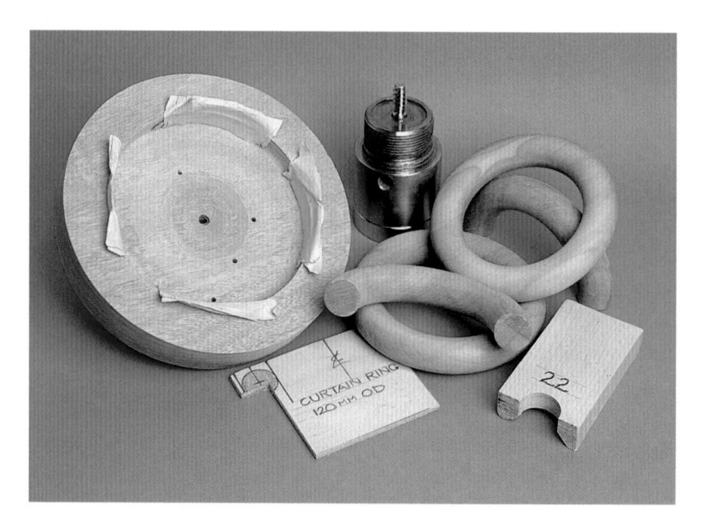

Figure 5.2 Radially-grained rings. *Left to right*: a jam chuck, a pencil gauge, a screw chuck, finished rings, and a template.

When using circular rings as curtain rings, screw the hooks into side- not end-grain.

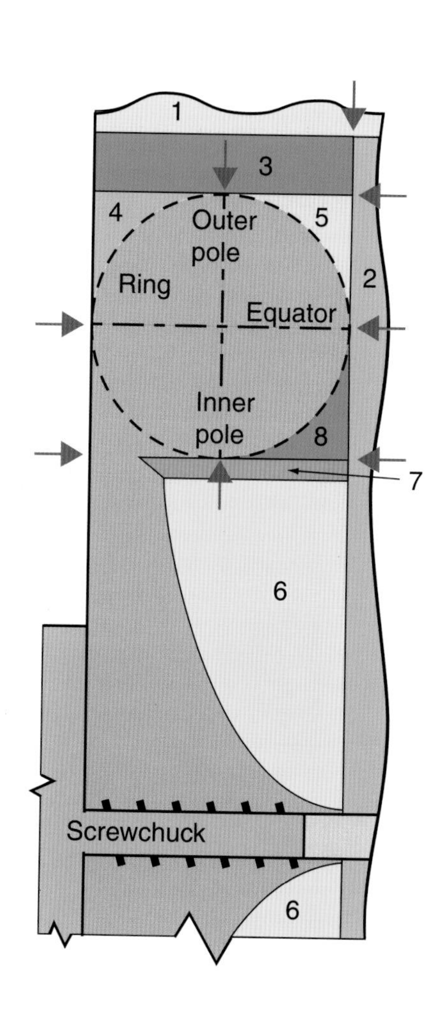

Figure 5.3 **The cuts and chucking to finish-turn the first three-quarters of a radially-grained ring of circular cross section.** This diagonal section shows the workpiece mounted on a screwchuck after the left-hand face has been planed or turned flat. The cuts are:

1. The initial rim-skim to produce a cylindrical surface on which to pencil the ring's thickness.
2. Face-peeling and/or -scraping to bring the workpiece to the ring's finished thickness.
3. Rim-skimming to the ring's finished overall diameter.
4. Cutting the left-hand outside of the ring, the later cuts start as face-scrapes and finish as rim-skims.
5. Cutting the right-hand outside. The cuts used are similar to those in 4.
6. Clearing most of the internal waste.
7. One or more pointing cuts with the gouge fully on its side and its bevel parallel to the lathe axis in plan. The cuts penetrate far enough for the inner pole to be marked.
8. A series of arcing pointing cuts. The finish-turned surface is then sanded. After dechucking, the workpiece is reverse-chucked as shown in the next figure.

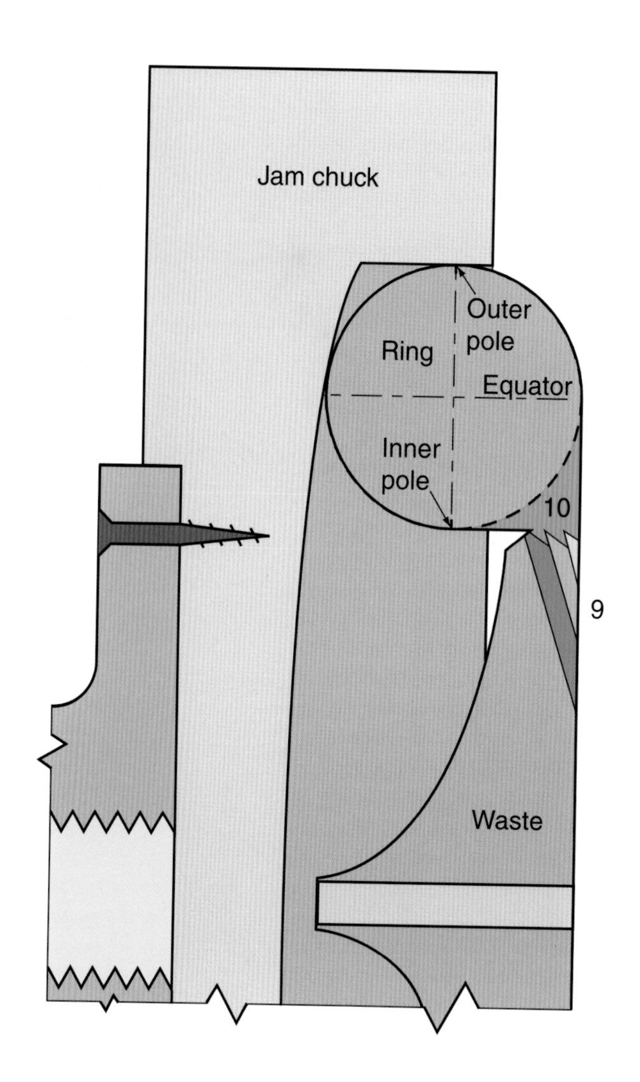

Figure 5.4 **Turning the last quarter of a ring's surface** with the ring's outer pole held by a jam chuck or a contracting-jaw chuck. The cuts shown in diagonal section are:

9. A series of several straight pointing cuts made with a detail gouge on its side. The waste disk when freed will be pushed safely inwards. The lathe can then be stopped and the waste disk removed before restarting the lathe.
10. Arcing pointing cuts. The area is then sanded.

Figure 5.5 **Rim-skimming the workpiece's bandsawn periphery to a true cylinder** (figure 5.3, cuts *1*). The finished thickness of the disk is then marked on the periphery from the disk's left-hand face using the pencil gauge.

Earlier the workpiece was bandsawn from a sawn plank, drilled, mounted on the screwchuck, and its right-hand face turned flat. The workpiece was then reversed on the screwchuck.

The workpiece is here held on a Vicmarc screwchuck. Like the Glaser screwchuck on which it is modelled, an outer flange (*back right*) can be screwed off to decrease the chuck's effective outside diameter. If your screwchuck's outside diameter is too large to allow tool access for you to turn the left-hand half of the ring's outer surface, mount a packing disk between the chuck and the workpiece. The radius of the packing disk should ideally be less than that from the lathe axis to the ring's inner pole.

Figure 5.6 **Using face-peeling cuts *2* to flatten the right-hand face,** and bring the workpiece to the ring's finished thickness.

Figure 5.7 **Marking the ring's equator, and the inner and outer poles.**

Figure 5.8 **Rim-skimming the periphery** to the ring's finished outside diameter (cuts *3*).

Figure 5.9 **Marking the equator and inner pole** on the left-hand face of the workpiece.

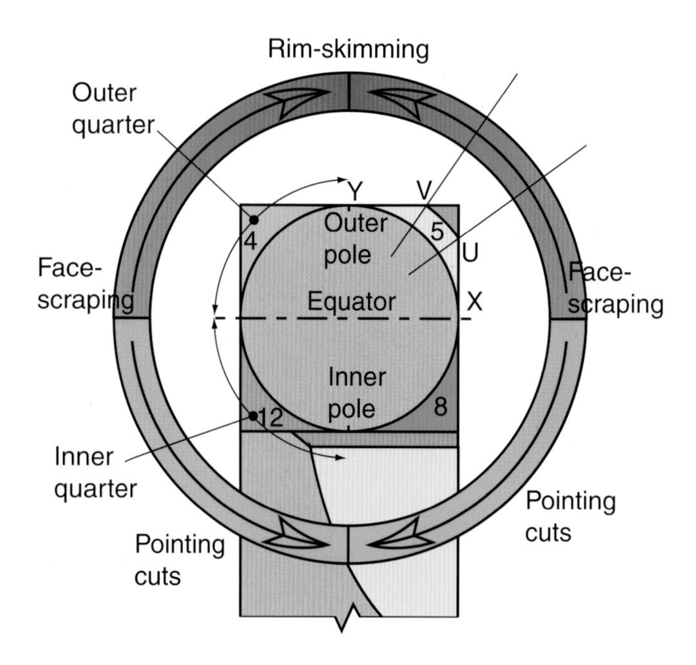

Figure 5.10 **The cuts used to form the surface of the ring** shown in diagonal section. The two outer quarters of the ring are cut from the left- and right-hand sides of the equator to the outer pole as shown in figure 5.11. An early cut, such as *UV* above, starts with a gouge presentation about midway between that for face-scraping and that for rim-skimming, This presentation barely changes through the cut *UV* as signified by the red/blue shading. As later similar cuts increase in length, their starting presentations will become closer to that for face-scraping. Similarly the presentation at the end of each cut will become closer to that for rim-skimming. The last cut *XY* should start as a face-scrape, and finish as a rim-skim.

When rings are turned inboard, the gouge presentations are restricted by the bed, and you have to use pointing cuts for finish-turning both inner quarters (figures 5.16 and 5.18).

Figure 5.11 Cutting the right-hand outer quarter as described in the preceding figure (cuts *5*). (The left-hand outer quarter has already been cut).

You will achieve a more accurate semi-circular outer profile if you leave the final cuts for both outer quarters until the end, and then finish-turn both quarters together taking the cuts on each quarter alternately. If the ring's cross section must be a true circle, you should monitor the profile with a template.

Figure 5.12 Clearing the inside waste (cuts *6*). Two types of pointing cuts are alternated: deepening cuts as here; and clearing cuts as shown in the next figure. Series of alternating deepening and pointing cuts are often used in faceplate turning.

Figure 5.13 A waste-clearing pointing cut. Have the flute pointing a little above horizontal. You need to take this series of pointing past the inner pole.

Figure 5.14 A pointing cut *7*. This may be a single cut or one of a series of similar cuts depending on the thickness of waste to remove. Cut with your gouge horizontal, its flute facing horizontally to the right, and its bevel parallel to the lathe axis in plan. Your gouge tip must first contact the workpiece at lathe axis height if the tool is not to catch.

Figure 5.15 **Marking the line of the inner pole.**

Figure 5.17 **One of the series of straight pointing cuts *9*.** As the central waste comes free, it will be pushed in and held there safely by the gouge bevel. Keeping the gouge in place, then stop the lathe and remove the waste.

The masking tape packing was needed because I cut the jam chuck a little oversize.

Figure 5.16 **Cutting the right-hand inner quarter of the ring** (cuts *8*). Then sand the finish-turned area.

The workpiece is then dechucked before being reverse chucked by its outer pole in a jam chuck or a contracting-jaw chuck.

Figure 5.18 **One of pointing cuts *10*.** The last cut sweeps from the equator to the inner pole. After any checking of the circularity of the cross section with a template, and any further cuts, sand, and gently lever the ring out of the chuck.

5.2 NON-CIRCULAR RINGS

Rings are often designed with non-circular cross-sections (figures 5.19 and 5.20), and are turned using techniques similar to those described in the previous section. Some rings are produced with figurative cross-sections (figures 5.20 to 5.22), although this is usually done with axially-grained disk-like workpieces, and is described in the next section.

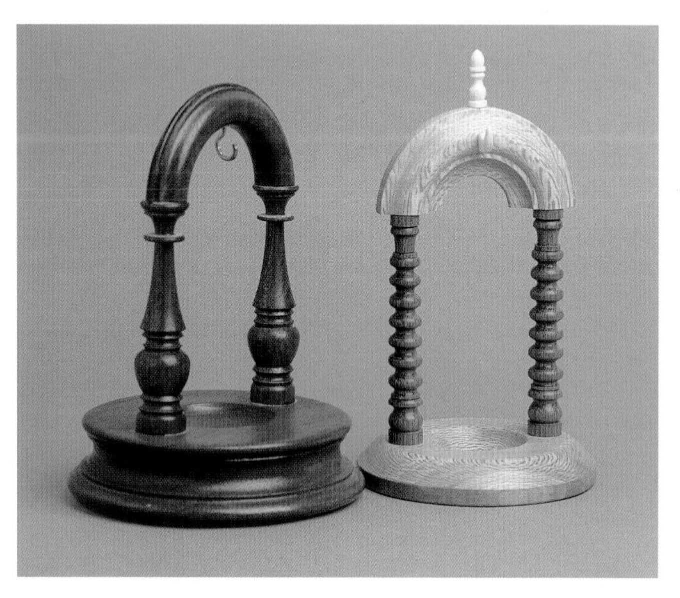

Figure 5.19 **Watch stands with arches made by halving non-circular rings.**

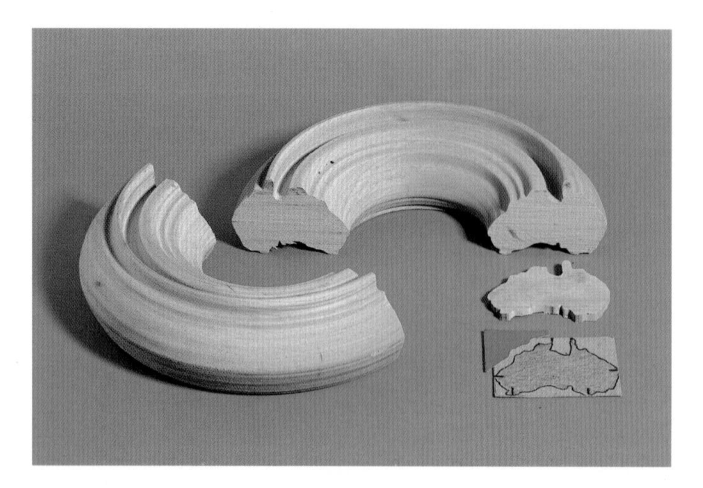

Figure 5.20 **An Australia-cross-sectioned ring for slicing radially into brooches.** The rectangular card gauge and the green card template were used to mark out and monitor the turning of the ring's cross-section.

Figure 5.21 **A disk being turned to an Australian cross section.** I first turned the southern half of the continent into a disk mounted on a screwchuck. I also turned the coast of Queensland before demounting the workpiece.

To achieve a more accurate match you need to monitor your turning with templates. You may need special *cutting* tools and scrapers to turn very detailed and deeply-indented cross sections. Workpieces such as this usually have to be chucked twice. The second and any later chuckings use a jam chuck or similar.

Figure 5.22 **Holding the workpiece in a jam chuck to enable the northern half of Australia to be turned.** I had to pack the ring with masking tape to achieve a tight fit in the chuck recess which I had cut a touch too big.

The grain direction through this ring is radial. Therefore the grain direction and the resistance to splitting will differ from one radial slice to another. Usually, however, the workpieces are short logs mounted with their piths running along the lathe axis. As the next section describes, this yields radial slices which are all quarter cut.

5.3 RIVED RINGS

Rived rings are axially-grained rings which are turned to a precise profile, and then radially rived into sectors or slices. The slices are later often carved, mainly by having their edges chamfered, into figurative forms such as farmyard animals and even royal heads (figure 5.23). The technique is still practiced professionally in central Europe, particularly in the Erz mountains of Germany.[1]

This turning technique could validly have been included in spindle turning's chapter 3 or in cupchuck turning's chapter 4 because the workpiece's grain direction is axial. The turning of a ring of horse's heads for knight chesspieces is described to illustrate the technique.

Professional central-European ring turners would turn two or more rings each hour, usually chuck them on sharp ring chucks (*Woodturning Methods*, p. 28, figure 1.47). Special tools are sometimes used (figures 5.24 and 5.25). Accurate setting out and monitoring with templates is required to achieve the desired shapes, as is shown below in figures 5.26 to 5.37.

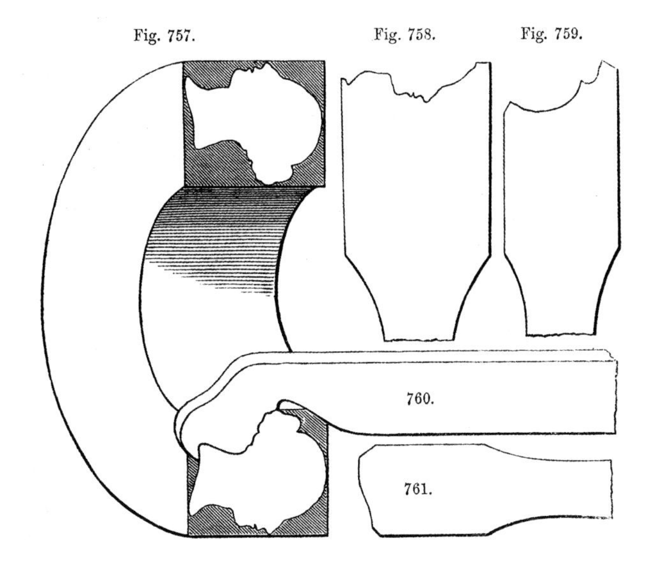

Figure 5.23 **A profiled ring of Queen Victoria** by a Mr Wyon.[2] The scrapers and a ring are in the possession of The Society of Ornamental Turners, and are pictured on page 10 of *SOT Bulletin* No. 81. It is likely that the slices were cut very thin and mounted as silhouettes. These popular pictures are named after M. Etienne de Silhouette. He was appointed in 1757 as Comptroller-General to Louis XV, and charged with halving the State's expenditure. When it became known that one of his means of relaxation was cutting paper profiles, a wit suggested that his name should be given to this, the cheapest form of portraiture.[3]

Although this ring was profiled using scrapers, such rings are often turned in softwoods with *cutting* tools.

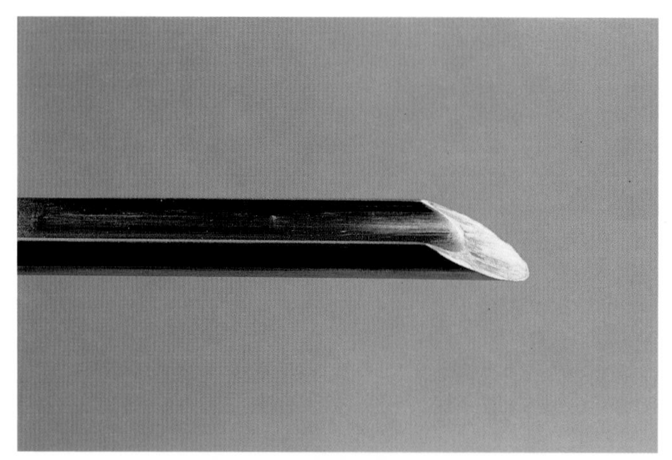

Figure 5.24 **An in-cannel-sharpened detail gouge.** The term in-cannel is defined in R.A. Salaman, *Dictionary of Woodworking Tools* (Mendham, New Jersey: The Astragal Press, 1997), p. 211. Having the bevel inside allows the gouge to make accurate in-line pointing cuts, especially along the sides of deep, narrow recesses. Gouges with the usual outside bevel are out-cannel. Gouges may also be ground to very narrow points.

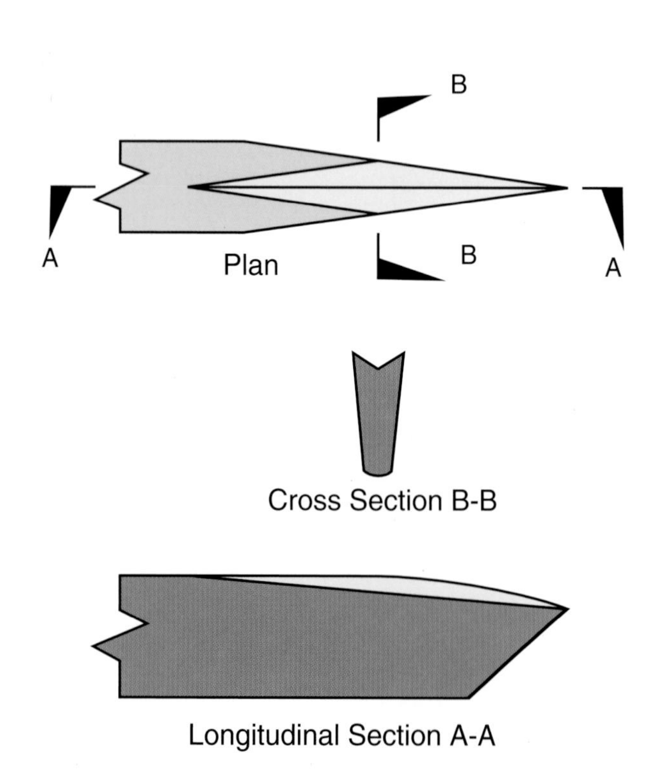

Figure 5.25 **A specially-sharpened narrow bruzze called in German a Pfannenstecher.**

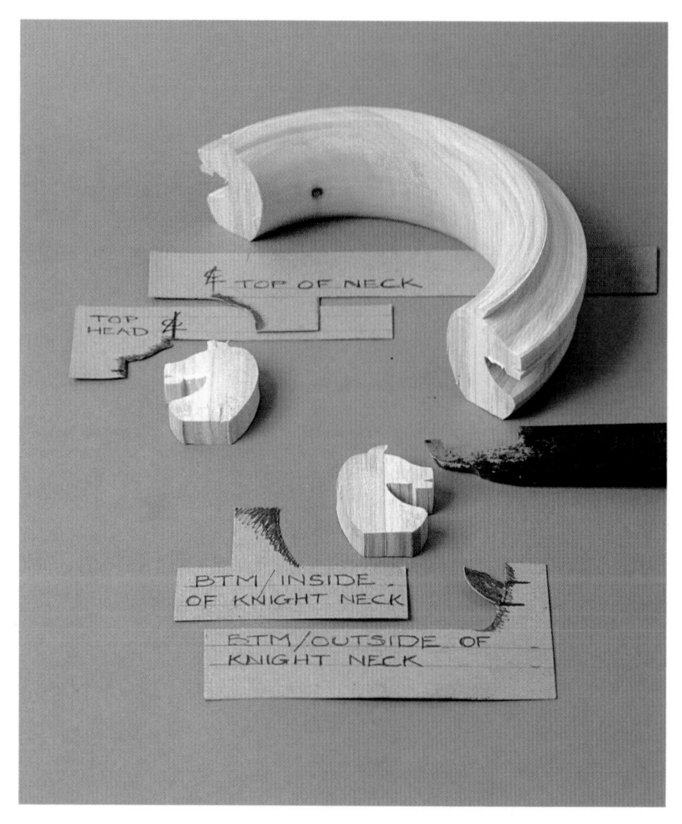

Figure 5.26 **Half a completed ring with two horse-head sectors,** the four templates used to monitor the turning, and the specially-ground scraper needed to shape the recess under the horse's head. Elsewhere I used normal spindle-turning tools, cutting deep grooves with parting-off tools.

The workpiece is typically a short log of easily rivable straight and axially-grained wood. It needs to be turned before its outer wood starts to crack. You could rough-turn rings from a wet log and season them with minimal chance of degrade, but riving will then be harder and less successful, and anyway the wet wood radial slices will season rapidly with minimal degrade.

You should consider how a ring's slices should be orientated with respect to the grain direction—for example slender legs and necks should run parallel to the grain. You must also decide which side of the slices should face radially inwards and which radially outwards; and, because rings are usually chucked twice, which parts of the ring should be turned on the first chucking and which when the ring is reverse chucked. Ideally complex details should face radially outwards so that access to them is better, and delicate areas should be turned when the ring is reverse chucked. For example for this horse's head, the head faces outwards and the top of the head with the delicate ear is turned when the ring is reverse chucked.

Rings can be turned and chucked singly, and in larger numbers

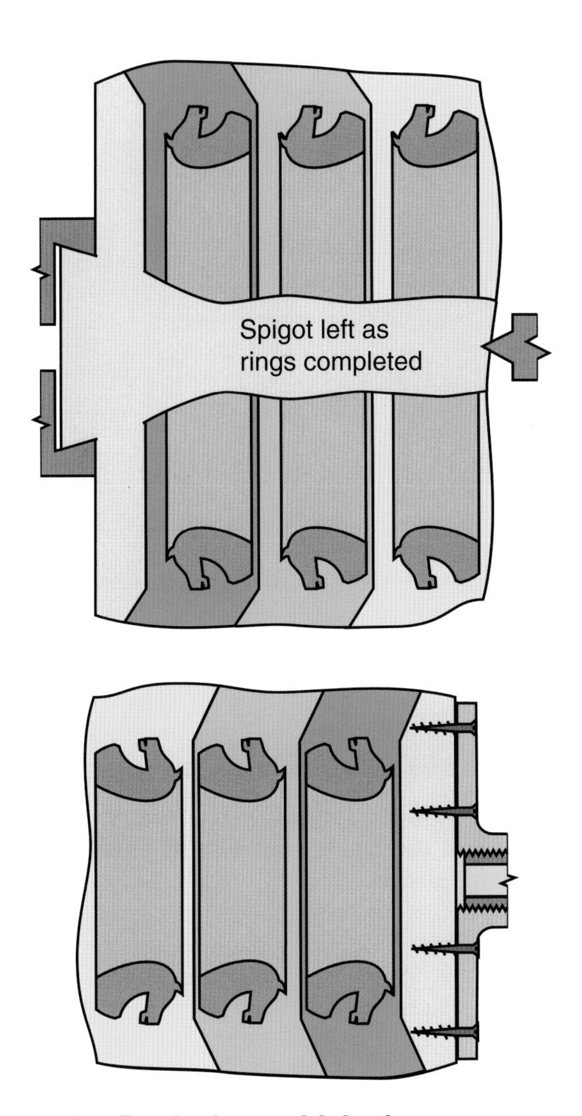

Figure 5.27 Producing multiple rings.

Figures 5.28 to 5.40 show the turning of a single ring. If you want to produce multiple rings, rather than saw the log(s) into disks, each which you then use to produce a single ring, you can:

1. *Top.* Mount a log or cylinder between centers and turn several profiled rings from it. For each ring you finish-turn the front and part the ring off. All the rings can be reverse chucked and completed afterwards, or you can reverse chuck each ring on the front face of what will become the next ring. For this second option the rings need to be relatively large in internal diameter and free from detail on the inside so that the central core left which the tail center thrusts against still allows sufficient access to finish-turn the remainder of the inside of the ring.
2. *Bottom.* Use the same procedure as above, but mount the workpiece on a chuck or faceplate, here outboard. The length of workpiece that you can securely cantilever is limited, especially if you mount the workpiece by screwing into end grain. If turning inboard, use tail center support when feasible.

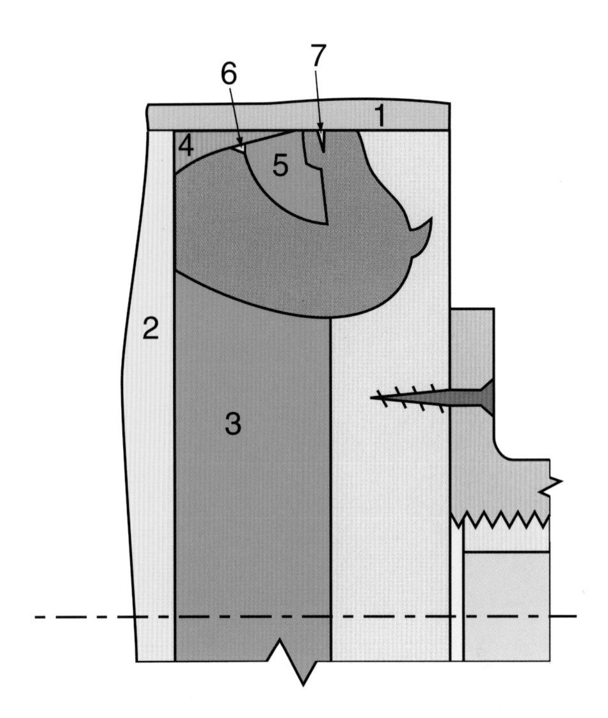

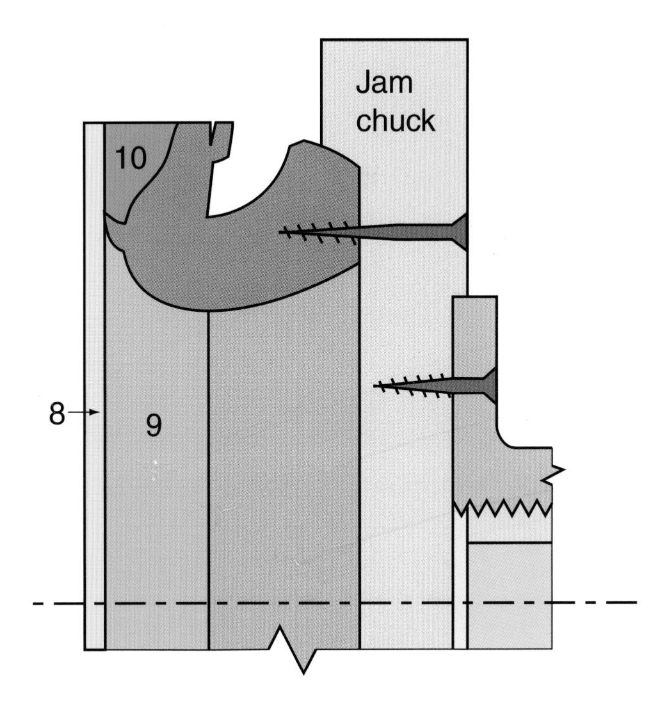

Figure 5.28 The chucking and cuts for producing a ring of knight heads. The ring is drawn being turned outboard, and the order of the cuts can be varied.

Figure 5.29 **Cutting away the central waste** using a face-scraping type of cut but on axial grain (figure 5.28, cuts *3*). The head has been marked out and the front of the chest (cuts *4*) turned.

Figure 5.30 **Monitoring the lower inside of the neck.**

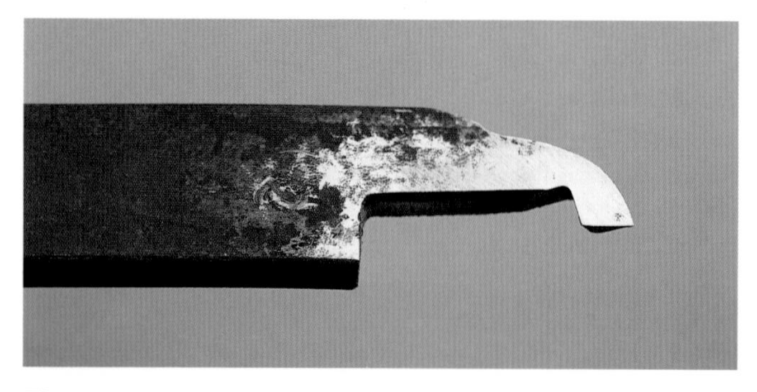

Figure 5.31 **The scraper used to cut the recess between the horses head and chin.**

Figure 5.32 **About to monitor the recess between the head and the neck** which was turned using the specially-ground scraper.

The ring is next reverse-chucked in a jam chuck or similar. Here the plywood jam chuck will be used to center the ring, but the ring is held in with four screws. The inner waste is then cut away.

Figure 5.33 **Monitoring the top of the head.**

Figure 5.34 **Cutting the ears.**

Figure 5.35 **Checking the profile of the top of the horse's neck.** After any sanding, the ring is dechucked and is ready for riving.

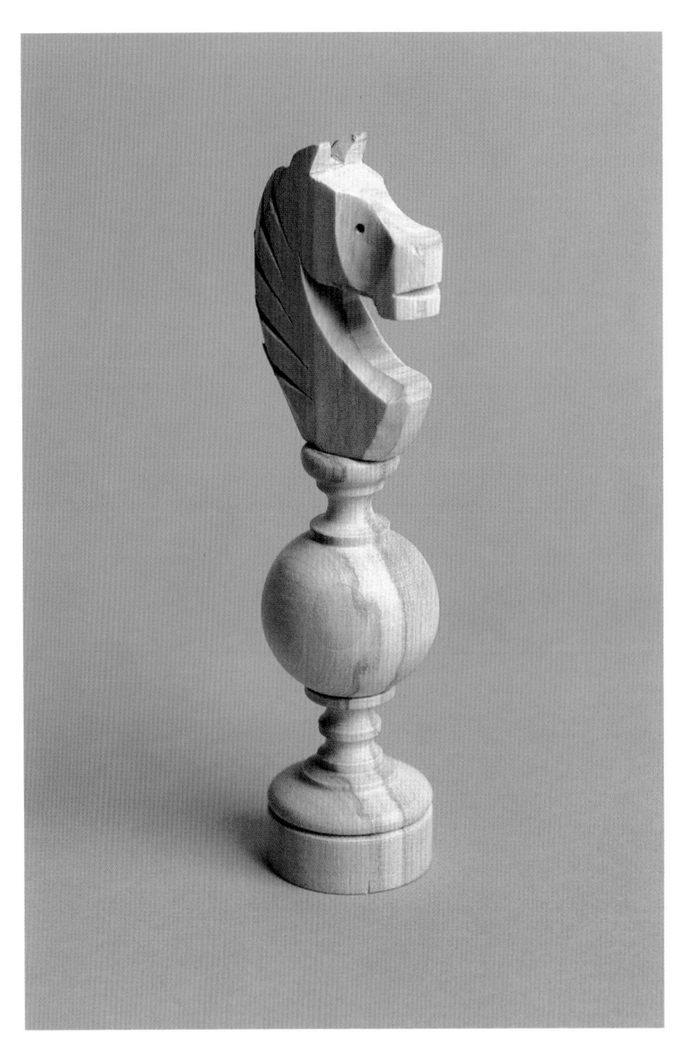

Figure 5.37 **A knight ready for polishing.**

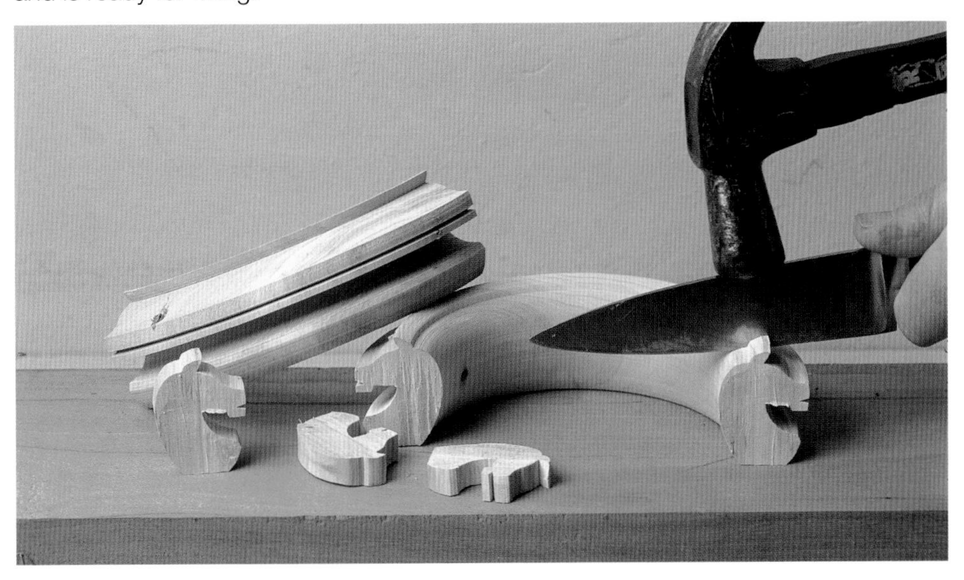

Figure 5.36 **Riving the ring into sectors** using a knife and hammer. The heads are then drilled and carved.

5.4 PICTURE AND OTHER FRAMES

This and the next section deal with rebated moldings. Most frames have one or more internal rebates to locate some combination of glass; slip; picture, photograph, tapestry, medal, mirror or plaque; and backing. The frame in figure 5.38 is one of those detailed in cross section in figure 5.39.

Frames are usually turned on two mountings. You first mount the blank on a faceplate, screwchuck or similar, and finish-turn the back of the frame, much of its through hole, and the rebate(s) (figures 5.40 to 5.47). You then reverse-chuck the workpiece to turn the frame's front (figures 5.48 to 5.56).

You can also turn frames on one mounting, scraping the rebate(s) after you have cut the through hole (figure 5.57)

Figure 5.38 A Regency-style gilt mirror by Mike Darlow Woodturning. This type of mirror was first produced in the middle of the eighteenth century in France. Only later in the century did it start to be made in Britain.[4] Its cross section is *C* in the next figure.

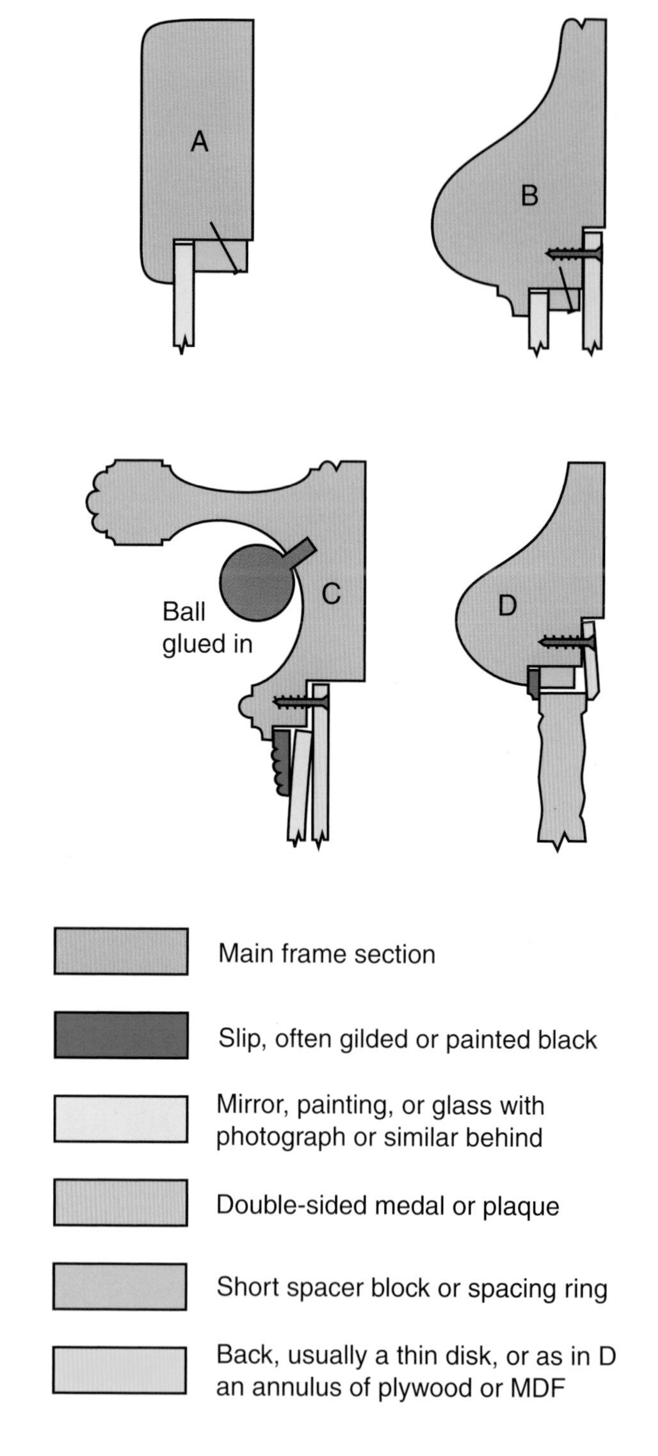

Figure 5.39 Cross sections through internally-rebated frames. Frame *C* is typical of the Regency-style gilt convex mirrors shown in the preceding figure. The annular back to frame *D* allows the reverse of medals or plaques to be seen.

Figures 5.40 to 5.56 show the turning of a frame similar to *B*. Figure 5.57 shows tools which can be used to cut the rebates from the front.

The back surfaces of slips and rebates should be blackened when a mirror will be mounted behind.

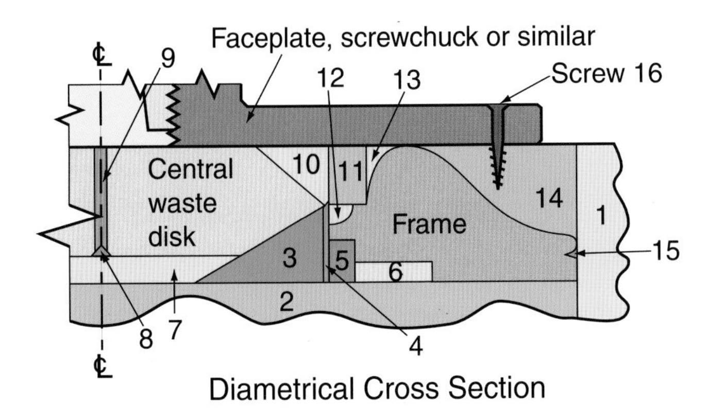

Figure 5.40 The order of cuts used to turn a frame similar to *B* in the previous figure. Cuts *10* to *15* are made with the workpiece reverse chucked on a backing plate which has a shallow, large-diameter, centering spigot. The rim of cut *6* should fit snuggly to the periphery of this spigot.

Cuts *7* provide the clearance to allow the workpiece to be reverse chucked on a backing plate spigot. Cut *8* is a pointing cut made with a detail gouge, and is used to provide a central start for drilling hole *9*. Hole *9* is optional, and is for screw which will prevent the central waste disk flying out. If you will be reverse-chucking the workpiece onto a backing plate which already has the centering spigot, do cut *7* before cuts *5* and *6*. This will allow you to trial fit the spigot as you turn the outer rebate with cuts *6*.

Take care with the placement and length of screws *16* so that they will not penetrate the surface of the finished frame.

Frames are best turned outboard, and figures 5.42 to 5.56 show that. Turning frames on a swivelling headstock is better than turning them inboard on a fixed headstock.

Figure 5.42 A deepening pointing cut made at lathe axis height along the boundary between cuts *3* and *4*. The detail gouge's flute should face horizontally to the left, the blade should be horizontal, and the bevel should lie parallel to the lathe axis in plan. Cuts *3* is a series of alternating deepening and clearing pointing cuts (next figure).

I started with a rough-sawn, seasoned disk cut from a plank, mounted it on an outboard faceplate, rim-skimmed it to diameter (cuts *1*). and trued the front face (cuts *2*).

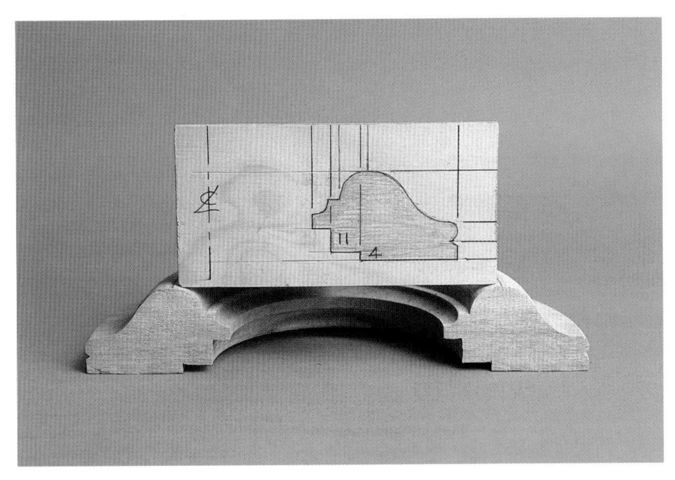

Figure 5.41 The pencil gauge and the finished frame in diagonal section.

Figure 5.43 Clearing a layer of waste to the bottom of the previous deepening cut. Cuts *3* is a series of pointing cuts made to deepen the vee and clear waste.

Figure 5.44 **A pointing cut *4*.** The tool presentation is the same as that in figure 5.42. The final cut *4* should be thin and made in one steady push to leave a fine finish to the frame lip.

Figure 5.45 **Cutting the deeper rebate.** A series of pointing cuts are made at axis height parallel to the right-hand boundary of cut *5*, The flute is facing horizontally to the left, the blade is horizontal, and the bevel is parallel to the lathe axis in plan. The next figure shows the second part of the cuts.

Figure 5.46 **Continuing the previous cut** by forcing the point to the left, at the same time rotating the tool clockwise about 30° to shear scrape parallel to the bottom of the rebate. Cuts *6* to form the outer rebate are performed in the same way.

Figure 5.47 **Drilling hole *9* for the waste-holding screw.**

Figure 5.48 **About to screw the rear, just-turned face of the workpiece against and onto a backing plate screwed to a faceplate.** The spigot on the backing plate mates snuggly with the largest-diameter rebate in the back of the frame. The four screws projecting through the backing plate will hold the workpiece securely.

Cuts *10* to *15* in figure 5.40 are done on this mounting. Cuts *11* to *13* can be done before or after cuts *14* and *15*.

Figure 5.49 **One of the series of clearing cuts *10*.** If you have not screwed in the waste disk, the bevel will tend to hold it against the backing plate until you have switched the lathe off.

Figure 5.50 **The waste disk cut free and unscrewed from the backing plate.**

Figure 5.51 A cut *11*, similar to cuts *5* shown in figure 5.45.

Figure 5.52 The second, shear-scraping part of a cut *11*.

Figure 5.53 Cutting the small hollow, cuts *12*.

Figure 5.54 A cut *13*. To produce the convex cross section the blade is rotated counterclockwise and the handle raised and moved to the left.

Figure 5.55 A cut *14*. The handle is low and the tip is presented to cut with minimal clearance and high side rake.

Figure 5.56 **The frame turned,** and ready for in-lathe sanding.

5.4.1 REBATING FROM THE FRONT

The reason for chucking frames by their front and then their back as shown in the preceding figures is to turn the rebates accurately by having good tool access. You can also turn frames in one operation by screwing frame workpieces onto a wood, plywood, or MDF backing plate and turning the whole frame including the rebate(s) from the front. You will need a simple rebating tool: two are shown in figure 5.57.

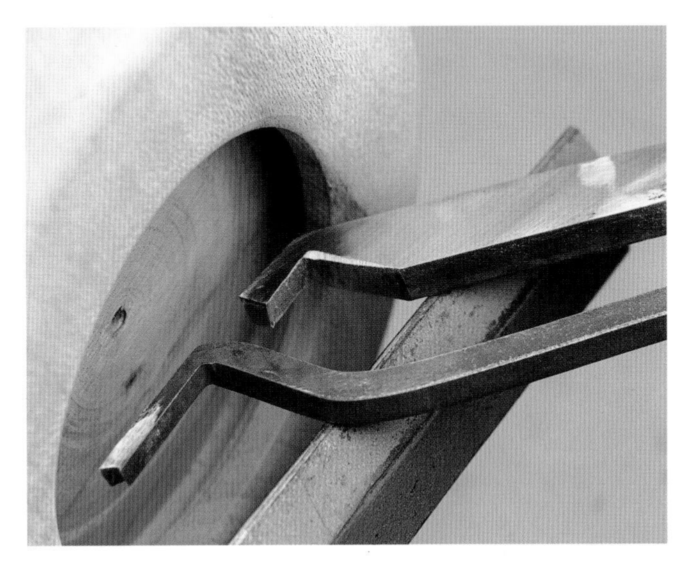

Figure 5.57 **Tools for rebating frames.** These tools are used from the front of frames mounted inboard, and avoid the need for reverse-chucking.

The front cranked rebating tool was marketed by Craft Supplies. Toolrest support must be taken under the straight part of the blade for the blade to be stable. The rear scraper is homemade.

You need to mount the workpiece on a wooden backing plate so that that the rebating tool does not contact the steel faceplate.

When cutting a double rebate from the front, cut both rebates to the same diameter, then cut the rest of the rear rebate. If you cut the rear rebate to its full diameter, then cut the front rebate, spelch (a frill of fibers) will be left at the corner between the two rebates.

5.5 BOLECTION AND INLAY MOLDINGS

Bolection and inlay moldings are used in combination to frame and hold in panels (figures 5.58 to 5.60).

Even now most circular moldings with traditional profiles are turned because they cannot be cut on overhead routers. Turning an inlay molding is shown in figures 5.61 to 5.74; turning a bolection in figures 5.75 to 5.85. The techniques described are relevant to the turning of all circular moldings and frames.

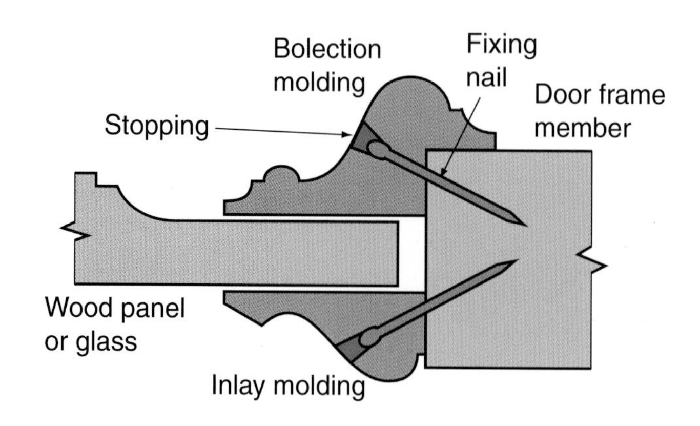

Figure 5.59 **A section showing how a panel is retained by a bolection and inlay molding.**

Figure 5.58 **A door of about 1880 with the tops of the panels held in by semicircular bolection and inlay moldings.** The circular moldings have to be turned to accurately match the straight moldings so that there is no discontinuity where the the two types meet.

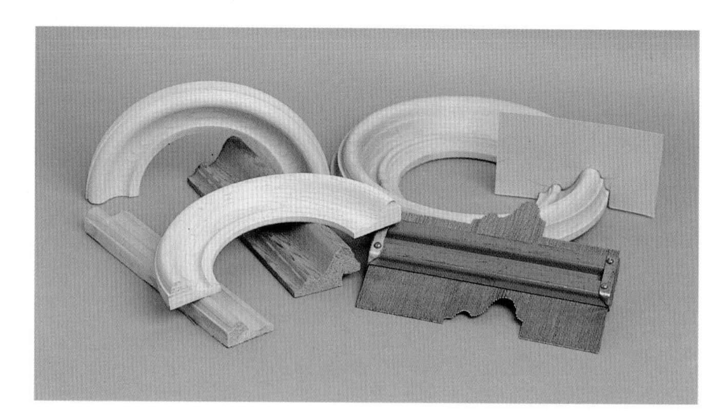

Figure 5.60 **Inlay and bolection moldings,** the matching straight sections, a cardboard template, and a mimic.

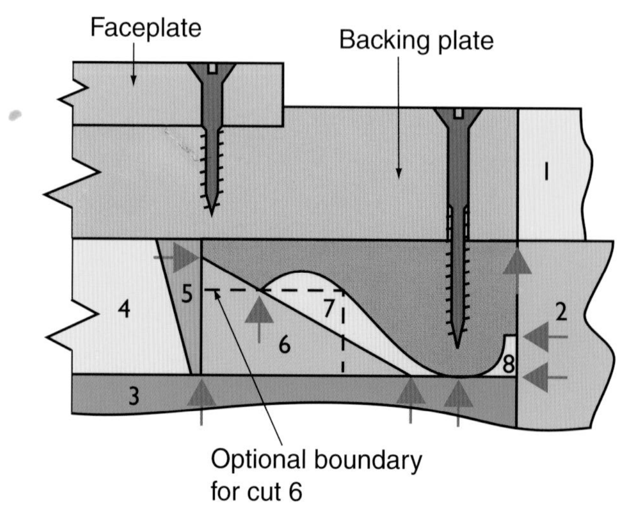

Figure 5.61 **The cuts for the inlay molding.** The order and form of the later cuts can be varied somewhat.

Figure 5.62 **You first turn a backing plate** to the outside diameter of the inlay molding (figure 5.61, cuts *1*). You should also skim the front of the backing plate if it does not rotate truly. The backing plate:

1. Gives a reference diameter for turning the outside of the moldings.
2. Enables you to positition the molding fixing screws, here four, so that they hold the thin inlay molding where it is thickest. Pack or recess the screw heads so that the screw penetration is sufficient to hold but will not marr the surface of the finished molding.
3. Prevents your tool hitting the faceplate when cutting away the central wastes.
4. Gives you a surface on which you can pencil the lathe axis which allows you to readily monitor the inside diameter of the moldings. If the moldings are to be sawn into two semicircles, draw a diameter through the lathe axis on the face of the backing plate, and return it onto the edges of the disk. When you screw the workpiece onto the backing plate align the grain correctly with reference to the marked diameter; the edge marks then define where to saw.

Figure 5.63 **Rim-skimming the periphery of the inlay workpiece to the diameter of the backing plate (cuts *2*).** You then mark on this periphery the inlay's maximum thickness and the position of the external fillet.

Figure 5.64 Peeling the face of the workpiece to the inlay-molding's maximum thickness (cuts *3*). Then mark on the face the lathe axis, the molding's inside diameter, the circle of maximum thickness, and the boundary of cuts *6*.

Figure 5.65 Driving a screw to hold the central waste to the backing plate. A hand-held drill was pushed in with the lathe running in reverse to drill the screw's pilot hole. Alternatively you can tack the waste to the backing plate or hold it in with the gouge bevel, your thumb, or the striking part of your hand.

Sometimes there is no central waste—it is better to jigsaw it out as a disk when the moldings' inside diameter is large. Also some large-diameter moldings are conglutinated from chord-like lengths.

Figure 5.66 Freeing the central waste (cuts *4*). Two types of pointing cut are used alternately: deepening cuts shown here and clearing cuts shown in the next figure. If the waste disk is not screwed or tacked to the backing plate, use the type of pointing cut shown in the next figure to free the disk.

Figure 5.67 The second type of clearing cut *4*.

Figure 5.68 The central waste cut free and unscrewed from the backing plate.

Figure 5.69 **Pointing cuts *5*** leave little spelching if the inner face of the workpiece is hard against the face of the backing plate. The inside diameter of these moldings must be accurate, and should be monitored continually during cuts *5* by checking the width as shown in the next figure, and/or better by checking the radius with a template as shown in figure 5.80.

Figure 5.70 **Checking the molding's width.**

Figure 5.71 **Cuts *6*.**

Figure 5.72 **Cutting the ogee, cuts *7*.** It is the need to make this type of cut with the handle down which makes outboard the preferred mounting.

Figure 5.73 **Cuts *8*.**

Figure 5.74 **Checking the inlay's profile with a mimic.** Alternatively you could use a template (figures 5.84 and 5.85).

Figure 5.76 **Checking the diameter of the workpiece.** It should equal the diameter of the backing plate turned in figure 5.62 plus twice the width of the rebate in the straight bolection molding sample.

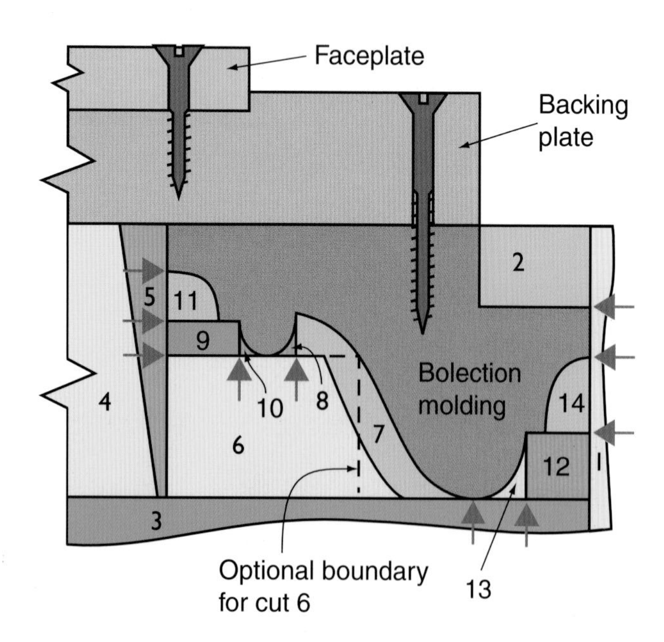

Figure 5.75 **The cuts to turn the bolection molding** shown in diagonal section. With a molding of this complexity there are several variations in the order and shape of the cuts.

Figure 5.77 **Rim-skimming the bottom of the rebate** in the bolection (cuts *2*). The second part of the cut is shown in the next figure.

Figure 5.78 **Face-scraping up the radial face of the rebate.**

Figure 5.79 **A clearing pointing cut *4*.** You should alternate clearing cuts with deepening cuts.

Figure 5.80 **Checking the internal diameter of the bolection** with a cardboard template. You can also use internal calipers, and check the radial thickness of the molding as shown in figure 5.70.

Figure 5.81 **Cuts *7*.**

Figure 5.82 **Cuts *11*.**

Figure 5.83 **Cuts *13*.**

Figure 5.84 **Monitoring the profile with a cardboard template.** You can also use a mimic, or if the molding is to be cut through, saw partially through along a radius and use a cardboard template as shown in the next figure.

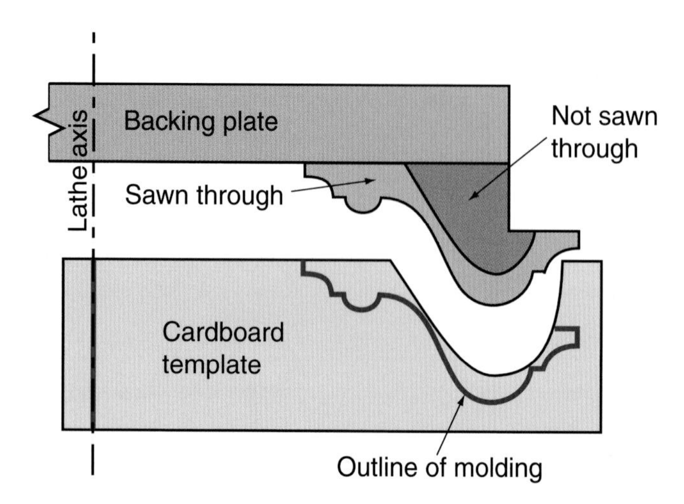

Figure 5.85 **Using an "internal" template.**

5.6 PATERAE

Not only are circular and elliptical frames turned, but turning is used to decorate the square paterae sometimes used at the corners of rectangular frames (figure 5.86) and doorways, and under the ends of mantlepieces. The turning of the paterae should echo the cross section of the moldings which butt to it.

Turned paterae (plate-like forms) can also have elliptical or circular peripheries. They can be turned by hand using tool presentations similar to those used to turn the moldings in earlier sections of this chapter. Many woods can also be scraped successfully. For large quantities you should consider using a profiled scraping cutter if your lathe has a carriage or if you can rig up a parallel slide (figure 5.87). Use a slow feed and a high lathe speed. A more secure method of chucking the square workpiece than a screwchuck will be necessary because of the high force exerted by the wide cutter.

If scraping the profile by hand, use several narrow profiled scrapers which each cut a short width of the profile rather than a full-width cutter which you could not control safely. The surface left off-the-cutter may just need sanding, or may need to be skimmed by hand-turning before sanding.

Figure 5.86 **A patera** (sometimes termed a corner block). The flush bead of the patera echoes the bead on the frame's edge moldings.

Elliptical and circular patera (see figure 1.27) with turned molded edges are frequently used as mounting plates for electrical and other fittings.

Figure 5.87 **Winding in a carriage-mounted cutter to produce a patera.** The patera blank is held in the outside gripping jaws of an engineers scroll chuck.

5.7 POLYGONAL PERIPHERIES

Faceplate turnings with polygonal peripheries can be bandsawn from one-piece turnings with circular peripheries. This wastes wood, and may force the finished piece to be smaller than desired. An alternative is to cut the piece's periphery first, and then mount scrap wood around this core to produce a circular blank. This avoids the problem of the cuts being discontinuous, and there could be dynamic imbalance were the scrap not used. This is a technique which has been popularized and described by Vic Wood of Melbourne, Australia (figure 5.88).[5]

There are three ways to attach the waste pieces:

1. Glue them onto the periphery of the workpiece core. This avoids the need for a supplemetary backing plate, but you have to saw the waste off, and plane and sand the core's edges .
2. Glue the waste pieces onto the core with paper joints. After splitting the scrap off, you have to prepare the core's edges for finishing. For safety at least screw the waste pieces to a backing disk which is in turn screwed to a faceplate or directly to the faceplate.
3. Fix both core and waste pieces onto a backing plate, the waste pieces just butting against the core's peripheral faces. There may be some tear-out along the core's edges which will need cleaning up.
4. Use a single waste piece which has a hole jigsawn through to accept the workpiece core. The core and the waste piece should each be fixed to a faceplate or backing plate.

Methods 2 and 3, especially, demand careful preparation if the composite workpiece of core and scrap is not to fly off the lathe. As a precaution keep the lathe speed low, wear a face shield, and stand not in the same plane as the workpiece, but in front of it.

The design possibilities are legion; for example a core need not have straight sides, nor need its two faces be turned on the same centers. The possibilities multiply again if the turning is a lidded box. It is essential however to fully design each piece and make accurate templates which you take care to work to. There are several chucking methods which you can use. You could for example glue waste disks onto the conglutinated workpieces to act as chucking spigots.

The making of a box in which the waste is glued to the core is shown in figures 5.89 to 5.96. Chucking is by screwing to backing plate.

Figure 5.88 A parallelogram-in-plan turned box by Vic Wood.

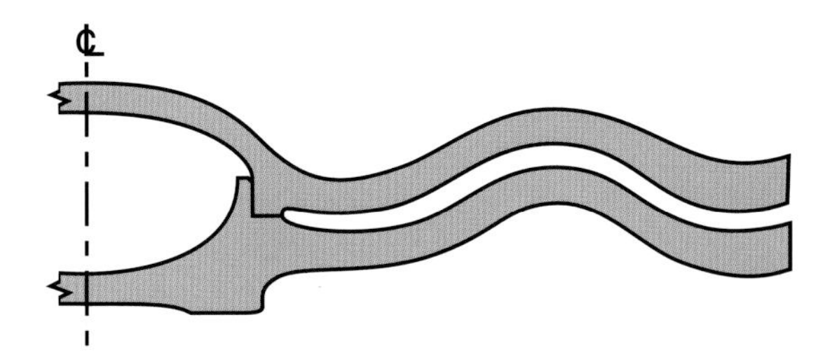

Figure 5.89 **The box which will be shown being turned in figures 5.90 to 5.96 shown in half cross section.** In this design the waves in the lid and base follow one another, whereas in the preceding box the waves in the lid mirror those in the base.

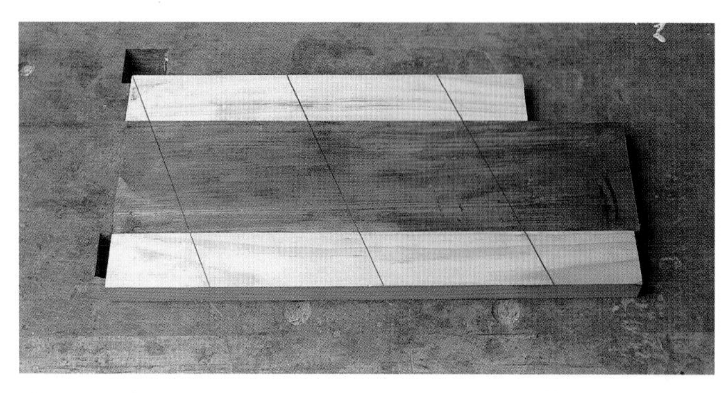

Figure 5.90 The first stage gluing finished. Two outer waste strips have been glued to the plank core. The pencil lines show where the conglutination will be sawn to yield one box lid and one base.

Figure 5.91 The second stage gluing finished and the bandsawing marked out. (The waste strips for the first gluing were too narrow). Had the waste used been more generous, an annular outer surface could have been kept which would have simplified and guaranteed the squareness of mounting of reverse chucked workpieces.

Figure 5.92 Checking the first-stage turning, the underside of the lid, with a template. The workpiece was screwed to a faceplate.

Figure 5.93 Trying the fit of the lid during the turning of the top of the base. The workpiece was screwed to the backing plate, with the screw positions and penetrations chosen so that the finished base would not be marred nor the turning tool tips chipped. A template was used to ensure that the top of the base conformed to the design in figure 5.89.

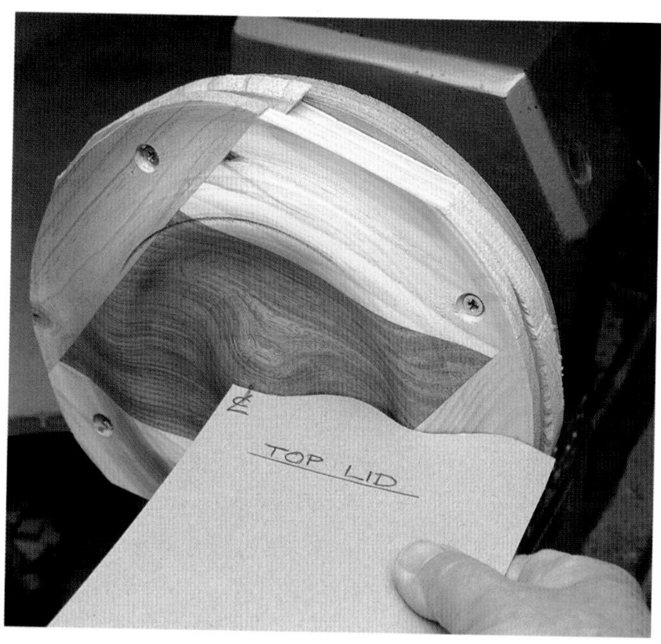

Figure 5.94 **Monitoring the top of the lid with a template.** A jam fit of the lid to the base would be insufficient to resist the forces generated during the turning. The lid conglutination has therefore been screwed to the base, with the screw heads well recessed.

Figure 5.96 **The finished box.** The waste has been bandsawn off, and the edges planed and sanded smooth.

Figure 5.95 **Monitoring the bottom of the base.** The upstanding lip of the workpiece was centered in a recess in the backing plate, and the workpiece then screwed to the backing plate.

5.8 ENDNOTES

1. Alan Lacer, "Turnings of the Erzgebirge," *American Woodturner* (Spring 1999): pp.12–15.

   Terry Martin, "The Ring Turners of the Erz Mountains," *Australian Wood Review* 29 (December 2000): pp. 84–85.

   Edward H. Pinto, *Treen and Other Wooden Bygones* (London: G. Bell & Sons, 1969), pp. 212–213, and pl. 227.

   Fritz Spannagel, *Das Drechslerwerk* (1940; reprint, Hannover: Verlag Th. Schafer, 1981), p. 242.

   R. Steinert and J. Volmer, "Decorative Folk Turning," *Fine Woodworking* 65 (July/August 1987): pp. 70–73.

   Rolf Steinert, *Drechseln in Holtz* (Leipzig: Fachbuchverlag, 1993), pp. 172–173.

   Johannes Volmer, "German Hoop Turners' Tools," *Woodturning* 16 (October 1993): pp. 51–55.

2. John Jacob Holtzapffel, *Hand or Simple Turning* (1894; reprint, New York: Dover Publications, 1976), pp. 560–562.
3. *From a Collector* (London: Weidenfield And Nicholson, 1965), p. 1.
4. Ralph Edwards, *The Shorter Dictionary of English Furniture* (London: Country Life Books, 1964), p. 377.
5. Vic Wood, "Making a Square Edged Lidded Container," *Woodturning* 1: pp. 40–43.

Chapter Six

BOWL TURNING

This chapter starts where chapter 9 of FOW ends, and, after a short diversion into the preparation of bowl blanks, explores the turning of nests of bowls and bowl chucking.

6.1 THE PREPARATION OF BLANKS

A thorough treatment of the preparation of bowl blanks was given in my first book *The Practice of Woodturning*, and will be revisited in a later book in this series. In the meantime figures 6.1 and 6.2 show a novel and useful burl slabber. Figures 6.3 and 6.4 then illustrate water blasting.

Figure 6.1 A burl slabber operated by Peter Herbert, president of the Sydney Woodturners' Guild in 2000 and 2001. (Yes, we all know he should be submerged in protective gear).

Figure 6.2 The slabber's clamping system, and the pivoting arrangement for the chain saw. A hole drilled through the chain bar is used to hold the chain saw onto the pivot. The slabber was built by Fred Robjent and Russ Torr. Constructional details are available on website www.sydneywoodturners.com.au.

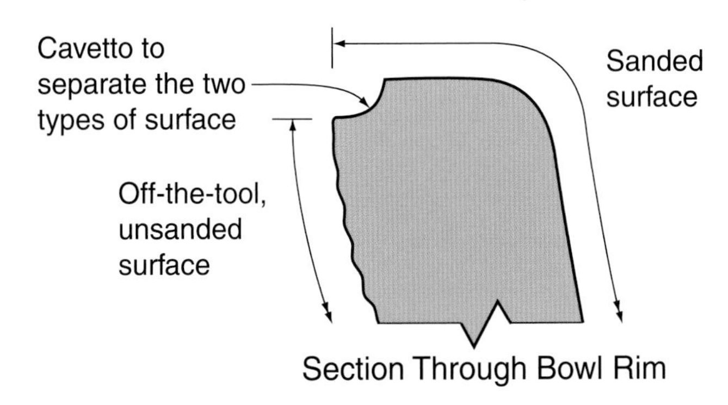

Figure 6.3 A bowl with the outer surface of the sapwood retained and undamaged. After removing the bark cleanly, the outside of the jarrah burl bowl was finish-turned using fine cuts with a small detail gouge presented with minimum clearance and high side rake to produce a rippled surface. This surface was not sanded as sanding would have destroyed the crisp boundaries between the turned and unturned surfaces. The cavetto turned into the outside of the rim creates a nice break between the sanded and unsanded surfaces.

Some turners like to leave bark on bowl rims, but leaving bark in the the outer or inner wall of a bowl is rarely aesthetically successful. Picking away the bark is tedious, and difficult to impossible if the bark has bonded hard onto the sapwood surface. Fortunately, as the next figure shows, there is a quick and efficient solution.

Figure 6.4 Water blasting bark off. A water pressure of 1700 psi (11,700 kPa) was needed to thoroughly remove the bark from these seasoned eucalyptus burls, although domestic water blasters may be sufficiently powerful for other woods. Apprentice Robert Campbell can confirm that the process is a soaking one even with waterproof clothing.

6.2 TURNING NESTS OF BOWLS

Turn one bowl from a blank and about 90% of the wood is wasted as shavings. Turn a nest of two or more nest bowls from the same blank and you produce more bowls with less waste; and the production time per bowl should be shorter. However, there are six factors which are apparent when a nest workpiece is viewed in horizontal diametrical section (figure 6.5):

1. Each separating cut must have a constant curvature if its width is to be constant and equal or close to the width of the tool's cutting tip. Therefore the blades of the tools in plan have to be arcs of circles.
2. The separating cuts are not taken to the lathe axis, but stopped short to leave a holding spigot large enough to restrain the bowl from flying free, but small enough so that it can be fractured to free the bowl after the lathe is stopped. The diameter of this spigot is therefore usually between $3/4$ in. and 1 in. (20 mm and 25 mm).
3. The grain direction through a holding spigot must be approximately radial for you to be able to fracture it with reasonable force.
4. If a nest bowl is to be finish-turned later, it must be left thick enough to:
   a. Accommodate the distortion due to internal stress relaxation, and the distortion and shrinkage due to any further seasoning.
   b. Be sufficiently rigid to allow the finish-turning.

c. Allow the turning of any required chucking feature.
d. Accommodate the bowl shape you intend. There is a conflict between maximizing the number of nest bowls cut from a blank and producing bowls with a strong, interesting shape—the thinner the nest bowls, the more nearly their finish-turned half diametrical sections must resemble sectors of annuli. However by altering the location of the center about which the cutter effectively revolves, you can change the basic shape and proportions of a nest bowl (figures 6.5 and 6.20).

The practice of turning nests of bowls using hand-held, curved-bladed hook tools (figure 6.6) is probably centuries old. An excellent sequence of photographs by Tony Boase on pages 28–37 of *Bowl Turning Techniques Masterclass* (Lewes: Guild of Master Craftsman Publications, 1999) shows Robin Wood of Edale, Derbyshire, hand turning a nest of four bowls on a pole lathe. The technique is safe on a pole lathe because the lathe speed is low and the turner can stop the lathe almost instantly. Also pole lathe turners usually use green wood which cuts more easily than dry. However motorized lathes were used,[1] and today even those who have yet to become supremely skilled can turn nests of bowls from seasoned wood on electrically-powered lathes. What makes this possible is the availability of modern versions of earlier equipment. Today's versions operate in either of two ways:

1. The groove-cutting tool is hand-operated but mechanically restrained to greatly lessen the probability of a mishap.
2. The path of the cutter is mechanically determined, although its movement is powered by hand.

With both these methods the cuts can be narrower than with hand-held hook tools.

The two earliest recently introduced nesting tools were by American Denis Stewart and Bruce Leadbeatter. The Stewart System includes a slicer which when used with the armbrace handle (*FOW*, figure 10.14) allows roughly conical nesting bowls to be cut (figure 6.7). Bruce Leadbeatter's system, introduced in 1984, used a curved-bladed tool (figures 6.8 to 6.11).

During 1988 and 1989 John Ambrose of Ely, Cambridgeshire, developed an apparatus (figures 6.12 to 6.15). The catalyst was a contract to produce spherical newel post tops for the British Museum. John then adapted his apparatus to produce graduated sets of ladles. The next step was to use it to turn nests of bowls. Rather than use curved-bladed parting or hook tools, John's apparatus uses cutting tips attached to a shell-like supports which approximate to an eighth of the surface of a sphere.

Interest in bowl nesting was aroused by two articles in 1990: one by Mike O'Donnell on John Ambrose,[2] a second by Richard Ewald on the The Granville Mill in America.[3] This timber mill in Vermont produces about 150,000 birch and maple bowls each year using a bowl-nesting lathe made in bowl which can be turned is 22 inches (560 mm). The nester is similar to John Ambrose's, but larger, and now equipped with pneumatic cutter changing.

Other apparatuses were developed including one by the late Cecil Colyer,[4] but the first internationally marketed bowl nester was produced during the early 1990s by Craft Supplies (figure 6.16). Currently I know of only two commercially available bowl-nesting apparatuses. Both, like all nesting devices, apply large eccentric forces to the workpiece which must therefore be chucked securely (figures 6.17 and 6.18). The device by Woodcut Tools International is shown in figures 6.19 to 6.23, that by Kelton Industries in figures 6.24 to 6.28.

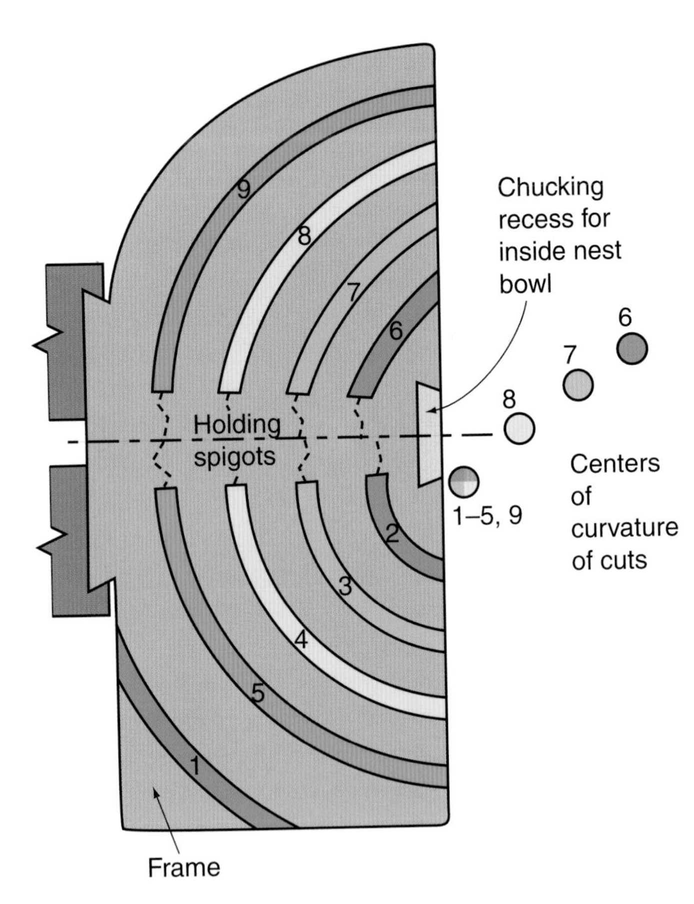

Figure 6.5 Two nests of bowls, each in diametrical section. The upper half shows a nest made with just one arc-bladed tool; the lower half a frame and a nest turned using a differently curved tool for each of the five cuts.

Any frame is usually parted free first. Then the nest bowls are partially parted in order, the smallest first. After each nest bowl is partially parted, it can be freed by fracturing its holding spigot, or be left attached as is usual when turning the whole nest between centers. If left attached, the spigots need to be stronger. A curved wedge might then be needed to fracture the spigots. If so the nest bowls' walls need to be left thick enough so that they do not fracture if the curved wedge is used.

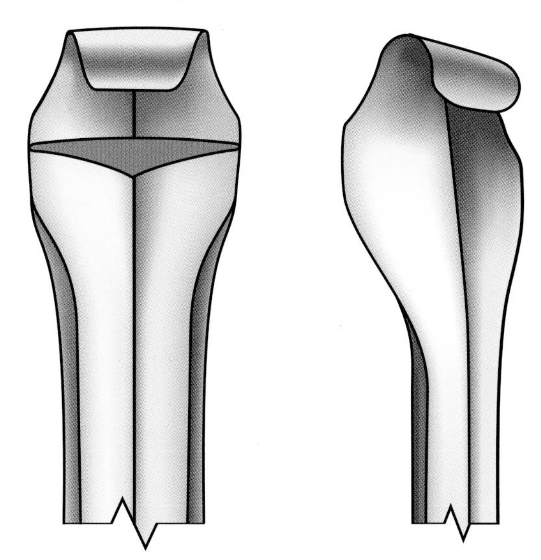

Figure 6.6 **The hooked tips used on hand-held, arced-bladed nesting tools.**[5]

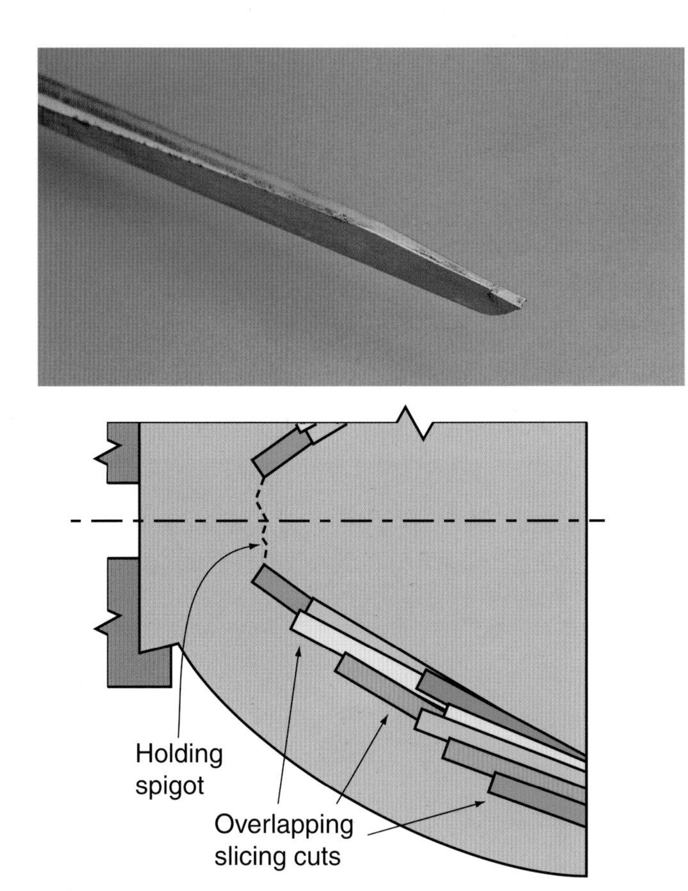

Figure 6.7 **Nesting with the Stewart System slicer,** a strong tool which can be controlled at long overhangs, especially if the armbrace handle is fitted.[6] Because the tool blade widens towards its handle, a series of leapfrogging plunging cuts at lathe-axis height is used to widen and slightly curve the groove.

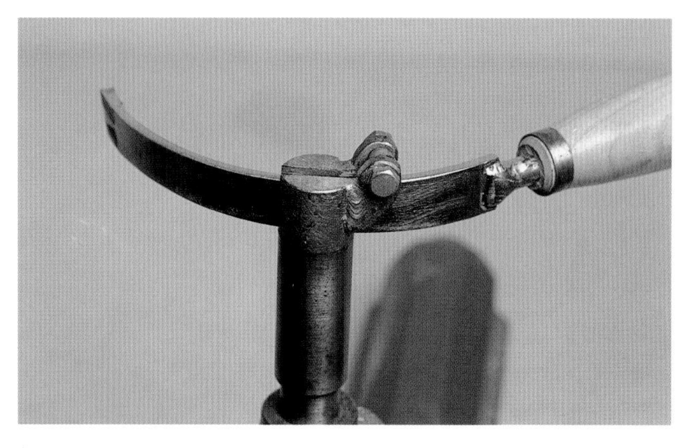

Figure 6.8 **The Leady bowl nester** is a curved-bladed parting scraper of radius 6 in. (150 mm) which locates in and is pushed through a slot in its mating toolpost. There is a device on the top of the toolpost which prevents the tip of the parting scraper from being forced down by the descending wood.

Figure 6.9 **Setting out a cut.** The wooden toolpost extension bodily raises the tool. By looking down and adjusting the position of the banjo and the orientation of the toolpost in the banjo, where the cut will finish can be estimated and adjusted. The toolpost extension is then removed leaving the banjo and toolpost locked in position, ready for the nesting cut to start.

Figure 6.10 Making the cut. The lathe speed is fairly low. As the tool is pushed forwards, the tool handle is slightly rocked up and down to give clearance.

Figure 6.12 John Ambrose operating his bowl nester.

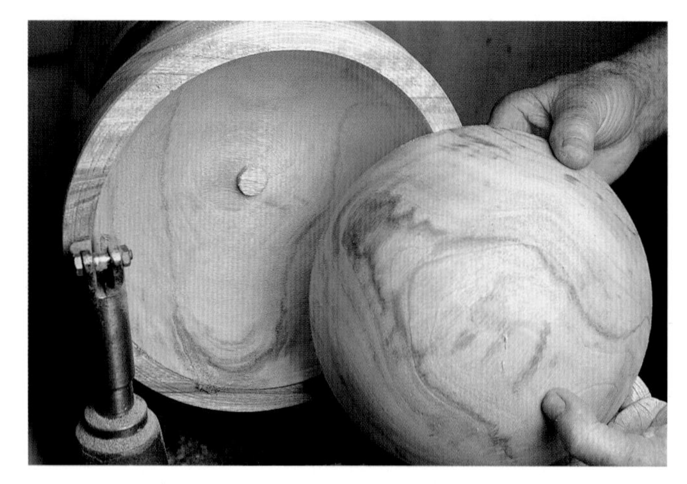

Figure 6.11 The inner nest bowl freed. After completing the arcing cut, a crisp tap on the end-grain edge of the inner nest bowl fractured the holding spigot. You can also use a wedge or lever to free nest bowls, but the walls need to be strong enough to take the stresses.

Figure 6.13 The five cutters of John Ambrose's bowl nester, and a nest cut with them. The bowl blank was held in a 3-jaw scroll chuck with its cambium surface facing the tailstock. The final cut was taken through the back of the blank, to just clear the scroll chuck jaws. The resulting ring could have been turned into a frame or molding.

Figure 6.14 **John Ambrose's apparatus** is simple in principle, effective, and is further described in the next figure.

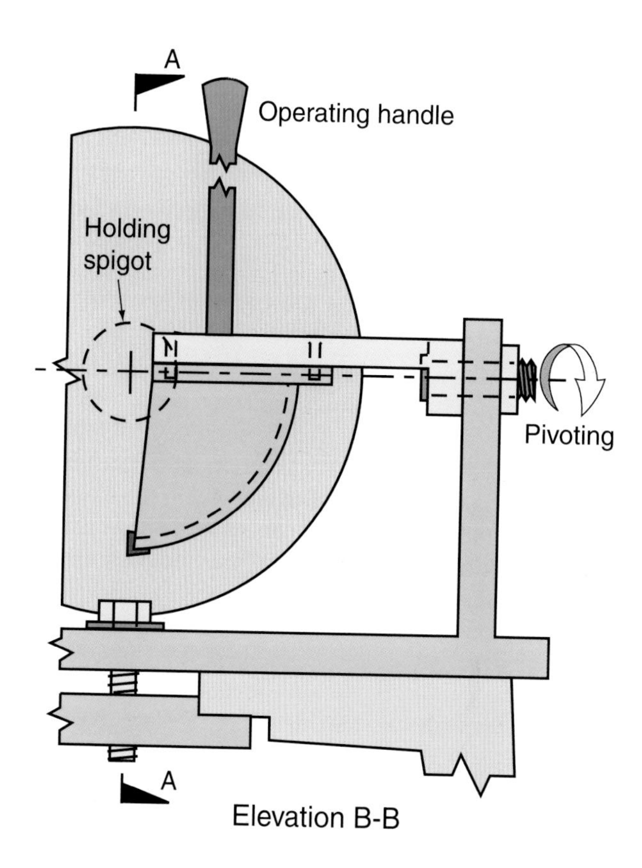

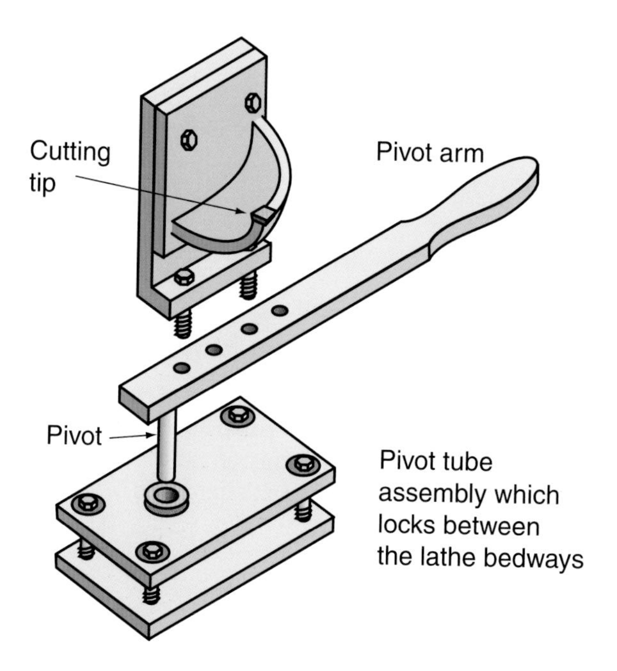

Figure 6.15 **The Ambrose bowl nester in an exploded view.** The cutter shell is welded onto a plate, which is screwed onto the L-shaped plate, which is in turn bolted onto the pivot arm at the correct radius.

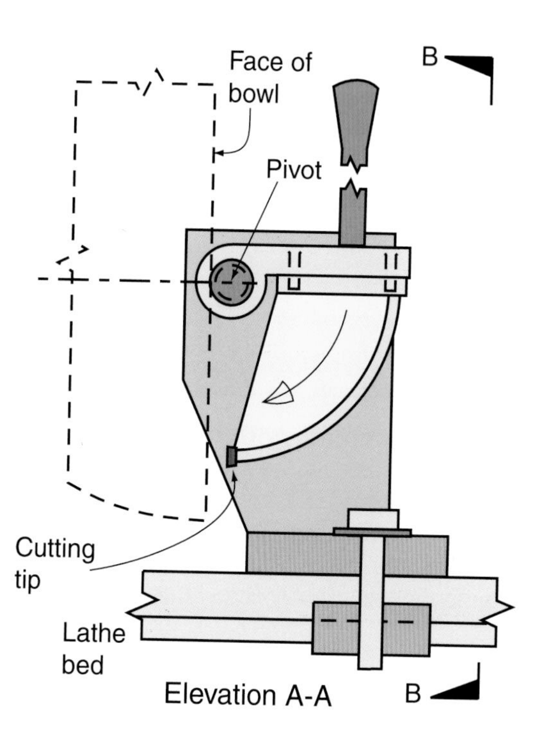

Figure 6.16 **The Craft Supplies bowl nester** is similar to that designed by John Ambrose, and was designed in consultation with John. However, its pivot is positioned behind the bowl and has a horizontal axis, not a vertical one.

6.2.1 CHUCKING FOR BOWL NESTING

Bowl nesting stresses chucking perhaps more than the hand turning of bowls. Therefore:

1. When holding a bowl blank by its bottom on a faceplate, you generally don't want to use long screws. By drilling extra holes through the faceplate at the largest sensible diameter you can hold securely using short screws (figure 6.17).
2. If using a jaw chuck to hold a bowl workpiece by its bottom, use jaws which contract onto a spigot or shoulder (figure 6.18). The diameter of this chucking feature should not be less than about a quarter of the blank's diameter or it may shear. If you use jaws which expand into a recess, they can split the bowl blank.
3. If considering other chucking methods, choose from those which will give a secure grip.
4. Use tailstock support when possible.

Figure 6.17 **A faceplate with extra holes,** here four, will hold the workpiece securely using even 1 in. (25 mm) screws. One of the new holes is deliberately not drilled midway between two adjacent original holes. Therefore if you remove the workpiece from the faceplate and later want to remount it, it will only screw back in its earlier orientation.

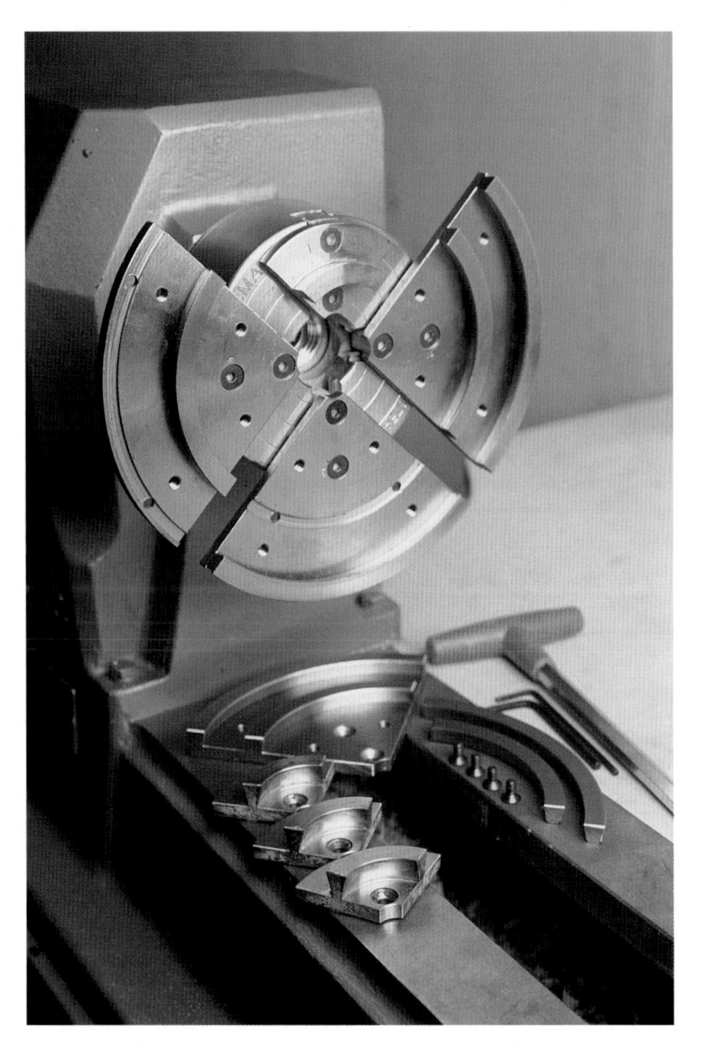

Figure 6.18 **A Vicmarc VM 120 Uni-Chuck with extra-large diameter multi-purpose dovetail jaws.** Either of the two dovetailed rings can be removed. Large-diameter dovetail jaws are available for most brands of chuck.

6.2.2 THE WOODCUT BOWL SAVER

Invented by Errol Udy, designed by Ken Port, and manufactured in Matamata, New Zealand, by Woodcut Tools International, this nesting device was introduced in 1996. It mechanically grips and guides a blade which is arced in plan and has a replaceable Stellite tip along an arc with the same radius as the blade. The device is simple to use, requiring minimal skill but some care.[7]

Figure 6.19 The Woodcut Bowl Saver.

Two blades are supplied, and are locked into arced grooves in the black rotating plate by screwing the small black handle-holding plate down with two hexagon-head screws. The active blade, whether the larger or smaller in radius, should project from the nearside of the rotating plate with its tip up; the other blade is stored over the rotating plate with its tip down.

A small replaceable piece of hard wood supports the active blade at the edge of the base plate. The base plate has a stem which is held in the lathe banjo, and is further steadied using a support bracket and a short length of screwed rod which is held in a Jacobs chuck in the tailstock ram. The support bracket is fastened through the arc-shaped slot in the right-hand side of the base plate, and the screwed rod is fixed through the support bracket using two nuts.

The positioning of the Saver is explained in the next figure.

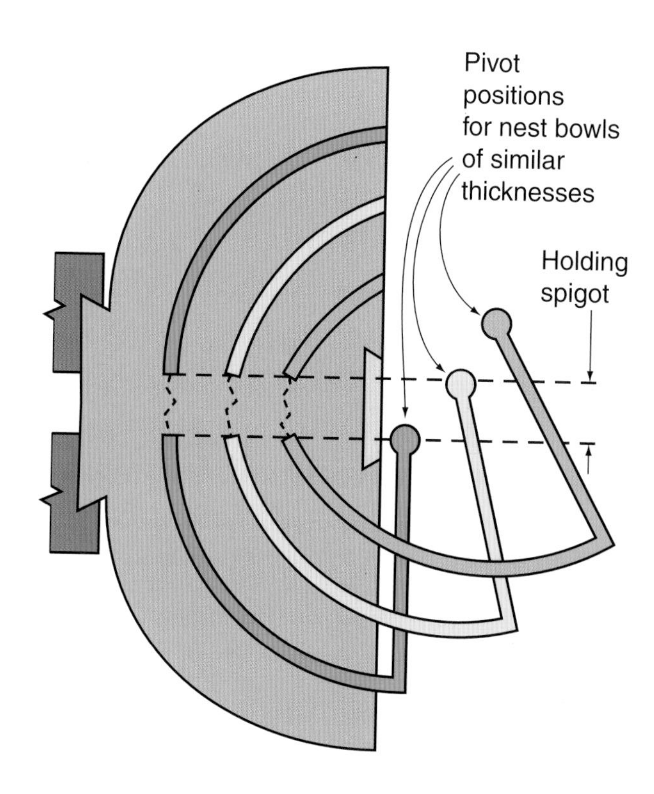

Figure 6.20 Positioning the Woodcut Bowl Saver.

Because the pivot is at lathe-axis height and its axis cannot be located effectively closer than $1/2$ in. (13 mm) to the face of the workpiece, the nest bowls must be shallower than semicircular unless the center pivot is moved to the right and towards the back of the lathe from the line of the nearside of the holding spigot.

The larger blade cuts a spherical groove $5/16$ in. (8 mm) wide with an external diameter of 10 in. (254 mm); for the smaller blade the cut is also $5/16$ in. wide, while the cut's external diameter is 8 in. (203 mm). Assuming a holding spigot of 1 in. (25 mm) diameter and because the pivot cannot be positioned closer than $1/2$ in. (13 mm) to the right of the blank's face, the maximum inner nesting-bowl outside diameters are approximately $10^1/2$ in. (265 mm) and $8^1/2$ in. (215 mm) respectively. To cut smaller nesting bowls, the pivot has to be repositioned further away from the face of the blank and/or further back as indicated.

Figure 6.21 **The Saver positioned to cut in at the chalked circle.** Have the front nearside edge of the base plate square to the bedways. The base plate should be raised so that the blade's cutting edge will cut at lathe-axis height. The supplied collar should then be permanently locked onto the stem so that the base plate will automatically be at the correct level in the future.

With experience you will be able to informally position and cut with a bowl-nesting device and get the nest bowls you intended. Alternatively you can use a technique based on that described in figure 6.9 to position your bowl-nesting device. A toolpost extension is shown *bottom right,* and can be used to position the Saver as described in the next figure.

Figure 6.22 **Checking and setting where the cut will finish** after raising the Saver with the toolpost extension without moving the banjo. Keep the baseplate aligned as in the preceeding figure. You can pencil on the baseplate where the front of the rotating plate should finish for the holding spigot to be cut to the required diameter.

Figure 6.23 **Cutting with the Woodcut Bowl Saver.** Holding the base plate and pressing the blade down onto the small piece of supporting wood minimizes noise and vibration. Feed slowly. Stop the lathe and clear any clogging shavings when required. As the holding spigot becomes smaller in diameter, the sound produced by the turning changes and provides an additional means of monitoring the cut.

6.2.3 THE NEW KEL McNAUGHTON SYSTEM

Similar to Bruce Leadbeatter's nester described earlier in figures 6.8 to 6.11, the McNaughton equipment is shown in figures 6.24 and 6.25. Its use is described in figures 6.26 to 6.28. Available in two weights, there are several curvatures of arc-bladed parting tool. The same toolpost will restrain both weights of blade. The first system was introduced by Kelton Industries of Kaitaia, New Zealand, in 1995, the "New" system in 1998.[8]

The McNaughton System requires more skill for safe use than the Woodcut Saver, but is more versatile and can be used to produce bigger nest bowls.

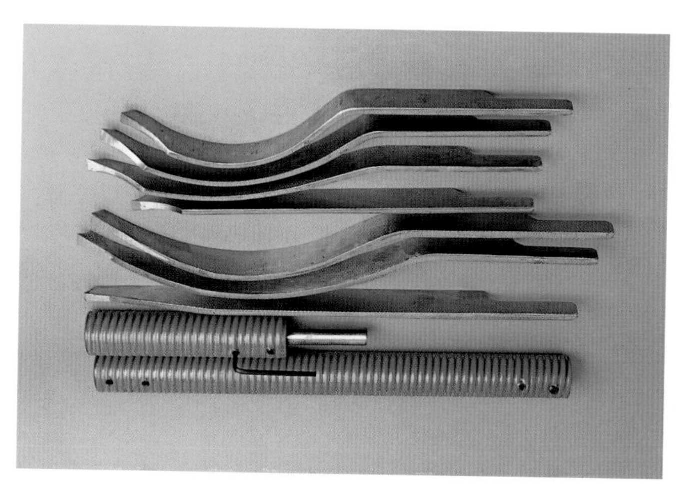

Figure 6.24 **The New MacNaughton System blades, handle, and handle extension.** The smaller blades are $1/4$ in. (6 mm) thick and 1 in. (25 mm) deep, about 13 in. (320 mm) long, and suited to cutting nesting bowls of up to about 16 in. (400 mm) diameter. The larger blades are $9/64$ in. (7 mm) thick and $1\,1/4$ in. (32 mm) deep, and about 17 in. (430 mm) long.

The radiuses of curvature of the blades are between 4 in. and 10 in. (100 mm and 250 mm).

The blades are fixed into the handle with two socket-head screws. The same toolpost, shown in the next figure, is used for both thicknesses of blade.

Figure 6.25 **The McNaughton toolpost.** The three vertical pins on its top form two gates. The deeper gate is for the deeper, thicker blades; the shorter gate for the shallower, narrower blades. The horizontal T-bar prevents the force applied by the descending wood pushing the cutting tip down and jamming the blade.

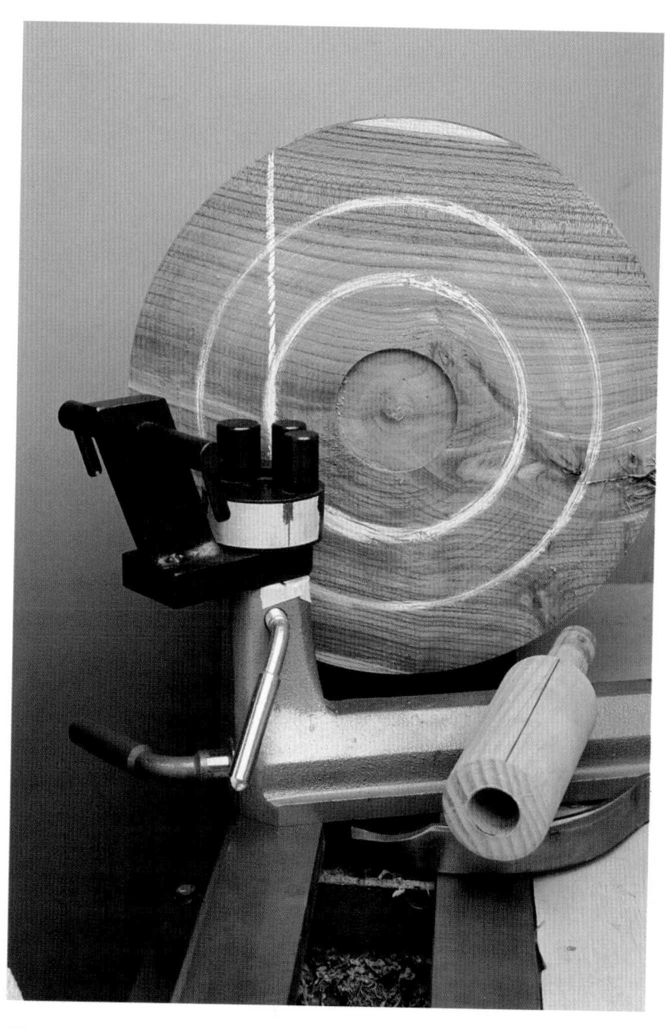

Figure 6.26 **Positioning and angling the toolpost in plan to achieve the desired cut.** Most experienced users seem to do this informally. You can however adopt the method shown with both the Leadbeatter and Woodcut devices. Here the inner chalk circle represents where the first nesting cut will start, and a vertical has been chalked from its left-hand side. The toolpost was then positioned and angled to cut the inner nest bowl with the appropriate gate close to the face of the bowl blank. The next step will be to check the correctness of the toolpost's position and angle by raising the toolpost with the extension shown *bottom right*. The line on the extension and the reference marks on the masking tape on the toolpost and banjo will help in raising the toolpost without altering its angle in plan.

A recess has been turned in the face of the inner nest bowl so that the bowl can later be readily chucked for finish-turning. Alternatively, you could leave in place any faceplate, chuck, or dovetailed ring which you used to earlier to prepare the blank for nesting, but this would increase the effective weight of the inner nest bowl. It would also increase the likelihood of the holding spigot snapping prematurely.

Figure 6.27 Checking where the cut should finish.

The toolpost has been raised without altering its angle in plan or the banjo's position. If the position of the cutting tip at the estimated completion of the cut is unsatisfactory, adjust the angle of the toolpost and the position of the banjo, ensuring that the blade passes through the projection of the vertical chalk line. Then without changing its angle, lower the toolpost so that the cutting tip will cut at or slightly above lathe-axis height.

Rather than use a toolpost extension which fits between the banjo and the toolpost, you could design one which more closely resembles that in figure 6.9 and locates onto the three pins on the top of the toolpost

Figure 6.28 Cutting out a nest bowl. The lathe speed should be fairly low. You slowly force the blade in. By oscillating the handle slightly from side-to-side and up-and-down you widen the groove and lessen the possibility of jamming. You can also widen the groove with an overlapping cut along one side, usually the outside, of the first. As you force the tool forwards you must continue to pull it upwards against the T-bar. This maintains the cutter at lathe-axis height. If you cease this pull, the weight of the handle can cause the tool tip to rise, jam in the cut, and then be slammed down by the descending wood with dire consequences.

If the groove becomes clogged, clean it out with the lathe stopped.

6.2.4 RECHUCKING NEST BOWLS

Figure 6.28 shows a recess which had been preturned into the face of an inside nest bowl. After freeing such a bowl, it can be readily and axially chucked by its top; and its outside finish-turned. If you hollow the inside nest bowl during the nesting process, you can later chuck it or any other nest bowl for finish turning by:

1. Mounting it centers. If the nest-bowl rim has been trued, the bowl can be chucked by centering the tail center in the stub of the holding spigot, and forcing the rim against the inside of the original bowl blank if it is still chucked, a faceplate or better a wooden disk mounted on a faceplate or similar, or a jam chuck. If the nest-bowl rim is irregular, force the inside of the bowl against a funnel or spigot chucked on the headstock.
2. Gripping the outside of the rim (if it has been trued) in a chuck with large-diameter concentrically-contractable jaws (figures 6.31, 6.32, and FOW, figure 9.5).
3. By using vacuum chucking to suck the inside of the bowl onto a funnel or suck the outside of the bowl into a recess.

6.3 REVERSE-CHUCKING BOWLS

You will need to chuck a bowl two or three times to finish-turn its whole surface. If you use the three chuckings, the last will be reverse-chucking. This will allow you to turn off any chucking features used earlier from the bottom of the bowl and to sand the freshly exposed area.

Your choice of reverse-chucking method should be influenced by the shape of the bowl and its rim, the bowl's size, and whether the rim is plane or irregular. The options are described in figures 6.29 to 6.35. A different but related chucking order is described in figures 6.36 and 6.37.

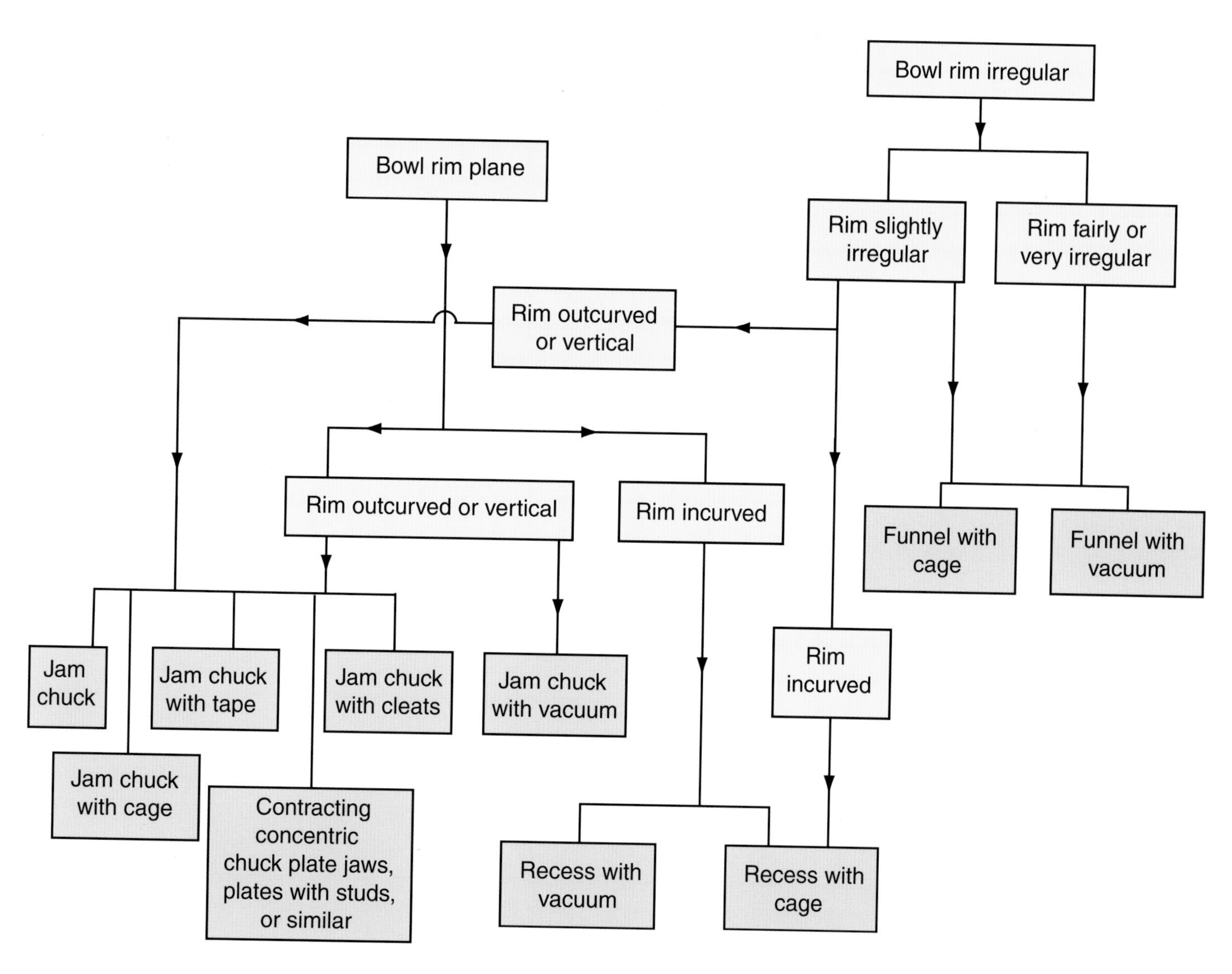

Figure 6.29 The choices for reverse chucking.

Reverse chucking can be inboard or outboard. When chucking with a recess for incurved bowls or with a funnel, it is best to chuck inboard so you can use the tail center to locate the bowl axially. When earlier turning the outside of the bowl you should therefore turn a central, small, conical hole for the tail center to locate.

The recess used to hold bowls with incurved or thick, rounded rims is a form of jam chuck, and is pictured in the lower half of figure 6.34.

A description of vacuum chucking is given in *FOW*, pages 33 to 37. Vacuum can be used to supplement the grip of a jam chuck, or replace or augment that of a cage.

If you are prepared to do a little hand carving, you can force the tail center against the waste spigot on the bottom of a bowl to hold the bowl into a jam chuck or recess or onto a funnel. After finish-turning all the bowl bottom except its very center, you can remove the bowl from the lathe, carve away the small disk of waste, and hand sand the center of the bottom.

Figure 6.30 **A jam chuck with cleats** which increase the chucking security. The padding prevents damage to the finish-turned walls.

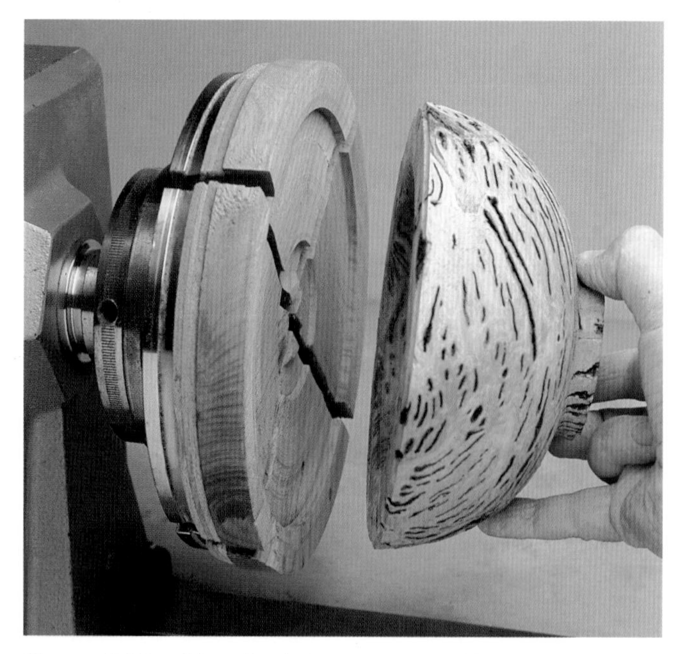

Figure 6.31 **Chuck plates are excellent for reverse chucking bowls with plane rims.** For very thin-walled bowls, turn the diameter of the recess to a touch less than the outside diameter of the bowl rim. Then gently tightening the jaws stiffens the bowl, and the bottom waste is easier to turn off.

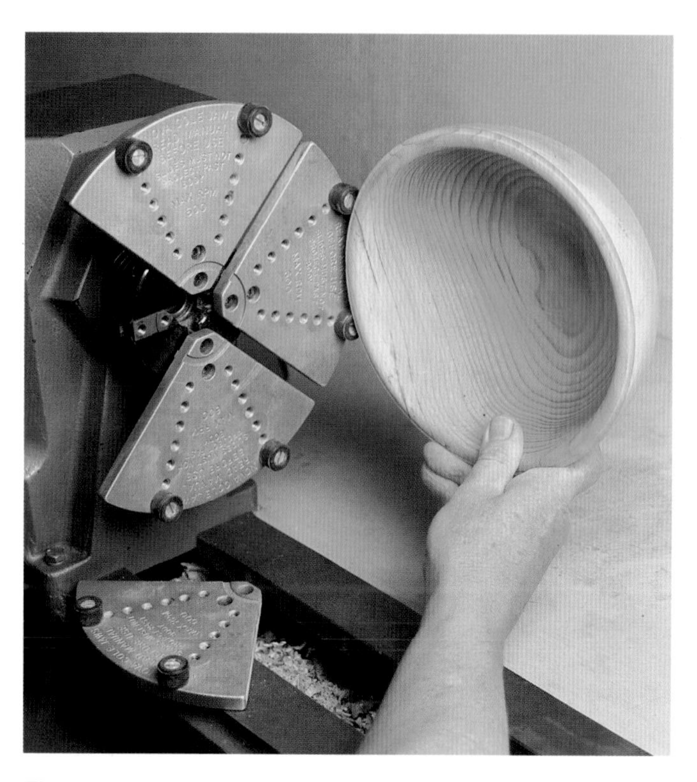

Figure 6.32 **Cole jaws, chuck plates with radially-adjustable rubber studs,** manufactured by Teknatool International of New Zealand. The studs exert force on a workpiece rim or periphery at eight points, and are therefore less suited for gripping very thin-walled bowls than chuck plates. Similar jaws are available from the manufacturers of other brands of woodturning scroll chuck.

Figure 6.33 **A cage chuck used with a funnel** to reverse-chuck a bowl with a waney rim.

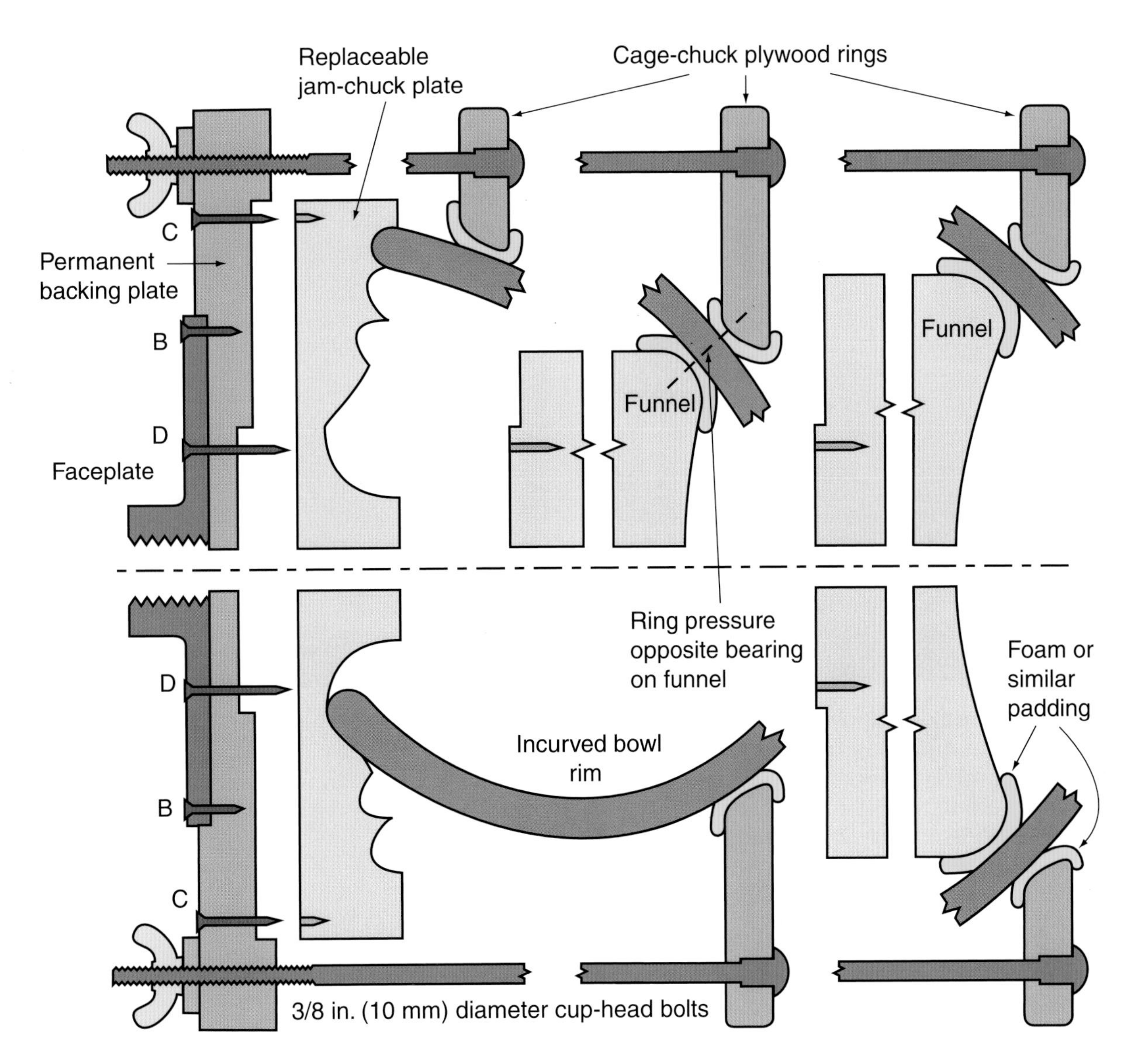

Figure 6.34 **A combined cage and jam chuck for continued reuse** shown in diametrical section. You can use this design to reverse-chuck almost any turned bowl. The chuck does not damage a bowl's surface or require any special chucking features to be left on a bowl.

The chuck parts are screwed and bolted together according to the chucking mode in use. Screws *B* permanently fix the backing plate to the faceplate. Screws *C* are only used to hold the jam-chuck plate into the backing plate; both the screws and the jam-chuck plate have to be removed before mounting a funnel into the permanent backing plate.

You turn suitably sized recesses into the jam-chuck plate to locate bowl rims, including those of incurved bowls. Once you have turned most of a jam-chuck plate away, you should replace it with a fresh plate. You could have several plates, each for a particular bowl geometry. When a bowl rim is so irregular that it will not allow the bowl to seat axially in the jam chuck, the bowl can be pulled against a funnel of suitable dimensions by the appropriately sized cage. You might have several differently sized funnels; each should have a short identical spigot to locate in the recess in the permanent backing plate, and is screwed into place from the rear of the faceplate with screws *D*.

Several plywood rings should be turned for the cages. Each ring should have a different inside diameter. All the rings should have the same outside diameter and bolt-hole positions (which should be evenly spaced around a circle). Three or four bolts are sufficient for almost any bowl. Cup-head bolts are preferred because they lock into the holes in the ring, making it easier to tighten the wing nuts; also they do not have dangerous projecting heads. You will need several different lengths of bolt, and may need to buy threaded rod if very long bolts are not available.

Vacuum can be used to augment the jam and the cage chucking. You could also replace the cage component with vacuum—however the secure holding of the cage has much to recommend it. If you will not be using vacuum, there is no need to bore the plates or the funnels and the funnels could then be termed spigots.

Figure 6.35 **The chucking shown in figure 6.33 with the workpiece cut away to show the glued-on foam padding** used to prevent damage to the inside surface of bowls. Also shown is the ideal situation with the bearing of the funnel and the ring on the bowl wall directly opposite one another. The tail center is only used here to ensure that the bowl is mounted axially.

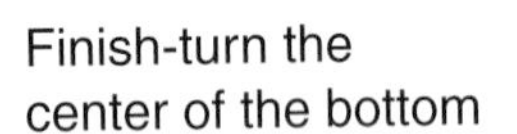

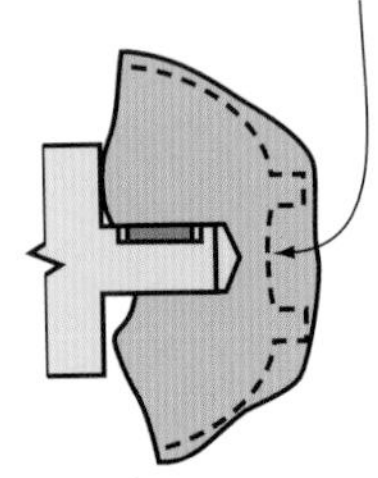

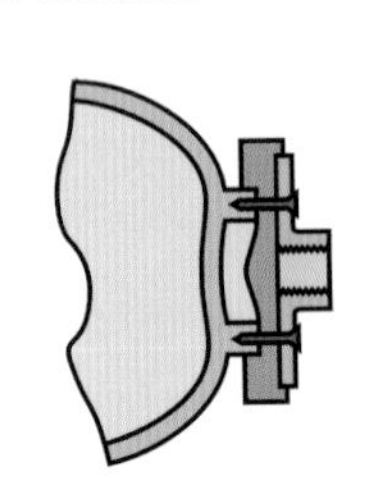

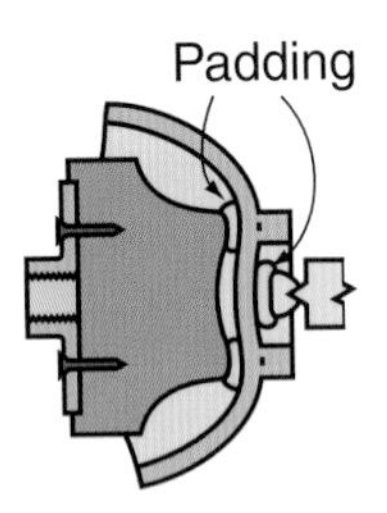

Figure 6.36 **An unusual three-stage bowl turning procedure** which uses the tail center instead of a cage to hold the bowl against a funnel or into a recess or jam chuck for the final turning operation (see next figure).

Figure 6.37 **Using the tail center** to push on a small waste disk to turn off the waste rim and finish-turn the area thus exposed. There is padding between the disk and the bowl to protect the bowl bottom's central finished surface.

6.4 ENDNOTES

1. Fritz Spannagel, *Das Drechslerwerk* (1940; reprint, Hannover: Verlag Th. Schafer, 1981), p. 82, figure 347, seems to show the turner using traditional hook tools to turn nest bowls on a motor-driven lathe.
2. Mick O'Donnell, "Nest of Bowls," *Practical Woodworking* (December 1990): pp. 32–35.
3. Richard Ewald, "The Granville Mill," *Fine Woodworking* 80 (February 1990): pp. 53–55.
4. Dave Regester, "Bowls by the Nest," *Woodturning* 17 (November 1993): pp. 38–42. An excellent article, but the illustration of Cecil Colyer's device is wrongly drawn.
5. Spannagel, pp. 80–83, describe nesting, and include a sketch on which this figure is based.
6. Dennis Stewart, "Turning a Concentric Bowl Set," *American Woodturner* (June 1988): pp. 4–6.
7. The Woodcut Bowl Saver is reviewed in Derek Phillips, "Nest-Egg," *Woodturning* 74 (April 1999): pp. 39-40.
8. The New McNaughton system is reviewed in Ray Key, "Star Turn," *Woodturning* 58 (December 1997): pp. 26–30; and Mike Mahoney, "McNaughton Center Saver," *American Woodturner* (Summer 1998): pp. 42–43.

Chapter Seven

THREADING

Page 19 of *Woodturning Methods* introduced the scroll, a mechanism invented in 1842. The scroll could be considered as a two-dimensional version of the screw, a much earlier and far more important device. The term "screw" includes a male screw with a helical ridge like a corkscrew,[1] and the mating female socket with a helical groove cut into its surface.

Screws are used to:

1. Convert rotary motion to longitudinal motion. For example, when you turn a screw within a fixed, like-threaded hole, the screw moves axially forwards or backwards through the hole. This facility is used to finely adjust the axial position of one of the two components—for example in micrometers. It is also usually nonreversible, so that attempting to push, say, the female-threaded component axially will not rotate the male component. There is also a large mechanical advantage which enables great force to be exerted by rotating one of the two components: vices and C-cramps are common examples in which the male thread is rotated.
2. Generate great friction between the long helixes of contact area on the flanks (sloping sides) of the male and female threads. This is utilized to prevent accidental loosening of lids, screws, clamps, and other fastenings. The axial force is resisted by the large area of shear resistance through the threads.
3. Convert a rotary motion about one axis to a much slower rotary motion about another axis at a right angle to the first by using a worm to drive a wormwheel (figure 7.1). This mechanism has a built-in brake because you cannot rotate the worm by attempting to rotate the wormwheel.

These useful properties have ensured that screws and the methods to produce them have had a long history.[2] This chapter outlines that history; it also details the geometry of threads, and how to cut threads in wood both by hand and with a range of devices and mechanisms. The final section in this chapter describes basic thread cutting in metal.

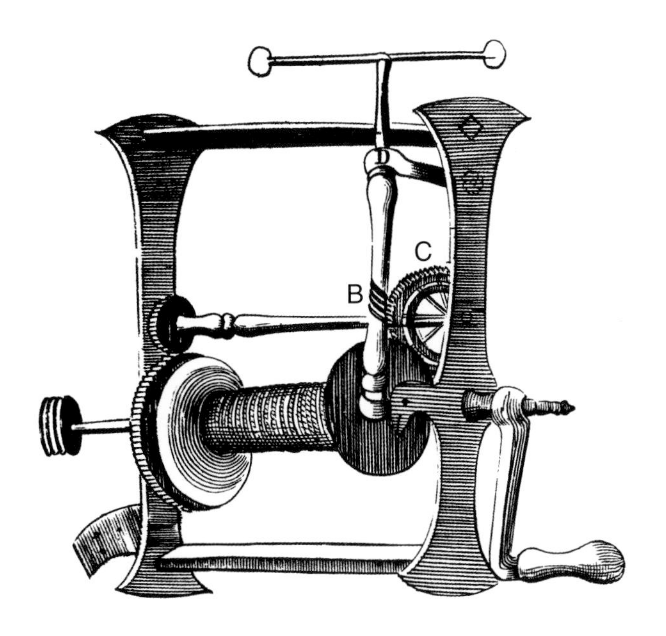

Figure 7.1 A windlass with a worm *B* and wormwheel *C*, pictured in Joseph Moxon, *Mechanick Exercises or the Doctrine of Handy-Works* (1678; reprint, New York: Praeger Publishers, 1970), Smith's Work, pl. 3.

7.1 THE HISTORY OF THREAD CUTTING BY HAND

The first screws were almost certainly hand carved in wood (figure 7.2). In the sixth century B.C. screw presses were used in Turkey for compacting cloth, and were described by the Greek natural philosopher Heracleitus.[3] Similar screw presses were in use around the Mediterranean by the second century B.C. for pressing olives and grapes.[4]

The setting out and carving of the male threads of these presses was relatively straightforward (figure 7.2), but to hand carve a female thread is impossible unless the female wooden component is first drilled and split longitudinally. The thread can then be carved on the insides of the parts of the female component, and the parts rejoined. Many early screw presses did not however use female threads, and instead used pins which projected into a cylindrical hole to engage with the male thread (figure 7.3).

The earliest description of a device for cutting female threads was written in about A.D. 62 by Hero of Alexandria (figure 7.4).[5] Hero's device was the forerunner of the tap (figures 7.5 and 7.6), the device most used to cut female threads in recent centuries. Taps are also used to cut female threads in the bodies of screw boxes, related devices used for cutting male threads in wood (figure 7.7). The equivalent of the screw box for cutting male threads in metal is the die (figure 7.8). Although screws were made in Ancient Greece and Rome, they were cut by hand[6]—taps and dies were not used until the fourteenth century.[7] Chasers, simpler devices pictured in figure 7.9 which enabled both male and female threads to be turned, may also have been in use by then. The fifteenth century saw the invention of the movable-type printing press (figure 7.10), an important application of the screw; and the application of threaded fasteners to armor and firearms. However screws were not used in clocks until the sixteenth century.[8]

There are four ways to cut threads:

1. Hold the wood still, and rotate and traverse a thread-cutting tool along the wood. A threaded section usually follows and is rigidly connected to the cutter. This threaded section engages with the thread just cut into the wood to ensure that the rotational and longitudinal movements of the tool produce a thread with the same pitch as that of the tool's threaded section.
2. Rotate and traverse the workpiece's circular internal or external periphery past a fixed or rotating cutter.
3. Revolve a fixed or rotating cutter while passing the workpiece axially past the circle of revolution of the cutter.
4. Rotate the wood and simultaneously traverse a cutting tool along the workpiece.

Hero's device uses the first way; and taps, dies, and screwboxes the first or the second. The traversing mandrel (figures 7.14 and 7.15) is also an example of the second way. The third way is rarely, if ever, used for cutting threads in wood. The fourth is used in hand chasing, and is the basis of the engine lathe (figure 7.24), the culmination of centuries of thread-cutting development.

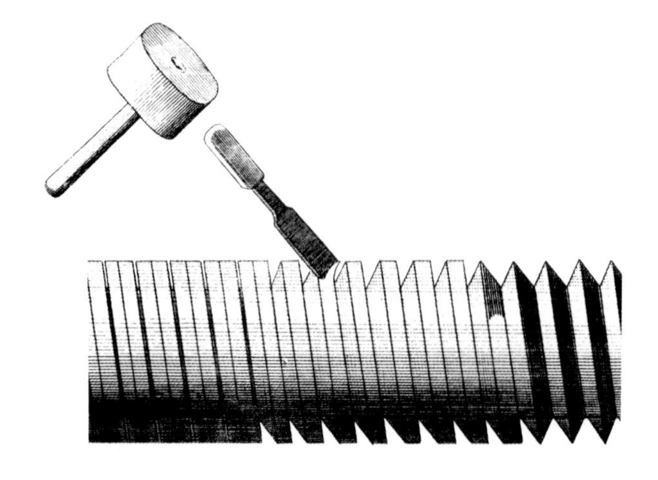

Figure 7.2 Hand carving a screw, from P. Hamelin-Bergeron, *Manuel du Tourneur* (1816; reprint, Nogent le Roi: Jacques Laget, 1981) vol. II, pl. VII. After marking out, a helical saw cut is made to the bottom (root) of the thread, and the waste is then chopped away.

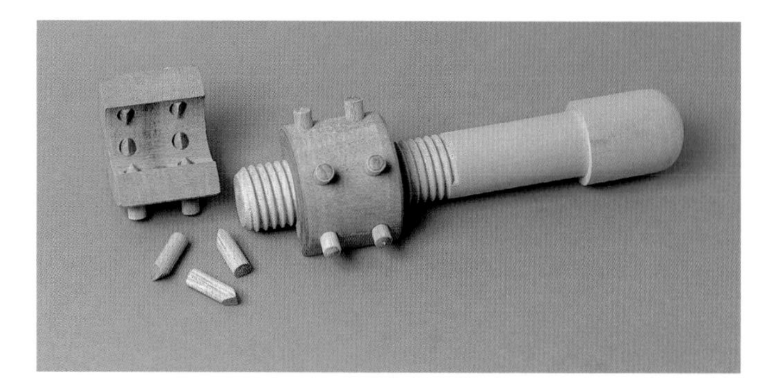

Figure 7.3 The earliest form of "nut" (here cut in half). The projecting thread pins have to have precisely carved wedge-shaped ends, and be accurately positioned if the screw is to be strong and free running. Also, the more thread pins, provided they do not weaken the nut body unduly, the greater the force which can be safely applied by the screw. A thread pin was called a *tylos* in Ancient Greece.[9]

The converse of this "nut" is the inclined knife, a device used in the eighteenth century to generate accurate lead screws as explained on page 140. An early form of lead screw is shown in the next figure. A lead screw with the same pitch as the thread it is used to cut is often called a *master screw*.

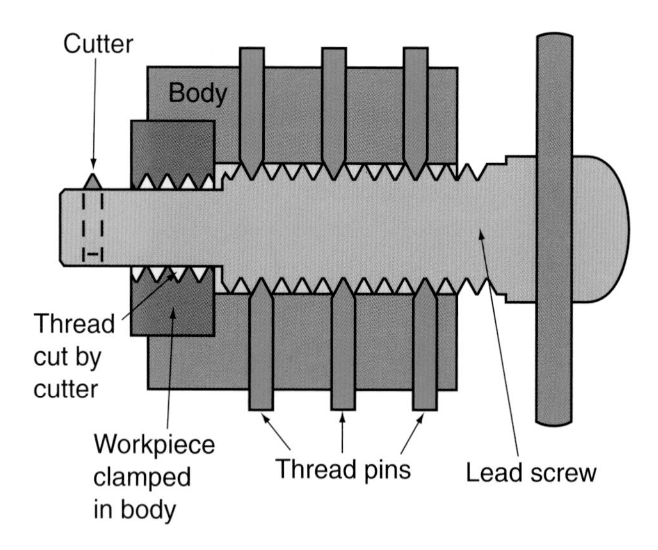

Figure 7.4 A wooden device for cutting female threads shown in diametrical section.[10] The body is similar to the "nut" shown in the preceding figure, except that a drilled workpiece can be chucked in and against the body's left-hand end. By winding the lead screw to the right, the metal cutter is simultaneously revolved and moved to the right, and cuts a thread. Threads would have been cut in several passes with the projection of the cutter being increased between each pass.

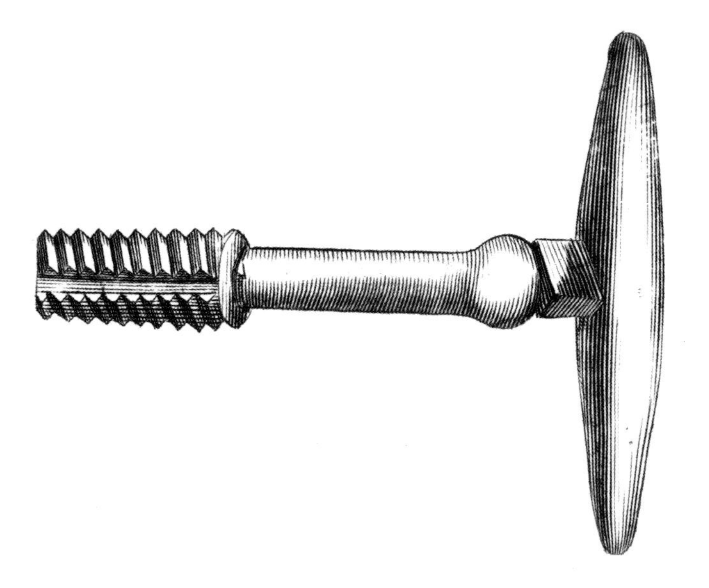

Figure 7.5 A hand tap for cutting female threads, pictured in Charles Plumier, *L'Art de Tourner* (1701; English translation, New York: Paul L. Ferraglio, 1975), pl. VIII. This scraping form of tap is used to thread both wood and metal. A *cutting* form of tap for wood is shown below.

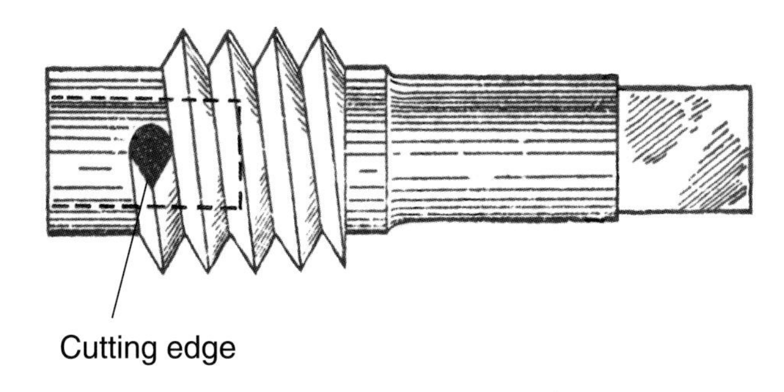

Figure 7.6 A hand tap for *cutting* wood. It leaves a much cleaner thread than the scraping tap shown in the preceding figure. The sharpening angle of the V-shaped *cutting* edge should be about 30°. After severance, the shaving passes down the hole between the two legs of the cutting edge and into the hole bored along the center of the tap. This type of tap was first pictured in Bergeron.

The *cutting* and scraping forms of tap are still in production. A third pattern of tap midway between the two is now made (figure 7.57), but seems to me to be less effective than the *cutting* type pictured here.

This illustration is reproduced from F.J. Camm, *Screw Cutting* (London: Cassell And Company, no date), p.173.

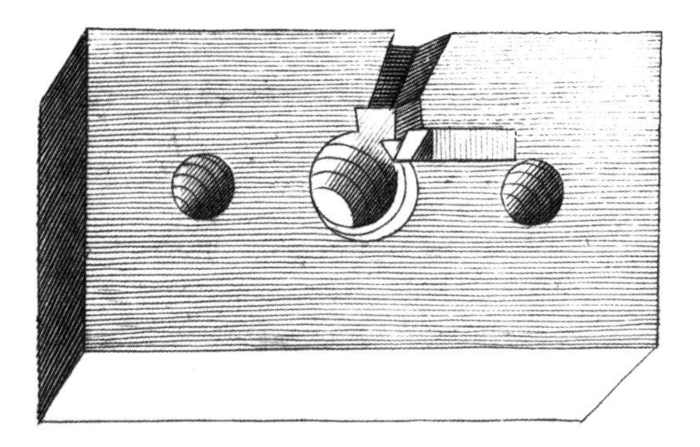

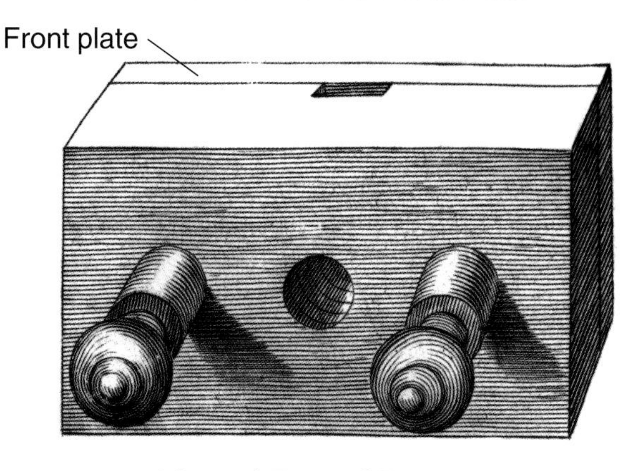

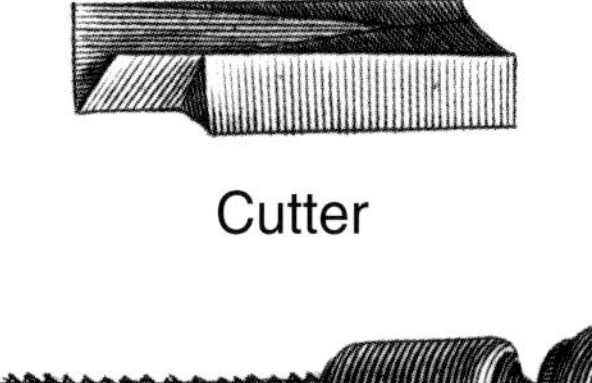

Figure 7.7 A screw box pictured in plate LXVI of Plumier. A modern screw box is shown in figure 7.51.

A tap (figure 7.5) is used to cut the female thread in the rear plate when a screw box is made. The same tap is sold with the screw box and used cut female threads which will mate with the male threads cut with the screw box.

When cutting a thread with a screw box, the length of the spindle to be threaded is first turned to a diameter equal to the screw box thread's outside (major) diameter. A lead-in chamfer is then turned on the spindle. The spindle is then pushed and rotated through the unthreaded hole in the front plate, and has a thread cut into it by the cutter. This male thread engages with the female thread in the rear plate, and thus dictates that the male and female threads have the same pitch.

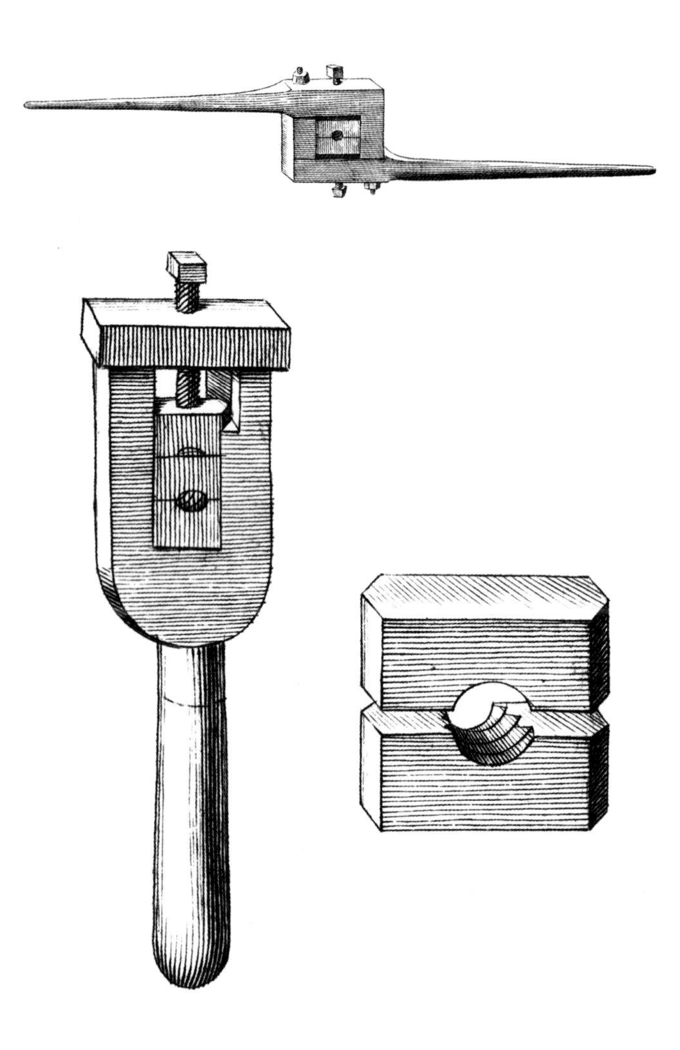

Figure 7.8 **A die, and dies held in die stocks,** pictured in plate LXVI of Plumier. Dies are used to cut male threads in metal.

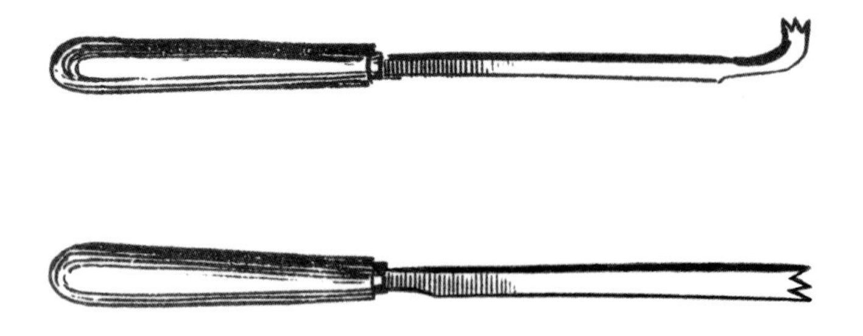

Figure 7.9 **Hand thread chasers** pictured in Moxon, Turner's Work, plate 15. Although machines for producing threads were still in their infancy, by 1678 hand chasers had achieved their final form. Their use is described on pages 173 to 178.

Figure 7.10 **An early printing press** showing its center screw.[11] There were two early improvements to this screw: by 1500 the single-start thread had been replaced by three- or four-start threads (see figure 7.30) so that the platen could be raised by a much smaller rotation of the bar; and in about 1550 wooden screws were superseded by iron screws.

Mechanical printing using wooden type (xylography) was not successful for text of normal size because the type quickly wore and fractured. Printing from blocks bearing the text of a whole page in relief, cast by pouring lead over a mold of the page, was tried between 1430 and 1440, but was unsatisfactory. The idea of assembling many small metal blocks of type, each cast with one letter in relief, in a form, and printing each page from such an assemblage, was being trialled by several European printers around 1450. In that year Johann Gutenberg borrowed money from Johann Faust (or Fust) to bring to fruition the concept of movable type and the printing press. After five years Gutenberg had still not produced a book, so Faust sued and bankrupted Gutenberg. Faust then worked in Mainz with son-in-law to be and type designer Peter Schoeffer, and in 1455 published the first printed book. Ironically and properly this book is known as the Gutenberg Bible.

William Caxton, who had learnt printing in Germany, returned home in 1473 to translate, print, and publish

Game and Playe of the Chesse, the first book printed in English, in 1474.[12]

Stephen Draye (or Daye) printed the first book in North America in about 1638 in Cambridge, Massachusetts, 1700 copies of *The Whole Booke of Psalms Faithfully Translated into English Metre*. Eleven copies survive.

Large print runs are not peculiar to today—the edition of Luther's Bible first printed in Wittenberg in 1534 ran to 100,000 copies.

7.2 THE EARLY HISTORY OF THREAD CUTTING IN THE LATHE

The boundary between hand working and machining is fuzzy. Hero's device in figure 7.4 has both stationary and moving parts and could properly be regarded as a machine. However the earliest thread-cutting device with the minimum complexity we might consider worthy of being called a machine is shown in a manuscript by Martin Mercz dated 1471. A similar lathe is pictured in the *Mittelalterliche Hausbuch* of 1480 (figure 7.11).[13] About twenty years later Leonardo da Vinci drew a screw-cutting device with two, not one, lead screws (figure 7.12). The next notable illustration of a screw-cutting device, by Jacques Besson, did not however appear until 1578 (figure 7.13).

During the sixteenth century two-bearing headstocks became more common, and the traversing mandrel was developed (figures 7.14 and 7.15). This mechanism continues to be used in modern ornamental-turning lathes, but has the restriction that it can only duplicate the pitch of a master thread. With the increasing need to produce threads in a range of pitches and diameters in metals, a more flexible principle was required. The development of the geared lead shaft will be described on pages 138 to 142.

The turning of metal with hand-held tools was common well into the nineteenth century, and was surprisingly precise (figures 7.16 and 7.17). The switch to a tool bit clamped to a cross slide, itself mounted on another slide parallel to the lathe bed or onto a longitudinally moving carriage, enabled the development of machine tools (machines used to make machines); this is also discussed on pages 138 to 142.

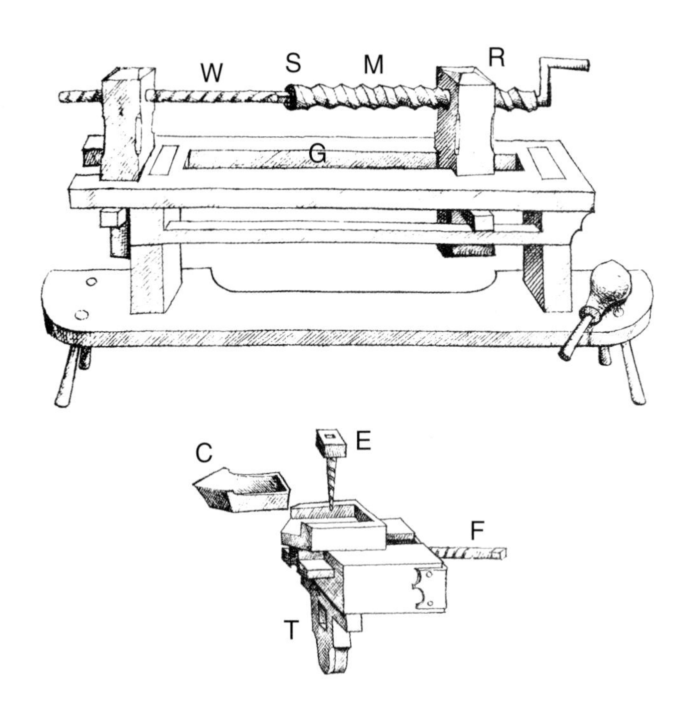

Figure 7.11 A clockmaker's thread-cutting machine of 1480.[14] In the upper engraving the larger-diameter threaded rod *M* on the right is the master screw. It passes through a like-threaded hole in the right-hand upright *R*. The right-hand end of the smaller-diameter workpiece *W* is rigidly chucked in a socket *S* in the left-hand end of the master screw. The workpiece is a sliding fit in an unthreaded hole in the left-hand upright. As the master screw's handle is turned, the workpiece is rotated and traversed past a fixed cutter *C*, and a thread having the same pitch and hand as the master screw is cut. The engraver has therefore erred with the hand of the thread on the workpiece.

The device in the lower engraving has to be rotated 90° clockwise in plan to be correctly orientated with respect to the machine above, and consists of the cutter *C* held in a cross slide. To clamp the cross slide and prevent it sliding longitudinally, its descending tongue *T* is located in the gap *G* between the bedways and wedged in the same way as the descending tongues of the master-screw and workpiece uprights. The cutter *C* is V-shaped in plan. It is fixed into the three-sided recess in the top of the cross slide by the screw *E*. The cutter is advanced to deepen the cut using the feed screw *F* projecting from the right-hand side of the cross slide.

Screw-operated cross slides remained a rarity until the nineteenth century, a trench in which the tool slid being the earlier norm.

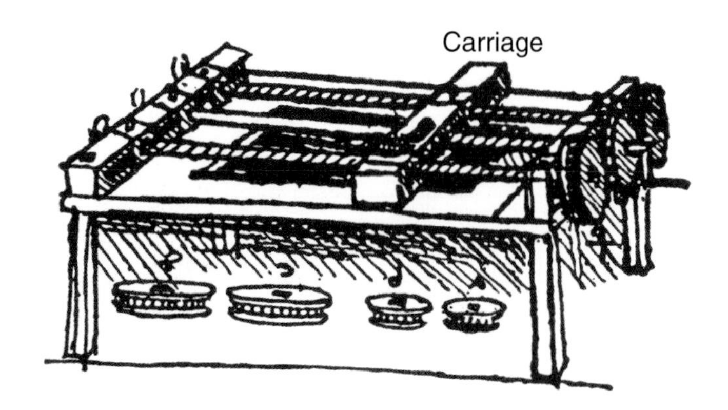

Figure 7.12 **A screw-cutting machine design by Leonardo da Vinci in about 1500.**[15] This was the first representation of screw cutting with the cutter mounted on a carriage. The central workpiece is rotated directly by the crank handle on the right. The carriage is traversed by twin lead screws, the lead screws being rotated through change gears.

Extra change gears are shown below the machine. By replacing the three equal-diameter change gears at the right-hand end of the machine with one large and two small or one small and two large, two additional screw pitches could be cut.

Although not drawn clearly, the carriage has a simple facility to advance the cutter so that the thread can be deepened with every traverse of the carriage.

A similar machine was later developed by David Wilkinson of Pawtucket, Rhode Island, in 1797, but lacked the change gears and therefore the ability to reproduce pitches other than that of its single lead screw.[16]

If you regard the crank handle as the equivalent of a headstock spindle, this machine is a forerunner of the conventional engine lathe which was developed between 1750 and 1850. However the use of separate lead screws seems to have been overshadowed by the traversing mandrel until the end of the eighteenth century; a notable exception is pictured in the next figure.

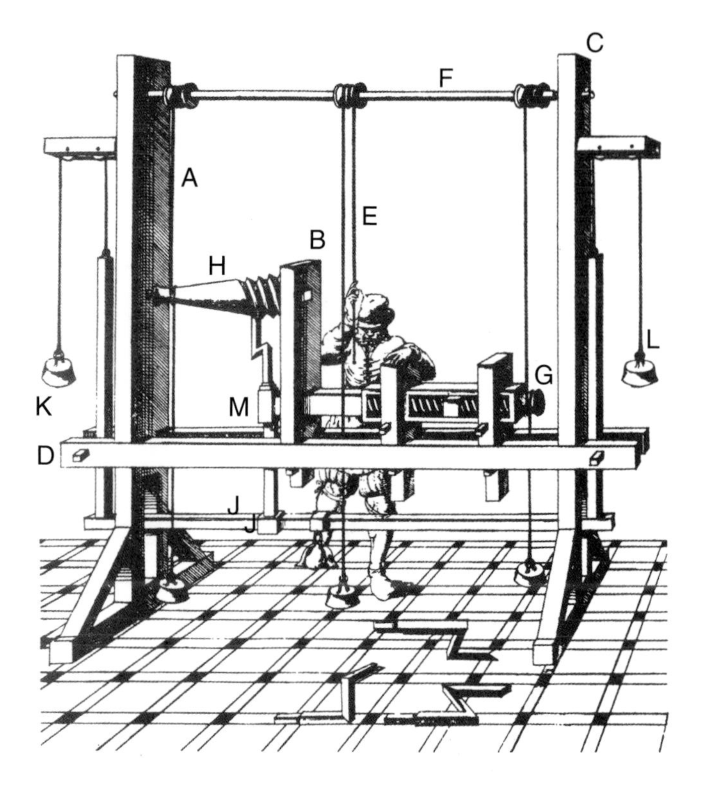

Figure 7.13 **A screw-cutting lathe pictured by Jacques Besson** in *Theatrum Machinarum* (Lyon: 1578).[17] Besson was Leonardo's successor as engineer to the French court. Although diagrammatic rather than practical, the elements necessary to cut a screw, here tapered, are present.

The three vertical supports *A*, *B*, and *C* are fixed to the bed *D*. When the operator pulls on cord *E*, the top shaft *F* is rotated, and, through two cords with weights attached, rotates the lead screw *G* and the tapered workpiece *H*. The housing of lead screw *G* is designed so that as *G* rotates it does not move axially, but screws cutter guide *M* to the left or right.

Below the bed is a suspended beam *J* which is pulled up and kept horizontal by two guides which are in close contact with the outsides of supports *A* and *C*. The two guides are in turn pulled up by cords with weights *K* and *L* tied to their ends. This upward pull on beam *J* is transferred to the cutter which can slide within the vertical cutter guide *M*. Spare cutters are shown on the floor beneath the lathe.

Although the development of successful screw-cutting machines was an essential precursor and part of the Industrial Revolution, the equipment to produce smaller-diameter screws in wood, ivory, and metal had been developed by 1800 as the next three figures show.

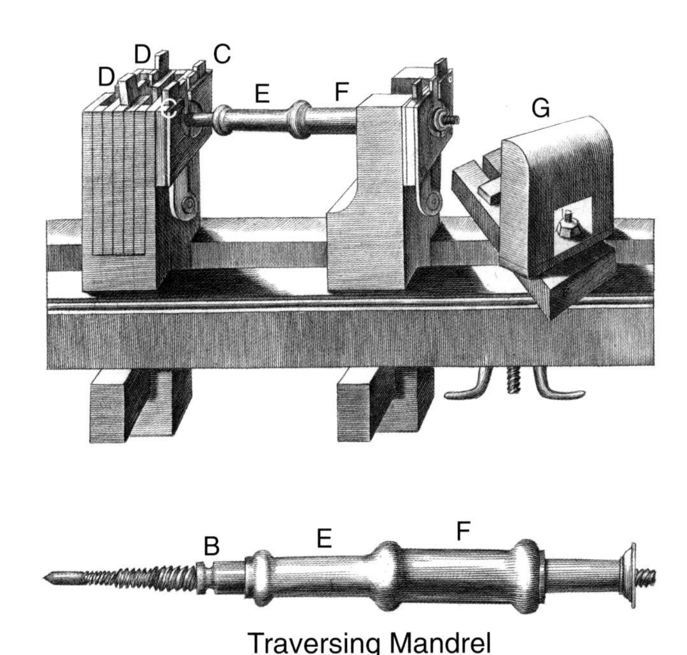

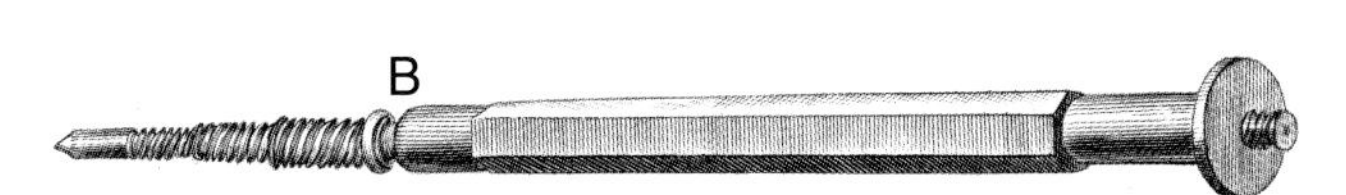

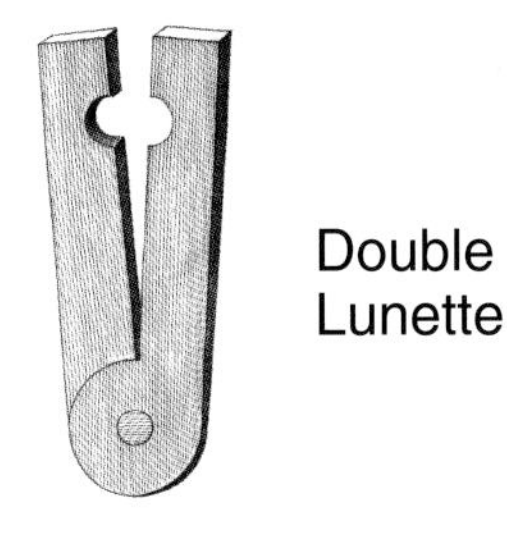

Figure 7.14 **A traversing-mandrel lathe shown in 1701** in plate XII of Plumier. The headstock mandrel (spindle) can both rotate within, and slide axially through, the headstock's two bearings (poppets).

The traversing mandrel has at its left-hand end three threaded sections each having a different pitch. Immediately to the right of the threaded sections is a pulley-like section *B*.

When the lathe is used for plain turning the arms of the right-hand double lunette *CC* are wedged together (wedges not shown) so that its two semicircular unthreaded recesses close into *B* and prevent the mandrel moving axially. To cut a thread, say having the pitch of the middle threaded section, double lunette *CC* is first opened. Double lunette *DD* is then wedged closed so that its semicircular checkouts (which are threaded and later called half nuts) engage with the central threaded section of the mandrel. Rotating the mandrel using a belt driving onto either wooden pulley section *E* or *F* would then cause a V-shaped tool held on toolrest *G* to cut the thread.

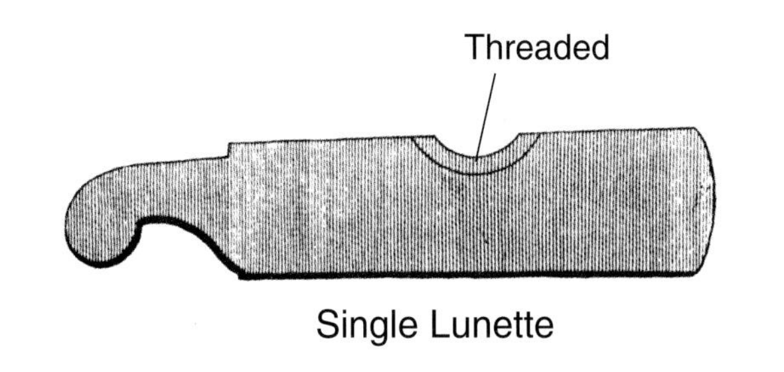

Figure 7.15 **A traversing-mandrel headstock which uses single lunettes to dictate the pitch of the thread cut on a workpiece.** This headstock, shown in plate XXIV of Bergeron, is a century later than that in the preceding figure, and is therefore more refined. The headstock mandrel has eight threaded sections. As with the preceding headstock, a lunette is held in contact with the corresponding threaded section on the mandrel with a wedge which is not shown.

Within a few decades the headstock spindle with several integral differently threaded sections had been superseded by a shorter headstock spindle with interchangeable threaded collars for ornamental-turning (figure 7.20).

Figure 7.16 A metalworking shop using traversing mandrels for threading screws and worms, plate 172 from Denis Diderot's *Encyclopedie* published in a first edition of 35 volumes in Paris between 1751 and 1777. An enlarged edition of 166 volumes was published between 1782 and 1832. This figure is scanned from a facsimile by Dover Publications. The engraving suffers from considerable draftsman's licence.

Back left, *fig. 1*, the workman is cutting into the surface of the metal rod to mark or start the thread.

Front left, *fig. 3*, the rod about to be threaded can rotate and slide axially within the center and left-hand blocks. The cutter is held in a cross slide fixed to the bed between the same two blocks. By rotating the capstan at the master screw's right-hand end, the workpiece is screwed past the cutter, and a thread is cut.

Front right, *fig. 4*, shows a thread being hand turned. The part of the traversing mandrel housed in the headstock on the right is threaded. It possibly has three threads, each with a different pitch, cut into it. The three lunettes each incorporates a threaded semicircular recess which can be engaged with the appropriate threaded section on the mandrel. When a lunette is engaged, the spindle traverses axially as it is rotated, and a "fixed" tool thereby cuts a thread. The lathe is powered by a hand-turned Great Wheel (*fig. 5*) which is cammed to reverse the workpiece's rotation each time the threaded section on the mandrel completes a pass through the lunette.

The hand turning of metal is described on the next page.

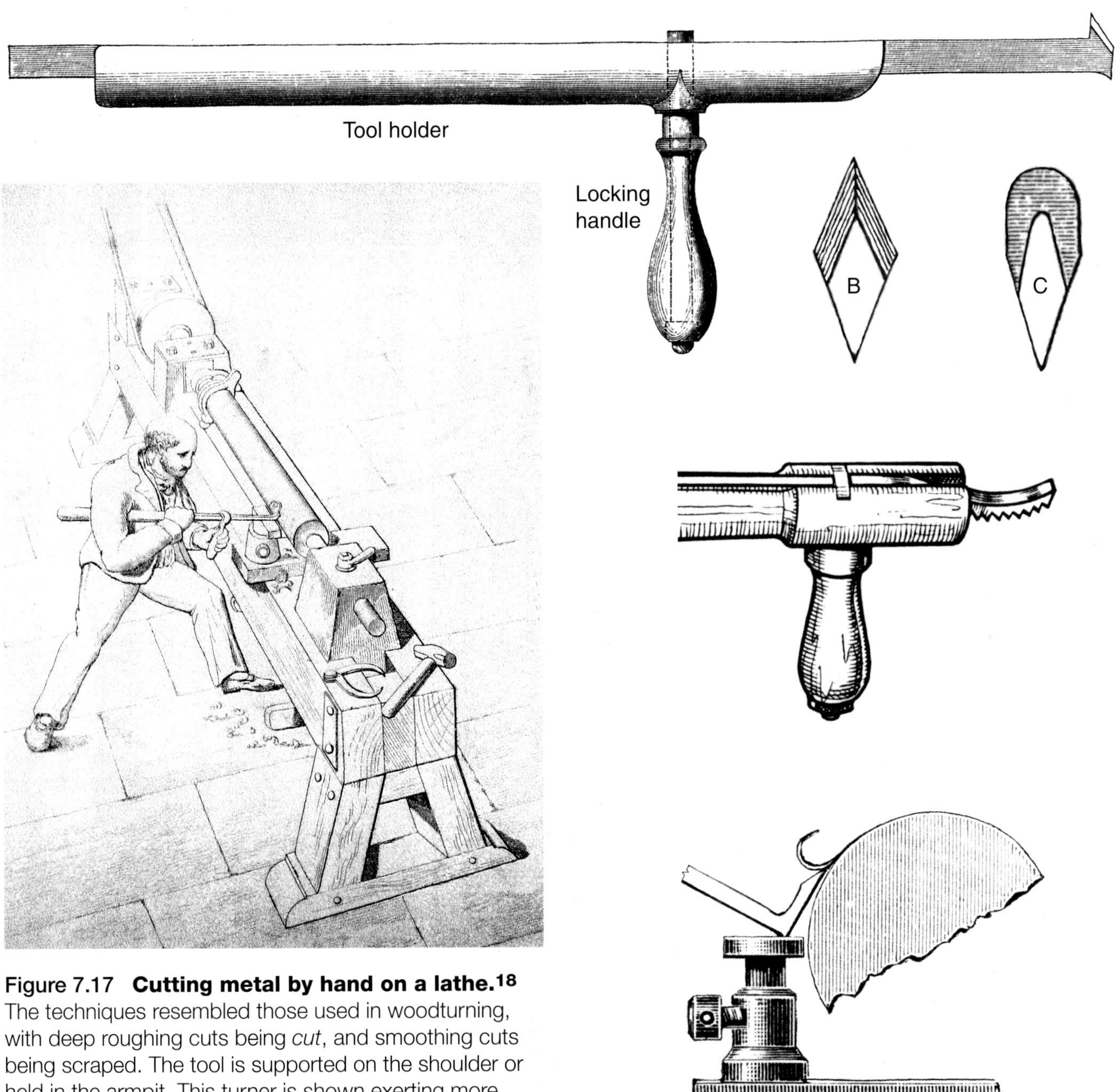

Figure 7.17 Cutting metal by hand on a lathe.[18] The techniques resembled those used in woodturning, with deep roughing cuts being *cut*, and smoothing cuts being scraped. The tool is supported on the shoulder or held in the armpit. This turner is shown exerting more effort than necessary because this illustration was paired with that in figure 7.18 to illustrate the ease by which metal is turned with a cutter held on a slide rest.

When *cutting* wood in the lathe the cutting force is applied by the turner thrusting along the tool. With the much higher forces which have to be applied to turn off metal, the tool tip was levered. To create a steady fulcrum the underside of the tool tip was pointed (*top right*) or serrated (*center right*) to bite into the toolrest which was a horizontal surface of flat wrought (soft) iron (*bottom right*).

Northcott explains[19] that the tool shown *top* is the ordinary hook tool used for roughing wrought iron, steel, cast iron, and malleable iron. The tool blade slides in a groove in the holder, and was locked in position by twisting the handle. The angular tip *B* was used to rough small workpieces; and to true ends, the sides of collars, and flat shoulders. Tip *C* with the rounded cutting edge was used entirely for roughing.

Northcott's remarks on catching are worth quoting: "Beginners find it very difficult to prevent the tool 'catching in' and taking a much deeper bite than desirable. When this occurs in certain cases the operator is lifted off his feet before he knows what the matter is." And "what the matter is" is that the turner presented his tool with too much clearance.

7.3 THE MODERN ERA OF THREAD CUTTING

During the eighteenth and nineteenth centuries the manufacturing focus was on metal. The demise of the hand turning of metal was forced by the development of machine tools and better tool steels which enabled and beds and metal slides to be made accurately and relatively cheaply (figures 7.18 and 7.19).

In the threading of metal, the traversing mandrel was further refined (figure 7.20), but chasing, in which a cutter is traversed along a rotating workpiece, was more flexible and more efficient. The screw-cutting device pictured in figure 7.21 and developed by Jesse Ramsden (1735–1800) chased accurate threads. However it was complicated and limited despite its clever sidestepping of the need for an accurate lead screw. Fortunately the ideal threading machine for general use had been foreseen by the beginning of the eighteenth century; it was a cutter mounted on a cross slide, with the cross slide mounted on a carriage driven along bed by an accurate lead screw driven from the headstock spindle

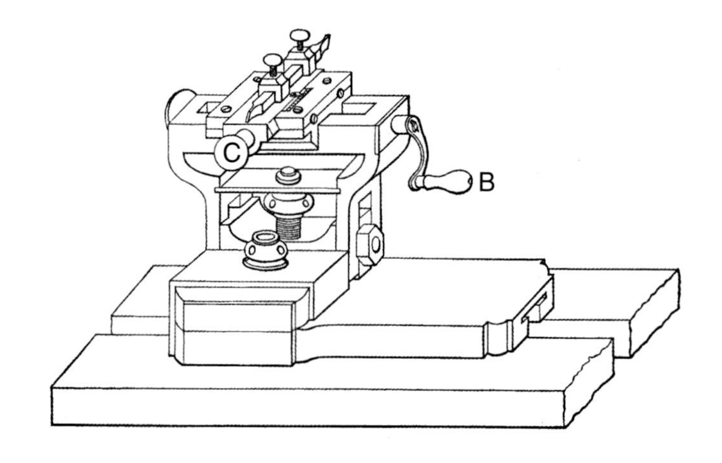

Figure 7.19 A compound slide of about 1800 pictured in plate XXXI of Bergeron volume II, and reproduced as figure 9 on page 50 of John Jacob Holtzapffel, *The Principles & Practice of Ornamental or Complex Turning* (1894; reprint, New York: Dover publications,1973). With the slide fixed onto a lathe bed as shown, cutter movement along the bed is controlled with the handle *B*, and the depth of cut with knob *C*.

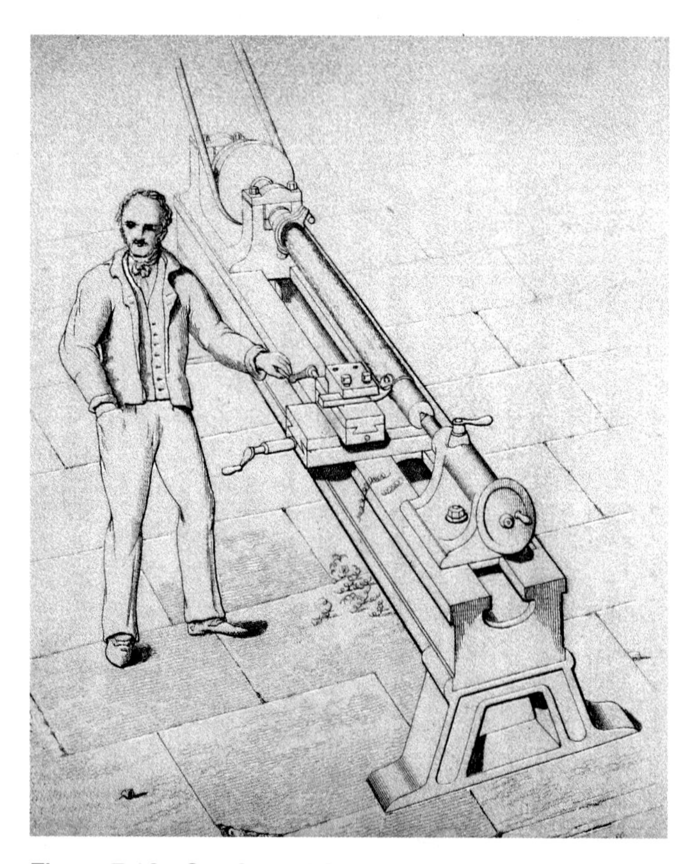

Figure 7.18 Cutting with a compound slide. This illustration was originally printed alongside that in figure 7.17 to demonstrate the ease of turning metal with a compound slide when compared with the effort required for hand turning.

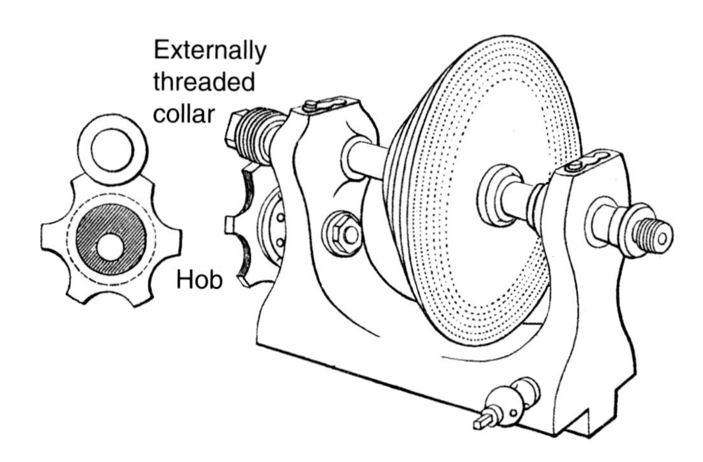

Figure 7.20 A traversing-mandrel headstock using loose collars in place of the threaded sections on the headstock spindle shown in figures 7.14 and 7.15.[20] Each loose collar has an external thread of a particular pitch. The threaded lunettes have been replaced by a hob which has six semicircular recesses. Each recess is threaded to mate with a particular collar.

To cut a thread on a workpiece chucked on the right-hand spindle nose, the collar with the thread of the desired pitch is locked onto the projecting left-hand end of the spindle. After rotating the hob until the recess with the mating thread is upwards, the hob is raised using the eccentric until the recess and collar mesh. Rotating the headstock spindle will then cause it to also move axially, and a fixed or rotating cutter to cut a thread with the same pitch as that of the collar on the workpiece.

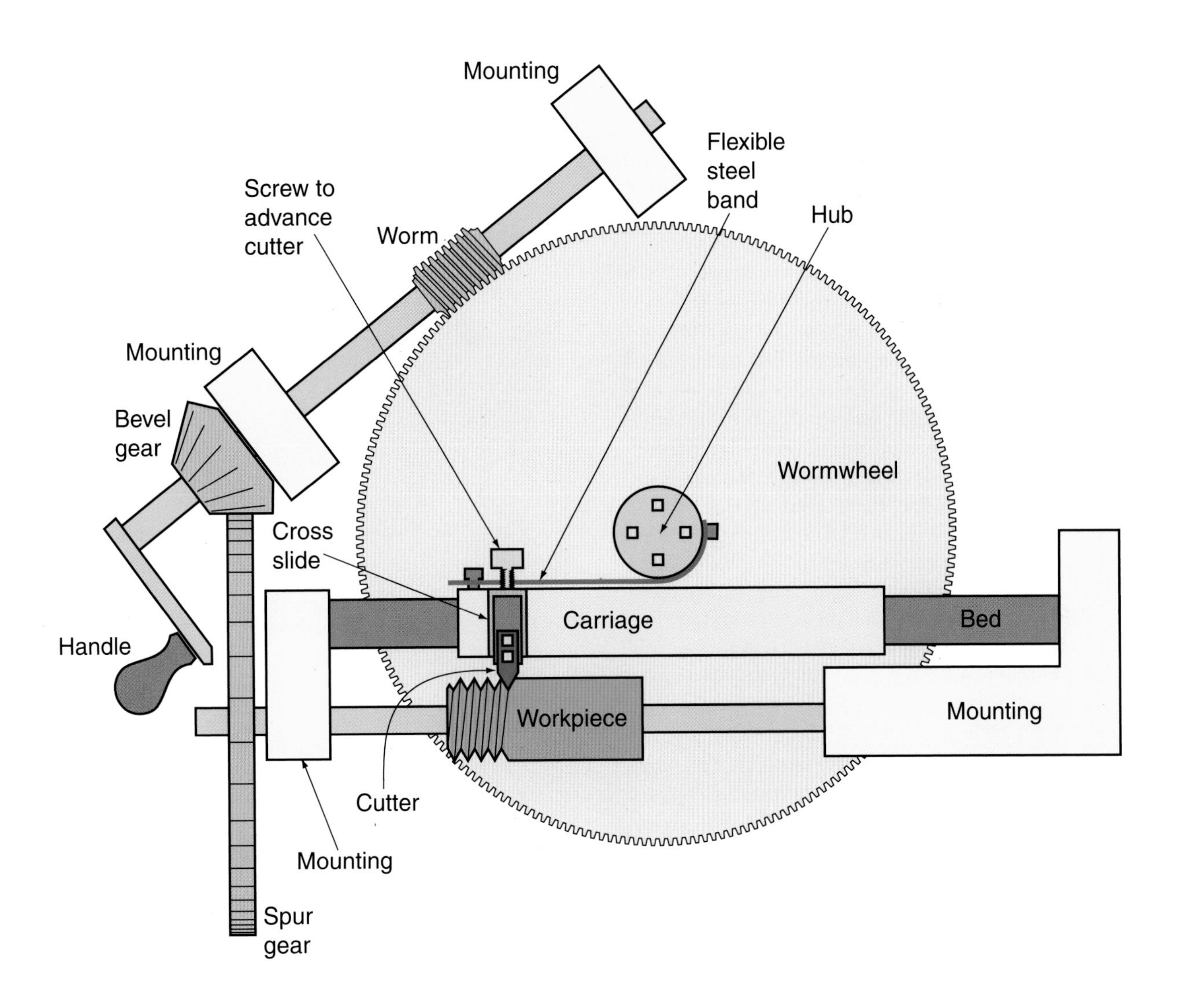

Figure 7.21 **Jesse Ramsden's screw-cutting machine of 1778.**[21] Although the worm is a thread, it is here used only as a reduction gear. This machine does not therefore depend upon a threaded component such as a master or lead screw to govern the pitch cut on the workpiece.

Turning the handle clockwise (looking from the left) rotates the bevel gear. The bevel gear in turn rotates the spur gear and the workpiece counterclockwise. (The workpiece is fixed onto the spindle driven by the spur gear).

Turning the handle clockwise also rotates the worm, which in turn rotates the large wormwheel and its hub counterclockwise. Fixed to the hub is a flexible steel band which is attached to a tool-holding carriage which is thereby pulled along a guide bed to the right. The gearing was such that 600 turns of handle traversed the carriage 5 in. (125 mm). The pitch of the thread cut on the workpiece was varied by varying the diameter of the hub.

through a gear train. Its embodiment is the engine lathe. This, the essential machine tool, can cut accurate screws of many pitches, and in a range of diameters and lengths only limited by the lathe's swing over the carriage and length between centers. However the development of the engine lathe was not well advanced until early in the nineteenth century. The saga started in Sweden, moved to France, developed in England, and culminated in America.

The evidence for the first engine lathe is in an unillustrated manuscript of 1710 by Swede Christopher Polhem. After describing how the rollers for rolling strip were forged, the manuscript continues: "Thereafter the rollers are set aside for turning. This is best done with a turning lathe run by a small waterwheel. The cutting tool is held by means of a block [carriage], which is gradually drawn forwards along the roller by a long screw and controlled by the rolling master's own hand. However, it can also be done so that the waterwheel itself is used to turn the screw".

Polhem also describes the making of lathe lead screws. A pattern or replica was first made in hard wood. The wooden screw and the length of round steel bar which was to become the lathe lead screw were mounted end-to-end between centers. A combined cutter and follower, perhaps similar to that in figure 7.144 or 7.145, was then used in many passes to chase the thread into the steel shaft. The steel screw was then mounted alone between centers and rotated slowly to allow the thread to be dressed with files. Finally the screw was hardened and tempered.

The lathe technology which Polhem described seems to have gone unnoticed because the next appearance of a lathe with a carriage driven by lead screw is in France. Jacques de Vaucanson (1709–1782) built a lathe between 1765 and 1780 which is still extant. Also in the Conservatoire des Arts et Metiers in Paris is the first engine lathe built by Francois Senot in 1795. It incorporates change gearing so that the rotation of the headstock spindle (and workpiece) can be transmitted directly to the lead shaft which in turn drives the tool-holding carriage along the bed. By varying the change gearing, the ratio of the rotational speed of the headstock spindle to that of the lead shaft can be altered, and different thread pitches cut.

By the end of the eighteeth century Britain had become the center of engineering progress. In 1796 in Birmingham the world's first comprehensive heavy-engineering works was opened to build Watt's steam engines. At that time Henry Maudslay (figure 7.22) was working in a factory almost as illustrious, that devoted to manufacturing Joseph Bramah's patent lock.

Refused a wage rise, Maudslay left Bramah is 1797 and opened his own business in London. Like Ramsden, Maudslay realised the importance of accurate screws. He built an apparatus in which an inclined knife incised the thread into wood or soft metal.[22] (An inclined knife is closely related to the thread pins of the "nut" in figure 7.3). Maudslay then hand cut the thread and used the resulting screw as a

Figure 7.22 **Henry Maudslay (1771–1831).** *Courtesy Science Museum, London.*

Figure 7.23 **Sir Joseph Whitworth (1803–1887).**[23]

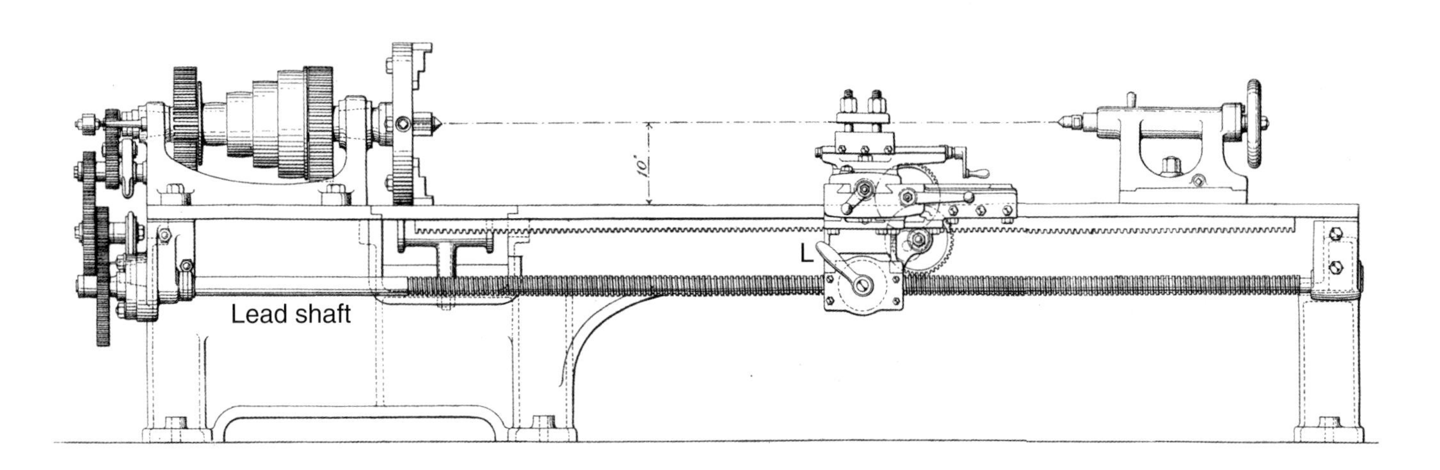

Figure 7.24 **An engine lathe,** originally pictured in plate V of Wilfrid J. Lineham, *A Text-Book of Mechanical Engineering* (London; Chapman & Hall Ltd, 5th ed,1900). The change gears connecting the headstock spindle to the lead shaft are mounted on the left-hand end of the lathe, and were supplied loose before gearboxes became standard (figure 7.26). This arrangement for the change gears was introduced by Richard Roberts in Manchester in 1818.[24]

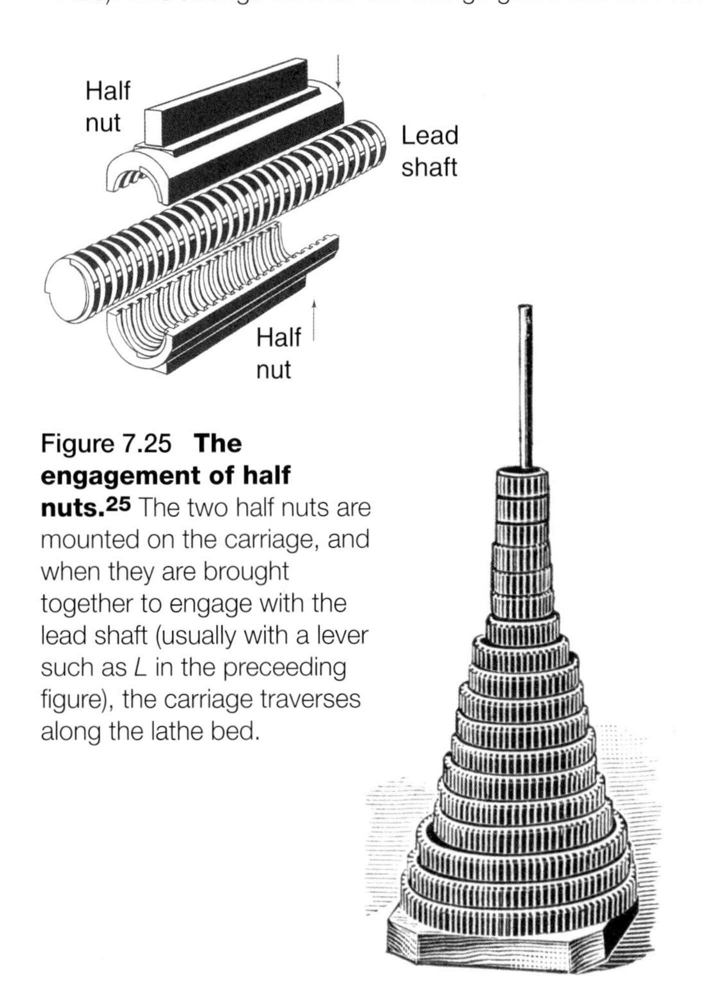

Figure 7.25 **The engagement of half nuts.**[25] The two half nuts are mounted on the carriage, and when they are brought together to engage with the lead shaft (usually with a lever such as *L* in the preceeding figure), the carriage traverses along the lathe bed.

Figure 7.26 **Change gears** allow the lathe operator to vary the ratio between the speeds of the headstock spindle and the carriage lead shaft, and so vary the pitch of the helix cut.[26]

Figure 7.27 **William Sellers (1824–1905).**[27] *Engraving courtesy Linda Hall Library of Sciences, Engineering and Technology, Kansas City.*

lead screw in his lathe to cut screws and to generate further lead screws. In 1800 Maudslay built a second screw-cutting lathe. It had a single, permanently-installed lead screw, and like Senot's lathe, used change gears to cut screws of different pitches. Maudslay standardized the threads used in the machines he built, and produced the necessary taps and dies which were later improved by Maudslay's ex-employee Joseph Clement(s) (1779–1844).

Maudslay's work on screw threads had lead to each major manufacturer standardizing its own threads, but there was still no interchangeability between the threads of individual manufacturers at the time of Maudslay's death. That giant step was due to Joseph Whitworth. He had worked for Maudslay, Charles Holtzappfel, and Clement between 1825 and 1833, before starting his own toolmaking business in Manchester. Whitworth saw the necessity for a national series of threads with definite pitches and similar forms. He measured the threads from all the leading manufacturers, and proposed a thread form with a 55° thread angle and rounded crest and root (figure 7.28) to a meeting of The Institution of Civil Engineers in 1841. Within twenty years the Whitworth (BSW) threads had been adopted throughout Britain and in America.

William Sellers (figure 7.27), born in Pennsylvania, has been called the Whitworth of America[28]. In 1864 in a paper titled "A System of Screw Threads and Nuts" he proposed a thread system which differed from Whitworth's. Sellers' thread had flat crests and flattened roots, and a thread angle of 60° not 55°. Sellers showed that his thread pattern would be more cheaply and accurately machined than Whitworth's. Sellers' paper also proposed standards for bolt-head and nut sizes. A committee was appointed to investigate Sellers' proposals, and reported favorably. In 1868 the Sellers thread was adopted for United States Government work, soon after became the standard thread pattern used in America, and was also called the United States Standard. It was adopted in 1898 by the International Congress for the standardization of screw threads in Zurich. At that same congress the Systeme Internationale (S.I.) thread was also adopted. This metric thread system is similar in form to Sellers'. The Sellers' form was revised in 1920 and until after WWII was called the American National thread form. It is now designated as Unified National.

The development of machine tools could not have progressed rapidly without complementary inprovements in tool steels. Benjamin Huntsman of Doncaster between 1743 and 1751 developed the art of making carbon tool steel of consistent and controllable quality by melting iron with a carbon source in a clay crucible. Robert Forrester Mushet (1811–1891) in 1868 in Gloucestershire then discovered that the addition of tungsten (later analysed as 7% by weight) produced a crucible steel which was self-hardening and possessed superior cutting properties. After Mushet's Titanic Steel Company failed, his steel was manufactured in Sheffield by Samuel Osborne & Co. and marketed as R. Mushet's Special Steel. Mushet's steel was used by the Midvale Steel Company of Pennsylvania. Its president William Sellers supported the twenty-six years of research by Frederick W. Taylor starting at Midvale in 1880 and continuing at Bethlehem Steel Works.[29] This research hugely advanced the efficiency of machining and the development of high-speed steels.

The developments in engineering and particularly in the threading of metals has greatly influenced the threading of wood. The introduction of fast-rotating cutters driven via an overhead early in the nineteenth century also enabled threads with better surfaces to be cut and allowed a wider range of woods to be threaded successfully. The remaining sections in this chapter, except 7.9, explore the many ways to produce threads in wood.

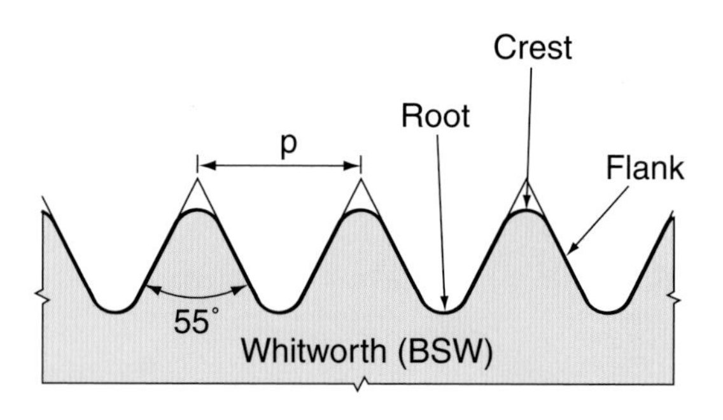

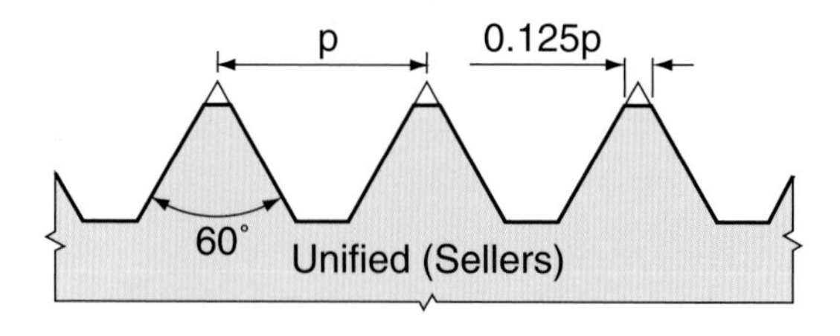

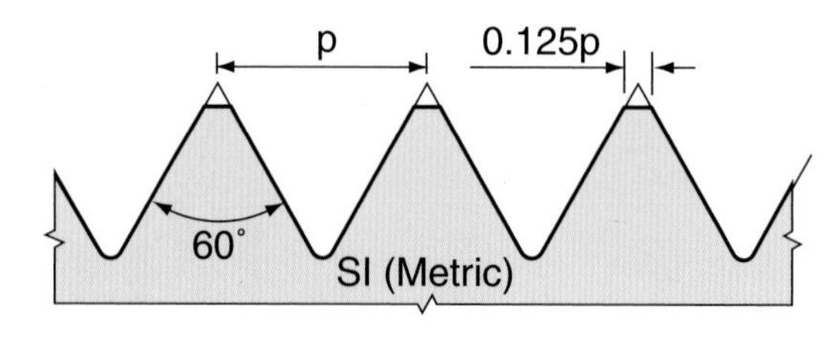

Figure 7.28 **The Whitworth, Unified, and SI screw thread forms.** The pitch of these threads, *p*, is defined in the next figure.[30]

7.4 THREAD GEOMETRY AND NOMENCLATURE

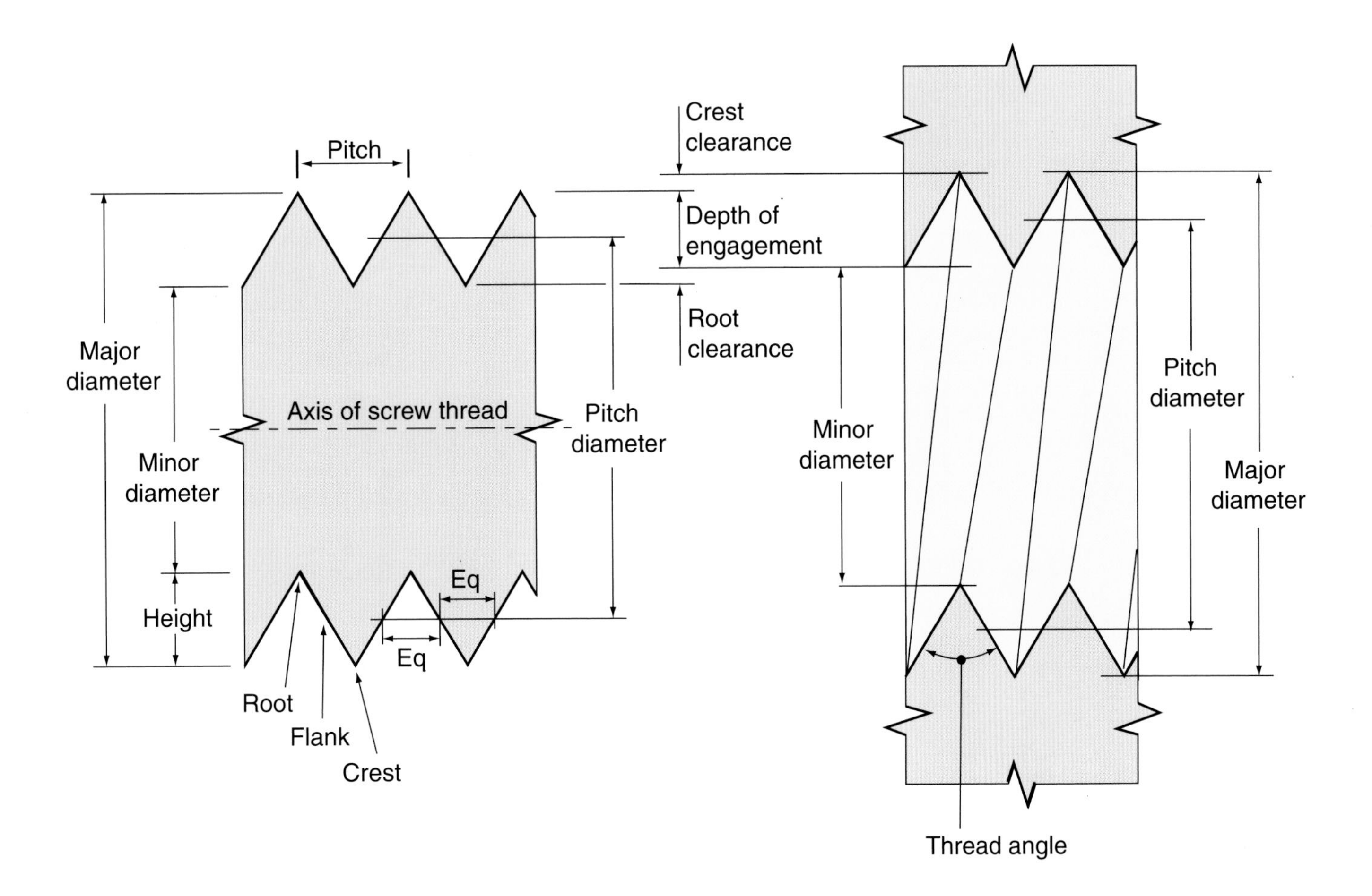

Figure 7.29 **The geometry and nomenclature of screw threads shown in longitudinal section.** This thread is single, and of sharp-V form. Its parts and dimensions are defined below:

Crest The outer surface joining the two flanks of a thread.

Crest clearance The distance in a thread assembly, measured perpendicularly to the axis, between the crest of a thread and the root of its mating thread.

Flank The sloping side of a thread connecting a crest to a root.

Height The height of a thread assumes that there is no truncation of the root or crest and that the thread is of sharp V-form. It can be calculated using the formula, height = pitch x cosine (0.5 x thread angle).

Lead The distance a screw thread advances axially in one turn. On a single-thread screw the lead and pitch are equal; on a double-thread screw the lead is twice the pitch.

Major diameter The largest diameter of a screw thread.

Minor diameter The smallest diameter of a screw thread.

Nominal size The designation used for the purpose of general identification. It is usually similar in size to the major diameter.

Pitch The distance from a point on a screw thread "tooth" to the corresponding point on the next thread "tooth" measured parallel to the axis.

Root The inner surface joining the adjacent flanks of a thread.

Thread angle The angle included between the flanks of the thread measured in an axial plane. It is 55° for Whitworth threads, $47^1/_2$° for British Association threads recommended for diameters below $^1/_4$ in., and 60° for Unified and S.I. threads. The 60° thread angle is preferred for wood.

Truncation The distance measured perpendicular to the axis between a sharp V-shaped root or crest and the cylinder which bounds the actual root or crest (figure 7.31). The root and crest truncations are not necessarily equal.

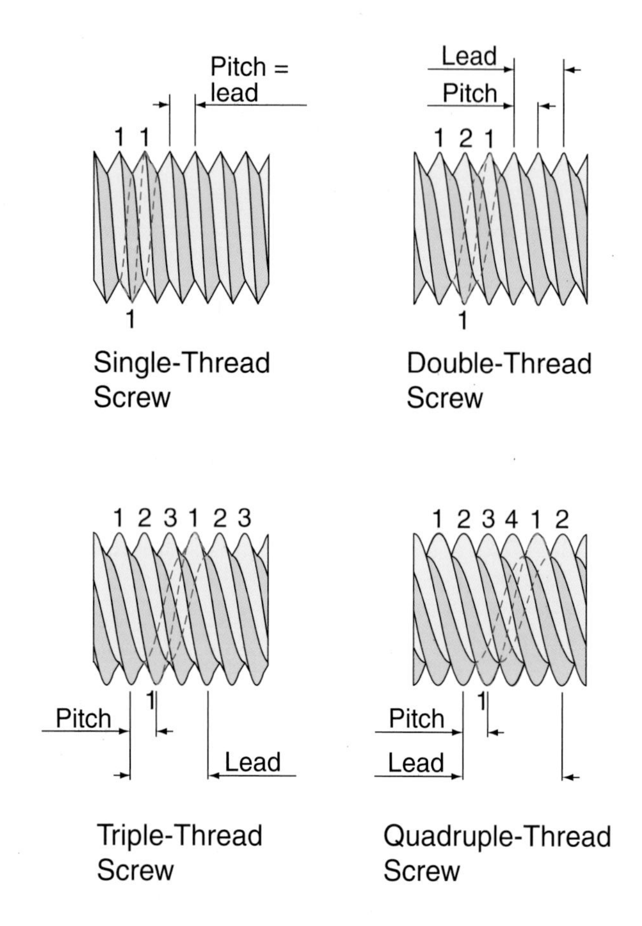

Figure 7.30 Pitch and lead, here illustrated with threads of V-form. The lead, the distance a screw advances in one turn, equals the pitch x number of threads. The pitch equals the distance between two adjacent thread crests irrespective of whether the crests belong to the same or to different threads.

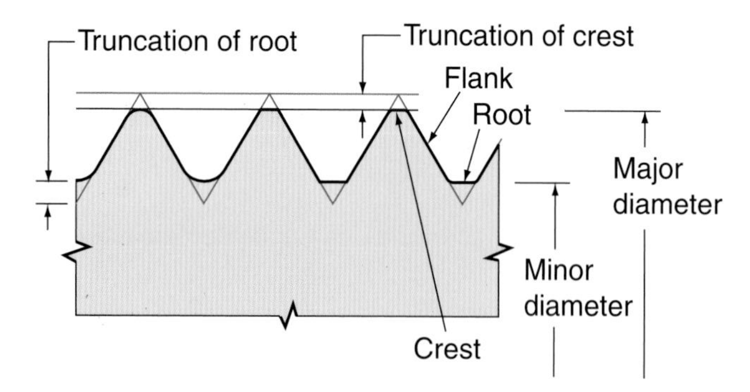

Figure 7.31 Truncation is usual with both male and female threads. *Left to right*: crests and roots are usually strengthened by being round, flat, or flat with rounded transitions into the flanks. Truncation also prolongs the life of thread-forming cutters.

When cutting threads in wood, pointed crests break away. They are also vulnerable during the life of the thread. It is better to leave flat crests by not cutting all the cylindrical surface of the workpiece away.

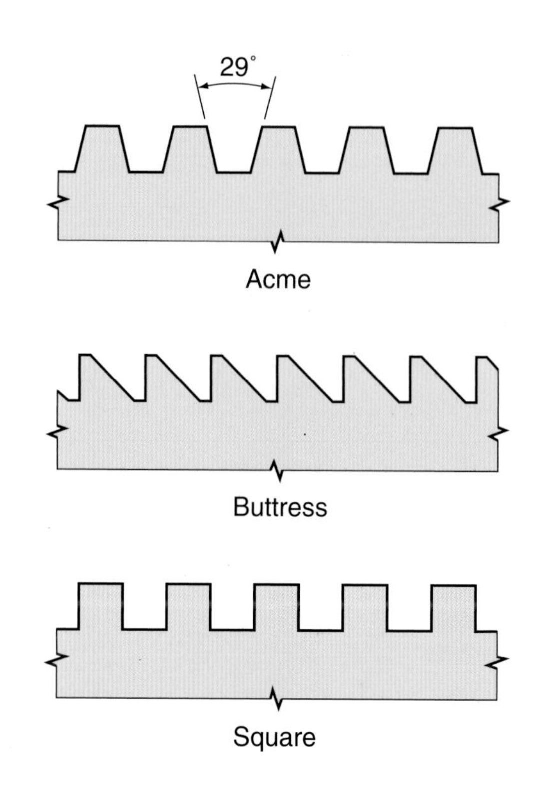

Figure 7.32 Three thread forms used in engineering. The Acme thread has largely superseded the square. The buttress thread is used where large forces are applied in only one direction, for example in woodwork vices.

7.5 CUTTING THREADS, THE BASIC METHODS

The four basic techniques for cutting threads in wood are listed earlier on page 130, and are repeated below:

1. Keep the workpiece stationary while simultaneously revolving the cutter around the workpiece surface and traversing the cutter parallel to the workpiece's axis. The cutter can either be fixed or rotating in this and the three following techniques.
2. Keep the cutter stationary while simultaneously revolving and traversing the workpiece surface past it.
3. Revolve the cutter while traversing the workpiece past it. This method is used in dowellors (*Woodturning Methods* figures 3.33 to 3.35) which use a helical cut to form the dowel surface, but does not seem to be used to cut threads.
4. Rotate the workpiece while traversing the cutter.

The thread quality should not be affected by which of the

four techniques is used, but is affected by other factors, primarily: the type and condition of the wood; the wood's grain direction; the sharpness, rake and side rake of the cutter; whether the cutter is fixed or rotating, and if rotating in what direction; and the form of the thread. These factors are introduced below.

Wood quality Very hard, cohesive, crisp-cutting woods thread best. Those which have their own internal oils or waxes, such as lignum vitae and olive, are especially suitable. For softer woods, producing the thread by deformation rather than by the cruder forms of cutting can be preferable. Trial your proposed wood and threading technique if you are at all doubtful. If the trial is unsuccessful, you may be able to change to a more suitable threading method and/or wood, inlet rings of a more suitable wood (figure 7.33), or use threaded plastic or metal inserts (figures 7.34 and 7.51).

Moisture content Seasoned wood is harder and takes threads better. If there are significant changes in a wood's moisture content after threading, the wood will go oval in cross section, resulting in fits which change from loose to tight and back every 180° of relative rotation between the male and female threads. Therefore if you are producing, say, a threaded box , you should rough-turn and hollow both the lid and the base, and allow both to fully relax and season before you thread and finish-turn them.

Temperature If you wish to produce a thread by deformation, you should heat the wood and the tool to above 80°C, the softening temperature of the lignin which binds the cellulose fibers together. This will make the wood plastic. When the wood cools the lignin will set and the deformation will become permanent.

Impregnation You may be able to improve the thread quality by impregnating the wood to make it harder and more cohesive. I tried impregnating camphor laurel, a hardwood

Figure 7.34 Plastic threads, here from a milk container. Because with screwing you can exert such massive axial forces, overtightening can separate a plastic thread section from its wooden socket or spigot.[31]

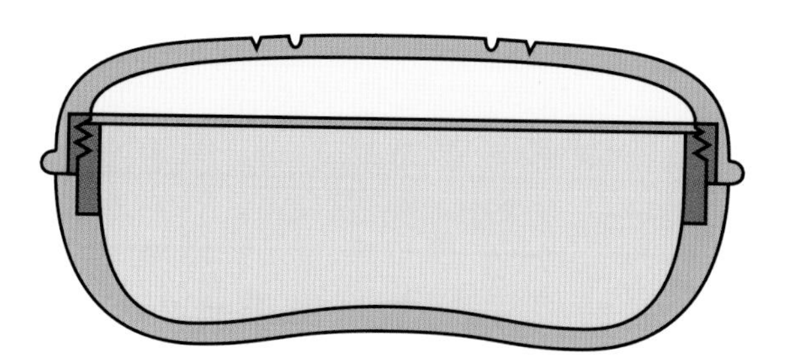

Figure 7.33 Inlet rings. A diametrical section through a box where wood suitable for threading was inlet into a main wood which was too soft or too contorted in its grain to thread well. The wood which is inlet should usually be similar in color to the main wood.

of average hardness and grain structure with olive oil, slightly diluted dishwashing liquid, slightly thinned polyurethane varnish, slightly diluted PVA glue, and thin cyanoacrylate glue. Only the first three penetrated the wood to any worthwhile depth. Unfortunately I found no significant reduction in damage when cutting the thread crests with any of the treatments, but this does not necessarily mean that the technique is without potential.

Grain direction Threads can be cut into axially- or radially-grained wood, although more easily and generally of higher quality into the latter. However for male threads of small diameters the grain of the workpiece must be axial or it will shear too readily.

Cutter type Wood is a relatively soft non-cohesive material with a tendency to spilt along the grain and the medullary rays. A sharp, fast-rotating *cutting* cutter will produce a cleaner thread than a fast-rotating scraping cutter. With either method you will minimize crest damage if you cut down into the wood or backcut (figure 7.79). Rotating cutters give a cleaner thread than a stationary or slowly moving *cutter*. A fixed scraping cutter will produce the worst thread, but in suitable woods the thread quality can still be good.

Lubrication With devices such as taps, dies, and screw boxes which have built-in guidance to determine the pitch, lubrication lessens the force which you have to apply to cut the thread and reduces damage to the thread.

Thread form Figure 7.31 introduced thread truncation and explained the advantages of leaving flat crests. To produce flat crests while still retaining ample engagement between the male and female threads you must:

1. Produce smooth male and female cylindrical surfaces of optimum and constant diameters.
2. Cut the threads parallel to the cylindrical surfaces, deep enough so that there is a substantial depth of engagement, but not so deep that all the original cylindrical surface is removed. Any truncation of the roots is determined by the form of the cutter.

Figures 7.35 and 7.36 detail the geometry and cutting of truncated threads.

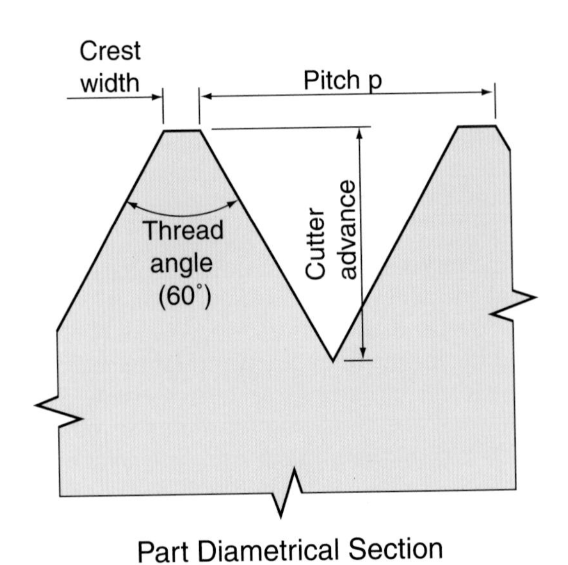

Figure 7.35 The geometry of flat thread crests. When you cut a thread with a V-shaped crest, crumbling and tear out will usually occur along the crest. There will be little or no tear out along the crest when the crest is left as a flat helical band of the original cylindrical surface.

For Metric and Unified series threads in metal the thread angle is 60°, and the crest width is 0.125 ($^1/_8$) of the pitch irrespective of the thread size. Whitworth threads have a rounded crest which is equivalent to a flat crest with a width of 0.167 ($^1/_6$) of the pitch.

Table 7.1 below tabulates the cutter advances required for various crest widths for single-start threads with sharp V-roots.

Table 7.1 The cutter advances required to achieve specified crest widths

Thread angle 60° (Unified and S.I. series)		*Thread angle 55° (Whitworth)*	
Crest width	*Cutter advance*	*Crest width*	*Cutter advance*
0	0.87p	0	0.89p
0.1p p/10	0.78p	0.1p p/10	0.80p
0.125p p/8	0.76p	0.125p p/8	0.77p
0.167p p/6	0.72p	0.167p p/6	0.74p
0.2p p/5	0.69p	0.2p p/5	0.71p
0.25p p/4	0.65p	0.25p p/4	0.67p

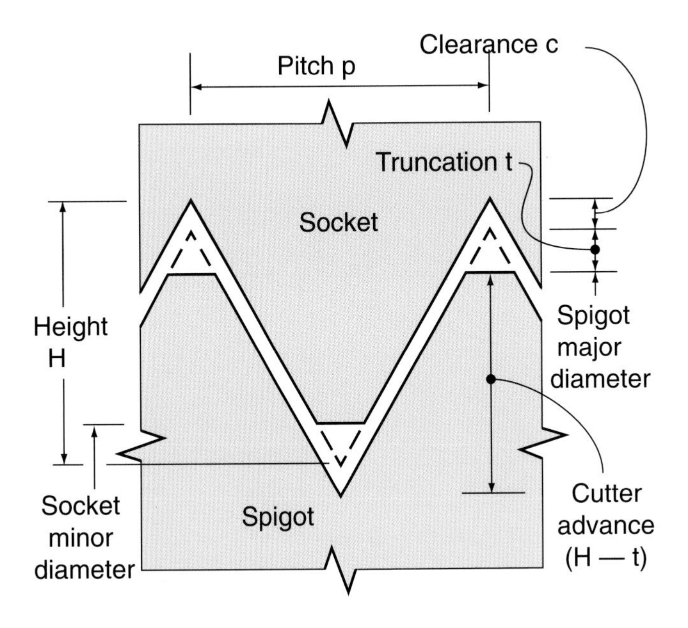

Figure 7.36 Thread mating. The diagram is a part diametrical section through a threaded socket and spigot, and the thread form is the sharp-V with straight crest truncations.

The importance of straight crests has been described. Another variable is thread clearance—without any, screwing will be very stiff. Both truncation and clearance are determined by the socket and spigot diameters you cut, and by how far you advance the cutter when you cut each thread. (I assume throughout that the cutter advance is the same for both the male and female threads; and that if the cutter produces truncated roots, this root truncation will not foul the crests of the other thread).

From the diagram:

$$\text{Socket minor diameter} = \text{Spigot major diameter} - 2(H - t) + 2c + 2t$$

$$= \text{Spigot major diameter} + 4t + 2c - 2H$$

For say a UNC thread in metal the standard truncation is 0.125H (= 0.125 x 0.87p = 0.11p), and the clearance is approximately the same. Using these values in wood for a 60° thread angle, and with a cutter advance from the preceeding figure of 0.76p

$$\text{Socket minor diameter} = \text{Spigot major diameter} - 1.1p$$

When visually inspecting a just-cut thread it is almost impossible to measure or judge the cutter advance directly. It is however relatively easy to assess the width of a flat crest as a proportion of the pitch. You can then use table 7.1 to estimate the true cutter advance you used.

7.6 CUTTING THREADS IN STATIONARY WOOD

You can cut a thread around the outside of a stationary cylindrical workpiece or around a hole by simultaneously revolving a cutter around and traversing it along the workpiece. This method is used in hand-carving; also with taps, dies, and screw boxes, devices which have built-in features which dictate the pitch, form, and diameters of the thread (figure 7.37).

Figure 7.37 A screw-fixed knob from a late nineteenth-century chest of drawers. The male thread on such a screw can be cut with a screwbox, the female thread inside a knob can be cut with a tap.

Having the knob screw fixed allowed the drawer front and knob to be French-polished separately and more efficiently, and is convenient if you need to refinish the drawer front or replace a damaged knob.

7.6.1 HAND CARVING MALE THREADS

Hand carving is a sensible option when you need to produce short lengths of thread, particularly when coarse and non-standard.

The first step is usually to set out and carve the male thread—a process similar to hand carving the helical bines on Jacobean-style legs and spindles.[32] A male thread can be set out directly onto the wood (figure 7.38), or marked from templates or similar (figures 7.39 to 7.43). The carving is surprisingly easy as shown in figures 7.44 and 7.45.

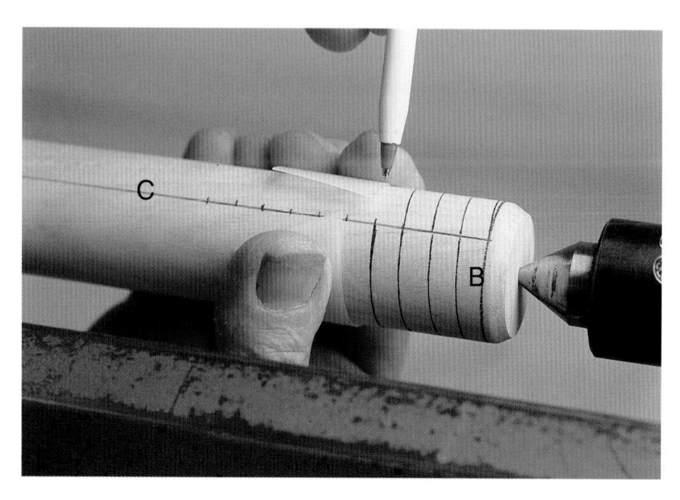

Figure 7.38 Setting out a male thread directly. I use a fine biro to draw on the wood—pencil tends to smudge during the carving. The steps are:

1. With the lathe running draw a reference circle *B* at one end of the thread.
2. Draw a horizontal line *C* along the cylinder using the top of a horizontal toolrest positioned close to the cylinder as a guide for the biro.
3. If the cylinder is large in diameter, you could draw a second line *D* along the cylinder on the opposite side. (If you have an indexing facility, use it to rotate the cylinder the 180°).
4. Dot where the crest crosses line *C*. The dots should be pitch distance *p* apart, and are best marked from a ruler using running measurements from the reference circle *B*. You could also use dividers.
5. If you have drawn line *D*, measure half the pitch along from the reference circle, and then mark the other dots *p* apart where the crest crosses line *D*.
6. Using a length of flexible card or better plastic as its edge will not crush, mark the center of the crest through the dots. Slope the card or plastic so that the thread will have the correct hand.
7. On coarse threads the root or even the edges of the crest can be drawn similarly. On smaller threads these features are not drawn, but are sawn or carved "by eye".

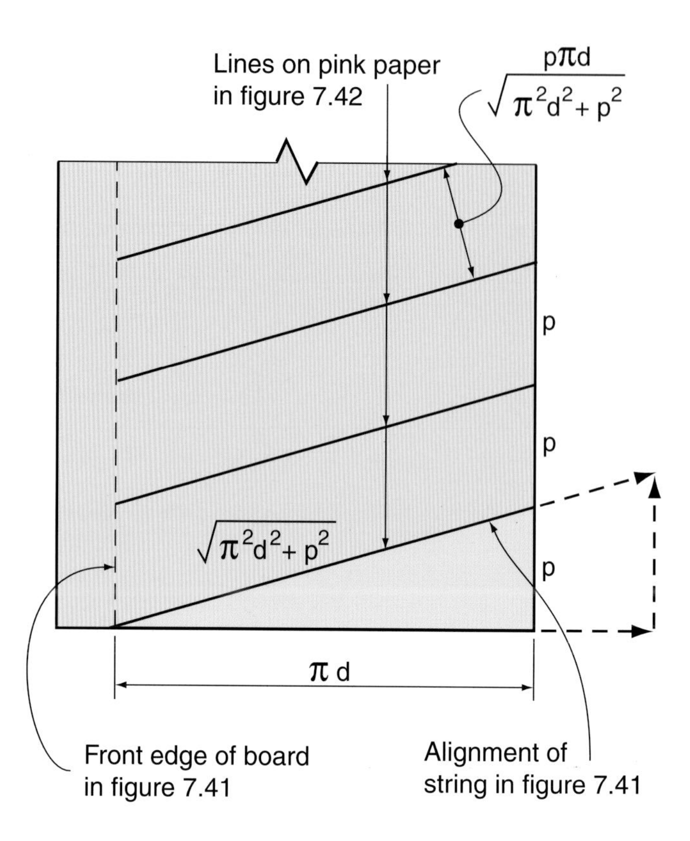

Figure 7.39 The geometry of templates. The dotted lines show how the long triangle used in the next figure is drawn. *d* is the major diameter of the male thread.

Figure 7.40 Setting out a male thread using a triangle of thin card with the geometry of the green triangle in the preceding figure. This method is a little innacurate because as the number of times the card is wound around increases, the pitch lengthens.

To use this method first wind the card around, then mark the helix of the crest from the angled edge of the card as you unwind the paper.

Figure 7.41 **Setting out a male thread using a taut string** smeared with a mixture of wax and a pigment, a method related to that described in the first century B.C. by Vitruvius.[33] The strips of grey cardboard are to prevent the workpiece seesawing on the string. The angle of the string is shown in figure 7.39.

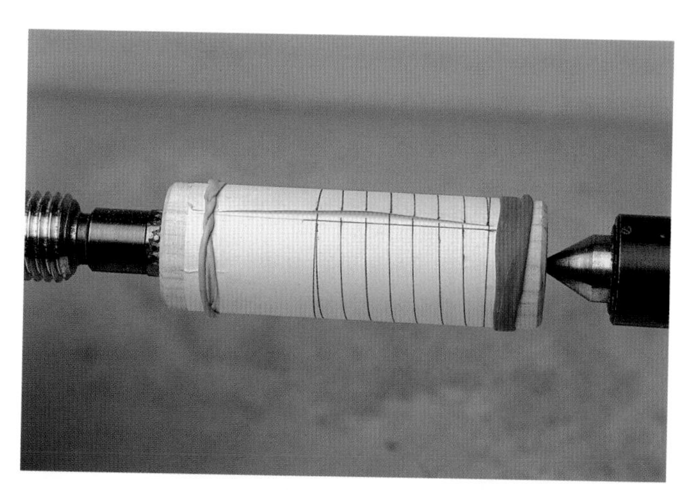

Figure 7.42 **Setting out a male thread using a band of paper with parallel lines drawn on it** as defined in figure 7.39.

Alternatively, for very large pitches you could wrap a long band of paper around the wood so that its edges touch. (The paper band's width is shown in figure 7.39).

Figure 7.43 **Marking a helix by cutting through the paper shown in the preceeding figure** with a sharp edge, here that of a skew chisel. The helix could define the root or the crest, and could also be marked by pricking through the line on the paper, or by using carbon paper between the pink paper and the wood.

Figure 7.44 **Hand sawing to the root** with a fine crosscut saw. I have not marked the root helix, and am sighting down the sides of the saw blade to keep it midway beween the adjacent sections of crest. If the thread pitch is large, you can draw the helix of the root, and saw along it with a strip of wood clamped to one side of the saw blade to act as a depth stop.

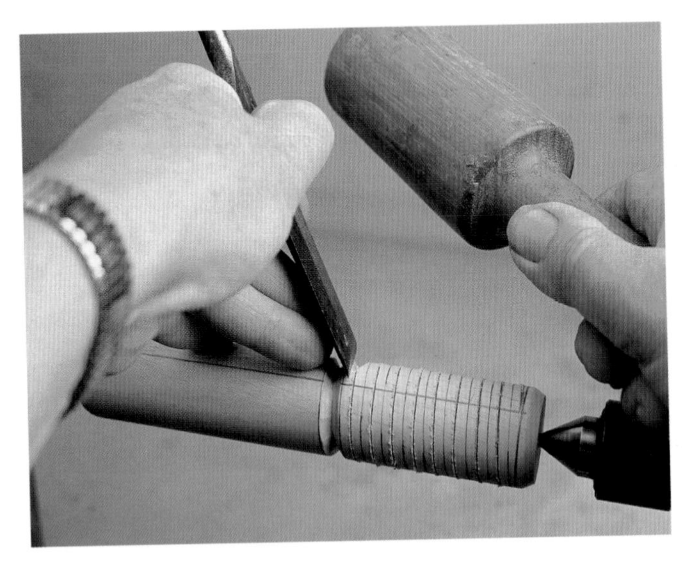

Figure 7.45 **Chopping the flanks.** I eye the crest width and thread angle. The final cuts can be made without a mallet.

7.6.2 HAND CARVING FEMALE THREADS

There are three ways to make a mating female thread by hand:

1. Conglutinate the workpiece with a diametrical paper joint. Bore the workpiece, split it along the paper joint, mark out and hand carve the female thread, then glue the workpiece back together (figure 7.46).
2. Make a nut with thread pins similar to that shown in figure 7.3 (figures 7.47 and 7.48).
3. Cast the female thread in a resin or a low-melting-point plastic or metal around the male thread. I have not described this method.

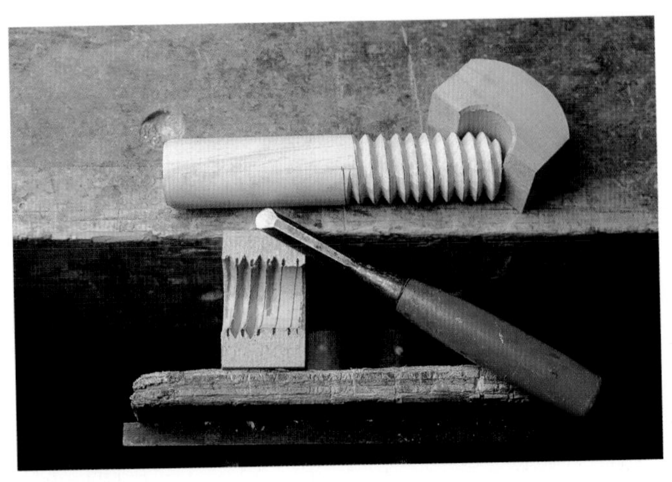

Figure 7.46 **Hand carving a female thread.** The steps are:

1. Glue together the two halves of the nut workpiece with a diametrical paper joint.
2. Bore a hole equal in diameter to the female thread's minor diameter (which should be a touch greater than the minor diameter of the male thread) axially through the workpiece. Also drill any holes for dowels or fasteners which will ensure that the two half nuts can later be easily and accurately registered.
3. Split the workpiece along the paper joint.
4. Mark the crest locations along both straight edges of the semicircular grooves.
5. Draw the lines of the crests on the curved surfaces of the grooves using the straight edge of a flexible strip of card or plastic.
6. Grind and hone a convex end on a chisel. It is then surprisingly simple to carve the threads.
7. Remove the paper from the joint surfaces, and glue the two halves of the workpiece back together inserting any registering dowels or fasteners.

The next two figures show making a "nut" with thread pins.

Figure 7.47 **Drilling for the thread pins.** The "nut" has been turned to a cylinder, bored to the male thread's major diameter, and marked outside with the root helix.

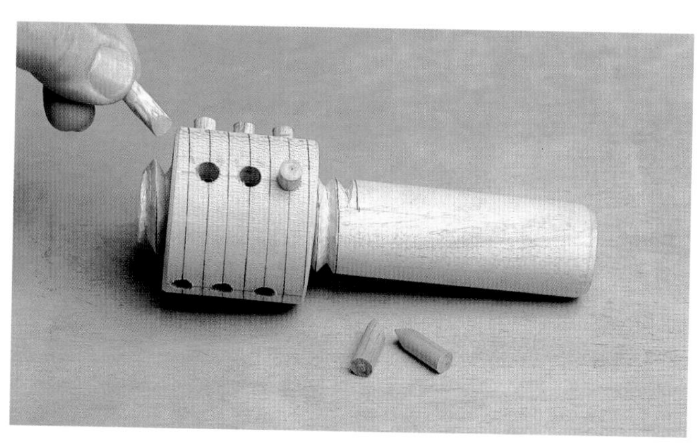

Figure 7.48 **Inserting the thread pins** with the male thread in place. To avoid gluing the male thread into the "nut", put glue only on the pins, not into the holes. The thread pins were cupchuck turned, with each pin's end being sharpened before the pin was parted off.

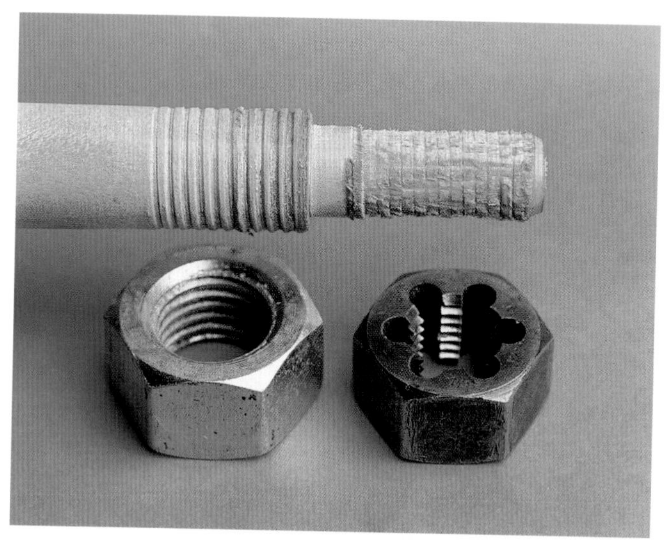

Figure 7.49 **Threads produced with a nut and a die.**

Left, a male thread made by deforming the heated surface wood with a heated and lubricated steel nut.

Right, the male thread cut using the engineers die is very poor with all but the densest woods as the thread shears close to the root. The spindle was first turned to diameters just less than the nut's and die's major diameters.

7.6.3 PRODUCING A MALE THREAD WITH A DIE, A NUT, OR A SCREW BOX

Male threads in wood can be cut with engineers dies (figure 7.49)—this property is exploited in the screw and spigot chucks invented by Bruce Leadbeatter (FOW, figure 7.5, and *Woodturning Methods*, figure 1.48). However on most woods, all the thread except the root will be sheared off during the cutting. A better solution in softer woods is to deform the surface wood into a male thread with a metal nut (also figure 7.49). On most woods, cutting the thread with a screw box should leave a good finish (figure 7.50).

Wooden screw boxes are fairly easy to make if you can readily cut the female thread. Each screw box is sold with a tap having the same thread as that which the screwbox cuts (figure 7.51). In wooden screw boxes, the accompanying tap is usually the one which was used to form the female thread in the screw box body.

Metal screw boxes are preferred for arduous use. Carl Heidtmann GmbH of Wuppertal, Germany, may be the only manufacturer of metal-bodied screw boxes.[34] They are available in a range of diameters up to 2½ in. (62 mm) and have two cutters. The front cutter should be adjusted to cut to about two thirds the depth of that of the rear cutter. The tap supplied with each screw box is of the type pictured in figures 7.6 and 7.56.

In addition to the screw box for general use, there is a second type for cutting a thread up to a flange (figures 7.53 and 7.54).

Both the cutting and deforming techniques could be applied to a radially-grained cylinder, but the wooden cylinder will usually shear either when producing the thread on it, or later when the cylinder is in use.

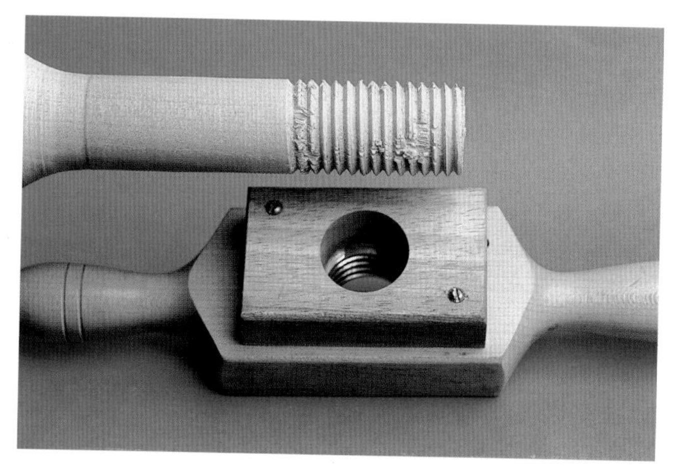

Figure 7.50 **A thread cut with a screw box.** The wood is kauri which is soft, squashy and crumbly. The male thread in figure 7.3 is in jelutong, a wood which is softer but cuts crisply, and which therefore has not crumbled during the threading.

Front View with Tap

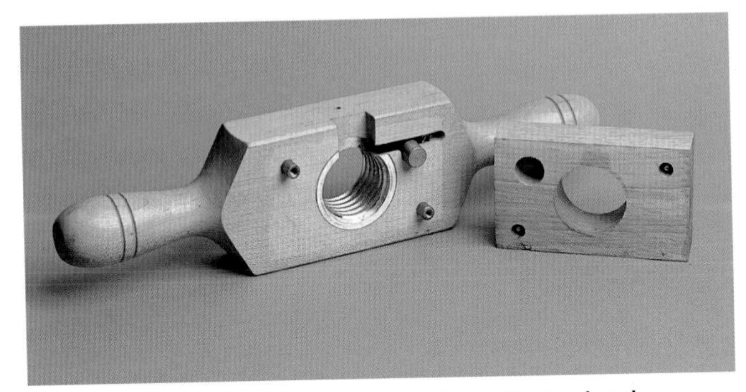

Front view with Front Plate Detached

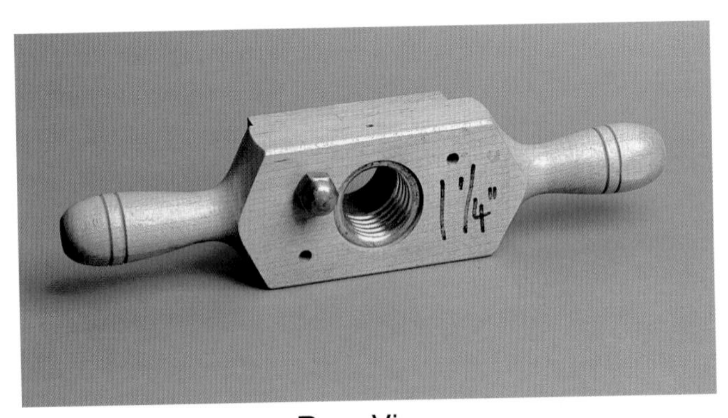

Rear View

Figure 7.51 A wooden screw box. The female thread in the body is machined into an aluminum lining. The tap is of tool steel. The front plate can be removed for threading up to a flange (figures 7.53 and 7.54).

A comprehensive article on the making of screw boxes is Richard Starr, "Wood Threads," *Fine Woodworking* (Spring 1977): pp. 22–28.

Figure 7.52 Cutting a thread with a screw box. To produce the cleanest threads the screw box cutter's advance should be adjusted to leave a narrow, flat crest. As you can only readily measure the minor diameter of the female thread in the main plate, the ideal major diameter of the spigot to be threaded is typically the minor diameter plus 1.1p (see the legend of figure 7.36). Fortunately you don't have to derive the spindle's major diameter in this way— just turn the spindle to slip nicely through the hole in the front plate. The required major diameter also ideally equals the nominal diameter of the screw box. It is best to trial cutter advance settings on waste wood.

One disadvantage of a screw box is that you cannot cut threads in two passes, advancing the cutter in between, because the first shallow thread will not pass throught the female thread in the screw box body. However, a sharp cutter cuts to the full depth with surprisingly ease.

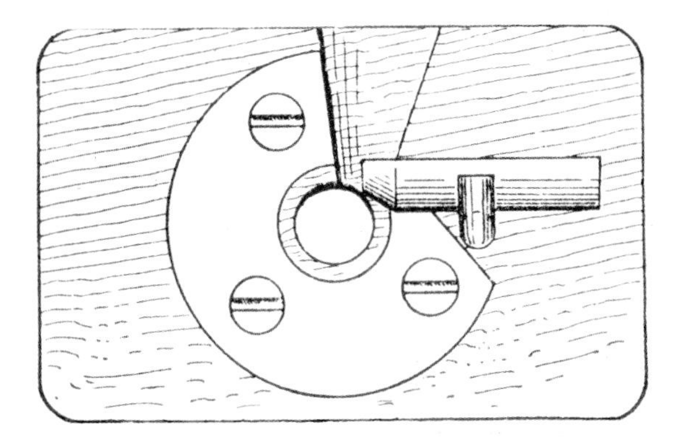

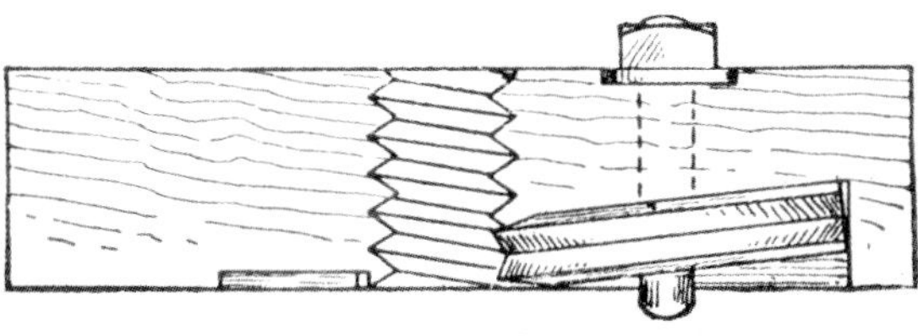

Figure 7.53 **A screw box used to extend or cut a thread up to a flange.** It can be used after the common type to cut the final length which the common type cannot reach, or alone. You may also be able to obtain the same facility by using a common screw box with its front cover plate temporarily removed.

Figure 7.54 **Cutting a thread up to a flange.**

Left, a flange from which projects a spigot which has been prepared for threading. The spigot has been turned to the appropriate major diameter. At the right-hand end there is a lead-in chamfer. At the left-hand end there is a groove with its left-hand flank vertical and its right-hand flank sloping. This recess ensures that the item will screw fully home into a female-threaded socket.

Right, the thread was cut with two passes of the screw box pictured in figure 7.51, the first with the front plate in place, the second with it removed. The section of thread cut in the first operation was damaged when screwing the screw box to the left for the second threading operation. It is therefore better and quicker to thread short projecting spigots only with a screw box suited or adapted for the purpose.

7.6.4 PRODUCING FEMALE THREADS WITH TAPS AND SCREWS

Engineers taps can be used to thread wood, but there are three tap types manufactured specifically for threading wood (figures 7.55 to 7.57). You can also make a tap from a bolt or screw (figure 7.58). However for soft and medium-hardness woods, machine screws (as opposed to wood screws) can be superior to taps, and cheaper. The grain direction of the workpiece also affects the ease of producing a thread, and its quality and durability.[34]

The desirability of leaving flat crests was detailed earlier. The diameter of the pilot hole should therefore be a touch bigger than the minor diameter of the tap. As the minor diameter is difficult to measure, the pilot-hole diameter can be looked up in an engineers tapping reference or be calculated (for a 60° thread) by deducting 1.1p from the tap's major (nominal) diameter.

To drill the optimum pilot-hole diameter you may need to source from both metric and inch drill sizes. Engineers suppliers will usually stock a much greater range of drill diameters than a local hardware store, for example in diametrical increments of 0.1 mm.

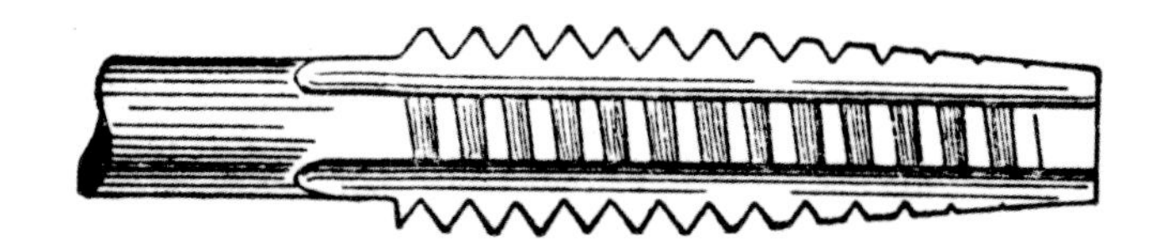

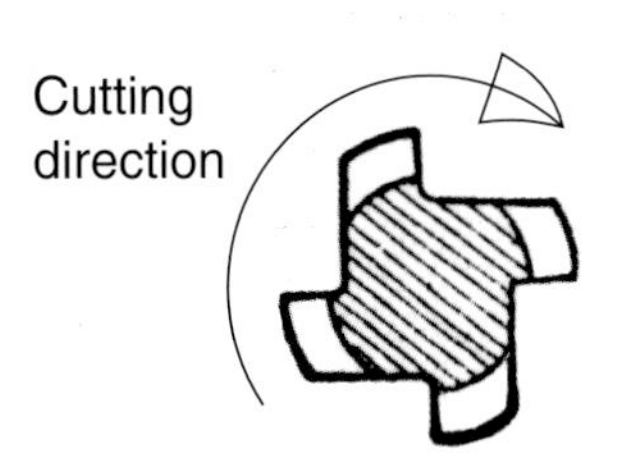

Figure 7.55 **A tap for wood,** similar to that shown in figure 7.5 and those used by engineers to thread metal. Taps produce better threads in radial grain than in axial grain (figures 7.59 and 7.60). Scanned from F.J. Camm, *Screw Cutting* (London: Cassell And Co., no date), p.173, figs. 171 and 172.

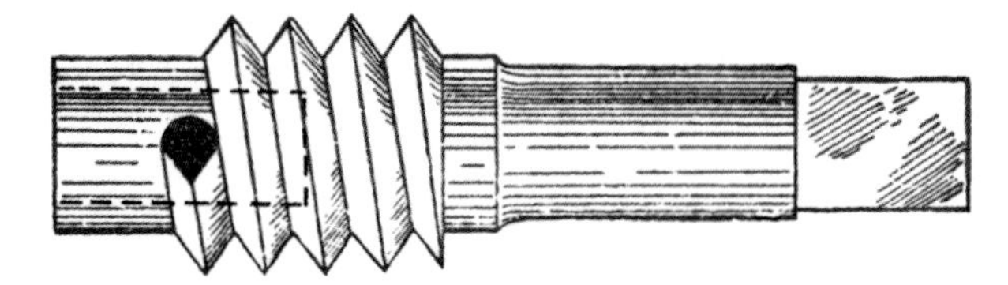

Figure 7.56 **A cutting tap for wood.** This design was pictured earlier in figure 7.6, and leaves a superior finish to those in the preceding and next two figures.

Figure 7.57 **The cutting tap supplied with the screwbox shown in figure 7.51.** It has a two long *cutting* edges.

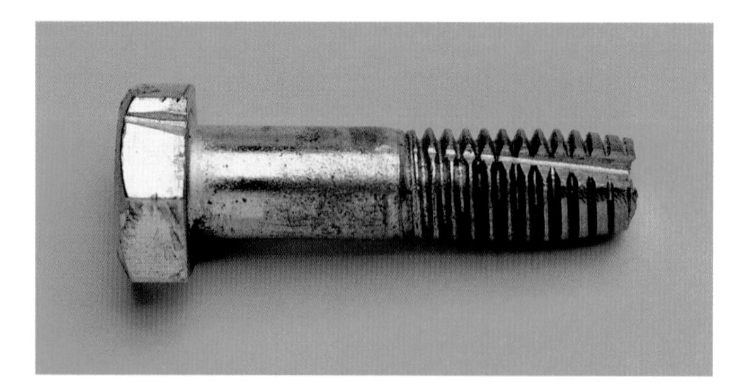

Figure 7.58 **Converting a fastener, here a machine screw, from a thread-deforming device into a thread-cutting device** by filing a groove and tapering the end of the screw.

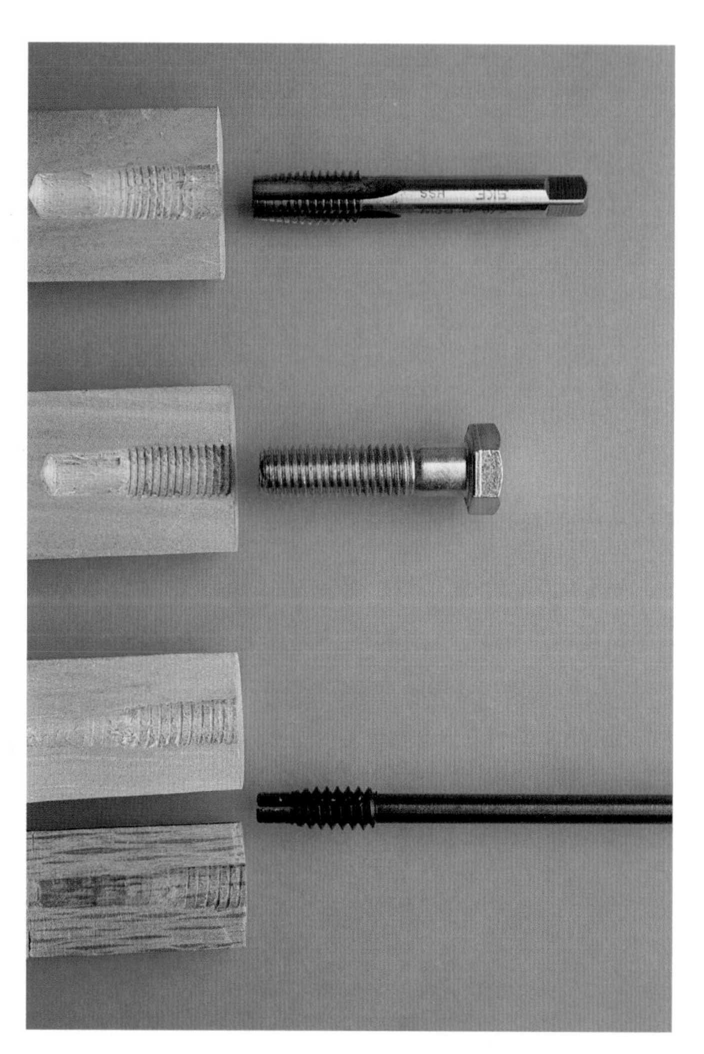

Figure 7.59 **Female threads in axially-grained woods,** here kauri, a soft, squashy softwood, and forest sheoak, hard and red-colored. The pilot hole should be bored to a diameter equal to or a touch greater than the minor diameter of the thread on the tap or screw.

Top and bottom, with all but the hardest woods the wood thread shears with the grain when using a tap.

Center, a superior thread is produced by deforming the wood with a screw. The wood is easier to deform if the hole and the screw are heated above 80°C to temporarily soften the lignin, and if hot oil or wax is used as a lubricant.

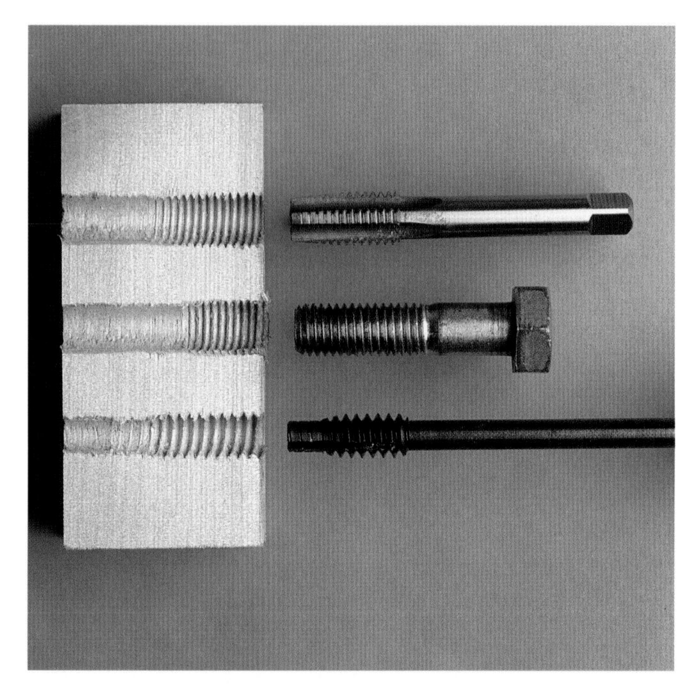

Figure 7.60 **Female threads in radially-grained kauri.** Radial grain threads far better than axial grain whether the thread is produced by tapping or by deformation.

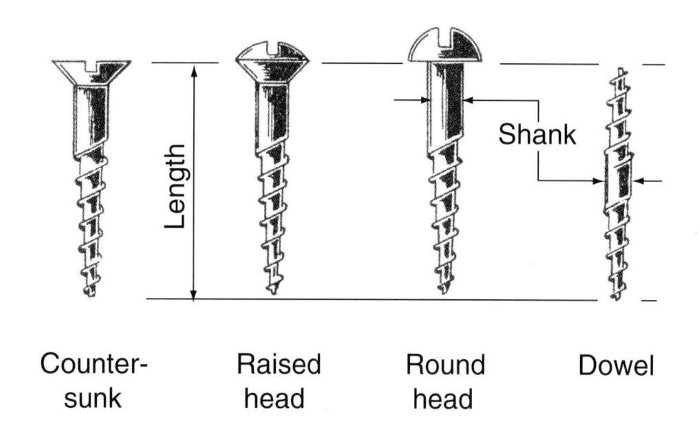

Figure 7.61 **The four types of wood screw,** scanned from Camm, p. 162, fig. 165. Typically for wood screws:

1. The diameter of the head is twice that of the shank.
2. The cone formed by the countersunk head has a 90° included angle.
3. The thread occupies about 60% of the screw's length.

Table 7.2 The clearance hole and pilot-hole diameters for wood screws.

Wood screw gauge	*Clearance-hole diameter*		*Pilot-hole diameter*	
	in.	*mm*	*in.*	*mm*
4	7/64	2.8	5/64	1.8
5	1/8	3.2	5/64	2.0
6	9/64	3.6	5/64	2.0
8	11/64	4.2	3/32	2.4
10	13/64	5.0	1/8	2.8
12	15/64	5.6	1/8	3.2
14	1/4	6.4	5/32	3.6

7.6.5 FORMING FEMALE THREADS WITH WOOD SCREWS

You form a female thread when you drive a steel or brass wood screw into wood. The wood screw does not cut away wood as does an engineers tap in metal, but compresses the wood along the interface between screw and the wood.

Several types of traditional wood screw are still manufactured (figure 7.61). Although they have been challenged or replaced by newer fasteners for many applications, the need to drill one, or two holes, and possibly countersink for the screw head before driving a screw into most woods remains for most screws, even those which are promoted as self-tapping. The sizes for the clearance holes through which the unthreaded shank should pass, and the pilot hole into which the threaded part of the wood screw screws are given in table 7.2.[35]

Screws are easier to drive if their points are first dipped in soap or wax. When using brass screws in hard woods, drive in an equivalent steel screw first, then replace it with the brass screw. Stainless-steel screws are a far stronger alternative to brass where rusting is undesirable.

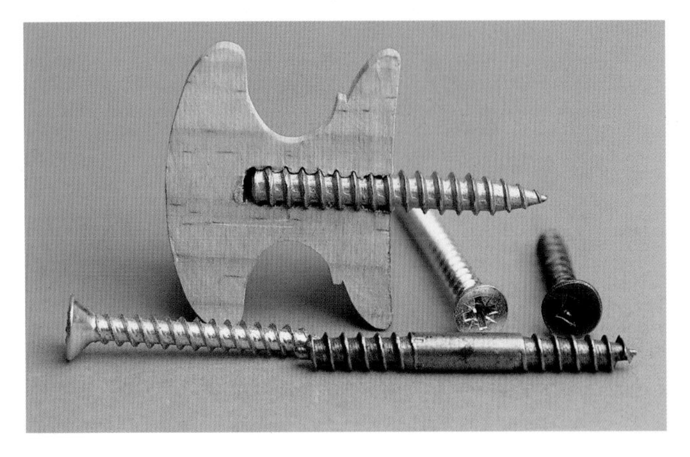

Figure 7.62 **Using a long wood screw to form a threaded spigot** projecting from the rear of a knob. This is commonly done because dowel (double-ended) screws are now available, if at all, only in a restricted range of sizes.

Right, cross-shaped slots such as the Philips and Posidrive have largely replaced single slots in the heads of newer fasteners, and have the feature that if too much torque is applied the screwdriver pops out. The square-recessed Campbell head does not have this pop-out feature and is in my view the best screw for fixing workpieces to faceplates and similar.

7.6.6 ADDING METAL THREADS TO WOOD

Figures 7.63 to 7.66 show some of the growing number of fasteners, some designated as knock-down, which you can use in woodwork and turning.

Figure 7.63 **Fixing with a cup head bolt.** The square section of the shank should lock in the clearance hole.

Figure 7.64 **A T-nut mated with a machine screw.**

Figure 7.65 **A lag screw** and a wing nut. To drive the wood screw part of the lag screw into the wood you can use two nuts tightened against each other, or an internally threaded driving socket similar to that shown in the next figure. The hole for the wood screw part can go through as shown, or be stopped.

Figure 7.66 **Screwing a nipple into the top of a lamp stem.** The driving device has a front steel plate with a threaded hole. There is a plain steel plate behind. Keep the thread in the front plate lubricated so that the nipple does not lock into it.

7.7 THREADING BY ROTATING AND TRAVERSING THE WORKPIECE

This class of methods uses some form of traversing mandrel; a spindle, traditionally but not necessarily a headstock spindle, which moves axially while it rotates.

7.7.1 EQUIPMENT

Figures 7.14, 7.15 and 7.20 illustrate early forms of traversing mandrel. More recent and related devices which hold, rotate, and traverse the workpiece while the lathe's headstock holds a rotating cutter are shown in figures 7.67 to 7.73. Various forms of rotating cutter are shown in figures 7.74 to 7.78.

Figure 7.67 **A home-built threading device based upon an inexpensive Taiwanese compound-slide vice.** The other essential component is a straight length of off-the-shelf threaded rod with nuts, here with a 30 x 3.5 mm thread which is the same as on my lathe's inboard headstock spindle nose. Take care to select a length of threaded rod which is truly straight, if not the thread height cut into the wood will vary around the 360°. The chuck which holds the workpiece screws onto the left-hand end of the threaded rod against the nut. The handwheel is off a lathe, and is locked onto the threaded rod by screwing it hard against a nut.

Threaded rod and nuts are available in the same threads as most headstock spindle noses. If not, you could get an engineer to turn a rod to suit, and choose whether the nose and main length can have the same or different threads.

The compound-slide vice is packed up on and screwed to a plywood base so that the axis of the threaded rod is at lathe-axis height.

Figure 7.68 **The underside of the base** showing the central guide which is a sliding fit between the lathe bedways. Clamping blocks are located at each end. Because they abut the central guide they do not tend to bind when the base is pushed along the bed. The clamping blocks have central lag screws which pass through holes in the base and have nuts and washers to pull the blocks up hard against the undersides of the bedways.

Figure 7.69 **Using the threading device** described in the two preceding figures. After turning the workpiece which was held in the chuck on the inboard headstock spindle nose, the chuck and workpiece were screwed onto the left-hand end of the threaded rod.

When cutting threads, you often want to do a trial fit. To obtain access move the workpiece transversely. Do not pull the whole threadcutting device back towards the tailstock because if you need to recut the thread you will not be able to register the cutter exactly with the previously-cut thread unless you have arranged an accurate stop to push the device back against.

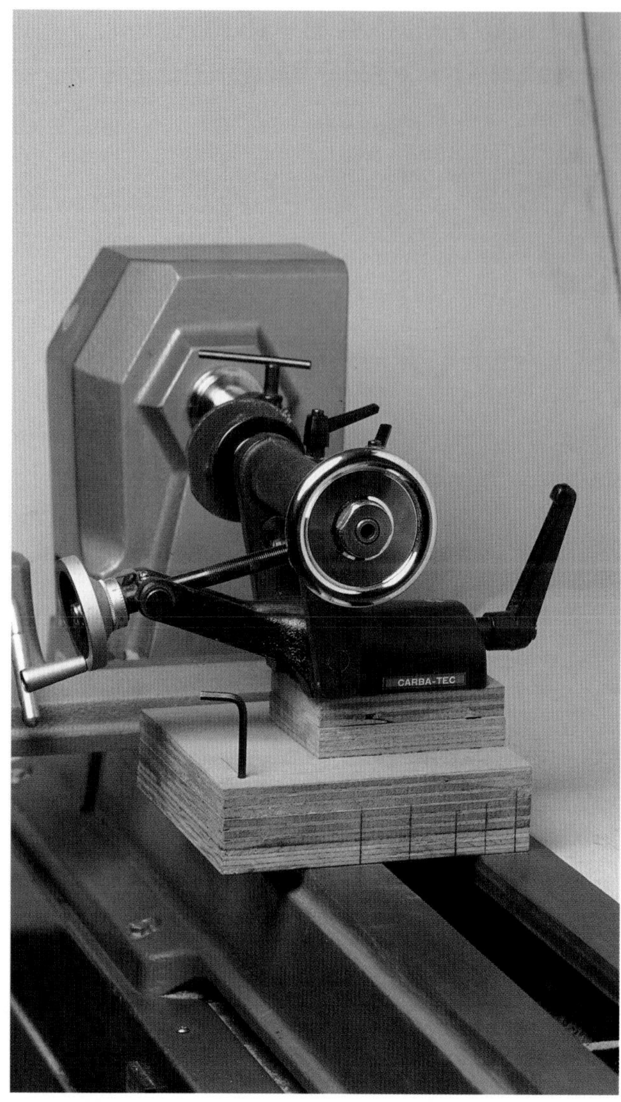

Figure 7.70 The Threadmaster, manufactured in Taiwan. Its cutter, shown in figure 7.74, is excellent for many woods being a *cutting* cutter.

The Threadmaster was made to be compatible with miniature lathes and therefore has to be packed up for the 200 mm center height of this Vicmarc VL200. The vertical pencil lines on both ends of the packing allow the Threadmaster's mandrel to be aligned parallel to the bedways in plan to cut a thread of constant diameter. Handle *H* at the rear operates a camlock to lock the device to the lathe bed. Mandrels are available with three different thread pitches, and are also threaded at their left-hand ends to take chucks which screw up against the integral flange. The mandrel screws through two internally and externally threaded collars which can be adjusted relative to one another to eliminate backlash. The collars are locked with handles *H1* and *H2*. Handwheel *HW1* rotates the mandrel and thereby also moves it axially.

The handwheel *HW2* moves the mandrel and its housing at 90° to the bed in plan. The handle is calibrated but because the main spindle moves in an arc, the calibrations are not as accurate as in the cross-slide arrangements in both the preceeding device and the Bonnie Klein device shown in the next figure. The Threadmaster should therefore be packed so that when the armature is vertical, the Threadmaster mandrel axis is at lathe-axis height. If you attempt to cut threads when the arm is not close to vertical and when the workpiece is not centered at close to lathe axis height, it is difficult to advance the workpiece into the cutter by the correct amount.

W is a washer I have installed; it is drilled allow two socket head cap screws to pass through and screw into two holes which I drilled and tapped into the rear of my chuck. This ensures that the chuck will not loosen on the mandrel's nose.

The cutter is held in a Jacobs-type chuck on a Morse taper arbor with drawbar bought from Peter Child, The Old Hyde, Little Yeldham, Essex.

Figure 7.71 The Bonnie Klein Threading Jig, available from Klein Designs Inc., 17910 SE 110th Street, Renton, Washington 98059-5323, USA. A traversing mandrel on a cross-slide, it is made for miniature lathes, but can be packed higher and used on larger lathes.

Figure 7.72 The Crawford thread-cutting jig, manufactured by Jack Crawford in Sydney, Australia. It produces a 30 x 3.5 mm thread. Because the depth of engagement between the threaded rod and the housing nut is below the maximum possible, there is noticeable slop which reduces the quality and accuracy of the thread cut unless you constantly push down on the chuck and/ or workpiece as you cut the thread.

When cutting a thread of constant major diameter, the traversing mandrel (here the threaded rod) must be aligned parallel to the bedways by sighting down to the bedways. Slackening the socket-head cap screw allows the mandrel to be tilted and the workpiece to be advanced into the rotating cutter. Another technique for advancing a workpiece mounted on such devices is described in figures 7.90 and 7.91.

Figure 7.73 A Latalex Ornamental Turner about to be used for threading. The arrangement is similar to that shown in figure 7.20.

Top right, a threaded collar is locked onto the mandrel. *Below*, the appropriately-threaded recess in the hob has been raised to engage with the collar so that the mandrel will move axially when rotated by its handwheel. Three differently threaded collars are shown below and to the left of the hob.

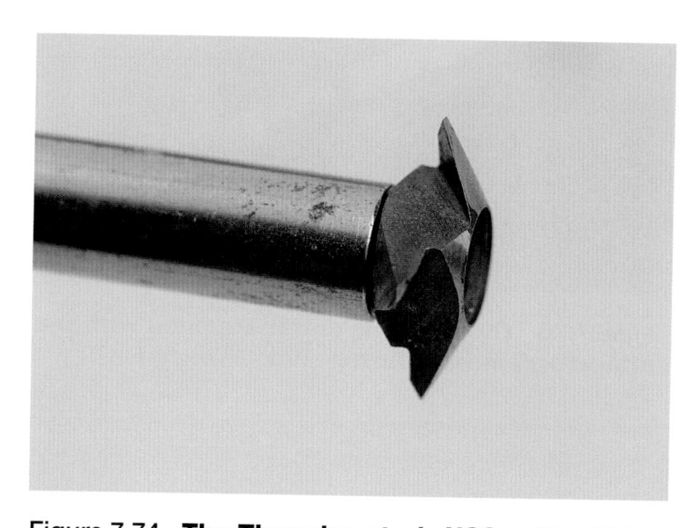

Figure 7.74 The Threadmaster's HSS cutter. This cutter leaves the best finish of any of the cutters shown, especially in softer woods.

Figure 7.75 **A 60° milling cutter** is readily available (this one supplied by Bonnie Klein). It produces a surface superior to that left by a scraping cutter, but inferior to that left by the Threadmaster type.

Figure 7.76 **The scraping cutter supplied with the Latalex Ornamental Turner** shown in figure 7.73.

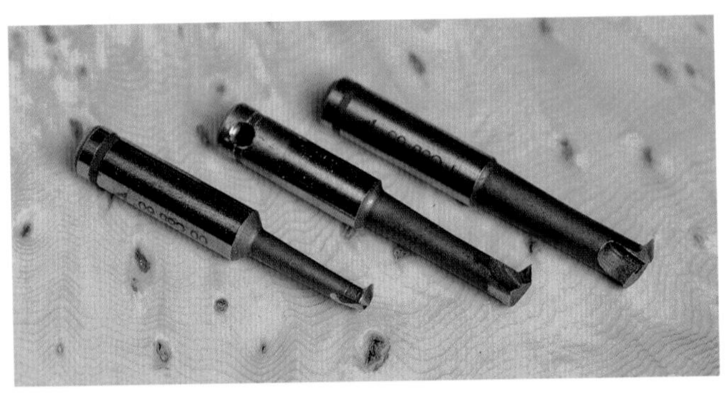

Figure 7.77 **HSS thread cutters manufactured to cut female threads in metal** also perform excellently in wood.

Figure 7.78 **A scraping cutter made by grinding an Allen key.** This solution was suggested by Geoff O'Loughlin of Beaumaris, Victoria, Australia.

7.7.2 CUTTING GOOD THREADS

Turned lidded boxes can have threaded lids. The threads can be scraped with chasers (pages 173 to 178), or cut with fast-rotating cutters. This second option enables a greater range of woods to be used, generally produces cleaner and more precise threads, and is described on pages 160 to 171.

To cut clean threads, especially in less cooperative woods:

1. The cutter should rotate at high speed (2000 rpm or higher for a cutter 3/4 in. (19 mm) in diameter).
2. Each thread crest should be a flat helical band of the original cylindrical surface.
3. The cutter should backcut down into the wood, not cut upwards on its way out (figure 7.79).
4. If the thread is coarse it is better cut in two passes.
5. The type of cutter is not too critical providing it is sharp, although a *cutting* cutter will give a better surface than a scraping cutter.
6. Impregnation with a suitable compound to improve the wood's hardness and cohesiveness may reduce any crumbling along the crest.
7. Because it is easier to turn the spigot's major diameter accurately, and if necessary recut the male thread to a smaller minor diameter, the female thread is usually cut first. However the advantage is small, and other factors can cause you to reverse that order.

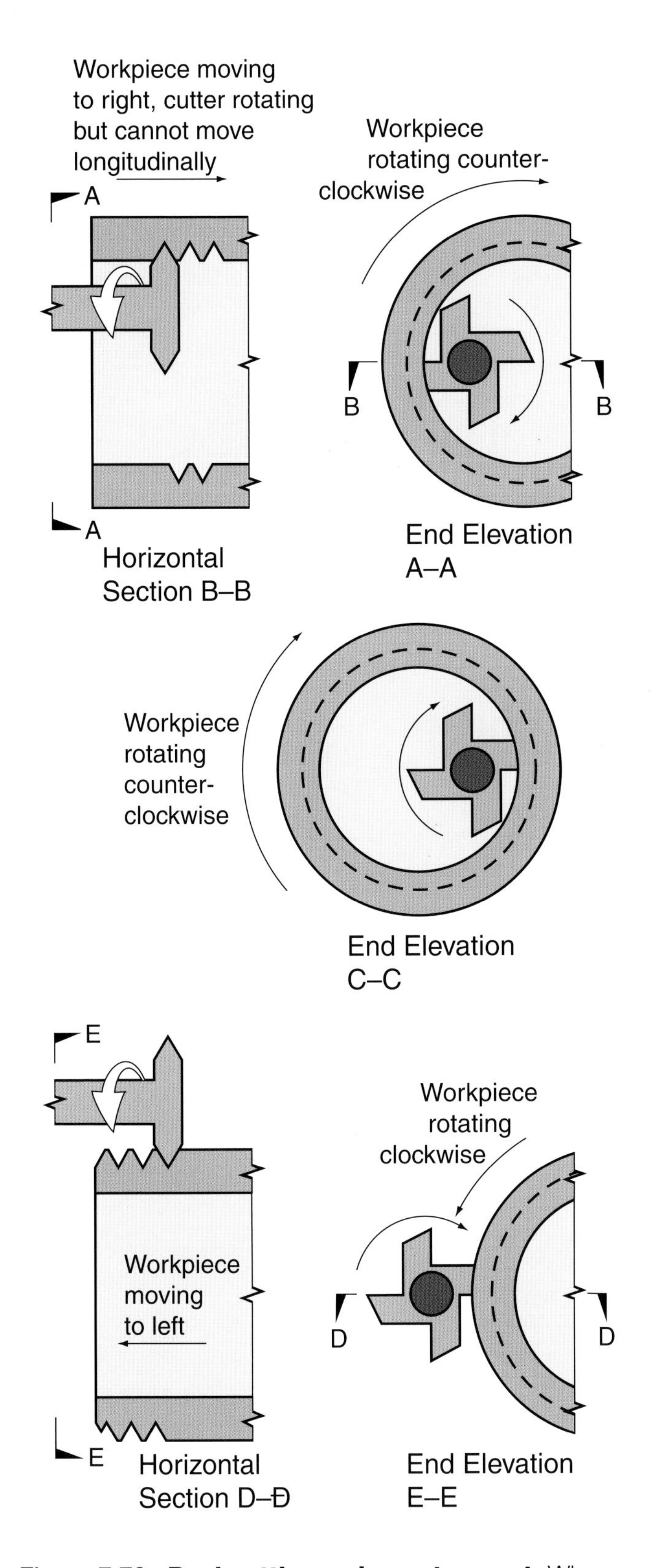

Figure 7.79 Backcutting reduces tear-out. When cutting a female thread (*A–A*, *B–B*, and *C–C*), the cutter should work out towards the rim of the socket: this is unchanged wherever on the socket surface the cutter is working (compare *A–A* and *C–C*). To cut a male thread, start the cutter at the rim of the spigot (*D–D* and *E–E*).

7.7.3 CALIBRATING YOUR EQUIPMENT

To cut threads accurately and repeatably you need to establish:

1. A method by which you can reliably advance the workpiece into the cutter to produce a thread with a narrow helix of flat crest of the required width.
2. The optimum difference between the socket and spigot diameters before they are threaded.

Therefore before starting to thread items which you intend to complete, you need to calibrate your equipment using the procedure shown in figures 7.80 to 7.89 . This procedure also takes you through the thread-cutting process, and is therefore doubly valuable.

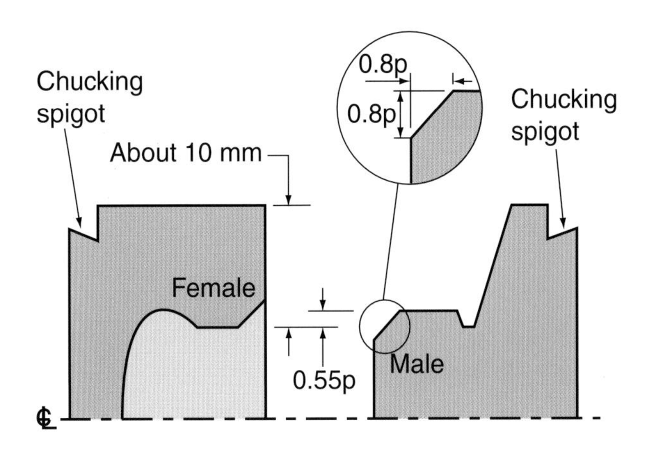

Figure 7.80 The test pieces resemble a simple box lid and base. The chamfers' dimensions are not critical. Theoretically the diameters of the socket and spigot don't matter as long as the difference between them is correct, but it is preferable to make the test pieces similar in diameter to the boxes you intend to make.

My traversing mandrel's thread was 10 tpi, and it therefore had a pitch of 2.54 mm. As the cutter produced a thread with a thread angle of 60°, I turned the male spigot's finished diameter 1.1p (= 2.8 mm) larger than the female's for the first test, based upon the equation in the legend of figure 7.36.

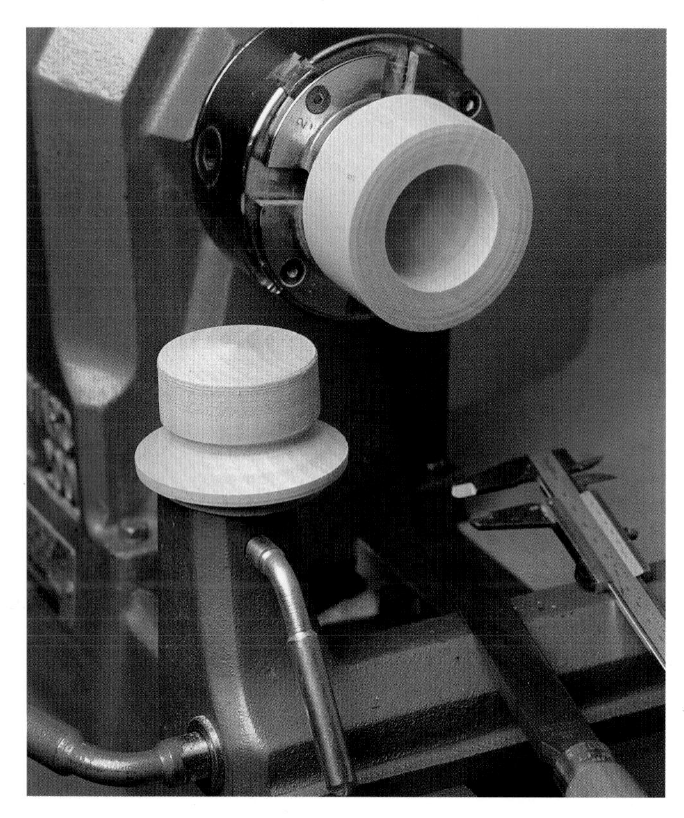

Figure 7.81 **The test pieces for the male and female threads.** They have been roughed, and allowed to relax and season.

Figure 7.82 **Shear-scraping the inside of the socket** to fine surface with a shear scraper of the type shown in the next figure. The depth of cut must be fine to achieve an excellent surface, and the tool is held with its blade horizontal, a little above lathe-axis height, and parallel to the lathe bedways in plan.

This shear scraper leaves a smooth surface even on wood with a difficult grain. It is better to *cut* an excellent surface than to sand one as the sanding leaves particles of abrasive in the wood's surface which will prematurely blunt your thread cutter.

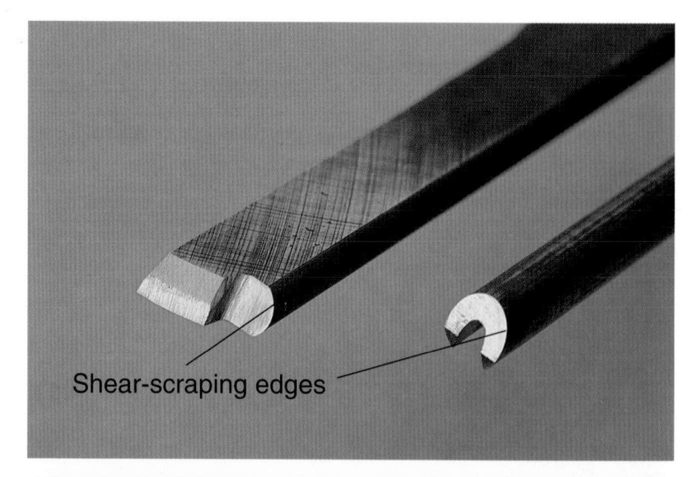

Figure 7.83 **Shear scrapers for socket walls.** One is ground from a surplus bowl gouge, the other from a scraper. Although such shear scrapers can be ground from worn-down tools, a long blade helps you to align the tool correctly as you push it forwards.

Top, when used to shear scrape the rounded edge just above the center of the blade is used. The face is ground to give a cut with 45° side rake, and is honed with a fine diamond lap.

Middle, the tools with their shear-scraping edges down. The rear tool doubles as an end-and-side flat scraper.

Bottom, the flat scraper in plan.

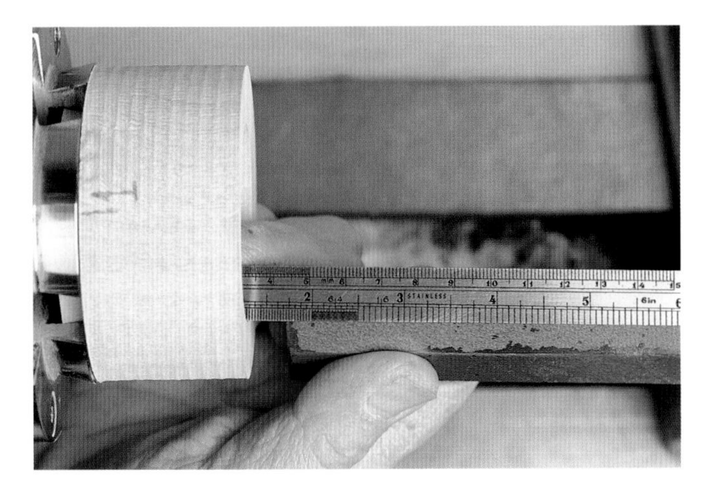

Figure 7.84 **Checking the alignment of the socket surface** by pressing a horizontal rule against the spigot surface, and sighting down to see if the rule lies parallel to the bedways.

Once the socket surface is true and smooth, you measure its diameter and chamfer the entrance before cutting the female thread.

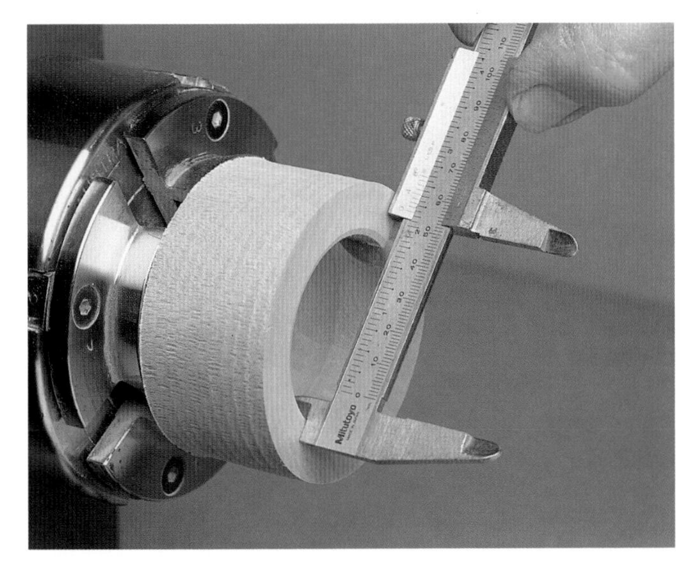

Figure 7.85 **Measuring the minor diameter of the female socket.** You can then calculate the major diameter of the male spigot, here by adding 1.1p.

To cut the female thread, the chuck still holding the workpiece has to be mounted on the traversing mandrel, and the thread cutter has to be mounted inboard on the headstock. I held the cutter in a Jacobs chuck on a Morse taper arbor. A drawbar was used to prevent the arbor loosening in the headstock spindle swallow.

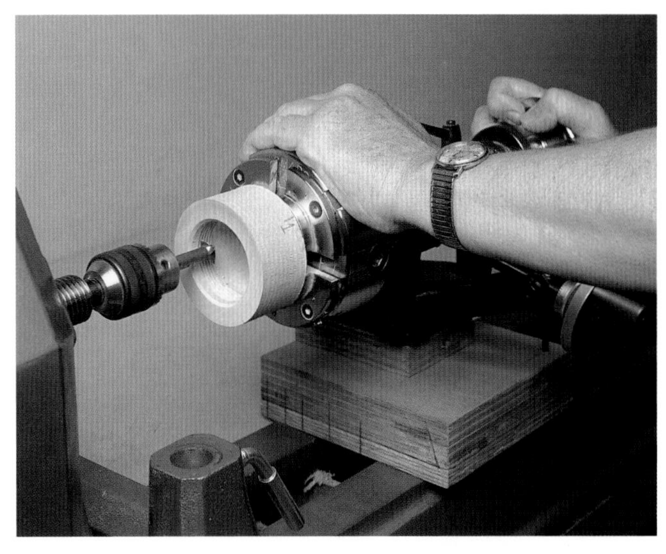

Figure 7.86 **Cutting the female thread.**

You must first position the workpiece so that the cutter is just touching the surface of the socket at the point from which you want to start backcutting the thread. To achieve this you have to:

1. Bodily move the threadcutting device (and thus the workpiece) along the bed, and lock it to the bed when the workpiece is in the correct position relative to the cutter. (To backcut the thread you cut the thread from the inside, back towards the entrance.
2. Finely adjust the lateral position of the workpiece. Rotate the cutter slowly by hand, and gently move the socket surface towards it at 90° to the bed in plan. As soon as you hear the cutter just touch the socket surface, stop and note the calibration on or mark the handwheel. The workpiece is now at zero cutter advance.

To leave a flat crest, the cutter needs to be advanced a particular amount which you can calculate using the information in table 7.1 on page 146. For a 60° thread angle and a crest width of 0.125p, the advance should be 0.76p (=1.9 mm). However this only holds if the workpiece's axis is maintained at lathe-axis height as it is advanced.

Run the cutter at 2000 rpm or more, and gently advance the workpiece the chosen amount. Dampen vibration by keeping your hand on the chuck holding the workpiece. Cut a couple of circles of thread. Stop the cutter and check the thread quality and crest width with a magnifying glass—you will be able to roughly estimate the crest width as a fraction of the pitch. Make any adjustments to the cutter advance, cut, check again, etc., until you have established and recorded the ideal advance. Cut the remainder of the thread at the chosen final advance.

Figure 7.87 **Cutting the male spigot to the calculated diameter** and a fine finish with a detail gouge presented with side rake. (Using a parting tool leaves a torn surface). You can also turn the male spigot to the required major diameter by using the female thread as a gauge—this less accurate method is described in the section on chasing in figure 7.138.

You should be able to eye the spigot to a constant diameter, although you could check its accuracy by eyeing the spigot surface or a horizontal rule held against it with the bedways as shown in figure 7.84.

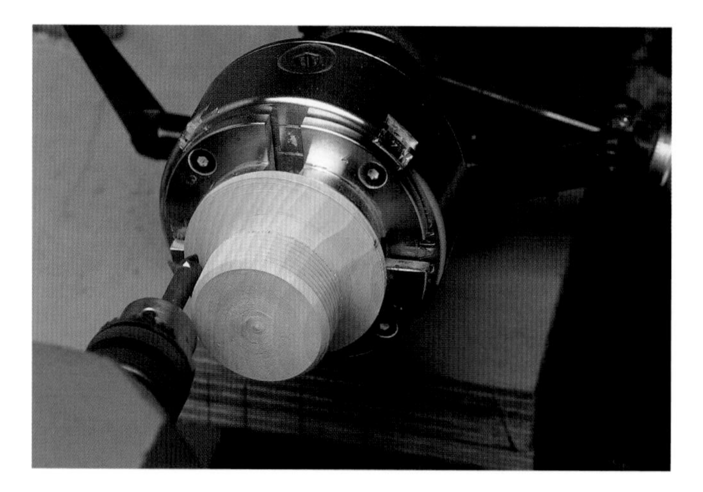

Figure 7.88 **Backcutting the male thread.**

The cylindrical section of the spigot is positioned close to the cutter. Then, as in figure 7.86, the cutter is spun by hand as the workpiece is slowly brought closer. The advancement is stopped when the cutter is heard to just touch the spigot. Then the cutter's blades are orientated so that they do not touch the spigot. The workpiece is then screwed back towards the tailstock until the cutter will just clear the chamfer at the front of the spigot. The workpiece is then adjusted by the cutter advance determined in figure 7.86 (1.9 mm here), and the lathe turned on. After cutting a couple of rotations inspect the threads. The thread form should be correct. But if the thread is too deep, reduce the advance and cut the remainder of the thread. If however the cut is too shallow, stop the lathe, wind back the workpiece, adjust its advance, and recut the first couple of rotations. If the thread form is now good, cut the rest of the thread.

Clean the threads in both the socket and the spigot with a toothbrush, and with another toothbrush apply a little wax. The threads should run smoothly.

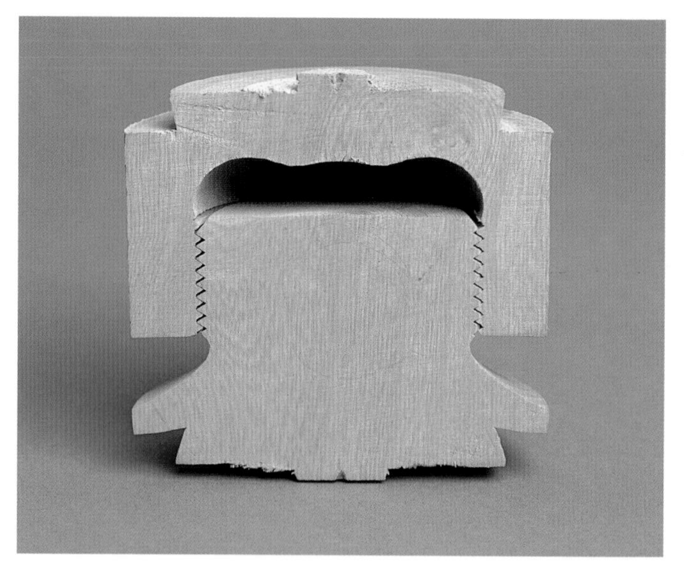

Figure 7.89 **A satisfactory fit of the test piece threads.** If the fit is too tight or loose, repeat the test with an appropriately revised difference between the socket minor diameter and spigot major diameter.

Threads are not usually polished, but if you intend to polish the threads in your completed boxes, do a trial polish with the test pieces. Apply the polish as thinly as possible to threaded areas. If after polishing the threads are too tight, repeat the threadcutting test with new workpieces, but decrease the difference between the socket minor diameter and spigot major diameter.

7.7.4 ADVANCING THE WORKPIECE WITH UNCALIBRATED DEVICES

There are traversing-mandrel devices similar to the Crawford jig in figure 7.72 which mount in a lathe banjo, but do not incorporate an accurate facility to advance the mandrel at 90° to the bed in plan. Another desirable facility would be the ability to temporarily move the workpiece out of the way to inspect the thread or do a trial fit. Both facilities can easily be gained by making a cutter-advance jig (figures 7.90 and 7.91).

Figure 7.90 **A cutter-advance jig.** The Crawford device has been locked into the banjo with its axis at lathe-axis height and at a right angle to the neck of the banjo. The banjo has been moved and locked to the bed so that the cutter tips glance the workpiece surface. The cutter-advance jig with its gauge bar down and pushed against the banjo, and its neck in close contact with the banjo's neck, is then locked to the lathe bed. The thickness of the gauge bar equals the cutter advance.

Figure 7.91 **The workpiece advanced.** The banjo was loosened on the bed, and slid forwards so that the gauge bar could be revolved out of the way. The lathe was then started, and the banjo pushed backwards, keeping its neck in full contact with the jig's neck, until arrested by the stop. Backcutting could then start.

7.7.5 MAKING A CASTER WITH A THREADED TOP

Making a box with a threaded lid is straightforward, and involves repeating the techniques used to calibrate your threadcutting equipment described on pages 161 to 164. The making of a caster with the male thread on the lid is outlined in figures 7.92 to 7.103. The wood used is bland in appearance, and therefore I have not attempted to ensure that the grain pattern in the lid and base align when the lid is screwed on tightly. How to achieve grain alignment is detailed on pages 169 to 171.

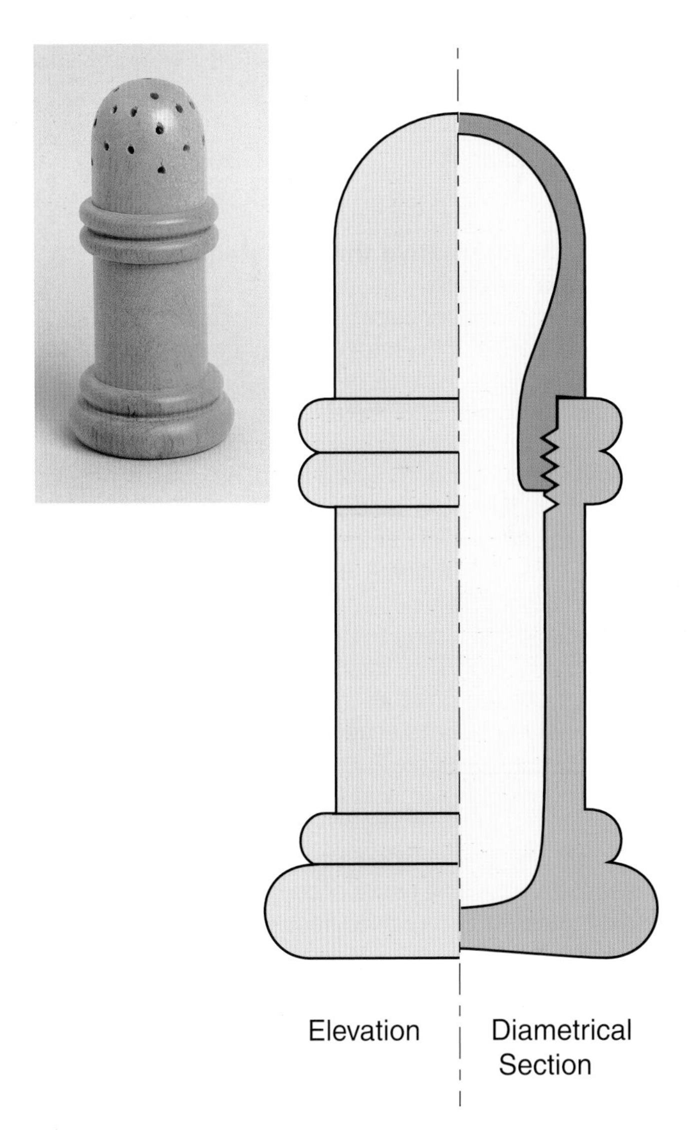

Figure 7.92 **A full-size drawing of a small caster for sugar or spice.** The wood used was New Zealand silver beech, *Nothofagus menziesii*, which is fine grained, and fairly hard. The 10 tpi threads (2.54 mm pitch) are shown enlarged in the next figure.

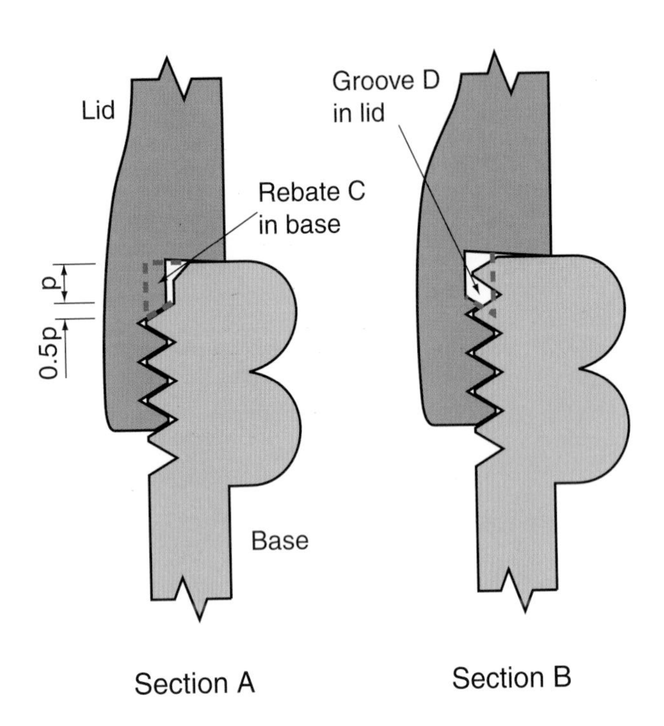

Figure 7.93 **Alternative thread details in diametrical section.**

You cannot usually cut a male thread right up to a shoulder because of the form of the cutter. So that the lid can close tightly, it is therefore necessary to modify the design of the socket or of the spigot.

In *section A* a rebate *C* has been cut into the entrance to the socket. It is good practice to cut a small chamfer at the rim of this rebate. In *section B* the unthreadable part of the spigot is cut away to the depth of the thread to leave a groove *D*. Solution *A* is usually preferred because the spigot is not weakened. When hand chasing threads, similar modifications have to be incorporated as shown later in figure 7.127. The dimensions of both the rebate and the groove assume that the root of thread cannot be cut closer to the spigot's shoulder than 1½p, a typical situation pictured in figure 7.110.

When designing screwed fastenings, consider the appropriate thread geometries from those possible, and also how many threads should engage—1½ to 2 is usually sufficient. (Here I have chosen three because I expect the caster to be refilled frequently and want the threads to last well).

The exposed length of the spigot should thus be the pitch multiplied by number of threads you wish to engage plus approximately two for the rebate *C* or groove *D*. Similarly the minimum number of female threads you cut measured from the rim should be the number of turns of engagement required plus two, although another turn or two are usually added.

Figure 7.94 **The base workpiece chucked and the lid workpiece below.** Both were rough-turned and bored earlier, and allowed to relax and season.

Figure 7.95 **Cutting the female thread in the base.** The hollow has been finish-turned and sanded. To keep the workpiece stiff for threading, I delayed finish-turning the outside of the base. The socket has been prepared for threading as described in figures 7.82 to 7.85. I first rotated the cutter by hand and gently advanced the workpiece to just touch it. The workpiece was then advanced into the rotating cutter.

Figure 7.96 **The lid spigot finish-turned to its calculated major diameter.**

It is usual to complete the hollowing before the threading. When the spigot wall is to be thin you may choose to trim the hollow to final size after the threading, or stiffen the spigot with a plug which fits snuggly into the finish-turned hollow.

Figure 7.97 **Cutting the male thread.** The workpiece has been advanced 0.76p into the rotating cutter, and is being moved to the left as it is slowly rotated so that the thread is backcut.

Clean both threads with a dry toothbrush, and do a trial fit. A light waxing with a paste wax will make the screwing sweeter. If too tight, recut the thread slightly deeper if the crests are wide enough, or, if the crests are not wide enough, mount the chuck and workpiece temporarily back onto the headstock spindle, skim the crests wider with a skew, and recut the thread. Do not move the threadcutting device along the bed unless you have an accurate stop to return it against because you will not be able to register the new threadcutting with the preceeding.

If the thread fit is too loose and there is enough spare length in the workpiece, cut off the spigot and cut a slightly larger-diameter one.

Figure 7.98 **Friction polishing the right-hand end of the top.** This is done early because access to this area is limited once the lid is screwed on. The top is then parted off.

Figure 7.99 **Pricking the positions of the holes in the lid.** The pencil lines and marks are then sanded off. The top is then finish-sanded and friction polished.

The turned section of the stem of the pencil platform fits snuggly in the hole in the banjo, and is stopped so that the top of the platform is at lathe-axis height. The platform's plan shape enables the setting-out lines for the holes in the lid to be drawn with ease and accuracy.

Figure 7.100 **Drilling the 3/64 in. (1.2 mm) diameter holes in the top.** This is done after polishing to avoid the polish clogging the holes.

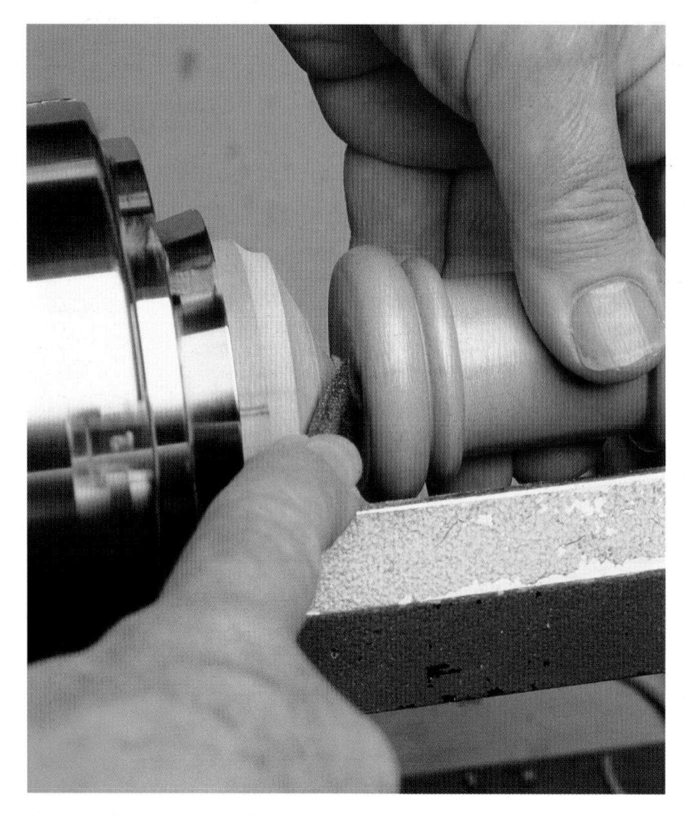

Figure 7.101 **Parting-off the base.**

Figure 7.102 **Threading a spigot in a piece of scrap wood on which to reverse-chuck the base.** The spigot was first turned to the same major diameter as the male spigot on the caster top. After the threading, the chuck still holding the scrap was removed from the Threadmaster, and mounted on the headstock, ready to receive the base.

Figure 7.103 **Finish-turning the bottom of the caster's base** with a small hook tool. The base is screwed onto the threaded waste spigot shown in the preceding figure. After the turning is completed, the bottom is sanded and polished in the lathe.

7.7.6 ACHIEVING GRAIN ALIGNMENT

To achieve grain alignment beween a box lid and base you must position the lid and the base correctly in the blank (figure 7.104)—this was discussed in FOW on pages 140 and 141. When grain alignment is aesthetically important but the grain is not straight and axial, one or two inserts should be glued in (figure 7.105). You will also need to decide which of the two thread details discussed in figure 7.93 to adopt. The steps are shown in figures 7.106 to 7.116.

Figure 7.104 **The positioning of the lid and base in a blank to minimize grain mismatch.**

The three red bands are waste for parting through or off. A chucking spigot is turned at each end of the blank before it is parted into two. However with very expensive woods, or where you don't have enough length to cut integral chucking spigots, you could glue on wooden waste disks into which you turn chucking spigots. This can be done before the blank is turned, or before or after the blank is parted in two. Most glues can be used, although cryanoacrylate allows a conglutinated workpiece to be turned within a minute or two.

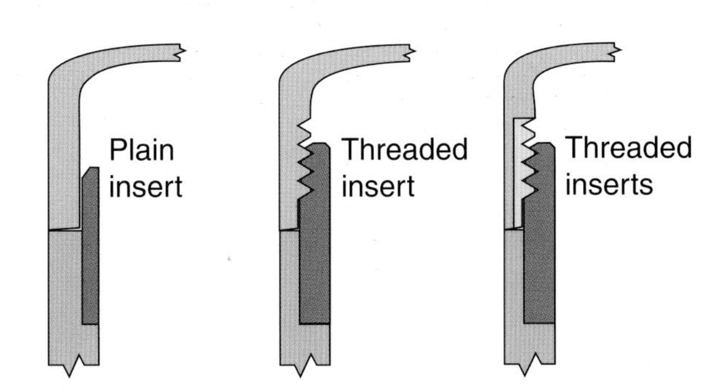

Figure 7.105 **Socket and spigot inserts.** Where minimizing grain mismatch is the sole problem, you only need to glue in a spigot insert. Where the main wood will not thread nicely, you will need to glue in socket and spigot inserts turned from a wood which threads well and is similar in color to the main wood.

Figure 7.106 **The lid socket ready to thread.** The lid is completed apart from some finish-turning and sanding to its outside. The diameter of the socket has also been measured.

The joint detail chosen is that in section A of figure 7.93 turned upside down. However the lid might need to be screwed further on by up to one full rotation to achieve a grain match. The rebate at the entrance to the lid should therefore be $2^1/_2$p to 3p deep.

Figure 7.107 **Backcutting the female thread inside the lid.** The chuck (still holding the lid workpiece) has been removed from the headstock spindle and mounted onto the Threadmaster. I use the loupe to inspect the width of the thread crest.

7.108 **Parting off the almost completed lid.**

Figure 7.109 **The box base hollowed, internally sanded, and the spigot cut to a diameter 1.1p larger than that of the socket's minor diameter.** The chuck and workpiece are then mounted on the threadcutting device, and the cutter is mounted inboard.

Figure 7.110 **Backcutting the thread on the spigot of the base.** The thread cannot be cut closer to the shoulder because of the projecting end of the cutter. If using a one-piece cutter you may the able to grind its end back to enable the cutter to thread nearer to a shoulder.

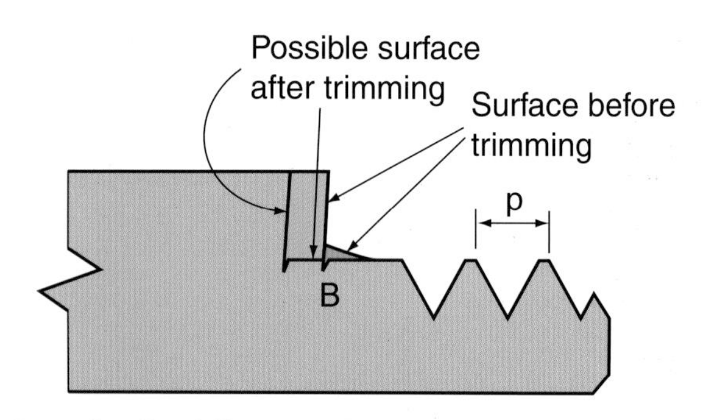

Figure 7.111 **Cutting a shoulder.** The red-colored wood should not be cut off when the spigot is first cut, or, when the green-colored wood is trimmed off to achieve the grain match, an unsightly V-cut will be left at *B*. The need to clear this red wood is another reason for cutting a slight chamfer at the entrance to the socket.

Figure 7.112 **The lid is screwed on fairly tightly and reveals a grain mismatch.** To achieve a grain match the lid would have to be screwed on a further x°. Therefore the shoulder and/or lid rim need to be shortened by a total of x p/360. Here x is 250 and the pitch is 2.54 mm, the total to be trimmed off is therefore 2.54 mm x 250/360 (= 1.8 mm).

As in most cases the lid cannot be accurately rechucked, the majority of the trimming must be done by cutting back the shoulder (or rim) of the chucked workpiece as shown in the next figure. I therefore decided to cut the shoulder back by 1.5 mm, allowing about 0.3 mm to be removed from the lid rim by sanding (figure 7.115).

Figure 7.113 **Trimming the shoulder back by 1.5 mm.**

Figure 7.114 **Rechecking the grain mismatch** with the lid again screwed on firmly. The mismatch is now about 20°, and therefore about 2.54 mm x 20/360 (= 0.14 mm) needs to trimmed either from the base shoulder or from the rim of the lid. As the amount is so small it is better to sand the lid rim as this can be done gradually.

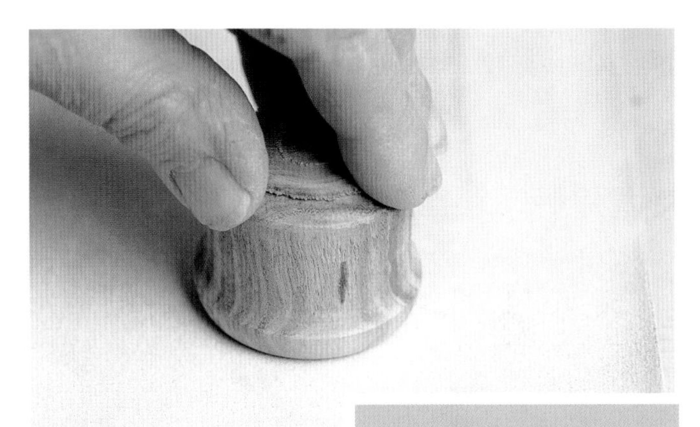

Figure 7.115 **Sanding the rim of the lid** on flat abrasive paper. Trial fit the lid regularly to ensure a perfect grain match.

Figure 7.116 **Excellent grain alignment** between lid and base when the lid is screwed fully on.

7.7.7 DUPLICATING UNUSUAL THREADS BY MAKING THE WORKPIECE THE TRAVERSING MANDREL

You can easily make a traversing mandrel with little more than a bolt or screw, and a nut. To match an existing thread, measure its pitch, say by measuring the distance between eleven crests and dividing by ten. Then search a reference with thread tabulations for a matching or close pitch. Buy a bolt or screw and a nut of this pitch and use them as the basis for a traversing mandrel. You could similarly use existing threaded components in wood or plastic, or carve threaded wooden components, which you then use as masters to make new items with the same pitch.

In constructing a traversing-mandrel device, the workpiece can be:

1. Separate from the traversing mandrel and chucked onto it, perhaps just by gluing.
2. An integral part of the mandrel.

Figures 7.117 to 7.118 show an example of the second arrangement, and how it was used to thread replacement parts (figure 7.119) for the lignum vitae wassail bowl in figure 7.120. This huge bowl was without its five dipper cups, their stub columns which were threaded into the main lid, and the five taps which screwed into the bottom of the upper syphon chamber. The threaded sockets for the taps and stub columns had a major diameter of 15.5 mm and a pitch of close to 9 tpi (2.8 mm), which is the pitch of the $^7/_8$ in. British Standard Whitworth thread. I found a $^7/_8$ in. BSW nut and bolt, set up the traversing-mandrel device, and successfully completed the job.[36]

Figure 7.117 A traversing-mandrel device.

Left, a Threadmaster cutter (figure 7.74) is held in a chuck mounted on the inboard spindle nose.

Center, The workpiece was turned to fit snuggly through the $1^1/_2$ in. (37 mm) wooden bearing on the left, and turned down to 14.3 mm (15.5 mm – 2 x 0.76 x p + 1.1p [see figures 7.36 and 7.37]) where it was to be threaded. The right-hand end of the workpiece was turned to 13 mm diameter and squeezed into a $^1/_2$ in. (12.7 mm) diameter hole drilled into the head of the 7/8 in. BSW bolt so that the two became integral.

To cut a thread, the device was located so the the correct thread height would be cut. The workpiece was then rotated by hand. The engagement of the bolt with the clamped nut ensured that the desired pitch was cut. After threading, each traversing mandrel was detached from the bolt, and finish-turned.

Figure 7.118 Another view of the threading device.

Figure 7.119 Replacement taps and dipper cups.

Figure 7.120 The wassail bowl fitted with the replacement parts, and then in the collection of John Hawkins Antiques. Turned in about 1640, the bowl's lid diameter is 14 in. (350 mm), and the bowl's overall height is 31 in. (790 mm). Pulling up the handle at the top draws punch from the lower bowl into the upper chamber. Punch is then dispensed into a cup using the tap above.

"Wassail" is derived from the old English "waes hael" meaning "be well". Wassailing was a ceremony held mainly at Christmas. A decorated bowl was carried through the streets by maidens singing carols and wishing onlookers well. What the maidens did after helping consume the punch in the bowl is not recorded.

Numbers of antique wassail bowls are pictured in Owen Evan-Thomas, *Domestic Utensils of Wood* (East Ardsley, Yorkshire: EP Publishing, 1973); Edward H. Pinto, *Treen and Other Wooden Bygones* (London: G. Bell & Sons, 1969); and Johnathan Levi, *Treen for the Table* (Woodbridge, Suffolk: Antique Collectors' Club, 1998). Eighteen wassail bowls made by members of The Society of Ornamental Turners are shown in the Society's *The Bulletin* Number 103, September 2000, pp.120–129.

7.8 THREADING BY ROTATING THE WORKPIECE AND TRAVERSING THE CUTTER

You can cut a thread on a workpiece which is being rotated slowly in a lathe but not being moved axially. There are five techniques:

1. Chasing, in which a thread cutter, known as a chaser, is repeatedly traversed (chased) by hand along the workpiece. With each traverse the cutter is advanced a little deeper into the workpiece. Once the thread is partially cut (struck), the speed of traversing of the chaser is governed by the engagement of the teeth of the chaser with the thread just cut on the workpiece.[37]
2. A form of chasing in which the the speed and constancy of the traversing is governed by a master thread which, like the workpiece, is in line with the lathe axis.
3. Using Dombleton's apparatus or a modern equivalent in which the movement of a fast-rotating cutter is governed by a master thread.
4. Using an engine lathe with change gears and a lead-shaft-driven carriage. You can mount a fixed cutter in the carriage's toolpost, but a rotating cutter is generally preferred for wood. This method is not further detailed.
5. Temporarily converting a plain lathe without a carriage into the equivalent of an engine lathe.

7.8.1 HAND CHASERS

Figure 7.9 showed hand chasers pictured by Moxon in 1678. As figures 7.121 and 7.122 show, their design remains unchanged today.

The technique of hand chasing became better known in the 1990s due largely to the writings of Bill Jones in the magazine *Woodturning*. Some who have tried hand chasing have been disappointed, probably not because of poor technique, but because they were not aware that chasing only works on the axial grain of the hardest woods.

You can make chasers (figures 7.123 and 7.124) or source them from:

1. Woodturners suppliers. Chasers are being produced in 2000 by woodturning tool manufacturers, among them Robert Sorby and Crown Hand Tools, both of Sheffield.
2. Suppliers of engineering equipment, both new and used. In engineering, thread chasers are used to clean-up threads, and may be held in an engine lathe's toolpost, or be hand held and traversed along a toolrest.

Chasers are easy to sharpen (figure 7.125). A chaser is also often supported and guided when cutting a female thread by a device called an armrest (figure 7.126).

Figure 7.121 **Hand chasers:** *left*, made by grinding down an engineers tap; *back right*, an chaser from an unknown source; *front right*, four BSW engineers hand chasers. You should fit wooden handles to chasers to give an overall tool length of about 12 in. (300 mm).

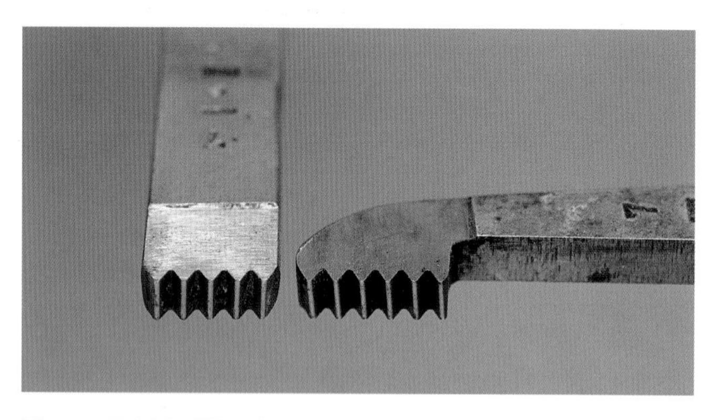

Figure 7.122 **The business ends of hand chasers:** *left*, an outside chaser with a pitch of 7 tpi (3.6 mm); *right*, the corresponding inside chaser. The slope of the teeth from the vertical rarely influences the quality of the thread if the chaser is held horizontal.

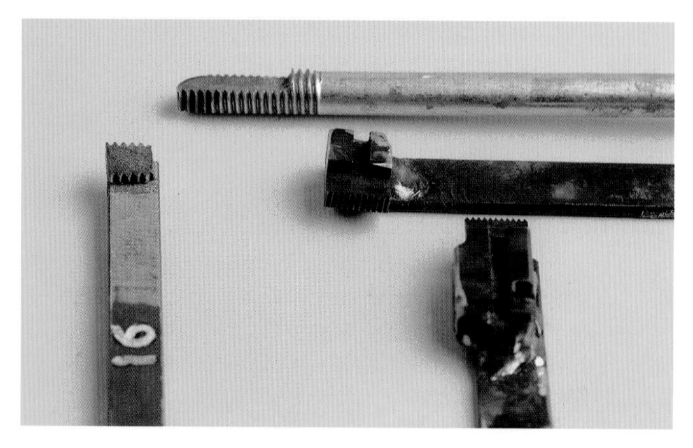

Figure 7.123 **Homemade chasers:** *back*, a ground-down fastener; *left*, a tip glued on with epoxy-resin glue; *right*, chasers from a die head welded onto rectangular blades.

Figure 7.124 **Chasers made by filing and grinding** teeth into annealed carbon tool steel which was then hardened and tempered.

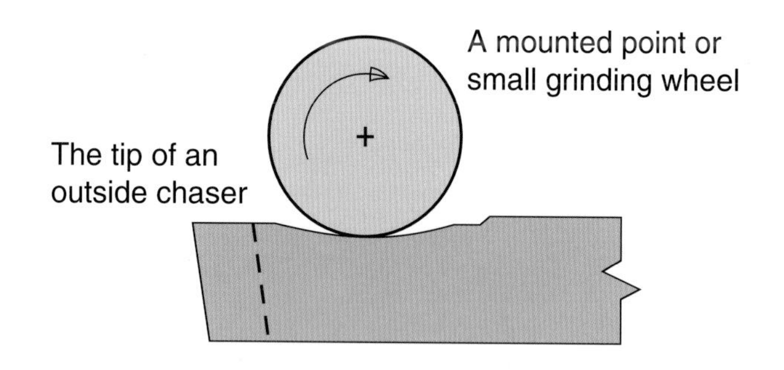

Figure 7.125 **Sharpening an outside chaser** in longitudinal section. Only hone or grind the top face. Honing with a diamond hone is excellent, and should be sufficient for most turners. To speed honing you can hollow-grind the top face. Hold an outside chaser face-down onto the periphery of a grinding wheel with its blade parallel to the wheel's faces. For an inside chaser the blade is held parallel to the grinder's spindle. You can also use a small mounted rotating grinding wheel or point.

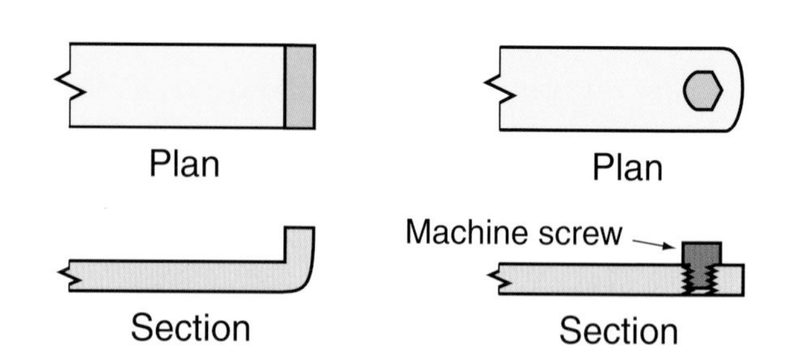

Figure 7.126 **Armrest ends:** *left*, the usual form of commercial armrest; *right*, a homemade version. The left-hand side of the head of the machine screw has been filed smooth. It might be better to file it to a vertical edge into which locates a vertical V-groove you cut in the back edge of the inside chaser. Handles are fitted to armrest blades to give a total tool length of about 12 in. (300 mm). An armrest is shown in use in figure 7.137.

7.8.2 CHASING BOX THREADS

Although not critical, it is slightly better to chase the female thread first as the male spigot and thread are easier to access and adjust.

The "secret" of chasing is to be able to traverse the chaser along the workpiece surface at the ideal speed relative to the lathe speed. A lathe speed in the range 150 to 450 rpm is recommended. Chasers for coarser pitches will traverse faster, and therefore the lathe speed is better slower; however the cut will be better with a faster lathe speed. If you have a variable-speed lathe, you can use a different lathe speed with each pitch of chaser. Choose these speeds so that the traversing speed is the same for all your chasers.

The method I show in figures 7.127 to 7.142 for chasing the threads of a box is unorthodox, and involves first cutting a temporary reference thread on the outside of both the lid and the body. You then use this thread to memorize the chaser traversing speed and path immediately before chasing a permanent thread. The reference thread is then turned off when you finish-turn the outsides of the lid and the base. Once you are a skilled chaser, you can dispense with the temporary reference thread.

Chasing requires sensitivity, not massive force. Therefore smooth slippage of the chaser across and along your toolrest is essential. Smooth and wax the top edge of your toolrest, the undersides of your chasers, and your armrest if you use one.

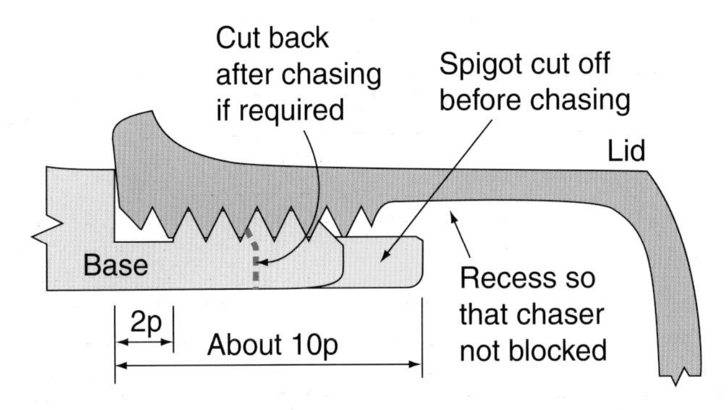

Figure 7.127 **The design of the box threads.** The chaser I shall use has a 9 tpi (2.82 mm pitch) BSW thread form.

A minimum of five circles of thread will chased because five circles increases the engagement of the chaser. The spigot can then be shortened so that the lid tightens in the required number of turns.

You can calculate the thread diameters using the formulae in figures 7.35 and 7.36. If you cut the socket first, the spigot major diameter can be obtained by adding 0.67p (from p[2 x 0.74 – 4{0.167 x 0.89} – 2 x 0.11]) to the socket's minor diameter. However figure 7.138 shows how to cut the spigot to diameter without calculation.

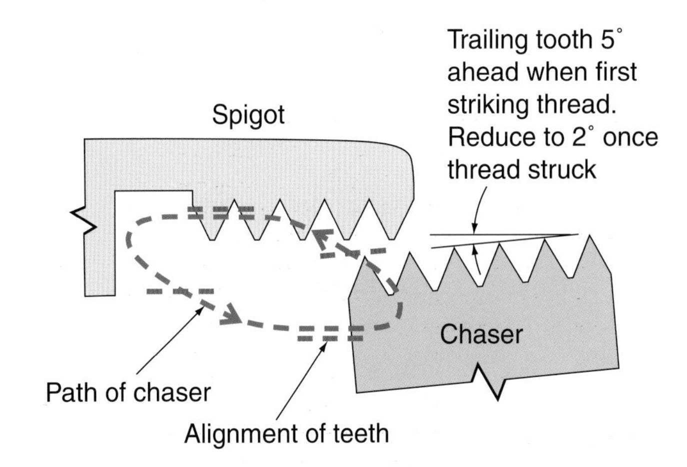

Figure 7.128 **The path of a chaser should be like a rhombus with rounded corners.** The entry and exit sections of the path are at about 30° to the lathe axis. Try and keep the chaser moving at the same speed around the whole path.

As you bring the chaser towards the wood, your grip should be relaxed and the trailing tooth should be slightly ahead. (The alignment of the teeth is indicated by the purple lines). Engagement of the chaser with the thread is smoother if three or more teeth are involved. The leading or trailing tooth does most of the cutting, but generally keep the teeth aligned parallel to the lathe axis.

Chasing is not difficult, but you need to establish the traversing speed and chaser path in your muscle memory. An hour's practice on scrap will greatly increase your probability of success.

Figure 7.129 **Chasing the temporary reference thread** on the outside of the combined workpiece. The top face of the chaser should point to a little below the lathe axis. All the chasing for this box was done at 300 rpm.

Many hold chasers in an underhand grip with the blades held between the thumb and forefinger of their left hand.

Figure 7.130 **Parting through to separate the lid and base workpieces.** Ideally the two workpieces should then be roughly hollowed, and allowed to relax and season before threading and finish-turning to ensure that the threads will operate smoothly long-term.

Figure 7.131 **Refining the area of the socket's surface** to be threaded after scraping the recess to its left (see figure 7.127).

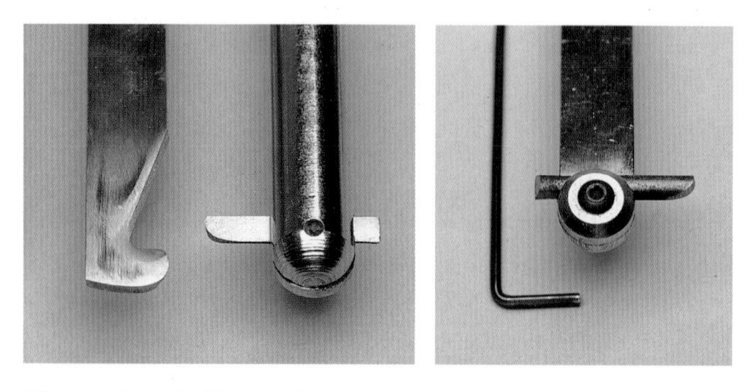

Figure 7.132 **Two of the many scrapers which can be used to cut the recess:** *left*, a round side-cutting scraper by Henry Taylor; *center and right*, a multi-tip shear scraper by Robert Sorby.

Figure 7.133 **Checking that the minor diameter of the area to be threaded is constant** by pressing the nearside edge of the shear scraper against, holding the shear scraper horizontal, and sighting how it aligns with a bedway.

Figure 7.134 **Chamfering the socket entrance.**

Figure 7.135 **Memorizing the traversing speed with the chaser held upside down.**

Figure 7.136 **Chasing the female thread.**

The top face of the chaser is a little above lathe-axis height to give a slightly negative rake to the cut. The chaser is held lightly until it is safely engaged. Move the chaser continuously in the rhombic path shown in figure 7.128, cutting on the push, until the thread is fully developed.

You can either support a chaser on a toolrest angled at 90° to the bed in plan as here, or use an armrest as shown in the next figure.

Figure 7.137 **Using a chaser on an armrest to cut the female thread.**

The chaser is pressed against the head of the armrest and both tools are moved almost as if welded together to take the chaser tip around the rhombic path.

The outside of the lid is then finish-turned, the lid parted off, and the base workpiece chucked.

Figure 7.138 **Testing the fit of the base spigot.**

The right-hand end of the spigot (colored yellow in figure 7.127) has been reduced until it fits snuggly within the crests of the female thread. This reduced diameter is approximately equal to the male thread's minor diameter. The rest of the spigot is then trimmed so that the height of the shoulder equals the depth of the chaser teeth (the cutter advance). The 2p wide groove is then cut to the left of the section to be threaded.

It is better to cut the section which will be threaded a touch too big because if the thread cut into it is too tight, the lathe can be speeded up, the crest skimmed, the lathe slowed, and the thread chased deeper.

Figure 7.139 **Memorizing the traversing speed.**

Figure 7.140 **Chasing the male thread on the spigot.**

7.141 **Trialling the fit of the lid.** Repeat the steps described in figures 7.112 to 7.116 to get the grains in the lid and base to align.

Figure 7.142 **The box ready for parting off.** To reverse chuck it and finish-turn the bottom of the base, turn and thread a socket in scrap or use the lid of the next box immediately after threading if the thread diameters are suitable.

7.8.3 CHASING FROM A MASTER SCREW

In the traversing mandrel the master screw is used to rotate and traverse the workpiece past a stationary cutter. Unscrewing a chuck holding a workpiece past a stationary but rotating cutter to cut a thread of the same pitch and hand as that of the lathe's right-hand spindle nose is perhaps the simplest example. However the converse, in which the master screw is used to traverse the cutter along a rotating workpiece, can be as useful as figures 7.143 to 7.147 show. With both types of application the pitch and hand of the master screw are replicated on the workpiece, but there is one exception which is described in figure 7.146. With all applications the thread form and diameters can be different from those of the master screw.

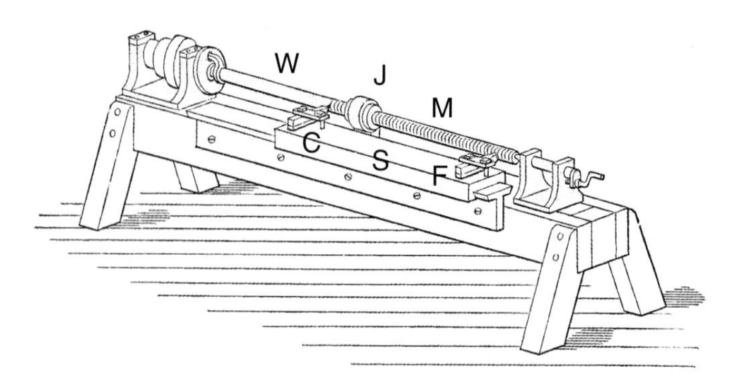

Figure 7.143 **The converse of the lathe shown in figure 7.11.**[38] The master thread *M* is joined to the workpiece *W* at *J*. A follower *F* when engaged with the master screw causes the slide *S* to move parallel to the lathe bed and the cutter *C* to cut a thread with the same pitch as the master thread.

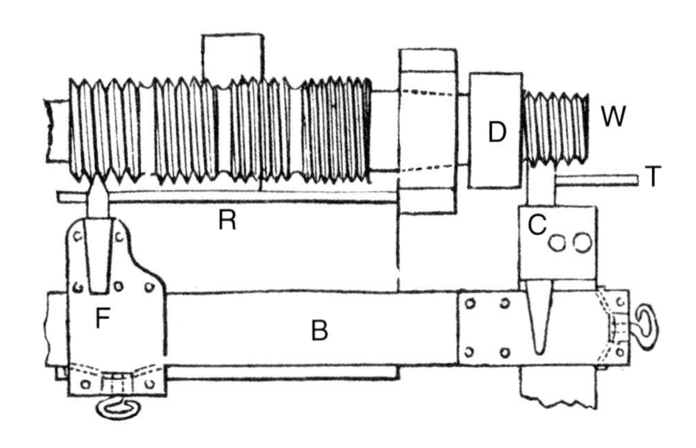

Figure 7.144 **The master thread apparatus invented by Mr S. Varley** and described on page 620 of Charles Holtzapffel, *Turning and Mechanical Manipulation,* Volume 2. On the same page is a diagram showing how the Varley apparatus can be used to cut female threads with an inside chaser.

The spindle above has four sections of master thread on it. A follower *F* is attached to the left-hand end of a bar *B,* and a chaser *C* is fixed to the bar's right-hand end. A workpiece *W* is held in a chuck *D* held on the spindle. The distance between the follower and the chaser on bar *B* is set so that the chosen of the four master pitches will be cut on the workpiece. Both the follower and the chaser are supported by rests *R* and *T*. If the spindle is slowly rotated and the combination of bar, follower, and chaser are moved in a rhombic path similar to that shown in figure 7.128, a thread with the master thread's pitch will be replicated on the workpiece.

Although the exact arrangement shown above is of limited relevance, two related arrangements are of more interest: the master thread could be held in a chuck at one end of the headstock spindle and the workpiece held in a chuck at the opposite end; or the master thread and workpiece could both be held next to one another between centers or be chucked next to one another as shown in the figure below.

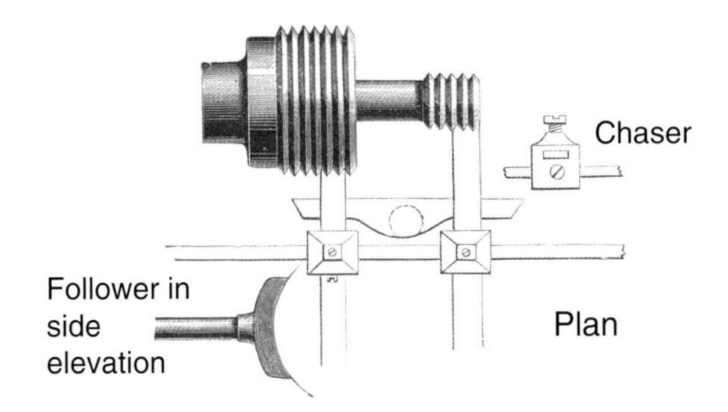

Figure 7.145 **A variation on Mr Varley's apparatus** in which the master thread and workpiece are both chucked inboard.[39] A more complicated version is shown in the next figure.

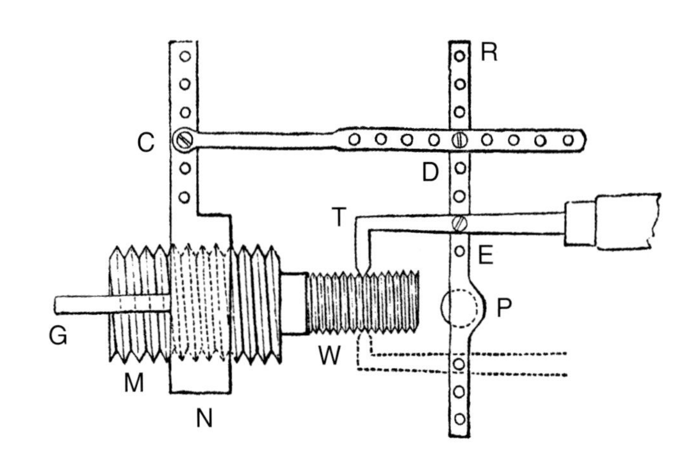

Figure 7.146 **An apparatus for cutting threads which differ from the master thread** developed at the end of the eighteenth century by a Mr Healey of Dublin. In his description, Charles Holtzapffel[40] calls this apparatus, " one of the least perfect of the modes of originating screws", but it is not without interest or potential.

M is the master thread which is rigidly and axially connected to the workpiece *W*. *N* is a nut which runs on *M*, and has an arm rigidly attached. Guide pin *G* ensures that the nut's arm remains horizontal as *M* and *W* are rotated. A horizontal arm *R* is pivoted at *P*. A connecting rod is pivotally fixed at *C* and *D* so that it lies parallel to the axis through *M*,*W*, and *P* when arm *R* is at 90° to that axis.

If a tool *T* is screwed to horizontal arm *R* at *E* so that it can pivot, and the master thread and workpiece are rotated clockwise and counterclockwise, *T* cuts a thread. The thread will have the same hand as the master thread, but because *PE* is half *PD*, the pitch of the thread cut on *W* will be half the pitch of *M*. To cut a thread of the opposite hand to that of *M*, the tool *T* (shown dotted) is pivotly fixed on the left-hand side of arm *R*.

Although the pitch of the thread cut by tool *T* decreases as connecting rod *CD* is positioned further away from the axis through *M*,*W* and *P*, the pitch cut by tool *T* also varies during a single cut, and is greatest when arm *R* lies at 90° to the axis through *M*, *W* and *P*.

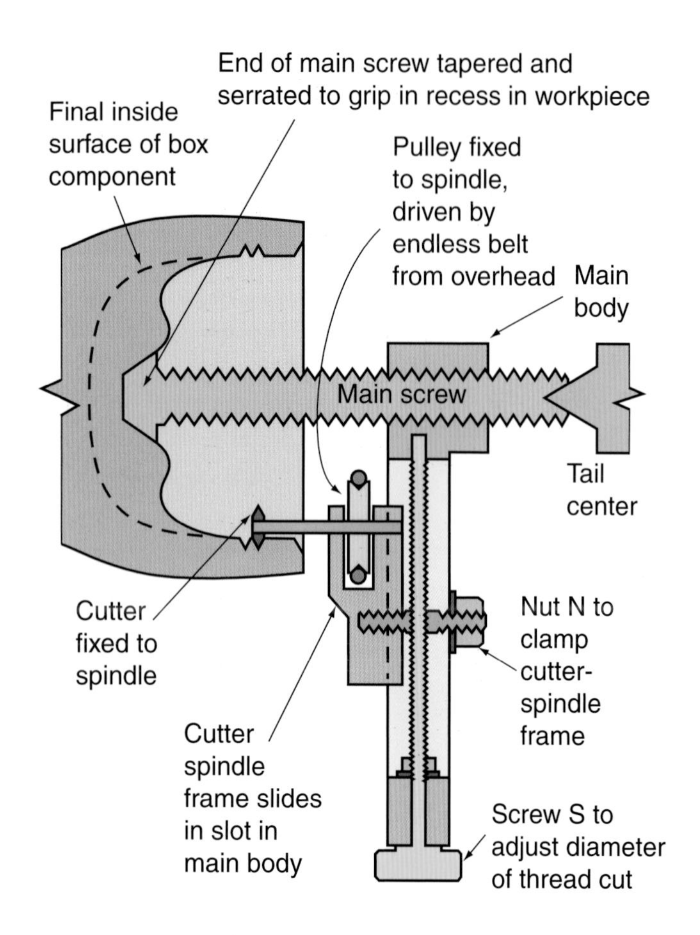

Figure 7.147 A thread-cutting apparatus, patented in England by General C. Dombleton in 1872. The Norwich firm of Hines catalogued it in 1890 for three guineas with three interchangeable master screws of 12, 16, and 20 tpi.[41]

The workpiece, here a box lid, is held in a chuck, and the workpiece's inside is partially hollowed. A recess is turned in the hollow, and the left-hand end of the apparatus's main screw is entered into the recess. Winding the tail center forwards into the conical hole in the right-hand end of the main screw then locks the main screw into the recess. The offset of the cutter is adjusted using the screw *S*, and locked with nut *N*. Then with the cutter being rotated at high speed from the lathe's overhead (see *Woodturning Methods*, figure 1.11), the apparatus is held lightly while the workpiece is rotated slowly. Rotating the workpiece causes the main screw to rotate, and the rest of the apparatus to move to the left or right parallel to the lathe axis. After the thread is cut, the tail center is retracted, the apparatus removed, and the inside and outside of the box lid finish-turned. The mating workpiece can then be similarly turned and threaded.

A modern version incorporating a high-speed electric motor to drive the cutter could be quicker to use than the devices shown in pages 157 to 159. However, the Dombleton apparatus cannot cut small-diameter female threads.

7.8.4 CUTTING THREADS WITH AN ENGINE LATHE EQUIVALENT.

Figures 7.148 to 7.150 show how a range of threads can be machined using a lathe with a plain headstock to mimic an engine lathe. You need to take care when setting up an apparatus of this type that it will cut the threads with the correct hand.

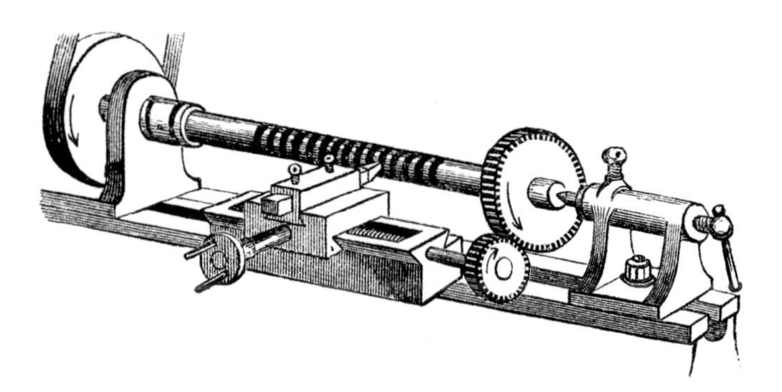

Figure 7.148 Cutting a thread with spur gears mounted on the workpiece and on the lead shaft of a longitudinal slide.[42] The pitch of the thread which will be cut is varied by varying the relative diameters of the two spur gears. Interposing an additional spur gear will alter the hand of the thread cut on the workpiece.

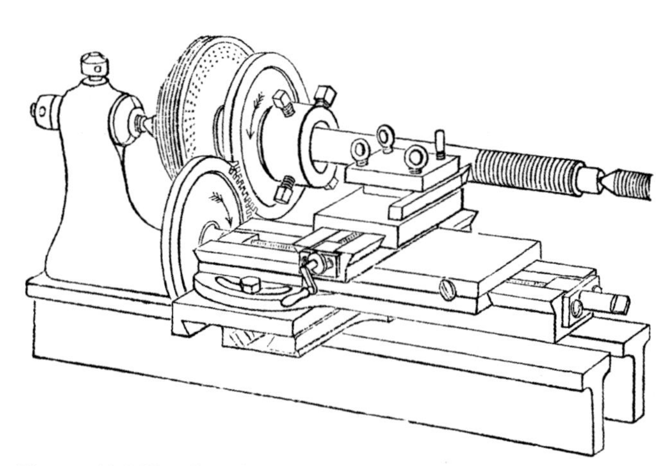

Figure 7.149 Cutting a thread using one gear mounted on the right-hand headstock-spindle nose and another on the lead shaft of the longitudinal slide of a compound slide.[43] Whether an even or odd number of gears is needed in the gear train will depend on the hand of the lead shaft thread.

If your lathe has an outboard nose, it could be more convenient to mount the first gear, a sprocket, or a pulley on it. Whichever is chosen would in turn drive another which is fixed on the end of a shaft. This shaft, if necessary via universal joints, then drives the longitudinal slide of a compound slide either directly or via gears, a chain and sprockets, or a belt and pulleys.

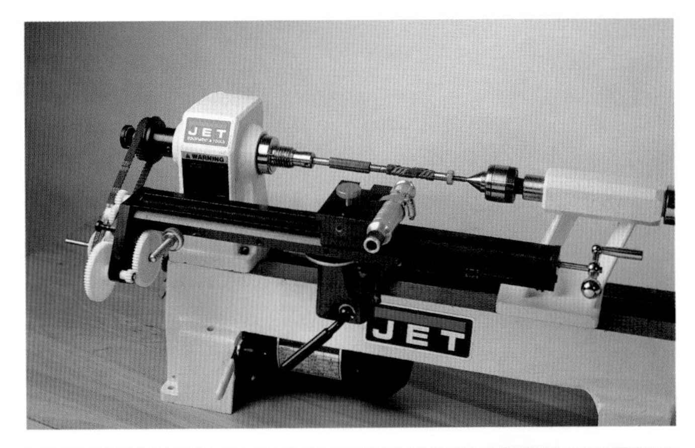

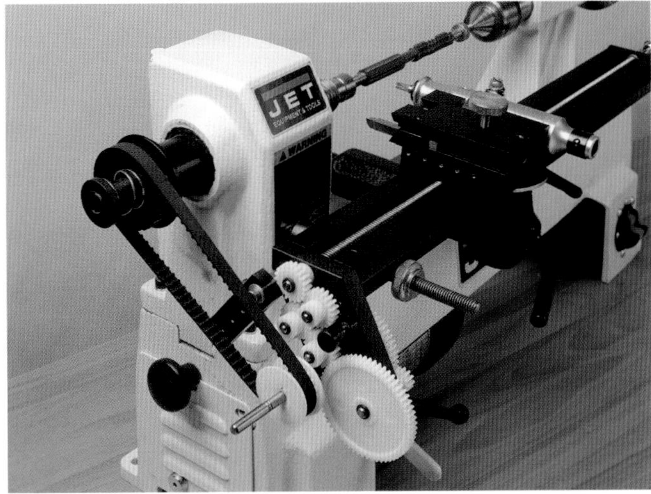

Figure 7.150 The Model A Lathe Attachment, manufactured by The Beall Tool Company of Newark, Ohio, converts a small plain lathe into the equivalent of an engine lathe, and allows threads of various pitches to be accurately machined.

7.9 THREADING METAL

Most woodworkers find it necessary to do some threading in metal, usually in mild steel, cast iron, or brass; hence this section.

7.9.1 TYPES OF METAL THREADS

Whitworth's dream of a standardized thread form has been partially realised in that all current threads now used belong to standardized systems, but he would surely be dismayed by the excessive number of systems.

During WWII the problems of thread incompatability had become painfully apparent. The 55°-thread-angle Whitworth did not mate with the 60°-thread-angle American National, and for larger nominal diameters the pitches of the two systems were different. In 1948 a Unified National thread was adopted by America, Britain, and Canada. The Unified form has a 60° thread angle, and is interchangeable with the American National. Within this UN system there are various series and classes of fit. An example of the full nomenclature is shown below:

$^1/_2$ in.–13UNC-2A

where: $^1/_2$ in. is the nominal diameter, 13 is the number of threads per inch, and UNC is a contraction of Unified National Coarse. (UNF represents the fine version which has a smaller pitch and is used to lessen the risk of a fastening vibrating loose). 2A is the class of the thread, and is related to the clearance between the male and female versions. Clearances are reduced in some applications, but need to be large where the threads are to be electroplated or galvanized. As 2A is the most common class, the title of this thread is usually shortened to $^1/_2$" UNC.

The S.I. thread system based on metric measurements has pitches which are not compatible with inch-based pitches.

In addition to the Whitworth, Unified National, and metric thread systems, there are:

1. Tapered threads for pipe joints.
2. Special miniature threads which have smaller thread angles to ensure sufficient depth of engagement.
3. Special threads for hose fittings, spark plugs, microscopes, etc.

7.9.2 THREAD IDENTIFICATION

If you know the country of origin of the item with the thread you wish to match, this can suggest whether the thread is inch based or metric. A thread with rounded crests will usually be a Whitworth. The outside diameter of a male thread usually approximates to its nominal diameter. For a female thread you must estimate the major diameter of the helical groove.

To find the pitch you can measure it directly, say by measuring the distance between eleven crests and dividing by ten, or determine the item's thread with a screw pitch gauge (figure 7.151). If you don't have access to a gauge, compare the thread with fasteners, taps, or dies with known threads. If you wish to check the thread, lie a male-threaded round bar, fastener, or a tap alongside—the two threads will mesh along their full lengths if their pitches are the same.

Figure 7.151 A screw pitch gauge. Most gauges cover only one thread system.

7.9.3 TAPPING FEMALE THREADS

The basic tool for cutting female threads is the hand tap (figures 7.152 and 7.153). Before you can tap, you need to drill a tapping or pilot hole, and it is critical that its diameter be correct—too large and the depth of engagement will be small and the threads will easily strip, too small and you will jam or break the tap. Tapping-hole diameters are commonly tabulated in metalworking references, and engineers suppliers may offer cards or charts. Details of the threads I have used most often are given in table 7.3.[44]

To drill a hole accurately, punch its location with a center punch. You will drill a true hole if you use a drilling machine and clamp the workpiece to its table. You can drill in your woodturning lathe. Some workpieces can be safely held in a chuck or on a faceplate, and be drilled with the drill held in the tailstock ram. Some workpieces can be safely held against a drill pad, with the drill mounted inboard in the swallow or in a chuck. If you use a hand-held electric or hand drill, make a metal or wooden guide in your woodturning lathe to enable you to drill perpendicularly by hand into a surface.

If the threaded hole is to be blind (that is stops within the thickness of the workpiece and does not go through), the hole needs to be about 4p deeper than the required threaded depth. Do not force the drill, and clear the chips to prevent the drill jamming and breaking. Ideally you should drill with the recommended lubrication, and it is essential when threading. For steel, wrought iron and most non-ferrous metals it is better to use a cutting fluid. Cast iron and brass are drilled dry.

Tapping will slightly dome the surface around the hole. To avoid this countersink the hole, or counterbore it 2p deep at the major diameter of the thread before tapping.

If you have used a drilling machine to drill the pilot hole (7.154), you should also tap with the workpiece still in the machine. Many taps have a small hole in their square ends into which you can locate a conical point, say of a center punch. When a tap is held in a tap wrench (figure 7.155), a conical point can also locate in the square hole left between the wrench jaws. Tapping can then proceed with the certainty that the tap is axial with the pilot hole (figure 7.156).

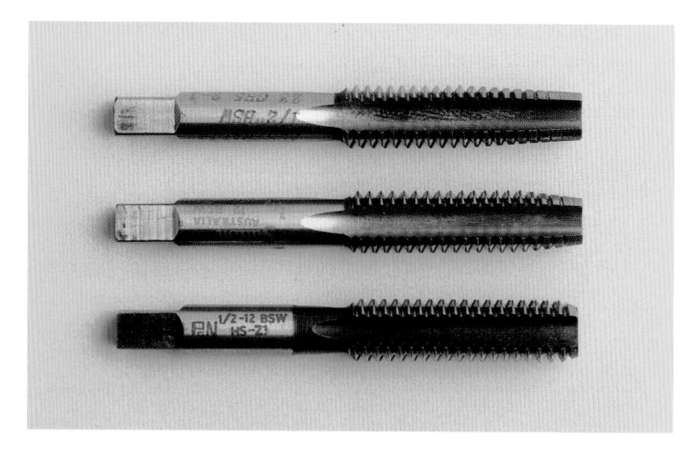

Figure 7.152 The types of hand tap. *Top to bottom*: taper, second-cut or intermediate, bottoming or plug. Taps are usually available in carbon tool steel for occasional use or dearer HSS for more arduous use. Most taps have three or four straight flutes.

Ideally, the land between the flutes in taps for hand operation should not be relieved, so that on reversing the tap rotation to break the chips, the chips cannot get wedged.

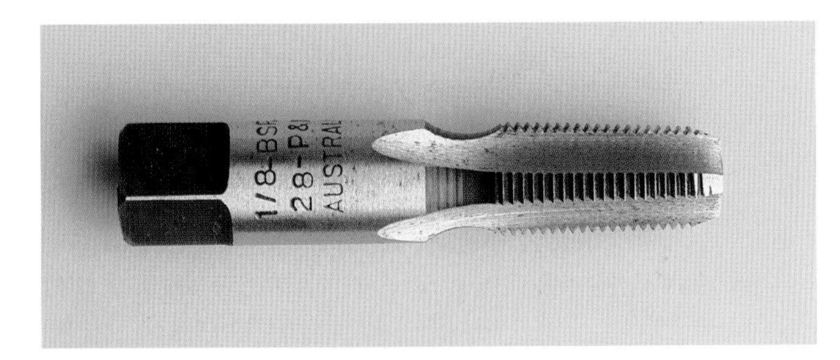

Figure 7.153 A taper pipe tap used to form pipe threads which do not leak even when the gas or liquid is under high pressure.

Table 7.3 Pilot- and clearance-hole diameters for tapping in metal.

Thread	*Pitch mm*	*Pilot-hole diameter*		*Clearance-hole diameter*	
		mm	*inches*	*mm*	*inches*
BSW					
1/4"	1.27	5.1	13/64	6.5	17/64
5/16"	1.41	6.5	1/4	8.1	21/64
3/8"	1.59	7.9	5/16	9.7	25/64
7/16"	1.81	9.5	23/64	11.3	29/64
1/2"	2.12	10.5	13/32	13.0	33/64
UNC					
1/4"	1.27	5.1	13/64	6.5	17/64
5/16"	1.41	6.6	17/64	8.1	21/64
3/8"	1.59	8.0	5/16	9.6	25/64
7/16	1.81	9.5	3/8	11.3	29/64
1/2"	1.95	10.8	27/64	13.0	33/64
Metric					
6 mm	1	5.1	13/64	6.1	1/4
7 mm	1	6.1	15/64	7.1	9/32
8 mm	1.25	6.9	17/64	8.2	21/64
9 mm	1.25	7.9	5/16	9.2	3/8
10 mm	1.5	8.6	21/64	10.2	13/32
11 mm	1.5	9.5	3/8	11.2	7/16
12 mm	1.75	10.2	13/32	12.2	31/64
14 mm	2.0	12.0	15/32	14.2	9/16

Figure 7.154 Drilling a pilot hole with the workpiece fixed to the drilling machine table. There are recommended drill speeds for different hole diameters in different materials.

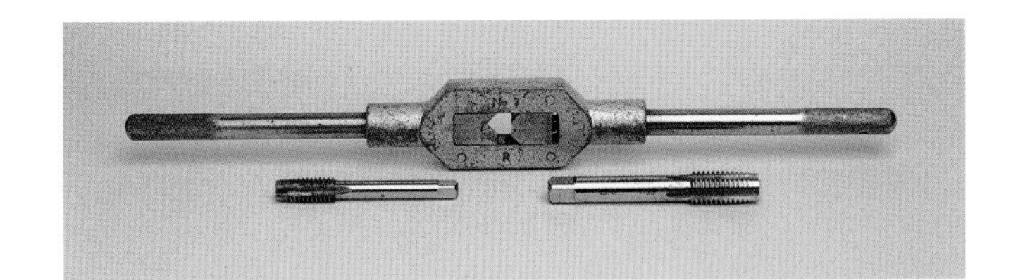

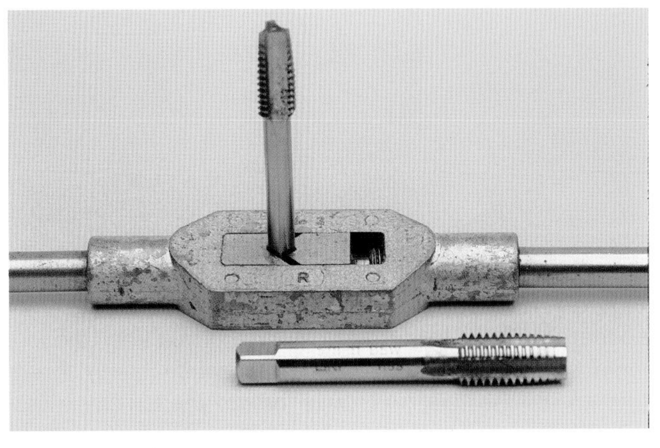

Figure 7.155 A tap wrench. The square ends of taps are gripped by screwing one handle (here on the right) and its attached jaw to the left towards the fixed jaw.

Tapping is easiest with a taper tap, although you can also use an intermediate tap. After using a taper tap, you may need to extend the thread with an intermediate or bottoming tap.

You can also tap between centers in your woodturning lathe if it has, or you can manufacture, a strong method to lock the headstock spindle.

Figure 7.156 **Tapping the hole shown being drilled in figure 7.154.** A center punch is held in the Jacobs chuck and locates the top of the tap. The quill is pushed down while the tap wrench is rotated.

7.9.4 CUTTING MALE THREADS

Dies are used to thread round bar or the outside of tubing. The workpiece's outside (major) diameter must be within the range specified for the particular die—you will find these tabulated in engineers references. When you need to extend an existing thread, say along the shank of a bolt, the diameter of the unthreaded section may already be suitable. When cutting a fresh thread, grind a chamfer on the end of the workpiece to help the die start more easily.

Various types of die and die stock are manufactured (figure 7.158). Figures 7.159 and 7.160 show how to cut a male thread.

Male threads are easily damaged. Use the edge of a half-round file, or a triangular saw file if the thread angle is 60°, to repair minor localized damage to a male thread. If the damage is greater, run a die or die nut along the thread. If you don't have a die or die nut, hacksaw a nut in half, lightly clamp the halves around an undamaged part of the male thread, apply some lubricant, and then screw the damaged part through the nut a few times.[45]

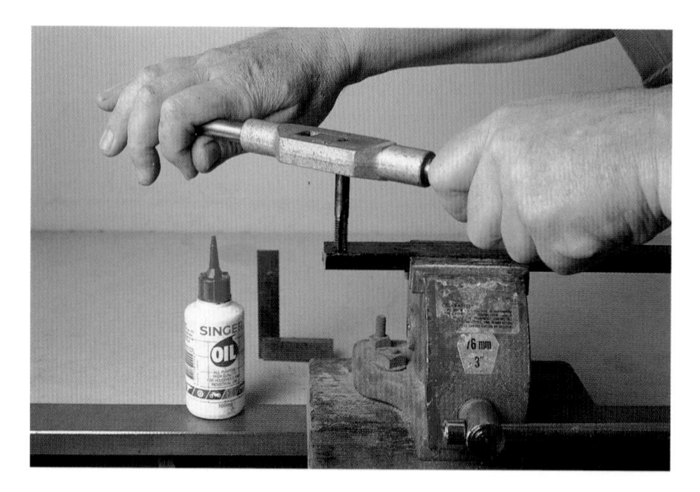

Figure 7.157 **Tapping by hand.** Clamp the workpiece so that the drilled hole is vertical—then if you keep the tap wrench horizontal you will not cut a drunken thread. Insert the tap into the hole, and rotate the tap wrench clockwise with some downward force. After two or three complete rotations, eye that the tap is still vertical with a square placed on the workpiece in two directions at 90° to one another in turn. Always use cutting oil or a light oil, except with cast iron. Reverse the tap rotation a little after every turn or two to free the chips. When the hole is deep, interrupt the tapping occasionally to wind the tap out, invert the workpiece, and tap out the chips.

When tapping a blind hole, use an intermediate tap before the plug tap. Also, the chips will need to be removed from the hole frequently.

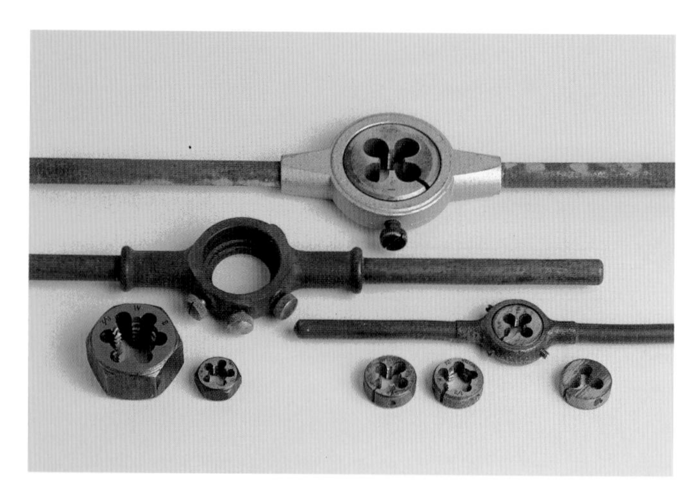

Figure 7.158 Button dies, button die stocks, and die nuts.

Bottom left, die nuts are intended for repairing damaged threads rather than for cutting fresh threads.

When using a die, the stamped size should face in the direction of threading to make use of the chamfered entry.

Figure 7.159 Adjusting a split-ring die. The compatible die stock has three screws. The plain side (no numbers or letters) of the split-ring die should be put against the flange in the die stock, and the split in the die aligned with the central expanding screw which should have a conical tip. There will be two holes in the outside cylindrical surface of the die into which the die stock's two locking screws locate.

Screwing the expanding screw in firmly before tightening the locking screws will cause the die to cut an oversize male thread. To reduce the diameters of the male thread cut, slacken off the locking screws, unscrew the expanding screw as required, retighten the locking screws, and rethread.

Figure 7.160 Extending the male thread on a bolt. If the workpiece is short, as here, hold it vertically in a vice; if the workpiece is long, you may need to clamp it horizontally.

When cutting a fresh thread, start to rotate the die stock with downward pressure. Keep the die stock square, or the thread will be "drunk" at the start. Lubricate liberally.

7.10 ENDNOTES

1. The geometry of the helix was first developed by the Greek mathematician Apollonius of Perga about 200 BC (*Encyclopaedia Britannica*).
2. The history of mechanical engineering and particularly thread cutting is spread over many sources. The most useful single general source that I have found and used is L. T. C. Rolt, *Tools for the Job* (London: B.T. Batsford Ltd, 1965). Other general sources include: Joseph Wickham Roe, *English & American Tool Builders* (1916; reprint, Bradley, Illinois: Lindsay Publications,1987), and Aubrey F. Burstall, A *History of Mechanical Engineering* (London: Faber and Faber, 1963). Charles Holtzapffel, *Turning & Mechanical Manipulation, vol 2, The Principles of Cutting Tools* (1847; reprint, Radford Semele, Warwickshire: TEE Publishing, 1999), pp. 577–681, provides a comprehensive account of early nineteenth-century thread cutting. A book which concentrates on the screw as a fastener is Witold Rybczynski, *One Good Turn: A Natural History Of the Screwdriver and the Screw* (New York: Scribner, 2000).
3. The writings and views of Heracleitus (b. c. 540 B.C.–d. c. 480) survive in short fragments quoted and attributed to him by later authors (*Encyclopaedia Britannica*).
4. S. Lilley, *Men, Machines and History* (London: Lawrence & Wishart, 1965), p. 31.
5. Hero of Alexandria flourished around AD 62. He wrote on mathematics, geometry, surveying, light, clocks, turbines, and mechanics (*Encyclopaedia Britannica*).
6. Burstall, p. 77.
7. Burstall, p. 115.
8. G. H. Baillie, C. Clutton, and C.A. Ilbert, *Britten's Old Clocks and Watches and Their Makers* (New York: E.P. Dutton, 1956), p.14.
9. Burstall, p. 78, fig. 28, provided the information for me to make the "nut". Rybczynski, p. 121, states that a thread pin was called a tylos in Greek.
10. This illustration is also based on fig. 28 on page 78 of Burstall. A similar device, but with the body internally threaded instead of having chisel-ended pins, is described in Oscar E. Perrigo, *Modern American Lathe Practice* (London: Crosby Lockwood & Son; and New York: The Norman W. Henley Publishing Company, 1907), pp. 36–37.
11. The woodcut of the printing press is reproduced from R.W. Hart, *The Industrial Revolution* (Hove, East Sussex: Wayland Publishers, 1978), p. 108. Much of the information in the legend was distilled from Grant Uden, *Understanding Book-Collecting* (Woodbridge, Suffolk: Antique Collectors' Club, 1982).

12. Gerald Donaldson, *Books* (Oxford: Phaidon, 1981), p. 21.
13. This book is now accessible through Christoph Graf zu Waldburg Wolfegg, *Venus and Mars: The World of the Medieval Housebook* (Munich: Prestel-Verlag, 1998).
14. Reproduced from the excellent Klaus Maurice, *Sovereigns as Turners* (Zurich: Verlag Ineichen, 1985), p.17, figure 4.
15. Reproduced from Rolt, p. 29, figure 11.
16. Rolt, pp. 162–163; and Roe, pp. 119–120.
17. Reproduced from Rolt, p. 27, figure 9.
18. The illustrations are sourced as follows: *top and top right*, W. Henry Northcott, *A Treatise on Lathes and Turning* (1868; reprint, Fresno, California: Linden Publishing, 1868) p. 84, fig. 80; *right*, Rolt, p. 65, figure 31; *right bottom*, James Lukin, *Turning Lathes*, 5th ed. (Colchester, England: Britannia Company, 1899) p. 55, fig 2; *bottom left and figure* 7.18, Robertson Buchanan, *Practical Essays on Mill Work and Other Machinery* (London: John Weale, 1841), p. 396.
19. Northcott, pp. 84–85.
20. Reproduced from John Jacob Holtzapffel, *Hand or Simple Turning* (New York: Dover Publications, 1976), p. 107, figs. 111 and 112.
21. Redrawn from Charles Holtzapffel, *vol* 2, p. 640, fig. 611.
22. An apparatus for generating screws with an inclined knife invented by a Mr Allan in about 1816 is described in Charles Holtzapffel, vol 2, pp. 581–582.
23. Reproduced from Roe, figure 25. An excellent biography of Whitworth is Norman Atkinson, *Sir Joseph Whitworth* (Stroud, Gloucestershire: Sutton Publishing, 1997).
24. *Handbook Encyclopedia of Engineering* (New York: The Industrial Press, 1929), p. 539; and Rolt, pp. 106–107.
25. Half nuts reproduced from Herbert D. Hall and Horace E. Linsley, *Machine Tools* (New York: Industrial Press, 1957), p. 202, fig. 25.
26. Lukin, p. 82, plate XI.
27. A short biography of William Sellers is included in Roe, pp. 247–251.
28. Rolt, p. 175.
29. Robert Kanigel, *The One Best Way* (New York: Viking Penguin, 1997).
30. Most of the information on the geometry of threads was sourced from *Machinery's Handbook*, 20th ed. (New York: Industrial Press Inc.,1976), p. 1275–1277.
31. Mike Darlow, "Threading Made Easy," *The Australian Woodworker* (February 2001): pp. 40–41.
32. Stuart Mortimer, *Techniques of Spiral Work* (Hertford: Stobart Davies, 1996).
33. Vitruvius, *The Ten Books on Architecture*, trans. Morris Hickey Morgan (New York: Dover Publications, 1960), p. 295–297.
34. This subject was introduced in Pat Warner, "Threading Wood for Machine Screws," *Fine Woodworking* 126 (September/October 1997): p. 63.
35. The information in table 7.2 was sourced from Ernest Joyce, *The Technique of Furniture Making* (London: B.T. Batsford, 1970), p. 343; and John A. Walton, *Woodwork in Theory and Practice* (Sydney: Random House Australia, 1990), pp. 68–69.
36. Mike Darlow, "Waes Hael, Wassail," *Woodworker* (April 1994): pp. 52–54.
37. The many references to chasing include:

    Charles Bell, "The Gentle Art of Thread Chasing," *Woodturning* 61: pp. 56–60.

    Fred Holder, *Making Screw Threads in Wood* (Lewes, East Sussex: GMC Publications, 2001).

    Fred Holder, "Getting the Thread," *Woodturning* 53: pp. 55–56.

    Fred Holder, "Uncommon Cutters," *Woodturning* (October 1999): pp. 59–60.

    Fred Holder, "Chasing Threads," *American Woodturner* (Summer 1999): pp. 33–36.

    Bill Jones, *Bill Jones' Notes from the Turning Shop*, (Lewes, East Sussex: GMC, 1996), pp. 14–19.

    Bonnie Klein, "Screw-Top Boxes," *American Woodturner* (March 1994): pp. 16–19.

    Terry Porter, "Getting the Thread," *Woodturning* 77 (July 1999): pp. 63–64.

    Richard Starr, "Chasing Large Wooden Threads," *Fine Woodworking* 60 (Sept/Oct 1986): pp. 53–57.

    John Swanson, *Turning Threaded Boxes* (Atglen, PA: Schiffer Publishing).
38. Perrigo, fig. 10. A hand-operated version is shown in fig. 11.
39. Lukin, pp. 42–45. Derek Pearce describes a modern and simpler version in *Woodturning* 15: p. 73.
40. Holtzapffel, vol. 2, pp. 618–620.
41. "Thread Cutting," *The Society of Ornamental Turners Bulletin* 101: pp. 40–42.
42. R.W. Hart, p. 86.
43. Holtzapffel, vol. 2, p. 622, fig 599.
44. The information was abstracted from Ian Bradley and Norman Hallows, *Screw Threads and Twist Drills* (Hemel Hempstead, Hertfordshire: Model and Allied Publications, 1974); and a tapping data card supplied by Boral P&N, East Bentleigh, Victoria, Australia.
45. *The Home Metalworker*, ed. Julian Worthington (London: Orbis Publishing, 1982).

Chapter Eight

WHERE NEXT?

Woodturning Techniques with FOW and *Woodturning Methods* should help you to gain most of the technical skills and knowledge you will need in hand woodturning. The fourth book in the series will not be technical, at least not in the same sense, but will focus on design. And I agree with those who shout, "Not before time". I could have included a design chapter in FOW, but did not because I wanted to provide a more thorough and integrated treatment than that in chapter 2 of my first book, the out of print *The Practice of Woodturning*.

There is a wrong and commonly held belief that only a few are born with designer genes, and that the rest of us can never design well. This excuse is of course self-fulfilling, and those who believe that they can't design never put in the necessary thought and effort. The result is depressingly familiar; well turned but poorly designed works which surely have far less merit than the converse.

Good design is like a sound turning technique, it is a means not an end. The next book will therefore attempt to unleash readers' design potentials through showing how design should be integrated with the other processes involved in producing turned items.

Figure 8.1 shows a design from the next book. The design looks simple, and is. It resulted from a desire, which lead to an idea, which in turn needed work to finalize the design and the turning procedures.

The aim of the next book is therefore to persuade you that you can design well, and to show you how. The "how" requires directed work, just as do the in-lathe areas of turning. But whether you are a professional, an amateur, or a beginner, isn't the desire to work actively and successfully the reason you turn?

Figure 8.1 Lopez chessmen designed and made by your author. (Ruy Lopez of Segura was a Spanish priest who wrote one of the most important early works on chess. It was first published in 1561).

My original objective was to design a set which did not require any detailed turning or any carving. I also required the six types of men to be clearly differentiated and instantly recognizable; also stable, and easy to pick up and put down. The key piece was the knight. The first idea of a truncated cone for the head could not be used until I thought of tilting the axis of the body.

The Australian native woods used are: *red*, forest sheoak; *white*, silver ash; and *brown*, Queensland walnut.

INDEX